CW00550987

TWENTY-ONE SQUADRONS

By the same author

SERVICE SLANG
DEFENCE UNTIL DAWN
FROM HIND TO HUNTER
VETERAN AND VINTAGE AIRCRAFT

Twenty-One Squadrons

Squadrons

The History of the
Royal Auxiliary Air Force: 1925-1957

LESLIE HUNT

With a foreword by

AIR CHIEF MARSHAL
SIR CHRISTOPHER FOXLEY-NORRIS
KCB, DSO, OBE, MA, RAF

CRÉCY BOOKS

This edition published in 1992 by
Crécy Books Ltd
First published in 1972 by Garnstone Press Ltd

© Leslie Hunt, 1992
ISBN 0 947554 26 2

TO HONOUR ROGER BUSHELL AND ALL AUXILIARIES
WHO GAVE THEIR LIVES IN
DEFENCE OF FREEDOM

Printed and bound in Great Britain by
Hartnolls Limited, Bodmin, Cornwall

Contents

PHOTOGRAPHIC SOURCES

Ministry of Defence: 1, 4, 27, 40, 42, 50, 51, 91, 141, 160, 169, 180, 202, 212.

Flight International: 2, 3, 17, 26, 31, 44, 45, 54, 66, 88, 89, 139, 140, 148, 154.

Imperial War Museum: 12, 13, 23, 36, 37, 38, 39, 47, 48, 61, 67, 69, 82, 83, 93, 100, 104, 105, 113, 116, 122, 146, 151, 177, 178, 188, 197, 203, 209.

Glasgow Daily Record: 7. *The Sunderland Echo*: 77, 78, 86. R. W. Cranham: 64, 101, 173. John G. Johnson: 76. Canadian Forces: 94. Roger Levy: 95. BOAC: 96. D. A. P. Cooke: 118. Aberdeen Journals: 166. W. S. Earnshaw: 213. *Sport and General*: 125, 126. *Southport Visitor*: 128. *Guardian Journal*: 138. J. D. R. Rawlings: 152, 182, 210. Russell Adams: 164.

Foreword

BY AIR CHIEF MARSHAL
SIR CHRISTOPHER FOXLEY-NORRIS
KCB, DSO, OBE, MA, RAF

IT WAS WITH genuine pleasure that I learned that Leslie Hunt had written this book and that I accepted his invitation to contribute a foreword to it. Although the British people have a vague and general idea of the history of the Auxiliary Air Force and its magnificent contribution to our victory in World War II, there was a real need for a full historical record; and Mr Hunt has established a well-deserved reputation for the meticulous accuracy and diligent research that is needed for such an undertaking.

I myself had the honour of a close and long association with the Auxiliary Air Force. I flew with No. 615 Squadron in 1940–41; I commanded No. 603 Squadron in 1944; and as Wing Commander Flying at West Malling in 1956 I had No. 500 Squadron in my wing. No one could have been sadder than myself when the Auxiliaries stopped flying; but the RAuxAF still exists in embryo and with a few

7

ground-based units; and one can but hope that justification can once again be found for some expansion.

One last word. This book, and indeed the public interest, tend to concentrate on the more glamorous activities of the aircrew. In the Auxiliary squadrons the groundcrew played perhaps an even more valuable part than in any other RAF squadrons for they provided the essential continuity. Commanders and aircrew came and went, sometimes tragically; but the NCOs and airmen remained year after year, providing that local loyalty and tradition of squadron service that was unique to the Auxiliaries. God bless them.

CHRISTOPHER FOXLEY-NORRIS

Introduction

PROVISIONS FOR AN Air Force Reserve and Auxiliary Air Force were part of the Air Force Constitution Act of 1917, and Sir Hugh Trenchard, in his 1919 Memorandum, said that a reserve Air Force should be organised on a territorial basis. In 1922 a Bill was drafted, but owing to apathy and opposition it did not become law until 1924 when Sir Samuel Hoare (later Viscount Templewood) was Secretary of State for Air. As one of the staunch advocates of the Auxiliary Air Force (who was in turn Honorary Air Commodore of 601 and then 604 Squadron) Viscount Templewood has said:

> Trenchard envisaged the Auxiliaries as a *corps d'élite* composed of the kind of young men who earlier would have been interested in horses, but who now wished to serve their country in machines. He conceived the new mechanical yeomanry with its aeroplanes based on the great centres of industry. *Esprit de corps* was to be the dominating force in the squadrons and each, therefore, was to have a well-equipped headquarters, mess, and distinctive life of its own. Social meetings were to be encouraged and on no account was any squadron to be regarded as a reserve for filling up regular units. The experiment was successful from the beginning. The forebodings of the doubters and critics were soon proved groundless. So far from the non-regular units damaging the reputation of the regular squadrons they actually added some of the most glorious pages to the history of the Royal Air Force during the second world war.

Under the Auxiliary Air Force and Air Force Reserve Act provision was made for raising six Auxiliary squadrons and seven Special Reserve squadrons. The long-range intention was to found twenty Auxiliary squadrons. Although the first to come into being was No. 502 (County of Ulster) Special Reserve Squadron, the chapters of this book are arranged in the chronological sequence of formation in or transfer to the Auxiliary Air Force, consequently 502's history – although it began in 1925 – appears in the great build-up of 1937 when, after twelve splendid years, the squadron became part of the AAF. It should here be mentioned that four single-engine bomber and three twin-engine bomber squadrons were contemplated as the Special Reserve units; Nos. 505 and 506, the first to have been twin-engine, the other single-engine, did not form.

2. Auxiliary Air Force Camp at Manston in the biplane era.

Older readers may recall Air Ministry Pamphlet No. 2 of June 1925 (A.P. 1108) *Notes for the information of candidates for commissions in the General Duties Branch for service in Special Reserve Squadrons*. It read as follows:

Special Reserve Squadrons will be raised and maintained in certain localities as part of the air defence of Great Britain. In peace-time each of these squadrons will be located at an aerodrome in the vicinity of the town from which the Special Reserve personnel of the squadron are recruited. Each squadron is associated for purposes of Home Defence with a regular air force aerodrome which will form its war station and to which it will proceed when called out to take its place in the air defences of the country. Each squadron will, normally, be commanded by a regular officer of the RAF and will have a strong nucleus of regular officers and airmen, but approximately two-thirds of the squadron will be composed of Special Reserve personnel living in the neighbourhood of the aerodrome and keeping themselves efficient by attendance at the aerodrome and compliance otherwise with the conditions of their service. These conditions are made as elastic as possible to mimimise interference with the civil life

of officers and airmen. Normal ages 18–25 but up to 31 if candidates have served as officers RAF. Initial period 5 years, extended
with consent of the Air Council for further periods each of not
more than 5 years. Officers taught to fly at public expense and
who do not complete 5 years' satisfactory service are liable to
pay liquidated damages of £20 for each year by which their
period of satisfactory service falls short of 5 years.

Obligatory uniform . . . breeches and trousers. Boots, ankle,
black. Puttees, Shirts, white. Walking stick (RAF pattern). A
grant of £40 for those not previously commissioned in the RAF.

There were differences in the conditions for the Auxiliary Air Force
squadrons, in that they were to be raised and maintained by the
County Territorial Associations and manned by locally recruited
non-regular personnel, with only a small cadre of regulars as permanent staff, and a non-regular commanding officer. The Auxiliary Air
Force Reserve was formed on 17th January, 1939.

3. Westland Wapitis in the 1932 RAF Display.
604 left, 600 centre, 601 right.

When, in January 1957, the Air Ministry announced that the
Auxiliary squadrons were to be disbanded, an outstanding contribution to Royal Air Forces' history ended. This book tells the story
as obtained from squadron records up to the first disbandings of
1945 and from newspaper cuttings and individual member's notes
for the 1946–57 period; since access to official post-war records
cannot be obtained until 1987 (due to the government's thirty-year
rule). There are, alas, omissions; for not all squadron histories were
kept by enthusiasts for the task and all too often the emphasis was
on what the officers achieved – in the air and on the ground. Nevertheless, the writer, who had to make-do with the RAF Volunteer
Reserve pre-war, hopes that former NCOs and airmen will accept
this book as a tribute to all who served, in peace and in war, in the
twenty-one squadrons.

That the first enemy aircraft to be shot down over Britain in World War II fell to Auxiliary Air Force pilots of 602 and 603 Squadrons on 16th October, 1939, followed by the further claim, on 28th October, 1939, of having brought down the first enemy on British soil, will be known to most. It may be worth mentioning here too that of the sixty-six RAF squadrons in the Battle of Britain, fourteen were AAF (the other six played a vital role as Army Co-operation or Coastal Command units, some on Air-Sea Rescue duties). Post-war evidence confirmed that the first U-boat sunk by ASV (Air-to-surface-vessel radar) was credited to 502 Squadron and few need to be reminded that it was 613 Squadron's Mosquitos which carried out the pinpoint bombing of Gestapo headquarters in The Hague. That 605's aircraft were first to destroy a V.1 flying bomb, that 602's pilots put Rommel out of action, and that 616 were first to get the jets are known facts. If some should comment that by 1941 there were very few pre-war AAF pilots in the twenty squadrons, it could stand repeating that a number of Auxiliaries were by this time commanding regular squadrons and that several had been promoted to command RAF stations or to hold key appointments in the Air Ministry, Command, or Group Headquarters. Never let us forget that it was an Auxiliary officer who was the inspiration of Stalag Luft III; and that other AAF members, when taken prisoner, caused the enemy to regret his scornful slurs on the 'long-haired amateurs' and 'weekend flyers', for some 'part-timers' were as active on the ground as they had been in the air and forced the enemy to retain extra personnel as guards, so weakening his strength elsewhere.

On outbreak of war in September 1939, recruiting for the AAF ceased and personnel became members of the RAFVR 'for the emergency'. On 2nd June, 1946, the AAF was re-formed as a force of thirteen fighter, three night-fighter and four light-bomber squadrons; all being converted later to day-fighter squadrons. It was on 16th December, 1947 that King George VI gave permission for the 'Royal' prefix and from that date until the squadrons disbanded in March 1957 they were RAuxAF units.

Some people will consider that the chapters which follow do scant justice to their own squadron, but to compress into one volume twenty-one detailed histories has not been easy. The writer hopes that, in time, the nineteen squadrons which, to date, have no separate books (the stories of Nos. 601 and 609 have been published) may help provide the material – especially photographs – to justify individual volumes. Offers of such material will be welcomed by the publishers but, in the first instance, send only the details so that an assessment can be made of a book's potential.

4. HM the Queen and HRH Prince Philip with Air Vice-Marshal Desmond Hughes, Commandant, RAF College, Cranwell, at the Golden Jubilee of the College in June 1970. Her Majesty was Honorary Air Commodore-in-Chief, Royal Auxiliary Air Force. Prince Philip was Honorary Air Commodore of No. 601 (County of London) Squadron; and AV-M Hughes was a flight-commander in No. 600 (City of London) and then Commanding Officer, No. 604 (County of Middlesex) Squadron.

Acknowledgements and Thanks

My warm thanks firstly to Air Chief Marshal Sir Christopher Foxley-Norris, KCB, DSO, OBE, MA, for so kindly contributing the Foreword. Very few senior officers have equal experience of the wartime Auxiliary Air Force. Then my thanks go to the Ministry of Defence's Air Historical Branch, Photographic Reproduction Branch, and Public Relations Branch, for access to official records 1925–45, for photographs of squadron badges, and for a sight of newspaper cuttings covering the post-war years. To the Imperial War Museum's Photograph Library, to Miss Ann Tilbury of *Flight* International, and to John Rawlings, I am grateful for many of the illustrations, also to Douglas Gillies and friends for photographs of the 'Caledonian Wing' of Nos. 602, 603, 612 Squadrons. To Peter Arnold for data on preserved Spitfires, to John Huggon for research into the Meteors, to Roger Levy and John G. Johnson for photographs of Vampires, and to Squadron Leader G. J. Wilson (Retd) for photographs of 601 and 500 Squadrons.

For assistance with illustrations and research for individual squadrons may I express thanks to Joe Kistruck, M. W. Hampton, Andrew McDowall and John Topham, for 602's chapter. To Ken Battrick, John Wright, Miss Judy Meakin, Larry Fears, 'Mog' Morgan and Bryan E. Laws for 600 Squadron. To S. G. 'Vic' Vickers, Sir Max Aitken, Aidan Crawley, Mrs Tom Hubbard and Norman Jones for 601's chapter. To Group Captain G. P. Marvin (Retd) and Flight Lieutenant 'Russ' Snadden, RAF, for help with 603 Squadron. To Lord Willoughby de Broke and Tom Cornish for 605's chapter; and to Group Captain John Cunningham, Chris Wren and Reg Padgham for help with 604 Squadron. To Wing Commander W. F. Blackadder for 607's chapter and Wing Commander Peter Hutchings for 608 Squadron. For assistance with 609's chapter to Syd 'Darky' Hanson, David Shaw, Gil Sunderland and to Frank Ziegler (whose squadron book is a classic). For 610's (and 611's) photographs to Dr D. A. P. Cooke, R. C. B. Ashworth, the late Group Captain T. F. U. Lang, Air Vice-Marshal Denis Crowley-Milling, and to H. O. Williams. For 611 Squadron my thanks go to Flight Lieutenant R. C. Gaskell, S. G. Jones, Aldon Ferguson, and, of course, Squadron Leader Robin Birley. To Mrs Kathleen Russell (widow of Wing Commander R. R. Russell), G. R. Thomson and Gordon J. Dorward for 612's chapter; to W. L. Drummond, Neil

McKay, J. Foakes, C. J. Holt and J. H. Owens for 614. To Air Vice-Marshal F. B. Sowrey, Keith Belcher, John Goldsmith, Ian Smith and J. R. Holloway for 615 Squadron; L. H. 'Buck' Casson, Air Vice-Marshal 'Johnnie' Johnson, and Maurice Clark for 616 Squadron; Brian Robinson, G. T. Holden, D. McCarthy, R. A. Scholefield, and W. R. Edge for 613's chapter.

For much help with the Special Reserve squadrons I am greatly indebted to Hunter McGiffin, F. E. Carlisle, Tommy Cameron, Mrs Betty Hunter, the *Belfast Telegraph*, and Group Captain Terence Corry, for the 502 chapter. To Wing Commander Douglas Allison, Squadron Leader Arthur Young and Harold Willers for 503 Squadron; Neville Franklin, Eric Sharman, George Cooke and Wing Commander W. B. Royce for 504's chapter. Mrs Douglas Crabtree and Raymond Rayner for 501 Squadron and Miss Daphne Pearson, GC, J. Weatherley, D. Robinson, and Squadron Leader Desmond de Villiers for No. 500 Squadron's chapter. If I have overlooked any helpers, my sincere apologies – together with my appreciation for their co-operation.

Finally, my gratitude to Michael Balfour of The Garnstone Press and to his editor, Miss Sally Rousham, for their consideration and encouragement; also to my wife for regular refreshment and for hospitality to visiting helpers.

LESLIE HUNT

90 Woodside, Leigh-on-Sea, Essex
July, 1972

602
(City of Glasgow)
Squadron

THE ENVIABLE DISTINCTION of being the very first Auxiliary Air Force squadron fell to No. 602 (City of Glasgow) Squadron when, on 12th September, 1925, Flight Lieutenant Martyn reported as adjutant to begin forming the squadron. Two days later Squadron Leader C. N. Lowe, MC, DFC, RAF, arrived to command and on 15th September thirteen NCOs and airmen came as the hard-core permanent staff with Flight Lieutenant H. Sleigh as stores officer – this date is now regarded by the Ministry of Defence as the actual date-of-birth of the squadron. The wartime 'acceptance aerodrome' at Renfrew on the Moorpark Road was chosen as headquarters, hangars and offices here being re-conditioned for 602's use.

On 7th October, 1925, Squadron Leader Lowe flew a D.H.9A serial H144 from Henlow, Bedfordshire, to Renfrew – the first aircraft ever flown by an Auxiliary Air Force squadron! To bolster recruiting of volunteers a Town Centre (a wooden hut in the precincts of No. 52 (Lowland Division) Signals' Drill Hall, Jardine Street) was erected and on 2nd November the first part-timers joined; more than two hundred applying in the first week. There were initial difficulties with the distance from the aerodrome and the lack of a really suitable Town HQs for social events, but there was tremendous enthusiasm and that was what was required. Captain J. D. Latta, MC, who had flown light Scout aircraft, became the first Auxiliary C.O. and quickly took dual instruction on the D.H.9A and went solo. By April 1926, Dr J. C. H. Allen had joined as medical officer in the rank of flight lieutenant and Messrs J. P. Drew, C. A. S. Parker, and H. G. Davidson began training for the A licence – normal condition for entry for pilots in the AAF.

Two more D.H.9As arrived, joined by two Avro 504Ks, and at

17

the first annual camp, held at Leuchars, Fife, *all* officers, AAF and RAF, made parachute descents – a feature of Royal Air Force training in those days. A total of 53 hours' flying was achieved at the camp and during the following March Mr D. F. McIntyre gained his A licence at Beardmore's Flying School. Squadron Leader J. Fullerton succeeded Squadron Leader Latta as C.O. and the squadron strength greatly increased during 1927 when Pilot Officer Lord Clydesdale (now Duke of Hamilton) and Messrs A. F. Farquhar and R. Faulds were gazetted. On 12th July HM King George V inspected a squadron guard of honour at the new Town Headquarters in Coplaw Street; and the *Glasgow Herald* gave considerable publicity to the formation flying of the four Lynx Avros as they left for that summer's camp – again at Leuchars. In October Mr J. K. Horsburgh joined and – to help find the right type of aircraft for the awkward steep approaches into Renfrew – the Fairey Fawn arrived.

5. Renfrew post-war.
The dark-roofed hangars were the first home of 602 Squadron.

A page of history was turned when Pilot Officers D. F. McIntyre and C. A. S. Parker became first to gain Auxiliary wings. Another – sadder – page records that during a practice aerobatic flight in May 1928, Pilot Officer J. P. Drew was killed, the first squadron casualty. Almost 200 hours were flown during July, though, and Squadron Leader (later Air Marshal Sir) Roderick Carr came to test pilots and air-gunners. Marshal of the RAF Viscount Trenchard paid the first of many visits and in 1929 the Westland Wapiti became the squadron's replacement machine. To show his delight at 602 being awarded the coveted Esher Trophy – competed for by all AAF squadrons – Lord Trenchard came to Glasgow City Chambers to present the trophy to the C.O.

6. P/O the Marquess of Clydesdale (left)
and P/O Norman Jones of 601.

During 1930 the Marquess of Douglas and Clydesdale became Member of Parliament for East Renfrewshire and on 7th June Nos. 26 (Army Co-operation) and 100 (Torpedo Bomber) Squadrons came up from Catterick, Yorkshire, and Donibristle to join 603 (City of Edinburgh) and RAF Leuchars' machines in a great flying display at Renfrew organised by 602 Squadron. In July the squadron proceeded to Hawkinge, Kent, for summer camp, flying 451 hours – a record! The following year Mr E. A. Howell was commissioned – he later transferred to the RAF and, in 1941, arriving in Crete to take over 33 Squadron of Hurricanes, he was badly wounded and left for dead. Found by German paratroopers he was flown to Greece virtually a complete cripple. His escape from imprisonment and eventual return to the Middle East are recounted in his book *Escape to Live*; he became a wing commander and received both the OBE, and the DFC for his flying and for his incredible escape. He now spends most of his time working for Moral Re-Armament in North America, coming back to St Andrews for occasional leaves.

January of 1933 saw the squadron moving to the new airfield at Abbotsinch and in April another page of history was written when Squadron Leader the Marquess of Clydesdale (with Colonel L. V. S. Blacker as observer) and Flight Lieutenant D. F. McIntyre (with a Mr Bonnett as photographer) became the first men to fly over Mount

Everest in two Westland Wallace aircraft as part of the Houston Expedition. Both airmen were awarded the Air Force Cross – a great triumph for them and for the squadron. In March 1934, the faster Hawker Hart was received and for the Empire Flying Display of 1935 about 1,500 spectators came to see the flying. The following month Mr A. V. R. Johnstone was commissioned and in July 602 became the first AAF unit to carry out an Armaments Training Camp at North Coates Fittes, near Grimsby. They dropped 529 bombs and fired 13,600 rounds in competition with RAF squadrons.

7. 602 v Scottish Flying Club, Fullerton Trophy Contest.
Left to right: Rintoul, Pinkerton, Farquhar, Cochran, unknown lady,
Robertson, Walker, Orr.

In October Flight Lieutenant A. D. Selway became adjutant, Flying Officer A. H. McHely, stores officer, and Messrs R. F. Boyd and J. M. Robinson joined for pilot training. April 1936 saw No. 17 (F) Squadron's Bristol Bulldogs flying in for fighter affiliation exercises. In May six of the squadron aircraft left Abbotsinch and joined with 603 and 607 (County of Durham) in a flight to Newtownards, Northern Ireland, for a luncheon with the Marquess of Londonderry and his guest – Herr von Ribbentrop (who was vastly interested in 'these weekend flyers'). In June the Hawker Hind became the squadron aircraft and as Squadron Leader the Marquess of Clydesdale retired – as was the AAF custom after five years of command – Squadron Leader D. F. McIntyre, AFC, took over. Messrs D. M. Jack and A. A. McKellar joined, and in February 1937 the squadron was transferred from No. 6 (Auxiliary) Group to No. 2 (Bomber) Group and flew down that summer to Rochford (Southend) for annual camp. Lord Stonehaven, the Honorary Air Commodore, visited the men in camp and Air Commodore S. Goble, CBE, DSO, a famous Australian pilot, presented the badge that had been approved by King George VI. A special Guest Night at The Palace Hotel, Southend-on-Sea, attended by the Mayor and Council, was a highlight of the summer camp.

Former members of this period will recall the visit of a well-known World War I airman – Squadron Leader D. S. Jillings, MBE, MC, for a pre-AOC's inspection – others will have happier memories of 12th December, 1937, when fifteen officers provided the guard of honour at the wedding of the Marquess of Clydesdale to the Lady Elizabeth Percy at St Giles' Cathedral, Edinburgh. At the end of the King's speech opening the great Glasgow Exhibition on 3rd May, 1938, the squadron flew overhead in company with Nos. 269 (RAF) and 603 Squadrons.

Flight Lieutenant H. S. Darley became assistant adjutant in June when the Hawker Hector was received. During summer camp at Hawkinge six officers and 150 airmen spent a day in Boulogne and, to the relief of the C.O., all turned up for the return boat! On 29th October, to mark the closing of the Glasgow Exhibition, three aircraft flew in co-operation with the searchlights over Ibrox Stadium, 602 creating a record for night-flying in the AAF. On 14th January, 1939, another page in the diary notes the transfer from army co-

8. A Flight, Abbotsinch, September 1939. Charles Hector McLean (standing in overalls), Marcus Robinson (seated centre, hatless), Findlay Boyd on his left, and Donald Jack on Boyd's left.

operation to the fighter role on transfer into No. 12(F) Group and re-equipment with the Gloster Gauntlet. The squadron was now affiliated to No. 22 (City of Sydney) Squadron, Royal Australian Air Force, and, to give the pilots some air-fighting practice, No. 41(F) Squadron and two Fairey Battle light-bombers flew up for exercise.

In April 1939 came the beginning of something new – the training of Leading Aircraftman Phillips as a pilot – the first to volunteer for the new NCO-pilot category in the AAF. In May a record crowd of over 20,000 saw an exciting Empire Air Day display and the excitement was increased when news came that 602 Squadron was to get the Spitfire – a considerable honour at a time when many regular squadrons were still flying the Gladiator biplane and many fighter squadrons would have been delighted to get the Hurricane. The summer camp was held at Church Fenton, Yorkshire, and included day and night defence exercises along the East Coast which were to prove invaluable in the future. On 24th August came embodiment into the Royal Air Force and the arrival, within days, of some of the AAF Reserve, including Flight Lieutenant J. H. Hodge who – in 1940 – was to join No. 11(F) Group (defending London and the South of England) as a controller, working alongside Wing Commander the Marquess of Clydesdale.

Twenty-two officers and 174 airmen were now under Squadron Leader A. D. Farquhar's command on active service, with Flight Lieutenants M. Robinson and G. C. Pinkerton as flight-commanders. The first few days of war were uneventful but the C.O. used them for testing a device he had evolved which overcame the obscuring of windscreens from airscrew vapour. Headquarters Fighter Command found this most satisfactory and so 602 Squadron made a notable contribution to fighter efficiency, not widely known. As 603 Squadron sent pilots over from Turnhouse on Spitfire 'know-how' attachments, the Padre, Squadron Leader (Rev) L. A. Sutherland, assisted by Sergeant R. Melville, organised a splendid variety show to relieve the monotony which was broken only by the despatch of one flight every day to Grangemouth. On 7th October the entire squadron moved there only to transfer again on 13th October, this time to Drem south-west of North Berwick on the East Coast.

Then came 16th October – a date which will always be remembered in RAF history. At 9.45 a.m. Blue Section of three Spitfires was scrambled under Flight Lieutenant George Pinkerton, B Flight leader, a farmer's son from Millerston, Glasgow. Sergeant Harry Henderson and his groundcrew had the aircraft 'on the top line' and, after one earlier alert which had come to nothing, every man now hoped that the City of Glasgow pilots would have the opportunity of combat. Imagine, then, the thrill when in the control room the cry 'Tally-ho' was heard over the radio from Pinkerton – indicating that the enemy had been sighted. When the Spitfires landed and it was seen that the guns had been fired excitement was intense, only to be disappointed as Pinkerton reported that the enemy machine had turned for home on seeing the Spitfires and that although he had ordered the Section to open fire, the enemy dived into thick cloud with smoke streaming from it and, in the absence of any photographic evidence or other confirmation of damage, no claim was made. Only a fraction of seconds – or yards – probably prevented 602 from making the first 'kill' over British territory since 1918.

The day, though, was by no means over, for just after 2.00 p.m. the scramble order was again received after the early warning had picked up the 'plots' of approaching aircraft. Both 602 and 603 Squadrons were ordered off and told to head for the Forth Bridge and Rosyth; earlier reconnaissance by the Luftwaffe had suggested to the Air Ministry and Admiralty that the naval base at Rosyth was likely to be an early target. Pinkerton was again first to spot the enemy and coolly led his pilots down as a Junkers Ju.88 started its bombing run, diving to only 5,000 feet above the water. Pinkerton got the plane into his sights and opened fire, the Junkers hitting the sea near Crail. Seconds earlier their friendly rivals of 603 had shot down a Heinkel, thus robbing the City of Glasgow of the honour of being first and making the morning's inconclusive sortie even more regrettable. However, to this day there are arguments about who really was first with a victory as, in the haste to get airborne, Pinkerton's flight take-off time was not recorded until after the Spitfires landed and it will always be claimed by 602's veterans that 'their Junkers' hit the sea before the Heinkel shot down by 603. Pinkerton, though, was happy that both the Scottish Auxiliary fighter squadrons had shared the first successes over the British Isles. One of the Junkers' crew was dead when the launch picked up his body and he was buried in Joppa Cemetery, Edinburgh. Military honours were accorded, and it was Harry Henderson and his comrades who carried the coffin. Pinkerton visited the pilot, Helmut Pohle, in hospital for, at this stage, the chivalry of World War I was maintained, by the Royal Air Force at any rate.

Telegrams arrived from the Chief of Air Staff and the Air Officer Commanding-in-Chief of Fighter Command; and the Air Officer Commanding No. 13(F) Group at Newcastle, Air Vice-Marshal Saul, flew up to congratulate both squadrons. Viscount Stonehaven, the Honorary Air Commodore and the AOC-in-C Coastal Command, added their congratulations with the newspapers headlining FIRST BLOOD TO THE AUXILIARIES throughout the country. On 28th October the two squadrons were again involved – this time in a genuinely shared combat, for after 602's pilots had scored hits on a Heinkel He.111, Red Section of 603 finished it off near Haddington, East Lothian. This was the first machine to be shot down on to British soil in World War II and how proud was Scotland that her sons achieved it. A month later came the inevitable penalty, for Pinkerton, awarded the DFC, along with his C.O. Squadron Leader Farquhar, was promoted to command No. 65 Squadron – a tribute to the AAF but a tremendous loss to the City of Glasgow squadron.

On 22nd December, Flight Lieutenant J. D. Urie, with Flying Officers C. H. McLean and A. Strong, sighted two Heinkels with underslung mines, fifteen miles east of May Isle. The nearest was promptly shot into the sea – the other making off for home at top speed. Our merchant ships had been saved from possible disaster once again and on 13th January, 1940, another solitary raider was badly damaged by Red Section off Carnoustie and then helped into the sea by No. 111 Squadron – another shared victory. On 9th February Squadron Leader Farquhar caught up with an He.111 twenty miles out to sea and so seriously did his attack damage the enemy that the Luftwaffe pilot turned round and crash-landed near North Berwick; one crew-member was killed, three were taken prisoner. On 22nd February, accompanied by Flight Lieutenant G. V. Proudman who was flying a cannon-armed Spitfire, Squadron Leader Farquhar shot down a Heinkel at Coldingham, Berwickshire, and, seeing the Luftwaffe crew trying to set their aircraft ablaze, Farquhar landed in the same field; unfortunately the Spitfire turned over on the soft ground and it was the Germans who helped free the C.O. from his position trapped upside-down in the cockpit!

On 26th February King George VI accompanied by Air Marshal Dowding, AOC-in-C, Fighter Command, arrived to present the squadron's first decorations – DFCs – to Squadron Leaders Farquhar and Pinkerton. In March the C.O. was promoted and left to command RAF Martlesham, Suffolk, and Pinkerton returned from 65 Squadron to lead 602 – a most popular move. Sergeant-Pilot R. F. P. Phillips also returned, from No. 7 Flying Training School, Peterborough, to become a squadron pilot, the first of the pre-war airmen volunteers to earn his wings. A Flight was moved up to Montrose and B Flight to Dyce, Aberdeen, with Flight Lieutenant M. Robinson promoted to lead No. 616 (South Yorkshire) Squadron which was soon to be heavily engaged in the air war.

By 28th May the squadron was back at Drem, sharing the airfield with No. 605 (County of Warwick) which was resting after a most hectic stay in France and over Dunkirk during May. Flight Lieutenant Archie McKellar of Paisley, a 1936 member, who had a part in one of the earlier engagements, was transferred to be a 605 Squadron flight commander and to make history. Said to be a pilot of intense likes and dislikes there was no middle course and he was always immaculately turned out as an example to his men. Although a strict disciplinarian McKellar was a true friend and another pilot said 'He would share his last bit of money with you.' Glasgow was proud of his later successes and only sorry they were not with 602.

It was on 25th June that Flight Lieutenant A. V. R. Johnstone opened his personal account with a Heinkel caught in searchlights and smartly deposited into the sea, the crew were taken prisoner. On 1st July, after a Ju.88 had jettisoned its bombs in the sea off Dunbar, it was intercepted and damaged by Flying Officer Webb and later crashed in France. A week later the same pilot, flying with Johnstone, destroyed a Heinkel. On the 9th, Red Section intercepted two Ju.88s ten miles east of Fifeness and both Flight Lieutenant Urie and Flying Officer Jack entered claims for damage to the enemy. 13th July saw efforts being made to disperse the aircraft in the nearby woods using all the natural camouflage available. 'The boys of Fettes College worked hard assisting ground personnel and ended their days with enormous appetites' quotes the diary. In the early hours of 24th July the searchlights picked up an He.111 at 4,000 feet and Sergeant Andrew McDowall, an engineer by trade but a first-class shot from his pre-war sporting days, was ordered to intercept. Confused by the beams he suddenly found himself not behind the enemy, but approaching head-on. Two parachute mines were jettisoned by the Heinkel but luckily did not hit the Spitfire. McDowall attacked without visible results but it was later reported that an aircraft was down in the sea. On 28th July the new aircraft were blessed by the clergy and in the evening Sir Harry Lauder gave the boys a much-enjoyed show attended by Sir David and Lady Kinloch and by Miss Jose McIndoe who gave £100 to start a 602 Squadron Benevolent Fund.

On 12th August the squadron was suddenly ordered down to Westhampnett, Sussex (now the Goodwood racing circuit), to relieve No. 145 Squadron. Arriving on the 13th the squadron was in action the next day and on the 15th – now known to have been Fighter Command's best day – a Dornier 17P (claimed as a Do. 215) was shot into the sea off Ventnor, Isle of Wight. On the 16th two patrols were flown: during the lunchtime sortie Ju.87s were caught dive-bombing Tangmere airfield, one was destroyed and another damaged. At tea-time about sixty Heinkels escorted by Messerschmitt Bf.110s were sighted and, without loss in the air, five Messerschmitts were brought down. One Spitfire was destroyed and one damaged on the ground during enemy bombing. Next day was a rest-day and on the 18th, when a mixed force of over fifty Ju.87s and Messerschmitt Bf.109s were attacking Ford airfield, eight dive-bombers were shot down and others were damaged. Five Spitfires were lost in the dog-fighting; Flight Lieutenant Urie baled out wounded, Flying Officer P. J. Ferguson, also wounded, crash-landed, and Pilot Officer H. M. Moody baled out unhurt.

19th August was a strangely quiet day for Fighter Command but 602 damaged a Ju.88 which force-landed in France, Pilot Officer Moody again baling out, this time with burns after return fire from the Junkers. On the 22nd the squadron entertained Group Captain HRH the Duke of Kent and next day Pilot Officer T. G. F. Ritchie collided with another Spitfire in action but he nursed the damaged aircraft down to a good landing at a time when Spitfires were more precious than gold. On Sunday, 25th August a solid mass of Luftwaffe aircraft was sighted between Swanage and Dorchester – perhaps three hundred in all – the squadron pilots singling out their own targets as they dived into the attack. The squadron claim afterwards was a mixed bag of twelve enemy destroyed or damaged but post-war research indicates that duplicated claims give the squadron only three 'probables'. Two Spitfires were shot down and Flying Officer W. H. Coverley and Sergeant M. H. Sprague baled out unhurt.

Next day, over Selsey Bill, about 150 of the enemy were sighted advancing towards London – the squadron managed to split this force and destroyed one Heinkel with another damaged, plus a Do.17Z. Flying Officer Charles McLean and Sergeant C. F. Babbage were shot down, McLean crashed and had to have his right foot amputated, Babbage baled out unhurt into the sea. Later that day an He.59 floatplane, bearing Red Cross markings but reported 'spotting', was shot down on the Prime Minister's personal orders. The next two days were rest periods and on the 29th the Luftwaffe showed little inclination to stay and fight it out. It was 31st August when, near Gravesend, a mixed force of bombers and fighters was turned back by 602 who claimed a Ju.88 and a Bf.109 for the loss of a Spitfire damaged which Sergeant D. W. Elcombe landed without personal injury.

9. Squadron at West Hampnett, September 1940. *Back, left to right:* unknown, Rose, McDowall, Hart, unknown, Proctor, Phillips, Lyall, Eade, unknown, Barthropp (with pup), unknown, Niven. *Front:* Micky Mount, Findlay Boyd, A. V. R. Johnstone (C.O.), D. Urie, D. Jack.

Squadron Leader A. V. R. 'Sandy' Johnstone had led the squadron since July with losses far less than many other units. On 4th September, for example, a force of Dorniers escorted by Bf.109s and Bf.110s was intercepted and dispersed without casualties to 602 personnel. On the 6th, though, it was a different story as B Flight was surprised by a force of Bf.109s, losing three Spitfires for only one certain Messerschmitt, Pilot Officer Ritchie baling out slightly wounded, the other pilots unhurt. Next day, over Mayfield, Sussex, there was a terrific battle in which, alas, Flying Officer W. H. Coverley and Pilot Officer H. M. Moody were killed, two other Spitfires were hit but without injury to the pilots. Two Dorniers were believed destroyed and it is possible the two dead pilots may also have achieved successes before losing their lives in defence of these islands.

Next day the Chief of the Air Staff came to thank and congratulate the squadron on their stout efforts and to announce a DFC for Flight Lieutenant Findlay Boyd. On the 9th – again over Mayfield – Flight Lieutenant P. C. Webb crashed after being wounded in combat with Dorniers, a bag of bombers and fighters being claimed as damaged. Then came a well-deserved award of the Distinguished Flying Medal for Sergeant Whall, but by 11th September only eight Spitfires were serviceable and the squadron joined with 213 Squadron to make a composite unit. Nevertheless the spirit was undaunted and six enemy were claimed destroyed or damaged for the losses of Sergeant M. H. Sprague, killed, and two other Spitfires lost, with Pilot Officer S. N. Rose wounded. There was a welcome award of the DFC, to Squadron Leader Johnstone and the chase of a Dornier which was left smoking (it is now known that it crashed on landing at Cherbourg).

In the heavy fighting on 15th September (commemorated for years as Battle of Britain Day because for a long time it was thought Fighter Command's greatest day) the squadron lost only one machine the pilot baling out safely. Over the airfields of Biggin Hill and Kenley – vital to the country's survival – several enemy aircraft were claimed (and probably re-claimed by other fighters who attacked them as they limped away). Then came a most welcome respite until 21st September when a Ju.88 was shared with 238 Squadron near Bosham. On the 24th a Bf.110 was damaged near Swanage and the next day another was hit near Brighton and is known to have crashed on trying to land back at its base. On the 26th the squadron intercepted an evening attack on the Supermarine works at Southampton, claiming four enemy hit without loss to the squadron. Next day, over Mayfield, Pilot Officer D. H. Gage was brought down, happily unhurt, the other pilots claiming three enemy to offset this loss. On 30th September the Luftwaffe resumed their large formations and a squadron of twelve Ju.88s, flying north, was sighted by the C.O. who ordered every pilot to select his own target – on landing the squadron claimed seven destroyed or damaged and post-war evidence reduces this to three confirmed destroyed and three damaged – with no loss to the City of Glasgow aircraft.

On 1st October, as the squadron flew head-on into an approaching formation, the enemy turned for home – next day a solitary Ju.88 approached Shoreham only to find Findlay Boyd and Paddy Barthropp on patrol. As the enemy turned the 602 pair overtook it and shot it into the sea 35 miles out. The following day another lone Ju.88 was chased to the French coast and left damaged, research indicating that it did not reach its base. On the 7th two Spitfires were detached to deal with a Messerschmitt Bf.109 which was shot down but, alas, only after it had brought down Sergeant B. E. P. Whall, DFM, who died next day – a grievous loss. Air Vice-Marshal Keith Park, AOC No. 11(F) Group, flew down in his Hurricane to thank the squadron and to announce a Bar to Findlay Boyd's DFC, and a DFM for Sergeant Babbage. Wing Commander the Duke of Hamilton (formerly Marquess of Clydesdale) visited his old squadron and was delighted when a moonlight sortie – no picnic in a Spitfire – resulted in a Ju.88 being probably destroyed off Beachy Head.

On the 26th Sergeant D. W. Elcombe did not return from patrol and was presumed killed by the enemy who reported two Heinkels missing, so Elcombe may have been victorious before losing his own life. Next day a Ju.88 was claimed as a 'probable' near Portsmouth and as, again, the Luftwaffe admitted losing two which could not be allocated one may well have been 602's victim. On the 29th came the squadron's best effort to date, for when they were flying at 28,000 feet they spotted two forces of Bf.109s at 25,000 feet and, diving out of the sun they claimed seven destroyed. Post-war research confirms at least five of these and, as the Luftwaffe fighter-bombers dumped their bombs haphazardly, many lives and much property was saved by the squadron's sharpshooting. At least three other Messerschmitts did not return from this engagement and could well be a trio claimed by 602 as probably destroyed. There was no loss to the squadron but next day Pilot Officer D. H. Gage and Sergeant W. B. Smith were brought down, Smith was slightly wounded and the Spitfire of Pilot Officer A. McL. Lyall was also damaged for only one of the enemy. 1st November brought tragic news – the death of former-member Squadron Leader A. A. McKellar who had gained the DFC and Bar with 605 Squadron; Archie's DSO was promulgated later, having been approved before his last flight.

The rain and mud kept 602 grounded until 6th November when Sergeant Andrew McDowall destroyed two Bf.109s and well-earned his DFM. Pilot Officers W. P. Hopkin and McL. Lyall each claimed probables and Squadron Leader Johnstone damaged a Ju.88, all near Bognor. Another Ju.88 was damaged on the 8th and on the 12th Flight Lieutenant C. J. Mount (whose eagle eyes had led to the great triumph of 29th October) was awarded the DFC. On the 13th Blue Section, led by Flight Lieutenant Findlay Boyd with Pilot Officer J. S. Hart and Squadron Leader J. D. Urie (who was visiting his old squadron), shared a Ju.88. On the 15th Sergeant McDowall was 'swiped' from above and slightly wounded and on the 28th November Pilot Officer McL. Lyall, climbing to 33,000 feet, was shot down and killed by a new high-flying type of Luftwaffe machine. On 1st December there was a double celebration as Sergeants Babbage and McDowall were commissioned and a Bar to his DFM was announced for Pilot Officer Andrew McDowall.

On 11th December Flying Officer A. L. Edy, DFC, was forced down but was unhurt and as instructions came for the squadron to move for a rest period to Prestwick, Pilot Officer Ian Cosby was transferred into 141 Squadron (getting a DFC later). Five other pilots who had not been long with 602, joined 610 (County of Chester) Squadron and Findlay Boyd was promoted to take command of the famous No. 54 Squadron. The hardened airmen were somewhat amused, on reaching Prestwick, to learn that the air-raid sirens which sounded soon afterwards were the first heard in that area – as a matter of interest it was a Blenheim and an Avro Manchester which caused the flap as the local Air Raid Precautions' organisation was not yet used to aircraft identification. Then, when the King and Queen passed through Glasgow, Squadron Leader Johnstone was invited to lunch with them to tell them something of the squadron's activities. Flight Lieutenant Mount, DFC, left to command No. 317 (Polish) Squadron, and in early March Glasgow newspapers came to photograph members of the squadron who were co-operating at this time with No. 600 (City of London) Squadron's Blenheims and also helping with the film *A Yank in the RAF* for 20th Century Fox.

On the well-deserved promotion of Squadron Leader Johnstone, Squadron Leader J. Kilmartin, DFC, a veteran of No. 1 Squadron's fighting in France – took command and on the 15th April, as the squadron moved over to Ayr, Andrew McDowall left to become a flight commander in No. 245 Squadron. B Flight was transferred temporarily to Montrose to defend the training sector and in early May, when the night blitz came to Glasgow, at least one bomber was damaged and probably did not make it back to Norway. Squadron Leader P. J. Simpson, commanding No. 504 (County of Nottingham), was flying from Northern Ireland to visit 602 when he met – and shot down – a Dornier 17, to the delight of all. Following his visit 602 also moved over to Limavady to co-operate with the Home Fleet and then, as Squadron Leader Donald Jack formed a new squadron – No. 123 – at Turnhouse, Squadron Leader Kilmartin also left to form No. 313 (Czech) Squadron and Squadron Leader P. E. Meagher took over. Flight Lieutenant Alan Deere, a New Zealand ace with the DFC and Bar from his 54 Squadron combats, came up to command a flight and during one of his first night patrols he was directed towards an enemy aircraft flying towards Glasgow. Before 'Al' could get within firing range the machine, a Bf.110, crashed – the pilot who had baled out being none other than Rudolph Hess!

Flight Lieutenant Glyn Ritchie, one of the few Auxiliaries now left, took over the other flight and as Pilot Officer Babbage, DFM, left for No. 41 Squadron, a batch of new Spitfire IIs came and the squadron flew down to Kenley in Surrey to begin a new phase: the offensive operations over Europe which Mr Churchill had ordered. The Kenley Wing comprised 602, 452 (RAAF) and 485 (RNZAF) under Wing Commander John Peel who according to some historians, fired the first shots in the Battle of Britain. The Wing's tasks included escort duties for our small forces of daylight bombers penetrating into Belgium, France and Holland, mainly Blenheims and Hampdens but with the four-engined Short Stirling about to make its debut in Bomber Command's day raids. 'Rhubarb' operations – flights of two or four Spitfires to beat up enemy airfields and ground targets including radar stations, enemy trains, flak posts, road transports and barges – broke the monotony of escorts and were designed to force the Luftwaffe to keep a strong defensive belt around the coastline, relieving pressure on Malta and, later, on Russia.

Squadron Leader Meagher got a Bf.109 on 14th July but Flight Lieutenant Glyn Ritchie was lost on the 21st, his flight was taken over by Flight Lieutenant T. D. Williams, DFC, from 611 (West Lancs) Squadron. Then on 30th July Spitfire Mk.Vs arrived and Flight Lieutenant Deere and Flying Officer 'Mitzi' Darling blooded their machines in a low-level sortie over France. On 1st August, when Squadron Leader Meagher entered hospital, Al Deere became C.O. and celebrated promotion by getting a Bf.109 over Gravelines – his first success from Kenley. Over St Omer on 7th August the squadron scored a double against the new Bf.109F with one destroyed and another probable, but Pilot Officer Thornton did not return. On the 9th, over Bethune, the squadron damaged three Bf.109s and claimed another damaged but Al Deere had to make an emergency landing at Manston – with forty cannon or bullet holes in his aircraft. The Kenley Wing lost five Spitfires that day for although we were on the offensive the Luftwaffe now had the advantage of being able to nurse crippled aircraft down to a French, Belgian or Dutch field, whereas the RAF had to cross the Channel – a reversal of the 1940 fighting. On 12th August, while escorting Hampdens to Gosnay Power Station, the squadron was jumped and Sergeant Bell-Walker was shot down (it was known later that he had been wounded and was a prisoner). On the 16th there was a morning show and Flight Lieutenant Williams and Sergeant Booty scored victories.

That, in brief, was the continuing story of 1941 with the squadron tally mounting slowly but with losses as the fight was taken right into the enemy camp. The Secretary of State for Air, Sir Archibald Sinclair, came to speak to the squadrons during early September when the new Focke-Wulf 190 was making life difficult. Happily not all of the missing pilots were killed or taken prisoner and Sergeant Bell, brought down in September, returned to England via Gibraltar after evading capture, thanks to the help of courageous patriots. On 14th January, 1942, the squadron moved over to Redhill and at the end of Al Deere's tour of duty, that great Irishman, Squadron Leader Brendan 'Paddy' Finucane, DSO, DFC and Bar, left 452 (RAAF) Squadron to take command – a fine tribute to the City of Glasgow men.

Group Captain Victor Beamish, DSO and Bar, DFC, AFC, one of four famous rugby players in the RAF, was then commanding the Kenley Sector and often flew with 602. On the morning of 12th February, in company with Wing Commander Findlay Boyd (the pre-war 602 Auxiliary), he flew a 'Jim Crow' early morning reconnaissance-cum-offensive sortie, looking for possible targets on the French coast. To their amazement they came out of cloud almost directly above a great German battle fleet – it was *Scharnhorst* and *Gneisenau* with their escorts trying to make for a German port under a cloak of poor visibility. Beamish and Boyd, ordered to maintain

10. Squadron at Kenley, 1942. *Standing, left to right:* W. J. Whitmore, E. H. Francis, A. Barton, Loop Schaefer, D. Buley, Willis, Kistruck, Meyere, T. W. Morrell, Phillips, Jones. *Seated in chairs:* de la Poype, John Dennehey, K. L. B. Hodson, Paddy Finucane, Osborne, Sqdn Doctor, Fifield. *On ground:* Intelligence Officer, H. Strudwick, Sqdn Adjutant, C. K. Tait.

radio silence, made for the nearest airfield and informed the Air Ministry. Within minutes an attempt was in motion to prevent the enemy convoy from reaching the North Sea but it was too late – a posthumous VC was awarded to the Fleet Air Arm pilot Lieutenant-Commander Esmonde, DSC, but his efforts and a series of do-or-die dives on the flak-ships by 602's Spitfires did not stop the Germans, although their battleships were seriously damaged in the later stages of their escape.

On 20th February Squadron Leader Finucane was wounded during a successful operation against FW.190s at Mardyck and on 13th March the squadron had a field-day over France claiming four FW.190s plus a probable and a damaged – Group Captain Beamish getting two victories with the squadron. On the 18th General Montgomery came to watch a fighter briefing and on the 28th, with a DFC signalled for Flight Lieutenant Bocock, a big dog-fight took place over France, Finucane getting a pair, although this sortie cost the Royal Air Force the lives of Group Captain Beamish and Sergeant Ptacek. No fighter pilot was better-liked or respected than Victor Beamish, a man who never differentiated between officers and airmen and who will ever be remembered with affection by 602's men.

Escorting Hurribombers against shipping brought few combats – the task being to wipe out the flak posts before the Hurricanes bombed. On 17th May Flight Lieutenant Major was shot into the sea and, seeing him in difficulties, Pilot Officer John Dennehey threw his own dinghy down. Regrettably, when the Air Sea Rescue got to the spot, Major was dead. Flight Lieutenant Keith Hodson left to command 401 (RCAF) Squadron and when 'Paddy' Finucane left to take over the Hornchurch Wing, Squadron Leader Peter Brothers, DFC, a Battle of Britain veteran of 32 and 257 Squadrons, assumed command. Australian Sergeant 'Loop' Schaefer scored his first victory during an escort to Boston light-bombers. Then came the Spitfire Mk.IX – the answer to the FW.190. Just as the squadron was beginning to take revenge for lost pilots news came of a move to Peterhead near Aberdeen which even the loyal Scottish ground personnel felt was a bit far north!

The news of Paddy Finucane's death in the Channel following his calm 'This is it, chaps' over the radio, cast a cloud over the squadron, for all ranks had contributed for a silver cigarette box for this popular leader and Paddy was to have flown over to receive it (it was sent, instead, to his father). Flight Lieutenant John Dennehey and Sergeant Schaefer left to strengthen No. 164 Squadron at Sumburgh, Shetlands, but soon after arriving Schaefer lost his life while giving the RAF Regiment gunners some practice in dealing with low-flying intruders. He hit the sea only yards from the gun-post and runway but was killed instantly. John Dennehey later commanded a Hurribomber squadron, getting the DFC, surviving the war to become a National Coal Board executive.

The squadron returned to the south for the Dieppe Raid of 19th August, 1942, getting five destroyed and ten damaged in four patrols but losing one of the last Auxiliaries, Flight Lieutenant Johnny Niven, DFC. To the joy of all, though, news came through next day that Johnny was, in fact, alive and in Brighton Hospital – the message telling of his survival had gone astray. Returning north to re-equip with the high-flying Spitfire VI to cope with the reconnaissance flights over Scapa Flow, Flight Sergeant Joe Kistruck and Sergeant Gerry Eames, a Canadian, damaged a Heinkel off Fair Isle. Then, as the squadron joined up flights in Orkney, at Skeabrae, Squadron Leader M. F. Beytagh took over and Johnny Niven left to instruct after logging 200 Ops hours in 602 from sergeant to flight commander.

11. Shetlands Flight at Sumburgh, 1943. *Left to right:* Condon, Kistruck, Rippon, Turner, Marryshow. *On wing:* Flight Sergeant unknown, Leslie Hunt, Sergeant unknown, Davey.

Down then to Perranporth in Cornwall for Bay of Biscay escorts. Sergeant Gerry Eames was lost on a shipping reconnaissance on 11th April, 1943, but he was picked up in his single-seater dinghy almost two weeks later, to establish an all-time record for endurance on his aircrew rations. Then came a move to Fairlop, Essex (the site originally purchased for the London airport, though never used as such). From here, on part of No. 121 Airfield, Allied Expeditionary

Air Force, the squadron was out every day under Wing Commander H. Bird-Wilson, escorting the bombing of pre-invasion targets. Moving into Bognor airstrip, Flight Lieutenant Freeborn, DFC and Bar, left to take over 118 Squadron and, on moving again into Kingsnorth, Flight Lieutenant W. W. J. Loud, DFC, a long-serving member, became a flight commander. By August 1943 there were only fifteen of the pre-war City of Glasgow airmen still with the squadron and they were asked to agree to serve anywhere (the original intention being that they would remain with the squadron they had joined pre-war). A DFC was awarded to Squadron Leader Mike Beytagh ('a friend and inspiration for over a year' to quote the diary) and as newly-commissioned Pilot Officer Joe Kistruck notched his hundredth sweep over Europe, the DFC came for Warrant Officer Blair with the Croix de Guerre for Sergeant J. Remlinger, Free French.

Another Frenchman who was to make a name for himself – Flight Sergeant Pierre Closterman – joined 602 at this time as Squadron Leader R. A. Sutherland was promoted from flight commander to command, getting a DFC shortly afterwards and travelling north in charge of a representative squadron party to meet Sir Patrick Dollan and to receive overwhelming hospitality in Glasgow. So few combats were possible with the Luftwaffe showing reluctance to fight that 602 put forward the suggestion that the Germans ask the Japanese to loan them a few pilots. After a spell at Detling, Kent, with No. 125 Airfield, another rest period was ordered and back to Orkney went 602 to take over old Spitfire Vbs; 'clipped and clapped' was the general comment! However, when a Bf.109 with long-range tanks ventured over Scapa Flow at 32,000 feet, two squadron Spitfires managed to climb up to bring the enemy down – for which they were warmly congratulated by the authorities. There were now aircrew from six countries – a cosmopolitan mixture working splendidly together.

In March 1944, a Ju.88 was brought down over Scapa after which the squadron was moved to Llanbedr in North Wales for a revolutionary experiment – the fitting of bombs to the sleek Spitfire – re-

12. Sgt W. W. J. Loud with Spitfire Vb BM124 'Queen Salote'.

garded by many as impracticable, but turned to brilliant account by 602 and others. Once trained the squadron moved back into Detling and were soon dive-bombing the 'Noball' sites – the ski-shaped launching platforms for a weapon then unknown but which later became the V.1 or doodlebug. No. 602 Squadron was first of the Spitfire units to carry out this dive-bombing, followed by 132 Squadron. Then came a move to Ford, Sussex, and Pierre Closterman was awarded the Croix de Guerre with two Palmes for his press-on flying, escorting the Mosquito fighter-bombers from Gravesend and Hartford Bridge (now Blackbushe airfield) and carrying out bombing with 250 lb or 500 lb bombs, against key targets.

13. Pilots being briefed for Spitbomber attack on V.1 site, 1944.

Before D-Day the aircraft, with their zebra stripes, were on the top-line and flew four sorties on 6th June as low-cover to the landing craft. Next day Pilot Officer L. D. Kidd landed in France and was reported 'missing believed safe' – a new expression. In fact he returned to the U.K. on 10th June having been in the American lines behind the beaches. On 25th June the squadron was flying from an airstrip known then as B.11, strafing everything within range of the Spitfires. On 29th June the squadron dived down on a German staff car near St Fey de Montgomerie. The car overturned and it was later discovered that the V.I.P. passenger was the enemy's commanding general, Erwin Rommel, who was flung into a ditch, fracturing his skull. He survived the injury but on 14th October committed suicide rather than face trial charged with complicity in the plot against

Hitler. Thus did 602 Squadron help shorten the war, for Rommel was
a magnificent leader whose death affected the enemy very considerably.

On 7th July a well-known South African, Squadron Leader
Chris le Roux, DFC and 2 Bars, assumed command, and with the
Spitfire IXe the squadron tore through German transports, destroying eleven on 31st July with the Headquarters 2nd Army Group
signalling thanks and adding 'We had a grandstand view of your
sharpshooting'. By the end of August the squadron held the record
for the 2nd Tactical Air Force's 'flamers' – including Tiger tanks and
other prize targets set ablaze. Now based at Vire, they became the
first squadron to have its own pub *The Getstuk Inn* – constructed
by the airmen from salvaged materials. In September over Belgium
and at the disastrous Arnhem drop, the squadron was in action protecting the airborne troops and bombing all the enemy positions
within reach.

14. Squadron pilots and ground NCOs, Detling, 1944. *Front row left to
right:* Aubertin, Maxie Sutherland, Bagget, Dumbrell, Spence, Jacques,
Gourly, Ted, Hook, Chieffy Macdonald. *Behind:* Penny, Jenkins, Fox.
On wing: Mouse, Manson, Sorge, Robson, Maconachie, Tommy. *On
fuselage:* Kistruck, Timmy Kelly, Ken Charney, Frank Woolley, Jonah,
Oste, Clostermann (cockpit).

With his score at 23½ confirmed victories, Chris le Roux lost his life in an aircraft accident and, after Squadron Leader A. R. Stewart had held the reins for a short time, Squadron Leader R. A. Sutherland, DFC, returned to his old command. Moving back to England, the squadron flew from Coltishall near Norwich and then from Matlask against 'Big Ben' sites – the new and terrible V.2 rocket launching pads. The Spitfire XVI was received, enabling the aircraft to carry a 1,000 lb bomb-load. DFC awards came for Flight Lieutenants T. A. Burke and B. J. Oliver and by early 1945, now from Ludham, the squadron was penetrating over Holland and, refuelling there, pressing into Germany, hitting bridges, railways and everything still working for the enemy. The C.O. got a Bar to his DFC, and when inevitably, after VE Day, 8th May, 1945, the orders came to disband, Wing Commander Sutherland left on promotion to command that great Battle of Britain airfield at North Weald, Essex.

When the Auxiliary Air Force re-formed in 1946 the squadron gathered volunteers old and new at Abbotsinch and, between June and August, Spitfires Mk.XIV were received and Squadron Leader M. Robinson, AFC, assumed command, the Spitfire F.21 coming in 1947 and the Mk.F.22 in the following year. Squadron Leader H. M. Stephen, DSO, DFC and Bar, from Elgin, who had flown in 605 and 74 'Tiger' Squadron, with a final tally of twenty-three victories, took over the squadron in 1950 and in that year the jet de Havilland Vampire FB.5 was received and the squadron moved to Renfrew for a time. Successful summer camps were held at places as far distant as Tangmere, Sussex; Pembrey, Wales; Celle in Germany, and as near as Horsham St Faith, Norfolk; Leuchars, Fife; and Woodvale, Lancashire. During 1952 Glasgow-born Squadron Leader J. A. Forrest took over after serving with Nos. 277, 137 and 174 Squadrons, and in 1953 he was succeeded by Squadron Leader R. B. Davidson, DFC, an Edinburgh man, whose DFC was gained with the tank-buster Hurricanes of 6 Squadron in 1944. Post-war the new C.O. had served with 603 (City of Edinburgh) and in 1956 he handed over to Squadron Leader C. D. Bartman who had flown with 245 Squadron during the war and 257 post-war. Unfortunately his command was cut short by the decision to disband the flying squadrons of the Royal Auxiliary Air Force in March 1957. A bitter blow to all, it must have been felt deeply by the Honorary Air Commodore, the Duke of Hamilton and Brandon, KT, PC, GCVO, AFC, LL.D, DL, who was first commissioned in the squadron in 1927, commanding from 1931 to 1936.

Happily, a few links were maintained – the squadron silver went to the Glasgow University Air Squadron and Group Captain Marcus Robinson, CB, AFC, who had left the squadron in May 1940 to command 616 (South Yorkshire) became chairman of the local Territorial Association which embodied some of the young airmen anxious to give voluntary service for their country. During 1961 the Queen graciously approved the appointment of the Duke of Hamilton as the first Honorary Air Commodore of No. 2 (City of Edinburgh) Maritime Headquarters Unit, Royal Auxiliary Air Force, formed in 1959 to provide backing for the RAF component of the Joint Naval-Air Maritime Headquarters at Pitreavie, Edinburgh, then functionally controlled by Coastal Command – now Strike Command's No. 18 (Maritime) Group.

15. Servicing radio of Vampire FB.5, Tangmere, 1953.

Some, of course, had stayed in the Royal Air Force after 1945, Air Vice-Marshal A. V. R. Johnstone, DFC, completing a full circle; after leading a Spitfire Wing in Malta during 1942, commanding major airfields at Fairwood Common, Wales, Middleton St George, County Durham, and Ballykelly, Northern Ireland, he became Deputy Air Defence Commander at Air HQs, Malaya, then being appointed Air Officer Commanding the Malayan Air Force. In 1965, returning from Borneo where he had been Task Force Commander during the emergency, he was appointed Air Officer Commanding No. 18 Group and Air Officer, Scotland, with vital responsibilities within NATO. Air Commodore C. J. Mount, CBE, DSO, DFC, who left 602 to command 317 (Polish) Squadron, also reached high rank, holding many key appointments (see the 600 Squadron chapter). Air Commodore Peter Brothers, CBE, DSO, DFC and Bar, who left the squadron to lead a Spitfire Wing at Tangmere and Exeter, resigned from the RAF, to join the Colonial Service in Kenya and was the first District Officer to own and operate his own aircraft. In 1949 he returned to the RAF, and, although he had always been a fighter pilot, was given the command of No. 57 (Bomber) Squadron, flying four-engined Lincolns during the Malayan Campaign. In 1951 he commanded the first 'V' bomber Flying Wing at Marham, flying Valiants, and, since 1968, has been RAF Director of Public Relations, Ministry of Defence. Air Commodore Alan Deere, DSO, OBE,

DFC and Bar, after leading the squadron and the Biggin Hill Wing, commanded the airstrip at Selsey, then North Weald, and was Assistant Commandant, Cranwell, and Commandant No. 1 School of Technical Training, Halton. He is currently Director of Sport and Recreational Grounds, Royal Air Force.

Some preferred civvy street and Group Captain Findlay Boyd, DSO, DFC and Bar, flew charter flights for Scottish Aviation, turned later to pig farming and then herring fishing before moving out to Skye. Wing Commander Andrew McDowall, DSO, AFC, DFM and Bar, wanted to stay in the Service but was offered by Rolls-Royce the job of testing the Meteors being sold to the world's air forces, for, after commanding a Spitfire Wing, Andrew had led the RAF's first jet squadron – No. 616 – in 1944. With his family he left for South America to assist the pilots there, afterwards going to Egypt. Later he became contracts engineer with Brush Electrical Engineering keeping up his flying (sometimes in the Rolls-Royce Spitfire) at Tollerton, Nottinghamshire, to which he commutes from Derby in the Bentley formerly owned by Sir Alan Herbert. Others, too, have made their marks, including Pierre Clostermann, who commanded No. 3 Squadron's Tempests, getting the DFC and Bar. Leaving the RAF he became a Member of the House of Representatives in France, writing three books about his combat flying, during which he claimed thirty-three victories in the air and twenty-four on grounded aircraft.

Mr K. J. Rosenfield of Raeburn, North Collingham, Nottinghamshire, has tried hard to keep former members in touch through reunions and one hopes these will long continue for it was always considered a special privilege to be posted to 602 and those who had never before seen Glasgow quickly felt that they, too, 'belonged'. Happily there are reminders of the squadron's great days in the shape of preserved aircraft. In the Imperial War Museum, Lambeth Road, London, is Spitfire I R6915 which was flown by 602 following use by 609 (West Riding) Squadron – probably the most 'operational' Spitfire in the world. Another Spitfire, a Mk.XVI serial TB382 coded LO-X, stood outside the RAF Hospital, Ely, for some years after being on the gate at Middleton St George (now Tees Side Airport). Perhaps 'Sandy' Johnstone was honoured through this machine during his command of Middleton St George? Yet a third Spitfire, Mk.F.21 serial LA198, flown by 602 in 1947 and later with the A.T.C. cadets at Worcester, is now preserved at Locking. It is of passing note that the Spitfire which acts as a memorial to 603 Squadron at Turnhouse, Edinburgh, Mk.XVI serial RW393, was once an instructional groundframe with 602 and was never with 603. The writer has been trying for many years to persuade the authorities to donate this or another appropriate machine to Glasgow and to move to Turnhouse or Edinburgh a genuine 603

Spitfire. The last preserved aircraft with City of Glasgow associations would appear to be a Vampire F3 serial VT812 (see also 601 and 614 Squadron chapters) which is at RAF Colerne, Wiltshire, as this is written, but which may one day be displayed in the Royal Air Force Museum at Hendon. It is thought that more ex-602 machines are preserved than for any other RAuxAF Squadron and perhaps it is only right that the 'senior' unit should be remembered in this way in addition to The Standard awarded by the Queen for the City of Glasgow's airmen-volunteers between 1925–57. They brought ever-lasting credit to the city and to Scotland.

16. Squadron Meteors at Tangmere, 1953.

REPRESENTATIVE SQUADRON AIRCRAFT

de Havilland D.H.9A		H144
Avro 504K		
Fairey Fawn		
Westland Wapiti IIa		J9601 J9860 J9862 K2239
Hawker Hart		K 3749 (Trainer) K3875 K3866
Hawker Hind		K4645 (converted to trainer) K5460 K5507
Hawker Hector		
Gloster Gauntlet II		K5301 K5352 K7833 K7879
Vickers Supermarine Spitfire	I	K9969 L1019 P9381 X4110 X4160 X4187 X4386 'G'
	IIa	P7660 P8047 P8396 P8574
	Vb	A A 910 LO-A BL310 BM649 EN904 EP244
	VI	
	IXb	MH736 MJ398 MJ881 LO-F MK255 ML252
	IXe	NH556 PL344 PL490 PT396

	XVI	SM276 SM350 LO-A RW358
	F.XIV	TX985
	F.21	LA227 LA269 LA315 RAI-K
	F.22	PK349 PK395 PK560 RAI-C
de Havilland Vampire	F.3.	VT812
	FB.5	VZ325 VZ345 WA137 LO-D WA453 LO-A
	FB.9	WR261
Gloster Meteor	T.7	WF773 W WF846 V WL378 U WL480 X

With the introduction of the Gauntlet, camouflage was used and the code ZT allocated, changed on outbreak of hostilities to LO which remained throughout the war. On re-forming in Reserve Command the letters RAI were allotted and then, on return to Fighter Command, LO was used and, unlike other RAuxAF squadrons, remained on the aircraft into the jet age. On changing from all-silver to camouflage the Grey Douglas tartan flash appeared either side of the squadron badge.

Badge: in front of a saltire, a lion rampant. The lion was adopted because of 602's association with Scotland; the saltire representing the cross of St Andrew, being fimbriated to show as white on a blue background.

Motto (translated): 'Beware the tormented lion'.

600
(City of London)
Squadron

ALTHOUGH SQUADRON RECORDS claim that 600 Squadron was formed at Finsbury Barracks in August 1925, the Ministry of Defence states that formation officially took place at Northolt on 14th October, 1925, when one hangar was allocated and Flight Lieutenant the Hon J. H. B. Rodney, MC, was appointed adjutant and flying instructor. D.H.9As and Avro 504Ks were provided and on 17th November Wing Commander A. W. H. James, MC, was appointed to command. The following year, when the first summer camp was held at Manston, Kent, Squadron Leader the Hon F. E. Guest became C.O., and on 18th January, 1927, the squadron moved to Hendon, a total of 1,008 flying hours being recorded that year including a camp at Lympne, Kent, and participation in the Royal Air Force Display.

In 1928 Flight Lieutenant H. B. Russell became adjutant; the annual flying total jumped to 1,117 hours (and in 1929 to 1,142 hours). Re-equipping with the Westland Wapiti and with Flight Lieutenant E. A. Healy as adjutant/instructor the hours rose to over 1,500 and by 1931 to 1,704 hours under Squadron Leader S. B. Collett, who moved over from 601 (County of London) on his promotion. During 1934 Flight Lieutenant J. B. M. Wallis arrived as adjutant/instructor and, tragically, during that year's RAF Display, Squadron Leader Collett lost his life. Squadron Leader Peter Stewart assumed command and a new record was set up when the annual hours exceeded 2,000 including the now-traditional camp, held in 1934 at RAF Tangmere, Sussex. On 20th February, 1935, came another grievous loss, in a civil air crash at Heston of Flight Lieutenant R. 'Jock' Faulds, mourned by all. The Hawker Hart light-bombers replaced Wapitis and for King George V's Jubilee

squadron members were chosen to line the Strand, Squadron Leader
Stewart, Warrant Officer Robinson and Flight Sergeant Hibbens
receiving the special commemorative medal. More than 14,000
spectators turned up for the Empire Air Display and the squadron
was invited to send representative aircraft and crews for the Royal
Review of the RAF at Mildenhall. The summer camp was held at
Sutton Bridge, Lincolnshire, mainly for air-firing and with an
average score of 96·3 per cent for front-gun drogue-shooting 600
Squadron's results were better than those of the competing regular
squadrons, Nos. 29, 54, and 56.

17. Westland Wapitis near Tangmere, 1932.

Flight Lieutenant John Marson (later Air Vice-Marshal) had
lectured the squadron on air-firing and, in addition to Squadron
Leader Stewart, Flight Lieutenants Lord Carlow, G. F. Anderson,
H. B. M. Wallis and H. Walter, with Pilot Officers D. de B. Clark,
S. C. Elworthy and R. G. Kellett, all performed brilliantly in this
friendly rivalry with the RAF full-timers. Following this eventful
camp, Pilot Officer Elworthy, a New Zealander and Cambridge
graduate with an honours degree in law (called to the Bar, Lincoln's
Inn, 1935), decided that he liked the Service life and applied for a
permanent commission. Posted to No. 15(B) Squadron he later
flew in 108 and 82 Squadrons, gaining the AFC, DFC, and DSO,
all in 1940, for his inspiring leadership and instruction on the Bristol
Blenheim. In 1936, as 'Sam' Elworthy departed to the genuine regret
of all, Mr C. J. Mount was interviewed and accepted for pilot-training.
In 1938, he, too, applied for and was accepted for a permanent
commission.

During 1936 a new AAF unit – No. 610 (County of Chester)
Squadron was forming at Hooton Park – their initial equipment of

Avro Tutor trainers being flown to them by 600's pilots. To strengthen the bonds already being forged between the weekend flyers nine of the City of London's Hawker Harts flew as far as Turnhouse (now the civil airport for Edinburgh and SE Scotland). Following

18. Intrepid Birdmen, Hendon, 1937. Air-gunners Peter Banbery, Jack Eames, Larry Fears, Ken Edwards, and Rufus Riseley.

this happy liaison with 603 (City of Edinburgh) Squadron the first night cross-country was recorded when Lord Carlow and R. G. Kellett flew the squadron's Tiger Moth from Hendon to Heston – from such a small beginning did great things materialise!

5th June, 1936, was Pilot Officer Elworthy's wedding day and the diary entry says that this ex-member was 'duly seen off with traditional informality'. The following day Mr Norman Hayes began flying – a pilot also destined to achieve considerable success in the air and on the ground. The August camp was at Hawkinge, Kent, and on 1st December came the welcome news that in view of the squadron's efficiency it was to be transferred from No. 6 (Auxiliary) Group to No. 11 (Fighter) Group. A few weeks later came the first Hawker Demon from Boulton & Paul's Wolverhampton factory and by Empire Air Day, 1937, eight aircraft were able to present a spectacular flying display, visiting no fewer than five airfields to give formation and dive-bombing programmes to delighted crowds. On 11th July the Rt. Hon Lord Lloyd of Dolobran, PC, GCSI, DSO, was flown into Hawkinge by the C.O., to be introduced to the squadron as the Honorary Air Commodore. A sadder occasion during 1937 was the passing of Captain the Hon Frederick E. Guest, former commanding officer, whose will had requested that his ashes be scattered over the Welsh Harp, Hendon, 'which has been such a wonderful mark and many times such a relief to squadron machines, homing in bad weather for Hendon'. His wishes were duly carried out.

19. Demon camera-gunning near Hawkinge, 1937. Flt Lt P. K. Devitt and A.C. Larry Fears.

20. Hawker Demon K5701, 1937.

In time for the Kenley exercises of February 1938, Pilot Officer Tollemache received his wings, and in May Air Commodore Lord Lloyd – soon imbued with the squadron spirit – went solo in a Demon! Special night-flying was laid on to recruit personnel for the Territorial Army's anti-aircraft units, and in June Lord Carlow became C.O. on Peter Stewart's completion of the usual AAF term of command. Camp was at Warmwell, Dorset, and on 26th September the squadron was embodied into the Royal Air Force and, by 1st October, at its war station – Kenley, Surrey – for the Munich crisis. As this panic died down, Pilot Officer P. H. Woodruff came as assistant adjutant and Flight Lieutenant Radford departed to form No. 616 (South Yorkshire) Squadron at Doncaster. Flight Lieutenant E. L. Colbeck Welch came in as adjutant and flying

21. Squadron officers and airmen, 1937. Sqdn Ldr Peter Stewart in centre.

instructor and in December history was made when Squadron Leader Lord Carlow went to RAF Bicester, Oxfordshire, returning with 600 Squadron's first Bristol Blenheim – the revolutionary fast bomber based on Lord Rothermere's privately-built aircraft 'Britain First' which he later handed to the Air Ministry who, fortunately, took the hint!

On 9th January, 1939, an Airspeed Oxford arrived for twin-engine training and by 5th March all pilots with the flying badge (and two not yet awarded wings) had soloed in the Blenheim. Training of the first airmen-pilots then began with Corporal Graham as the first volunteer. Lord Lloyd went dual in a Blenheim, and the April exercises at Northolt included the affiliation of Air Training Corps cadets from Watford who helped with ground duties in return for 'air experience'. 24th August saw the call-up of members and on the following day sixteen Blenheims were at Northolt ready for action. Flight Lieutenants Campbell-Orde, Anderson, and Devitt were posted to the Operations Rooms at Northolt, Tangmere and Filton, where their experience could be used until such time as civilians enlisted into the RAF Volunteer Reserve could be trained, to release pilots for a return to flying. Crews were sleeping under the wings of Blenheims at this time when every siren threatened large-scale Luftwaffe attacks but, alas, the only flight of note records that Pilot Officer Isaacs, practising approaches to Northolt, spun into the ground near Hendon and was killed. Pilot Officer Woodruff then flew all other ab initio pilots to St Athan, Wales, for completion of training.

On 2nd October the squadron moved to Hornchurch, Essex, continuing a few days later to the satellite airfield at Rochford (now Southend Municipal Airport) for defensive patrols and search-light co-operation. On 16th November Flying Officer Vickers was killed when an engine failed during take-off. And – top secret then and for some time – the first three Blenheim IVfs arrived for pilots and air-gunners to be trained in the use of airborne radar – chiefly at Manston, Kent, under Squadron Leader (later Air Marshal Sir Walter) Pretty. Sea patrols were flown over our convoys when the day fighters could not operate and when the first leave-boats began for the British Expeditionary Force in France, the squadron Blenheims flew overhead as protection. Lord Lloyd's Christmas present to the squadron was an all-star concert of West End artistes; and when Lord Carlow was posted to the Directorate of Intelligence, Air Ministry, Squadron Leader Wells took command – on St Valentine's Day, 1940.

11th March is entered in the diary as a day of heroism unequalled in 600's history, although tinged with tragedy. Flying Officer Anthony Tollemache was airborne with Leading Aircraftman Smith as his gunner, and with Lieutenant Sperling of the Welsh Guards as passenger, on a searchlight co-operation exercise. As the Blenheim approached the Manston flarepath for landing it struck a tree, crashed into a field and burst into flames. Both pilot and gunner were uninjured and managed to get clear of the blazing wreckage. Tollemache, realising that Lieutenant Sperling was trapped in the aircraft, endeavoured to break through the forward hatch, completely disregarding exploding ammunition and the intense conflagration. He persisted in his courageous attempts until driven away with his clothing alight. His valiant efforts, though alas in vain, almost cost him his life and made him one of Sir Archibald McIndoe's first 'Guinea Pigs' at the Queen Victoria Hospital, East Grinstead, Sussex. On 6th August, 1940, the Medal of the Order of the British Empire for Gallantry (EGM) was awarded to Flying Officer Anthony Tollemache (on the institution of the George Cross, 24th September, 1940, this automatically became a GC for Tollemache, all living holders of the EGM exchanging their medals at the first convenient investiture). Thus the squadron achieved a truly rare distinction, not only as first of the Auxiliary Air Force squadrons with a George Cross, but, as it transpired, one of only two ever to have this honour – second only to the VC and preceding all Orders of Knighthood.

22. Sqdn Ldr
A. H. H. Tollemache, GC.

After leaving East Grinstead, Anthony Tollemache served for a time as a Controller but pleaded to be allowed to fly again, subsequently becoming a Squadron Leader, and flight-commander in

No. 612 (County of Aberdeen) Squadron of Coastal Command –
happily surviving to become export manager of a large chemicals
company in post-war years. As he lay in the Queen Victoria Hospital
on 10th May, 1940, his comrades were meeting the enemy for the
first time when Pilot Officer Anderson, vectored (directed) towards
France by Control, spotted an He.111. He was about to attack when
his gunner, Leading Aircraftman Baker, sighted another Heinkel
behind, whereupon Anderson quickly turned to tackle his nearest
opponent – four more Heinkels by this time looming into view. The
nearest Heinkel opened fire some 600 yards from the Blenheim and
Anderson, closing-in to 400 yards, saw his tracer bullets entering the
Heinkel's fuselage and, seemingly, putting the gunner out of action.
He then dived below this Heinkel so that Baker could fire from 100
yards' range – after which burst the enemy machines turned for their
base. The Nazi invasion of Belgium and Holland had commenced
and 600 Squadron was ordered by Fighter Command to attack
Rotterdam aerodrome where parachutists had landed – the Blenheims
instructed to destroy all enemy aircraft seen, whether in the air or on
the ground.

At noon, 10th May, B Flight, led by Squadron Leader Wells and
comprising Flying Officers Hayes, Moore, and Rowe, Pilot Officers
Anderson and Haine, with their air-gunners (the C.O. also carrying
Sergeant Davis, observer), set out and, on reaching the Dutch airfield,
destroyed several Ju.52 transports. Twelve Bf.110 fighters, patrolling
high above, dived and 'jumped' the Blenheims, only Flying Officer
Norman Hayes (with Corporal Holmes) landed back at base, having
successfully outwitted three Heinkels, damaging all three in brief
combats. Pilot Officer Dicky Haine (with Pilot Officer Kramer as
gunner) made a forced landing in Holland and the pair made their
way back to England in the destroyer evacuating the Dutch Royal
Family. The three officers were awarded the DFC, Corporal (Later
Sergeant) Holmes getting the DFM. At 1.30 p.m. A Flight was
ordered-off under Flight Lieutenant D. de B. Clark, with Flying
Officers Clackson, Pritchard, E. S. Smith, and Hannay, plus Pilot
Officer Rawlence, and their gunners, Clark carrying Sergeant Wilson,
observer, as well as Corporal Riseley. Their target was Middlekerck-
Zeebrugge-Flushing and an He.111, destroyed on the ground, was
credited to this sortie.

On 16th May the squadron returned from Manston to Northolt
to defend London by night if – as then expected – the Luftwaffe
launched a follow-up offensive over England. Ferry flights were
flown into France by day taking replacement fighter pilots for the
casualties, returning with vital equipment as the allies retreated
towards Calais and Dunkirk. On 24th May Flying Officer Hannay
and his gunner, Leading Aircraftman Short, lost their lives during
a special convoy escort after the failure of their port engine. On 1st

June squadron aircraft were ordered over Dunkirk beaches at 4,000 feet, only to find themselves a target for Royal Navy guns – getting back to base after fifteen minutes of 'violent evasive action'. On 20th June three aircraft took off from Manston on 'Intruder' flights to Arras and St Pol – perhaps the first ever flown by Auxiliaries, though these patrols and others on 26th/27th June, failed to find the Luftwaffe aircraft on the ground. On 2nd July the Air Officer Commanding No. 11(F) Group, Air Vice-Marshal Keith Park, flew his Hurricane into Manston to present Sergeant Holmes with his Distinguished Service Medal – a landmark in squadron history.

On 20th July, after a respite, Pilot Officer A. D. McN. Boyd attacked an He.59 floatplane believed to be spotting for the enemy, though the Luftwaffe claimed it was on Red Cross work! Then, on 8th August, newly-promoted Flying Officer Boyd and Flying Officer D. N. Grice were flying two Blenheims on airborne radar practice when Control ordered them to land as enemy fighters were approaching. Boyd landed at Manston without his partner and the other Blenheim was next seen diving out of a cloud near Ramsgate with both engines ablaze. According to eye-witnesses Flying Officer Grice skilfully pulled the crippled machine out of its dive and, avoiding the main shopping centre and harbour, crashed out to sea. Grice with Sergeant F. J. Keast and Aircraftman J. B. W. Warren (airborne radar operator) were killed and it puzzled many that no posthumous award was made to this gallant pilot who undoubtedly saved many lives by his unselfish airmanship.

On 9th August Flying Officer S. Le Rougetel was at 6,000 feet over Margate when his starboard engine cut and stopped. He ordered Sergeant A. Smith to jump and, when he saw the parachute open, baled-out himself, both landing safely. On Monday 12th August Manston was repeatedly bombed; one Blenheim was totally destroyed and a second damaged. A Section of three aircraft was instructed to move back to Hornchurch for local defence and for defence of the capital. Those who have read *Nine Lives* by Air Commodore Alan Deere will know of his high praise for personnel of 600 Squadron who, notwithstanding the heavy Luftwaffe attacks on Manston, helped to refuel and rearm the day fighters as they touched down. Many of 600's men had been airborne or on ground duties throughout the previous night and should have been resting. In addition to working on the Spitfires, Hurricanes and Defiants, the men mounted their own Lewis gun and exacted a form of revenge for the loss of Flying Officer Grice and his crew as they brought down a Bf.110 with the gun on their dugout. On 14th August three more Blenheims were burnt-out during Luftwaffe bombing of Manston but, luckily, the only squadron casualty was a black-eye for the C.O. when a stone richocheted from the adjutant's tin-hat!

On 15th August Air Commodore 'Al' Deere recalls that he was almost shot down by 600's machine-gun when he came in to land close on the heels of a Bf.110 at which the City of London airmen were firing. 'How those 600 Squadron chaps stick it, I don't know,' was Al's comment at the time. 'Flying Officer Norman Hayes and Flight Lieutenant David Clackson were always on hand to give encouragement and valuable assistance, and when 54 Squadron landed on the 20th August after their fourth patrol of the day I missed the cheerful faces of 600 personnel and was told they'd been evacuated to Hornchurch.' What a compliment from one of the greatest of Churchill's 'Few'!

On 8th September one flight was detached to Redhill; one Blenheim having been destroyed with two others damaged in a further raid on Manston on 16th August, another damaged on 20th. Squadron Leader H. L. Maxwell, DSO, a very experienced pilot, was appointed to command as the first Beaufighter arrived, and the crews felt that here at last was a machine capable of inflicting damage on the Luftwaffe. A week later – 15th/16th September – Flight Lieutenant C. A. Pritchard, with Pilot Officer H. Jacobs and Sergeant Smith, destroyed a Ju.88 off Bexhill just after midnight (they actually claimed a Heinkel according to squadron records). This was a real tonic, especially as it was in the Blenheim. A Douglas Boston was loaned to speed up the training of personnel in airborne radar and as the men became impatient for their turns to train, great news came that an 'old boy', Squadron Leader R. G. Kellett, leading No. 303 (Polish) Squadron at Northolt, had been awarded the DFC and the Polish DFC (he later got a DSO, and a Bar to his DFC).

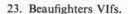

23. Beaufighters VIfs.

On 27th September a new pilot, Gordon Denby, claimed a probable near Hastings, the unidentified enemy aircraft disappearing into clouds on fire. Then, on 30th September, another red-letter day when Flying Officer Boyd and Pilot Officer Haine, DFC, flew the first 'Ops' in Beaufighters. On 1st October the squadron moved to Catterick for a rest and further intensive training, B Flight being detached to Acklington and, on the 24th, to Drem, near Edinburgh. In November Squadron Leader Maxwell became a controller at Headquarters No. 13(F) Group, Newcastle, and Squadron Leader Pritchard was promoted to command as the squadron was taken out of the line so that radar operators (known afterwards as Observer Radio, with flying badge RO) could be trained, using the squadron's Blenheims. January 1941 saw Squadron Leader David Clackson also promoted, to command No. 68 Squadron at Catterick, Pilot Officer Dicky Haine, DFC, going with him. In this squadron one flight was entirely Czech personnel and it was of interest that Squadron Leader Max Aitken of 601 later assumed command of 68 which became a fine unit at Coltishall and elsewhere.

In the squadron diary it is noted that the sole redeeming feature of February 1941 was that it only had 28 days; at the end of that month came Wing Commander G. Stainforth, AFC, the notable Schneider Trophy pilot, to take over on the upgrading of the C.O.'s post. In March one flight moved to Prestwick, Scotland, just in time for Pilot Officer Gordon Denby, with his operator Pilot Officer Gilbert Guest, to shoot down an He.111 which was raiding Glasgow. In early April both the C.O. and Flight Lieutenant Norman Hayes had indecisive combats, making no claims as they did not see the results of their fire. On the 27th came the welcome orders to move south, to Colerne, near Bath, a new airfield in No. 10(F) Group. Unfortunately it meant parting with newly-promoted Squadron Leader Norman Hayes, DFC, who joined 68 Squadron. However, it brought a DFC for Gordon Denby, a very popular award.

A good start was made from Colerne as Flying Officer R. S. Woodward – with Sergeant A. J. Lipscombe – brought down a Ju.88 near Shepton Mallet and three nights later Squadron Leader Pritchard – with Sergeant Gledhill – destroyed a Heinkel over Sherborne despite some very accurate return fire. The squadron's call-sign at this time was 'Gardener', the C.O. naturally being referred to as 'The Head Gardener'. On 7th May came the first double when two Heinkels crashed to 600's guns, one complete with its bomb-load. The next night a Ju.88 was damaged over Minehead and on the night of 9th/10th May Flying Officer Woodward – with Sergeant Lipscombe – were themselves shot down – by another Auxiliary squadron's night-fighter! The Beaufighter at this stage of the war was comparatively unknown and these mistakes were made, sometimes with tragic results. Happily, on this occasion, the squadron pair baled out to safety and their main comment was that they felt this burst of fire was carrying inter-squadron rivalry a bit far!

On 16th May Squadron Leader Pritchard was about to open fire on a Ju.88 when searchlights illuminated our Beaufighter, allowing the Junkers to turn and shoot down the 600 machine, both the C.O. and Sergeant Gledhill parachuting without injury. In addition to the growing numbers of Caterpillar Club members (those who took to silk in emergencies, as opposed to paratroopers) there was one consolation at this time in Flight Lieutenant Boyd and Flying Officer Clegg, a fine crew, getting a Ju.88 near Honiton, Devon, thought by Sector Controller to be the aircraft which had shot down the C.O. a few minutes earlier. June, though, saw only one combat – without claim – followed by the squadron's move to Predannack in Cornwall and the detachment of A Flight to Fairwood Common near Swansea. There was then a return to Colerne where night-flying was more suitable at this time. On 9th July Flying Officer Woodward, again aided by Sergeant Lipscombe, got a Heinkel near Abergavenny, the DFC being awarded to Woodward for his hat-trick of bombers.

The promotion of Wing Commander Pritchard, to be Wing Commander Flying at the night-fighter OTU, at Cranfield, Bedford-shire, was followed by the destruction of a Heinkel over the Scillies by Pilot Officer Ellis and Sergeant Houston. Then came a terrible blow as Flying Officer Woodward, in a spin, ordered Sergeant Lipscombe to bale out – Lipscombe losing his life, to the dismay of all; Woodward himself breaking a leg. A week later Squadron Leader G. E. T. Scrase, long-serving member, now a flight-comman-der, was testing the stalling-speed of a Beaufighter Mark V when he, too, got into a spin. His operator, Sergeant Ladymore, baled out safely, but the pilot was killed near Acton Turville, Gloucestershire. Then, as Wing Commander Stainforth left to take over 89 Squadron, Wing Commander H. M. 'Toby' Pearson came in to command after a tour commanding No. 54 Squadron's Spitfires and the summer of 1940 as Group Controller at No. 11(F) Group.

On 10th October Squadron Leader A. D. McNeill Boyd, with Flying Officer Clegg, shot a Heinkel into the sea off St Ives and in November Squadron Leader C. P. 'Paddy' Green, DFC, pre-war 601 and then 92 Squadron, came with observer radio Sergeant Reg Gillies. Paddy had been badly wounded over Dunkirk and, trans-ferring to night-fighters, had crewed with Reg Gillies at Operational Training Unit. Moving back to Predannack for operations against 'milk train' Luftwaffe reconnaissance aircraft which radioed weather reports as they headed for the Irish Sea and Atlantic areas, Flight Lieutenant J. G. Fletcher, AFC (with Sergeant Grant) experienced severe icing and, with one engine stopped, ditched in the sea. A search by air-sea rescue Lysanders escorted by 66 Squadron's Spitfires, failed to find the dinghy – one body came ashore later.

On 2nd December two Heinkels were brought down. On the 15th Flying Officer Ross, a civil pilot with 2,500 hours' flying, radioed that he'd 'Got a Hun' during a milk train chase. No further news was received and when the Beaufighter did not return a probable was claimed in the belief that possibly both machines had crashed during the combat.

On Christmas Day, celebrated with the traditional waiting on the airmen by officers, a signal announced DFCs for Squadron Leader McNeill Boyd and his observer radio, Flight Lieutenant A. G. Clegg. January's serenity was disrupted when an enemy intruder followed Flying Officer Arnsley into Predannack, dropping three 1,000 pounders as the Beaufighter was coming in to land; luckily without causing casualties or damage. With the arrival of the Beaufighter Mk.VI two crews came from No. 604 (County of Middlesex) Squadron, one being Sergeant (Count) Dunin Rzuchowski, a first-class pilot, with Sergeant L. Dixon as his Observer Radio. In early March V.I.P. aircraft en route for the Middle East were escorted to the limits of Beaufighter endurance, Boyd and Clegg getting a lone He.115 floatplane off Lizard Point as a minor consolation for the departure of Group Captain 'Toby' Pearson, who became Station Commander at Colerne. The diary reads, 'It was with great regret and a very real sense of personal loss that the squadron said goodbye to a most popular commanding officer.'

Hot-foot from Russia, complete with DFC and Order of Lenin, came Wing Commander A. G. Miller – 'old boy' of 1935–40 – to take over the squadron, a most experienced night-fighter who had instructed at the Fighter Interception Unit and had commanded No. 17 Squadron during the Battle of Britain. *The London Gazette* announcing the half-yearly Honours and Awards included a Mention in Despatches for Pilot Officer J. T. M. Wright (posted to RAF Cosford on being commissioned) but better known to the squadron as 800158 Flight Sergeant Wright, a tower of strength in peace and in war. Gordon Denby, promoted, left to instruct, later joining No. 125 (Newfoundland) Squadron as a flight-commander, losing his life off the Shetlands when his Beaufighter developed trouble – a tragic loss to the Royal Air Force.

On 7th June, 1942, another unique page of squadron history was written as Pilot Officer Harvey, a tobacconist in peacetime, flying with Flying Officer Bernard Wicksteed, a *Daily Express* columnist, as his observer-radio, shot down an He.111, only to be shot down themselves by the very accurate return fire of the doomed gunner. After incredible adventures the 600 Squadron crew reached Portreath beach, Cornwall, in their dinghy, Harvey receiving an immediate Distinguished Service Order and Wicksteed the DFC for a most courageous exploit. Wicksteed, who had been Flight Lieutenant PRO, Air Ministry, had volunteered for aircrew duties at a very ripe old age, reverting to two ranks lower to fly. He died in post-war years but his book *Father's Heinkel* gives a first-class first-hand account of his epic flight with Harvey and other squadron sorties.

Paddy Green was selected to form No. 125 (Newfoundland) Squadron, in which he was soon joined by Gordon Denby and Pilot Officer A. H. Drummond (and their observers). In June a reunion was held at the Polurrian Hotel, the squadron's Airspeed Oxford, flown by Flight Lieutenant Hanus, a Czech, picked up former members at Northolt, including Wing Commanders Kellett, Aste, and Hiscox. With combats during July the score mounted slowly but surely and in September Wing Commander Miller left to command No. 54 Operational Training Unit, Wing Commander J. R. Watson, his predecessor there, taking over the squadron. Squadron Leader Paul Elwell, who had opened his account with an He.111 destroyed and another damaged, flew off to pick up Sir Archibald Sinclair, KT, CMG, MP, Secretary of State for Air, flying him down from North Coates, Lincolnshire, on Sir Archibald's acceptance of the appointment as Honorary Air Commodore, 600 Squadron.

Then came a bolt from the blue – a move to Church Fenton, Yorkshire, to undergo intensive field training for aircrews and groundcrews alike. On 14th November the squadron was back in Cornwall, this time only to refuel and, on 17th November, seventeen aircraft flew off to Gibraltar continuing next day to Blida, Algeria, being allocated French barracks which were so filthy that de-lousing was essential. Groundcrews, who had sailed from the Clyde, arrived on the 27th and the top-secret airborne radar sets were flown in by Boeing B-17 Flying Fortresses. The personnel of No. 608 (North Riding) Auxiliary Squadron cheerfully lent a hand to get the Beaufighters ready for operations and Flying Officer Hilken co-opted another Auxiliary Squadron's observer – Pilot Officer Mason of No. 500 (County of Kent) Squadron – for a reconnaissance of the area which crews of 500 and 608 had flown over already. Cagliari Harbour, Sardinia, with its seaplane base, was found to be packed with potential targets and on the return flight to base Flying Officer Hilken shot down a Cant Z.506B tri-motor seaplane. Next day the same pilot tried hard to 'shepherd' another seaplane back into captivity but, on seeing it marked as a Red Cross machine, Hilken left it to its own devices.

On 7th December the squadron moved to Maison Blanche, Algiers, with 608's generous help. Patrols over the torpedoed troopship *Llanstephan Castle* and a flight from Bone to Algiers of General Alexander in a squadron Beaufighter, added to routine chores. Then, on Boxing Day – a new C.O. in the person of Wing Commander Paddy Green, with Pilot Officer Reg Gillies, two old members, who came out by Flying Fortress after their tour of duty with 125 Squadron at Fairwood Common and at Sumburgh, Shetlands. During the important Casablanca Conference the squadron did night guard patrols over the Prime Minister and other leaders and, in January 1943, another move, to Setif; the ground personnel going by train in a mixture of cattle trucks and horse vans. On 19th December came Squadron Leader Desmond Hughes, DFC, survivor of the 264 Squadron Defiants and former flight-commander 125 Squadron, bringing with him tremendous experience. Pilot Officer Laurie Dixon crewed with Desmond who took over B Flight and, after Flying Officer Thompson (with Flying Officer White) had destroyed a Piaggio 108 on 22nd January, the new firm of Hughes and Dixon became airborne on 23rd January and, before landing, destroyed two Ju.88s. There was a 600 Squadron camp concert with an award for the best turn of the evening . . . as Squadron Leader Hughes walked in towards the end of the variety programme he was unanimously judged to have taken first prize! Later came news of a Bar to Desmond's DFC, and a DFC for Laurie Dixon.

Wing Commander Paul Elwell, promoted to command Djidelli, was replaced by Squadron Leader A. W. V. Horne, who soon opened his personal tally with a Ju.88, Flight Lieutenant Hanus getting another, and Sergeants Owen and McAllister a Heinkel. The Luftwaffe had now brought the fast FW.190 into the area for protective cover but this did not stop Sergeant Parkinson and Flight Sergeant Stevens from shooting down a Ju.88 in broad daylight off Sardinia – reckoned the squadron's most exciting combat yet. Flying Officer J. H. Turnbull, a tall quiet Canadian, arrived from 125 Squadron and was quickly in action when he shot down a Cant Z.1007b north of Bone and, throughout April, rarely a night or day passed without a combat. Distinguished Flying Medals were promulgated for Sergeants Owen and McAllister on 29th April and then, on the 30th, came one of the war's outstanding patrols. Flight Sergeant A. B. 'Ace' Downing, with operator Sergeant John Lyons, intercepted five Ju.52 transports loaded with Rommel's Afrika Korps soldiery and, as dawn came up, all five were in the sea, making the squadron's total for the month up to eighteen destroyed. With another ten destroyed in May (including another Ju.52 for Downing/Lyons) morale was indeed high as Marshal of the RAF Viscount Trenchard found when he visited the squadron on 4th June.

A DFC for Flight Lieutenant Hanus was followed by transfer from Coastal Control to North African Tactical Air Force. On 15th June the groundcrews left in convoy to Sousse and on 23rd embarked for Malta, twenty aircraft flying over to the island from Bone the next day. The wretched 'Malta Dog' soon hit personnel at Luqa but flying had to proceed and Wing Commander Green took Generals Montgomery and Browning over to Kairouan, Tunisia, waiting to bring them back safely. The following day 600 Squadron covered the successful rescue from the sea of Sergeant Edwards, 73 Squadron, and as July progressed the enemy aircraft were thick on the ground – in flames! The night of 12th/13th added six to the tally with the C.O. getting a couple, Flying Officers Mellersh/Armstrong a couple and Desmond Hughes and Pilot Officer McKinnon one apiece. The next night Brigadier Bowen of the Airborne Forces flew with the C.O. and saw Paddy shoot down another enemy bomber. 'The most memorable moment of my life,' said the Airborne Force commander as he landed. Perhaps, though, he should have waited until the next night when Paddy and his operator Reg Gillies brought down four machines, damaging a fifth, whilst Flying Officer Johnny Turnbull/ Sergeant Fowler got three Ju.88s and Flying Officer Roberts/Flight Sergeant Burraston another Ju.88 – eight enemy destroyed and one damaged – an all-time record!

The following evening as the *Times of Malta* gave forth the good news, followed by a B.B.C. report of the combats, further bombers were biting the dust or hitting the sea, the squadron moving into Sicily (Cassibile) on the 26th, with awards of the DFC signalled in August for Flying Officers Turnbull, Gillies, Mellersh and Roberts, with the DFM for Flight Sergeant Fowler. When HMS *Delhi*, the flak cruiser, sent a party to look over the Beaufighters, a series of flights was organised for the sailors, in return for which hot baths were laid on for 600 Squadron aboard the cruiser. Control of the airfield's cookhouse had now passed to 600, the diary recording 'tea is drinkable for the first time here'. The night of 11th August was remembered for the triple successes of Desmond Hughes/Laurie Dixon, all three being Ju.88s, the C.O. got another and Johnny Turnbull a pair, with Mellersh also getting a Junkers. Pilot Officer Thomson was awarded the DFC, and a second Bar to his DFC came through for Squadron Leader Hughes, with a Bar to his DFC for Laurie Dixon. Air Vice-Marshal Harry Broadhurst flew in to present Flight Lieutenant Hanus with his Distinguished Flying Cross and Air Marshal Sir Arthur Coningham flew with the C.O. to see for himself the 600 Squadron technique; unluckily no enemy ventured out that night.

With detachments at Milazzo and San Antonio problems of servicing and administration occurred but the chaps pressed on as, with Downing/Lyons shooting down a pair of Ju.88s, the squadron's ninety-ninth and hundredth confirmed kills were registered – DFMs to both Flight Sergeant Alwyn Downing and John Lyons crowning their achievements. As the damaged HMS *Warspite* was taken in tow, 600's aircraft flew cover and afterwards, firstly at Monte Corvino, then at Brindisi, as the tally increased, DFCs came to Flying Officers Armstrong and Newhouse and to Flight Lieutenant Paton, with a Bar to the DFC for Johnny Turnbull and a Bar to the DFM – a rare award – for his operator Flight Sergeant Fowler. As Squadron Leader

Desmond Hughes became tourex Squadron Leader James Bailey –
also ex-125 Squadron – flew out with Flying Officer Ross, to take
Desmond's place: the squadron was now based at Gaudo. Sergeants
Bamford and Battersby, in trouble over Tortorella, baled out and
made their way across difficult country to allied forces. Christmas
Day saw the squadron at Foggia, a few miles from the Adriatic Sea,
with typical celebrations. 1st January, 1944, was the occasion for
'First Footing' with a vengeance, a cable from Sir Archibald Sinclair,
congratulating the squadron on ninety-four enemy destroyed by
night in a year, commented on the shining proof of the superb
efficiency and fighting spirit of the City of London squadron. The
Worshipful Company of Merchant Taylors presented the squadron
with twenty-four pewter tankards bearing their crest.

24. Squadron at Cassabile after 100th victory. Wg Cdr Green, Sqdn Ldr
Hughes, Flt Lt Turnbull, Flt Lt Gillies, Flt Lt Dixon in second row; Ace
Downing in third row, Lyons top right.

Authority was now obtained for the squadron to carry out long-
range 'Intruders' during which, with five changes of control, over
250 miles was covered in one successful chase. By the 25th January
the squadron's century of successes overseas and under Paddy was
celebrated and the ribbon of the Africa Star distributed – to the
appropriate comments of all! A move was made from Monte Corvino
to Marcianise and Lago and, on 1st February, a sad occurrence
marred the run of successes when Downing's machine developed
trouble and he and John Lyons baled out. Although both reached the
dinghy, Lyons was dead when picked up, despite all the efforts of
those in the rescue boat to revive him. He had been commissioned
before this last flight and was a tremendous loss to the squadron.
Awards of DFCs came through for Downing and the deceased Lyons

a few days later; the United States had earlier decorated both for their efforts in support of the American landings.

With the squadron score at 111 destroyed, Paddy was awarded the DSO, and was promoted to be Group Captain commanding No. 1 Mobile Operations Room. Wing Commander L. H. Styles came to take over the squadron and the introduction by the Luftwaffe of the 'Window' metallised-strips to confuse radar plots did not prevent the squadron from increasing its tally, the new C.O. and Squadron Leader James Bailey both notching victories during March. The great eruption of Vesuvius on 21st March caused the evacuation of Pompeii airfield as the Beaufighters transferred to Pomigliano to make room for day fighters whose airfields were also untenable as the lava poured down. On 28th April the first He.177 four-engined bomber (in tandem pairs) fell to the guns of 600 and occasional Ju.87 dive-bombers being thrown into the fight became easy targets for the Beaufighter crews.

As news came of the allies in Normandy (Desmond Hughes commanding 604 (County of Middlesex) on the first night-fighter strip in France) the City of London airmen began a series of moves which provoked the statement 'Our sympathies henceforth will always be with the gypsies'. From La Banca – with the song of nightingales – to Voltone (with visits for personnel into Rome) then on to Follonica and Rosignano (remembered for the 'Achtung Minen' signs). Storms blew tents and marquees over and only the regular additions to the squadron's tally of enemy aircraft kept the men happy. Squadron Leader James Bailey – now with DFC – caught a Bf.110 near Rome and a Ju.87 in the act of bombing. Then, with South of France landings on 15th August, the squadron detachment at Falconara brought down two Ju.87s, bringing up the total to 150. During September nine Ju.87 dive-bombers were shot down as they tried to get through to bomb the allied forces.

The squadron now turned to all-out attacks on transportation, hitting every enemy vehicle – train, barge, truck – which was seen, building up a fantastic run of successes in support of the armies in Italy. From Cesenatico pilots were detached to Foggia and operators (now called navigators) to Naples, to train on new equipment before flying the Mosquito Mk.XIX. Wing Commander A. H. Drummond – who had flown with the squadron earlier – came from 604 in Normandy to command and the first FW.190 was brought down as the Italians and Germans capitulated on 2nd May, 1945. The squadron totals stood at 165 aircraft destroyed, 13 probables, and 34 damaged, plus 77 trains, trucks, barges, destroyed or badly damaged. An interesting point is that 600's figures are not affected by the post-war revisions brought about by access to Luftwaffe files.

By 24th May the squadron was at Campoformido and a well-earned MBE was awarded to Warrant Officer Nelson, the squadron engineering officer. Some impressive flypasts were staged in connection with the Victory Parades and Wing Commander Hugh Drummond left to take over No. 114 Squadron, RAF, as orders came that 600 was to disband at Aviano by 21st August, 1945, after VJ Day which ended the war in the Far East. In the weeks which followed, as aircrew returned from various P.O.W. camps, some interesting stories circulated – one that a Ju.87 pilot, shot down by 600 Squadron in November 1944, was the Luftwaffe's 'Ace' on this type with over 300 'Ops'. Another, told by Flight Lieutenant Wilmer, who had left the squadron to fly with 256 Squadron, of how, when shot down and captured, a P.O.W. interrogator, on picking up the form on which he had written only his name, rank and service number, exclaimed 'And where is 600 Squadron nowadays?' Such was the City of London's fame with the enemy.

25. Squadron Spitfires F21/22, October 1949.

When the squadron re-formed as part of the post-war Auxiliary Air Force in June–July 1946, it was moved to Biggin Hill owing to the unsuitability of Hendon for the faster types of aircraft then in service. With a mixture of Spitfires Mks. FR.14a and F.21, under former Wing Commander Norman Hayes, DFC (who had commanded West Malling and No. 149 Wing in Europe 1944–45), there were very many who, like Norman, gladly rejoined in a lower rank. In 1948 Squadron Leader Hayes handed over command to Squadron Leader D. E. Proudlove, a wartime 91 Squadron Spitfire pilot, and in August 1949 Her Majesty The Queen graciously accepted the appointment of Honorary Air Commodore – an inspiring honour for the City of London's airmen. The Spitfire F.22 had replaced the earlier aircraft and in 1951 came the Gloster Meteor jets and a change in command as Squadron Leader J. P. Meadows, DFC – who had flown with 130, 604 (County of Middlesex) and 219 Squadrons in the war – took control, with some post-war 603 (City of Edinburgh) AAF flying already in his logbooks.

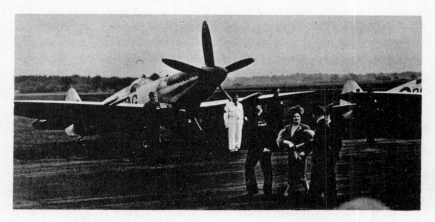

26. HM Queen Elizabeth, Biggin Hill, October 1949. Sqdn Ldr D. E. Proudlove on left, Flt Lt J. P. Meadows, right.

On 19th July, 1951, came a rare distinction as Air Ministry Orders authorised 600 Squadron to hold two badges including what was proudly nicknamed 'the dust-cart crest' seen daily in the City on the road-sweepers' carts. Whereas the original badge had included the sword together with a crescent moon, representing the squadron's night-fighter activities, the new badge comprised the City of London's own arms surmounted by the traditional RAF eagle. At the foot, a scroll worded '600 City of London Squadron' instead of the former motto. This was approved by the Queen who paid regular visits both to Biggin Hill and to Finsbury Barracks, as well as to the squadron's church, St Bartholomew the Great, where, on 26th July, 1950, the Queen had unveiled a memorial stone 'In Honour and Remembrance of those who gave their lives in the service of their country'.

On 31st January, 1952, Her Majesty presented the new squadron badge to Squadron Leader Jack Meadows at Finsbury Barracks and in October the C.O. in turn presented a squadron plaque to the Mayor of Hendon, marking the pre-war association with that airfield. It was at Buckingham Palace on 16th May, 1953, that the Honorary Air Commodore (now HM Queen Elizabeth the Queen Mother) presented a Squadron Standard with Battle Honours which included France and the Low Countries, the Battle of Britain, North Africa, Sicily, Italy, Salerno, Anzio and Nettuno. During 1953 Squadron Leader J. M. Cormack took command and a link was established with No. 1 (Auckland) Territorial Squadron of the Royal New Zealand Air Force. Summer camps had been held at places as far apart as Thorney Island and Tangmere in Sussex, Celle and Oldenburg in Germany and Takali in that old squadron haunt, Malta. Along with Nos. 601, 604 and 615 RAuxAF Squadrons, 600 put up a gallant fight to stave off disbandment of the twenty flying squadrons but it was of no avail and, on 10th March, 1957, No. 600 (City of London) Squadron ceased flying.

27. Meteors rehearse for Battle of Britain display, 1954.

The Standard was laid up in the Lady Chapel of St Bartholomew the Great on 5th November, 1957, and there were many who thought that (as, alas, with some RAuxAF units) the squadron would now pass into RAF history. The members of The City of London Squadron Association, however, were determined to keep alive the memories and traditions of this great squadron and, first at Croydon, then at Biggin Hill, they formed a Flying Group affiliated to the Popular Flying Association, with 120 members, about half of them qualified pilots, the others undergoing training. A Percival Prentice was used for touring into Europe and a Tiger Moth for pilot-training under the chairmanship of Wing Commander W. H. Wetton, Wing Commander A. T. Warburton, former adjutant, acting as secretary. Instruction was in the hands of Flight Lieutenant John Miles, a classics master at St Albans School and a squadron Meteor pilot. A plaque in the squadron premises at Biggin Hill carried the squadron badge and commemorated its wartime achievements. On the first

Friday in every month at *The Castle*, Cowcross Street – one of London's unique inns – squadron members have gathered for twenty years. The badge is displayed beneath three golden balls, for this pub has a pawnbroker's licence in perpetuity, granted by George IV who once borrowed money here on his watch. It is not recorded that 600's members have had to leave any of their possessions to raise the fare home! Thanks to the energetic Honorary Secretary, Ken Battrick, and Flight Lieutenant John Wright, MBE (a well-earned 1951 award for his great work as engineering officer in post-war years – in 1954 he had gained a second clasp to his Air Efficiency Award), and a committee including Messrs F. Moody, MBE, F. de Vroome, BEM, R. Aveyard, W. Cardew, A. Chantrey and R. Dougan, reunions and outings have maintained the links. A welfare fund, with trustees Association President Squadron Leader Jack Meadows DFC, AFC (the latter award for his splendid leadership in post-war years), Flight Lieutenants Norman Wheeler and John Wright, helps those in need and a magazine, edited by Lt. Colonel Charles Kirby, adds to the news issued frequently by Ken Battrick.

Perhaps only now is it possible to assess the true contribution of the squadron to Royal Air Force victory in World War II – the awards of a George Cross, two Distinguished Service Orders, forty-two DFCs (including Bars), nine DFMs (including Bars), three MBEs, and sixteen Mentions in Despatches speak for themselves. Yet this is by no means all, for many members held high commands – Marshal of the RAF Lord Charles 'Sam' Elworthy, GCB, CBE, DSO, MVO, DFC, AFC, MA, who became not only Chief of the Air Staff but Chief of the Defence Staff. Air Vice-Marshal Desmond Hughes, CB, CBE, DSO, DFC and two Bars, AFC, MA, is Commandant, RAF College Cranwell, as this is written; Air Commodore C. J. Mount, CBE, DSO, DFC, flew with 602 (City of Glasgow) after leaving 600, and later commanded 317 (Polish) and 260 Squadrons of fighters, before commanding 104 (Bomber) Squadron and, post-war, has held many high appointments. Air Vice-Marshal E. L. 'Ted' Colbeck-Welch who had left 600 to command 29 Squadron afterwards commanded a 2 Group Bomber Wing, Coltishall and Horsham St Faith fighter stations and then the Central Fighter Establishment. Group Captain G. M. Beer also held key appointments as did Group Captain Peter Stewart whose OBE, in 1967, recognised years of work for Auxiliaries and Territorials: Peter's death was a blow to every former member of the squadron. A few still give their spare time, one being Flight Lieutenant A. B. Clucas, RAFVR(T), who has commanded No. 120 (Hendon) Squadron, Air Training Corps, using the very hangar that was 600's original Hendon home – happily a part of the complex earmarked for the RAF Museum, due to open late in 1972.

At the movingly impressive funeral of Sir Winston Churchill

it was right that 600 should be represented as Group Captain Dicky Haine, DFC (who had commanded No. 488 (NZ) Squadron in war and a major Yorkshire fighter base post-war), walked with others of the illustrious 'Few'. Regrettably the powers-that-were have failed to preserve in U.K., as of now, any tangible link with the squadron, the Beaufighter (formerly of the Malta Communications and Target Towing Squadron, Luqa) repainted in 600's colours for the Abingdon Royal Review to mark the RAF's Golden Jubilee, having been donated to the National Aeronautical Collection of Canada. One hopes that it may be kept in squadron colours, though it is very doubtful. Maybe a genuine ex-600 machine will be found, or another be marked as a City of London aircraft at Hendon. In the Imperial War Museum, London, is the tail of a German glider which made a voluntary descent near Setif on 30th December, 1942. On this tail is painted a list of 'involuntary' descents brought about by aircraft of 325 Wing, Nos. 153, 255 and 600 Squadrons, recording many of the City of London's victories at this time.

28. Marshal of the RAF Lord Charles Elworthy, GCB, CBE, DSO, MVO, DFC, AFC, MA, the squadron pilot who became Chief of Air Staff and Chief of Defence Staff.

REPRESENTATIVE SQUADRON AIRCRAFT

de Havilland D.H.9A	J8184 J8165 J8223
Avro 504	
Westland Wapiti IIA	J9870 J9871 J9878 K1334 K1339
Hawker Hart I	K2473 K2979 K2984 K2985 K2987 K3040
Hawker Demon	K5700 K5701 K5703 K5704
Avro Tutor	K3391
Bristol Blenheim If	L1295 BQ–E L1429 L6791 L8698 BQ–M
IVf	L4906 P4829 P4846
Bristol Beaufighter If	R2076 R2256 BQ–F R2259 also BQ–F
VIf	V8388 BQ–6 V8891 X7920 X8128
de Havilland Mosquito XIX	TA133 X TA425 TA448 (Wg Cdr A. H. Drummond.)
Vickers-Supermarine	
Spitfire FR.14a	TZ141 RAG–E TZ175 RAG–D
F.21	LA228 RAG–N LA253 RAG–K LA278 LA323
F.22	PK392 PK405 RAG–Y PK670 RAG–X
Gloster Meteor F.4	VW256 VZ412 LJ–P VZ429 LJ–Q
F.8	VZ505 W WH474 P WH975 X WK951 Y
T.7	WA628 S WA696

The squadron Wapitis carried the squadron number on the fuselage but in the Hart and Demon era a squadron insignia of interlocking triangles of red and white was painted on the upper wing and fuselage. The code letters MV were used from the Munich crisis until outbreak of war when it changed to BQ which was used until 1943 when, for a time, figures replaced aircraft letters. The post-war Spitfires at first used RAG for the Reserve Command period but on transfer to Fighter Command the Meteors at first used LJ and then changed to the traditional pre-war insignia of interlocking triangles.

No. 600 Squadron was the only one to have two badges. The first was in front of an increscent, a sword in bend. The crescent moon representing the squadron's night-fighter activities whilst the sword commemorates the connection with the City of London. The motto, translated, was: 'More than six hundred.'

The second badge was the City of London arms, known as 'The dust-cart crest'.

601
(County of London)
Squadron

MINISTRY OF DEFENCE records tell us that No. 601 (County of London) Squadron was formed at Northolt on 14th October, 1925, as a light-bomber unit, though many of the original members would say that White's Club, St James's, London SW1, was its birthplace. Certainly it was right and proper that Lord Edward Grosvenor, Royal Naval Air Service pilot of World War I and holder of Royal Aero Club Certificate No. 607, became the first commanding officer of what was soon to become known as 'The Millionaires' Mob'. The Grosvenor Challenge Cup of 1923's Lympne light-aircraft meeting was 'Ned' Grosvenor's first endowment in support of British aviation; his next and most passionate interest was to see the implementation of Trenchard's non-regular air force plans and although 601 cannot claim to be the first of the weekend squadrons, few will deny that it was their first C.O. who played a tremendous part in the formation of the Auxiliary Air Force. Little wonder then that another sponsor of the part-time force, the then Sir Samuel Hoare, Secretary of State for Air, accepted Squadron Leader Grosvenor's invitation to be the first Honorary Air Commodore of the County of London Squadron. One feels that had 'Sammy' refused, Ned would have talked 'Boom' Trenchard into the appointment!

Flight Lieutenant H. G. Bowen was posted to the squadron as the first regular RAF adjutant, he arrived at Northolt supported by twenty-five RAF airmen on which nucleus the squadron was to be built. A temporary Town Headquarters was set-up at 1 Elverton Street, Westminster, the headquarters of the 22nd Armoured Car Company (Westminster Dragoons), and on 4th December, 1925, the first Auxiliary airman – 801000 Aircraftman 2nd Class Matthews

G. T. – was enrolled. Pilot Officer J. J. Parkes became the first Auxiliary to be awarded the flying badge although there were, of course, AAF pilots like Lord Edward Grosvenor and the first flight-commander, Flight Lieutenant S. B. Collett, who had qualified in the Royal Flying Corps or RNAS. In January 1926 Flight Lieutenant J. D. Driberg, OBE, MC, FRCS, joined as the medical officer, and by the first weekend camp, held in June, there were six Auxiliary officers and twenty-eight Auxiliary airmen on strength.

29. Early group of 'The Legion'. *Left to right:* Peter Ducane, Maurice Jackaman, Norman Jones, Nigel Seeley, Geordie Ward, Ashley Howard, Bill Collett, Bill Thornton, John Parkes, Rupert Bellville (puttees), Ian Murray, Gillow, Drogo Montague, Brian Thynne, Loel Guinness, Dickie Shaw, Bill Langdon.

In July 1926 solo flying was demonstrated by Flight Lieutenants Collett, H. B. Pett, and R. A. Grosvenor, MC, and by Pilot Officers J. J. Parkes, E. D. Reid and H. N. St. V. Norman, using the de Havilland D.H.9A bombers, and by Pilot Officers R. Bellville, A. Schreiber and N. H. Jones on the Avro 504N. History was made when the squadron gained the Viscount Esher trophy for the best all-round unit in the Auxiliary Air Force that year, the presentation being made by the Chief of Air Staff in December. On 18th January, 1927, the squadron moved to Hendon and in June new Town Headquarters at 54 Kensington Park Road were formerly opened by HRH The Prince of Wales (the late Duke of Windsor). In August six D.H.9As and four Avro 504s flew down to Lympne for summer camp, Sir Philip Sassoon, friend of Ned Grosvenor, entertaining the officers at his seaside residence, Porte Lympne.

30. Air-gunners, armourers, and instructors, August 1930. *Back, left to right:* LAC Franklin, S. G. Vickers, Geo Berry, unknown, Neville Shute, Wewege-Smith, G. Nicholas, L.A.C. Fisher. *Seated:* two RAF NCOs and Auxiliary Sgt Holmes.

Lord Edward's drawing for a squadron badge – based on the scarlet Sword of London – led to the naming of the first concert party 'The Flying Swords' with a public performance following dedication of a new church at RAF Hendon (St Alphage's) for the squadron parades. In 1928 the Esher Trophy was again won by 601 which the C.O. had nicknamed 'The Legion' after a perusal of the foreign-sounding names of some members. Squadron characters were by no means limited to the officers or pilots and an unforgettable airman was Corporal T. Wewege Smith, one of the young air-gunners who abruptly left and joined the Foreign Legion from which he soon escaped, returning to Hendon to face charges of desertion. To his great relief Lord Edward Grosvenor disposed of the case in a most unconventional manner and what the regular adjutant, Flight Lieutenant (later Air Vice-Marshal) Thornton, told Air Ministry is not recorded. 'Wiggy' Smith's book *The Green Hell of the Chaco* tells of this airman's flying in the Bolivian Air Force when, it appears, the 601 badge was first flown into battle – on the nose of the Junkers of which Wiggy was gunner, in the mid-1930s

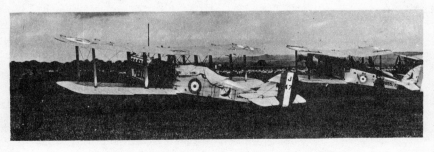

31. D.H.9A Wapiti and Avro 504N, August 1930.

Prior to Corporal Smith's second departure from the squadron, the commanding officer and founder, Lord Edward Grosvenor, died suddenly on 18th August, 1929, after a very short illness; he was only 37 years of age. The squadron, though, with a strength now of 21 officers (and a long waiting list) and 120 Auxiliary airmen, was Ned's memorial and dream-come-true. On 5th October Flying Officer D. A. Boyle came in as assistant adjutant, returning as adjutant after a short tour of duty at the RAF College, Cranwell, from which he had earlier graduated. Meanwhile Flight Lieutenant (later Air Chief Marshal Sir Francis) Fogarty had come as adjutant and flying instructor pending formation of No. 604 (County of Middlesex) Squadron, to which he moved on the return of Flight Lieutenant Dermot Boyle. The Westland Wapiti had replaced the D.H.9A and in November 1931 Flight Lieutenant Stanley Beresford Collett was promoted and given command of the sister squadron, No. 600 (City of London), also based at Hendon. Sir Philip Sassoon, the new C.O. of 601, marked his delight at the appointment by presenting the squadron with a Spartan three-seat biplane for private flying by the pilots. At this time, though, Sir Philip could not fly and it is said that the then Chief of Air Staff, Sir John Salmond, had Dermot Boyle posted to the County of London Squadron for the main purpose of seeing that Sir Philip Sassoon gained his flying badge – which he eventually obtained.

32. Visit of Oxford University Air Squadron, mid-1930s. *Standing:* extreme right: Roger Bushell; Tony Bellville tall and balding; centre, smoking: Archie Hope; third from left: Johnnie Hawtrey. *Seated:* right: Flt Lt Ira Jones; next: Noël Coward; centre: Wg Cdr Keith Park.

On being invited to become Under-Secretary of State for Air, Sir Philip handed over his command to Squadron Leader Sir Nigel Norman (of Heston Airport) and about this time the Hon G. R. Ward and the Hon E. F. Ward joined the squadron – both later transferring to the Royal Air Force on short service commissions. On 6th August, 1932, Roger Bushell went solo and obtained his A licence three days later, soon making his mark in a company already famous throughout the AAF, and the RAF, not only for brilliant flying at air displays and summer camps, but for a new 'high' in practical joking, hitherto mainly associated with the legendary Atcherley twins who would have fitted so smoothly into Legion membership. In February 1933 the first Hawker Hart arrived and a month later the squadron said a reluctant farewell to Flight Lieutenant Dermot Boyle who was posted to India after teaching many pilots his grass-cutting evolutions – crowd thrillers of the thirties. In May, alas, Hart K2974 was destroyed in a tragic fire, Pilot Officer Viscount Knebworth and Leading Aircraftman Harrison losing their lives.

33. Hawker Hart during exercises, possibly 1933.

During 1934 Sir Nigel Norman's business commitments – not only at Heston but with Airwork Ltd – brought his resignation and the new C.O. was Squadron Leader 'Dickie' Shaw, DFC (won in a D.H.4 of World War I). After only a year, though, he made way for a younger man, Squadron Leader Brian Thynne, one of Ned Grosvenor's far-seeing choices for eventual command. The Hawker Demon now replaced the Hart and, to the delight of all, the squadron was re-categorised as a fighter squadron from July 1934. In November of 1936 the approved version of the squadron badge was signed by King Edward VIII and was presented to the C.O. by the Rt Hon Sir Philip Sassoon – a wonderful moment for a former commanding officer and for Brian Thynne and all present.

On 11th February, 1937, another glorious page of squadron history was written when, in Demon K5722, Flying Officer Aidan Crawley (then a *Daily Mail* writer and Kent cricketer) flew off on a long-distance cross-country flight, with Pilot Officer Guy Branch. After refuelling at RAF Netheravon, Wiltshire, they took off in poor weather, just missing the hangars and crashing in flames on the nearby road. Guy Branch extricated himself from the wreckage but, finding Aidan Crawley trapped, climbed back into the flames to pull out the unconscious pilot. For this feat of gallantry, Guy Branch was awarded the Medal of the Order of the British Empire for Gallantry (EGM). Unhappily, Flight Lieutenant Branch lost his life leading a flight of No. 145 Squadron into action in August 1940.

In May of 1938 Flight Lieutenant Roger Bushell was selected to perform aerobatics at the Empire Air Display – a tremendous compliment to the Auxiliaries – and to the squadron in particular. Roger had other claims to fame at this time, one being that in trying to land Max Aitken's private aircraft, Aeronca G–ADZZ, near the Botolph's Bridge Inn on the Romney Marshes, he hit a signpost. The aircraft wreckage was immediately auctioned and sold for £5.0.0.; far more important, it seems, was the directional arm of the 'To Dymchurch'signpost as another much-prized trophy for the squadron crew-room. The wild exploits of The Legion did not always meet with the Air Ministry's approval but only the gentlest of reining was applied for many wisely realised that this 'press-on' spirit might soon be put to a real test.

34. Guy Branch, EGM.   35. Aidan Crawley, MBE.

On 26th September, 1938, the squadron was embodied into the Royal Air Force for the Munich crisis and was based at Biggin Hill, its war station. At this time the pilots included Flight Lieutenant

J. R. A. Peel, Flying Officers Michael Peacock, Sir Archibald Hope, Max Aitken; Pilot Officers C. P. 'Paddy' Green and W. H. Rhodes-Moorhouse (son of the first Air VC winner). On 31st October, returning to Hendon, the Gloster Gauntlets were received – K7888 arriving for the initial training sessions. Not long afterwards, however, and coinciding with the appearance in early 1939 of newcomer Pilot Officer Willard Whitney Straight, naturalised American millionaire racing motorist, news came that 601 was to re-equip with the twin-engined Bristol Blenheim If (Mark I) fighter. That summer the camp was held at Ford in Sussex and on 2nd September the Blenheims were ordered to Biggin Hill, the squadron again part of the Royal Air Force.

Squadron Leader Roger Bushell, on promotion, was appointed to command No. 92 Squadron, RAF, Brian Thynne remaining to lead 601 instead of handing over his command to Roger who was probably the first Auxiliary to command a regular unit. Unhappily, after getting his squadron operational on the Blenheim and then, from March 1940, on the Spitfire, Bushell was brought down during the Dunkirk fighting after probably destroying two Messerschmitt Bf.110s. Taken prisoner, his exploits as an inveterate escaper inspired others and in Stalag Luft III he became the legendary 'Big X' of the mass escape following which the Gestapo, on Hitler's orders, executed fifty officers in cold blood – Roger Bushell was one of the first to die. Although portrayed magnificently by Richard Attenborough wearing the DFC, in the film *The Great Escape*, this gallant South African-born barrister was never decorated; his name, though, lives forever: he was the ideal Auxiliary of Trenchard's vision.

Back to September 1939, though, with 601 liaising with the searchlights and gunners, occasional breaks including escort by Brian Thynne to an autogyro going to France for radar calibration work. Then – on 27th November – came the very first 'Op' with six Blenheims ordered to move from Biggin Hill to Northolt and then to Bircham Newton in Norfolk, to join with six Blenheims from No. 25 Squadron, RAF, in an attack on the Luftwaffe's seaplane base at Borkum. Squadron navigators and gunners were left behind and replaced for this occasion by more experienced Coastal Command navigators and Bomber Command air-gunners. Flight Lieutenant Michael Peacock led one Section, including Flying Officers Sir Archibald Hope and Raymond Davis, with Flying Officer Max Aitken leading the other, supported by Flying Officers W. Rhodes-Moorhouse and Tom Hubbard. The enemy defences were taken completely by surprise, the guns of the Blenheims straddling seaplanes at their moorings. All twelve aircraft made the return crossing of the North Sea to land at Debden, Essex, without damage or casualty to the crews. This was the first crossing of Nazi territory by British fighters and Flight Lieutenant Peacock, another South-

African-born barrister and a close friend of Bushell, was awarded the DFC, first war 'gong' to the squadron.

This unique sortie, made in extremely bad weather, was properly celebrated; runs to favourite taverns being rather easier for 601 than for others at this time as, on warning of petrol rationing, a complete filling station had been purchased to keep the fleet of Brough Superior motorcycles on the road. (The filling station was later sold at a profit by Willie Rhodes-Moorhouse, Treasurer of the Legionaires.) A few days after the Borkum raid Squadron Leader Thynne moved to Headquarters, Fighter Command, becoming a Sector Controller and, on promotion, C.O. of a fighter base. To take over 601, Squadron Leader Loel Guinness was promoted and after flying briefly from Gravesend the squadron moved into Tangmere for hectic reunions with Roger Bushell and his Blenheims/Spitfires. During January and February of 1940, the monotony of the 'Phoney War' period was relieved by the occasional duties of navigating Hurricanes en route to France as the squadrons there converted from Gladiators. During March, though, the squadron flew a record 560 hours by day and 26 by night as they themselves worked furiously to convert to the Hawker Hurricanes, regretting only that they had to part with their loyal navigators and gunners, some of whom took pilot courses, others going to new squadrons or to ground jobs with 601 Squadron.

So magnificently did the squadron ground personnel work on the Hurricane programme that the C.O. ordered a pint of beer to be served to each man – causing some eyebrows-raising on the part of Regular personnel – tinged, perhaps, with a little envy? On 8th April, Whitney Straight, sick to death of the inactivity, pestered Air Ministry for action, leaving soon afterwards for a secret destination – later discovered to have been Norway where, for his magnificent work, he was awarded the Military Cross. At this time, too, Aidan Crawley was appointed Assistant Air Attaché in Ankara (a post he managed to leave for command of No. 73 Squadron, Desert Air Force, later on).

On 10th May, as the Nazis systematically attacked in the Low Countries, 601 Squadron was moved into Hawkinge near Folkestone, to patrol the English Channel shipping. On the 13th three pilots left to strengthen the already-weakened fighter squadrons in France, Squadron Leader Michael Peacock, DFC, taking command of No. 87 Squadron, RAF. On the 17th the squadron was ordered over to Merville to become a temporary part of the Allied Expeditionary Air Force. Next day the new Air Officer Commanding No. 11(F) Group, Air Vice-Marshal Keith Park, flew his Hurricane down from Northolt to talk to the squadron and to congratulate the pilots who had carried out offensive sorties over Malines and Brussels, claiming ten enemy destroyed and two others damaged. Flight Lieutenant Sir Archibald Hope, leading the Merville A Flight, crash-landed in a field after return fire from a Dornier, making his way back to Merville on a motorbike he found in a deserted Amiens dump. On the 19th – in company with 145 Squadron – the Merville Flight fought against Heinkels and Junkers over Douai and five of the enemy fell, with three Hurricanes lost, two pilots making their way back to the U.K. later. Until the end of May patrols were flown over Dunkirk and over St Valery (where Max Aitken brought down a Bf.110 fighter-bomber and a Ju.87 dive-bomber). The Army complained at the absence of the RAF, but 601 claimed twenty Luftwaffe aircraft over the approaches to the evacuation beaches, often out of sight of the waiting soldiers whose lives would certainly have been even more at risk, but for 601 and the other squadrons trying their best to prevent the enemy aircraft attacking our almost defenceless men.

A Flight was ordered back to Tangmere and Flying Officer G. W. S. 'Mouse' Cleaver – responsible for the ground members – did a splendid job in organising their safe return via Boulogne. Flying Officers Charles Lee-Steere and Gerald Cuthbert gave their lives above Dunkirk's beaches and news came that former members and chums Roger Bushell and Michael Peacock were missing – Peacock soon confirmed killed as he courageously led his squadron only a day after having to bale-out following a victorious combat. On 31st May nine of the Hurricanes flew close-escort to Winston Churchill's D.H. Flamingo to Paris, returning next day. The pilots made the most of this unexpected chance to visit the gay city and were thanked by the Prime Minister before take-off from Villacoublay. On 1st June the squadron was moved to Middle Wallop, Hampshire, and as Loel Guinness moved to the Operations Room at RAF Catterick, Squadron Leader Max Aitken assumed command – a most popular appointment. On 7th June, with the miracle of Dunkirk safely accomplished, 601 Squadron penetrated into France with No. 43 Squadron in pursuit of the Luftwaffe and to attack the airfields they had occupied. Flying Officers Tom Hubbard and Peter Robinson were reported missing but both later returned (Robinson, who had come back from the U.S.A. to fight with his old squadron, was landed, wounded, from one of the last ships to leave France). Escorts to Blenheim light-bombers hitting and photographing airfields, brought the DFC for Flying Officer W. P. 'Little Billy' Clyde, who had come back from Mexico to rejoin The Legion. Then, from Tangmere, came the experiment of using single-seat fighters for night defence. On 26th June at 11.0 p.m. Max Aitken and Flight Lieutenant Tom Hubbard were airborne just in time for Max to intercept an He.111 and shoot it into the sea after the searchlights had illuminated the bomber. Three days later the AOC-in-C Fighter Command, Air Chief Marshal Sir Hugh Dowding, came to Tangmere to present the Distinguished Flying Cross to Squadron Leader Aitken for his victories and his fine example. On 7th July, this time in company with

Flying Officer Clyde, Max shot down another night raider – a Do.17, chased to within fifteen miles of Cherbourg.

On 10th July a Dornier 17P was damaged off the Isle of Wight and the next day Flight Lieutenant Rhodes-Moorhouse, Flying Officer M. D. Doulton and Pilot Officer J. W. Bland intercepted a Do.215 between Selsey Bill and Portland, shooting it into the sea beyond the Isle of Wight. An hour later, at 11.30 a.m., Mouse Cleaver and Sir Archibald Hope each destroyed a Stuka dive-bomber near Portland and Sergeant L. N. Guy damaged a third. About the same time Pilot Officers J. C. Lindsey and H. J. Riddle each destroyed a Bf.110 in this area. That evening the entire squadron was ordered off and Rhodes-Moorhouse led the attack on a force of Heinkels which were escorted by Bf.110s. Flying Officer C. R. Davis got a Bf.110; Flight Sergeant A. H. D. Pond, in destroying a Heinkel, saw it collide with another Heinkel, both falling in flames, Mouse Cleaver damaging another. Unfortunately our own anti-aircraft guns scored hits on Sergeant A. W. Woolley's Hurricane, the pilot baling-out wounded and burned.

On the 16th B Flight, led by Flight Lieutenant Rhodes-Moor-house, sighted three Ju.88 bombers, one of which Rhodes-Moor-house promptly shot into the sea, attacking a second without obser-ving final results as this and its companion hurriedly turned for France. Next day Squadron Leader Aitken was posted to the Air Ministry and was replaced by Squadron Leader W. F. C. Hobson, only for the new C.O. to be taken ill and for an old squadron member, Squadron Leader the Hon E. F. Ward, to assume command. A well-earned DFC came to Flight Lieutenant Willie Rhodes-Moor-house and on 20th July a change from routine when an He.59 float-plane, wearing German civilian registration D–AKAR, was shot down by Flight Lieutenant Tom Hubbard, Flying Officer M. D. Doulton and Pilot Officer T. Grier near the convoy code-named 'Bosom' (which had caused some interchange of comments between pilots and the Sector Controller).

On the 22nd Pilot Officer J. K. U. B. McGrath had to crash-land when his engine failed, Hurricane P1772 being a write-off, but the pilot happily unhurt. On 26th July Pilot Officer P. C. Lindsey was jumped by Bf.109s and killed in Hurricane P2753 – a great loss of an up-and-coming pilot. A few rest days followed, with 145 Squadron (including Guy Branch) taking over until, on Sunday 11th August, 601 was ordered to scramble as a complete squadron about 10.00 a.m. to help meet a large incoming Luftwaffe force. Although squadron records claim twelve destroyed and four damaged enemy machines, post-war investigations reveal duplicated claims with other units and it seems that only three Ju.88 bombers can be confirmed as 601 victories in this air battle off Portland Bill, tragically for the loss of four pilots, Pilot Officers R. S. Demetriadi, W. G. Dickie, J.

Gillan and J. L. Smithers, shot down by the Bf.109 fighters who outnumbered the squadron very heavily. Sadly this combat also saw the loss of former member Guy Branch, EGM, of 145 squadron.

On 13th August the enemy's planned destruction of Fighter Command and its supporting bases and radar stations was due to accelerate to pave the way for invasion and an early start was certainly made from the French airfields, though mainly against the Kent and Essex establishments at first. The County of London men were doing their bit without making extravagant reports on this vital day; Billy Clyde's machine was damaged but he nursed it down to a safe landing, saving a precious Hurricane to be repaired and re-flown. Pilot Officer Clive Mayers, an Australian recently in 601, baled into the sea and was saved thanks mainly to Archibald Hope's initiative in speedily directing air-sea rescue craft to the spot. Two Ju.88s and four Bf.110s were confirmed as destroyed by 601, with several others damaged – the combat reports were too confused to allocate successes to individuals. Next day was uneventful with the Luftwaffe licking its wounds, but an all-out onslaught was made on 15th August which has now been proved Fighter Command's highest-scoring day. On the 15th it was the Auxiliaries in NE England who made headlines, though at tea-time action moved to Sussex and Hampshire and 601 rendered claims for eight destroyed and six damaged. In the event this was watered down to five Ju.88s confirmed, shared between Carl Davis, Archibald Hope, Billy Clyde, M. D. Doulton, Sergeant Guy and Flight Sergeant Pond. Pilot Officer McGrath, whose DFC was signalled that morning, was brought down, making a good crash-landing. Mouse Cleaver, alas, returned with severe injuries to his eyes and did not fly again with the squadron; his DFC was a well-merited reward for some fine work.

On Squadron Leader Ward's departure for the Tangmere Sector Operations Room, Squadron Leader Sir Archibald Hope took over the squadron. On 16th August mass formations of Ju.88s and 87 dive-bombers escorted by Bf.109s were met over the Isle of Wight as they headed for Tangmere airfield, diving down out of the sun. Considerable damage was inflicted on the RAF base but 601 managed to bring down several of the enemy for the loss of only one Hurricane. Sadly it was piloted by one of the few American volunteers in Fighter Command, Pilot Officer William Mead Lindsley Fiske, a one-time Cambridge undergraduate well-known on the famous Cresta Run along with Roger Bushell and others of The Legion. Fiske joined 601 in mid-July and on this day was desperately trying to land his damaged Hurricane when Luftwaffe fighters dived down to attack it. With the aircraft ablaze Fiske was eventually freed by gallant (and unknown) heroes, but he was terribly burned and died the next day. He could so easily have baled-out, but wished to get the valuable aircraft back. In St Paul's Cathedral a tablet bears Fiske's name and the simple words 'An American citizen who died that England might live'. The squadron diary states that the Hurricane he had saved was painstakingly repaired and put back into squadron service as the groundcrews' own tribute to this splendid Legionnaire.

17th of August was, luckily, a respite period with the Luftwaffe failing to show up during daylight hours, but the following day Sergeants L. N. Guy and R. P. Hawkings were killed by overwhelming odds near Portsmouth, their comrades bringing down some of the raiders. On 19th August orders came to move back to Debden, Essex, for a so-called rest but this was a misnomer as East Coast convoys had to be protected throughout the hours of daylight. There was, in fact, a little relaxation and time for training and, until 30th August, no sign of the enemy. On this day B Flight, led by Rhodes-Moorhouse, intercepted and shot down a lone He.111 after a longish chase. The following breakfast-time, Debden itself came under attack from Dorniers, and aircraft and buildings were hit. Pilot Officer Grier managed to take off only to be brought down over Debden, happily surviving to fly again. In a later engagement over Essex, Flying Officer Doulton, who had shared three successful combats, lost his life, Pilot Officer H. T. Gilbert and Sergeants R. N. Taylor and A. W. Woolley all having to jump from their burning machines, Woolley being slightly wounded, his second visit to hospital in six weeks.

36. Maintenance at Exeter, 1940.

Flight Lieutenant M. Lister-Robinson, a newcomer, soon claimed three Messerschmitts and it is believed one was later made airworthy as part of the RAF 'Circus' of captured aircraft, flown to airfields for aircraft recognition exercises after being evaluated at the Royal

Aircraft Establishment, Farnborough. On 4th September, Flying Officer J. S. Jankiewicz, one of several Polish reinforcements, made a good landing near Worthing after being forced down, his Hurricane written-off, a Messerschmitt Bf.110 to the squadron partially balancing the accounts. Friday 6th September was one of the blackest in 601's history as, in the same fierce battle over Kent, Flight Lieutenants Willie Rhodes-Moorhouse, DFC, and Carl Davis, DFC, lost their lives, Flying Officer J. Topolnicki baling-out into a tree and Pilot Officer H. T. Gilbert also jumping from his crippled Hurricane. The loss of two of the remaining pre-war Auxiliaries was felt very much and one hopes that the country's debt to the Rhodes-Moorhouse family will never be forgotten. Next day came a move to Exeter and a chance to take things easier until an engagement near Plymouth on 25th September and a double victory over the Bf.110s near Portland on 7th October, Pilot Officer Clive Mayers having to make an emergency landing after meeting with return fire. The month ended with a disaster during a training flight near Exmouth when Sergeants May and Mills-Smith collided; both were killed before they could make their marks.

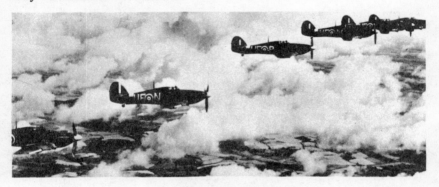

37. Hurricane IIbs, 1941.

On 17th December, after a useful defensive stay in the West Country, and a Heinkel added to the score by Whitney Straight on 12th December, the squadron returned to Northolt, a DFC being awarded to Squadron Leader Sir Archibald Hope, who handed command over to Squadron Leader J. A. O'Neill, DFC. On 25th January, 1941, Flight Lieutenant Whitney Straight, MC, was promoted to command B Flight and Flight Sergeant G. H. Harnden was awarded the British Empire Medal for his tireless example in keeping the Hurricanes serviceable, King George VI making the presentation at a Duxford investiture. On 2nd February another page of history was written as 601 participated in the first of the new 'Set Europe Alight' offensives ordered by Churchill as an escort to five Blenheims of No. 139 Squadron, attacking Boulogne harbour installations and ships. A yellow-nosed Bf.109 was sent into the sea by Whitney Straight to celebrate his return to offensive flying after several staff posts including one as Aide to Group Captain HRH the Duke of Kent. On 5th March the first of the more-powerful Hurricane IIbs arrived, to give real punch in the now constant gunning of ground targets along French and Belgian coasts. Regrettably, during the ferrying-down of the new Hurricanes from Carlisle, Flying Officer J. W. Seddon and Pilot Officer A. Smith lost their lives in a sudden blizzard near Keswick.

During a 'Rhubarb' (a sortie by a pair of Hurricanes into Occupied Europe) Sergeant Mares had an incredible experience when at only fifty feet he was jumped by four Bf.109s, one of which he managed to destroy. His tail, though, hit the ground and on the rebound the Hurricane caught a high-tension cable. Though wounded, he brought his aircraft back to base. 16th April saw a chapter of accidents when the C.O. shot down a Bf.109 only to be brought down by another and was forced to ditch off Dungeness after getting back across the Channel. Group Captain T. McEvoy, flying with the squadron, force-landed at Lydd and the Wing Leader (Wing Commander Manton) also crashed and was slightly hurt. Squadron Leader E. J. Gracie, DFC, a Battle of Britain 56 Squadron pilot, assumed command and on 1st May the squadron moved into Manston, Kent, for the dual role of offensive operations over Europe and the escorting of our convoys and air-sea rescue craft. Several Bf.109s were brought down as the Hurricanes guarded the slow-moving Lysanders dropping their dinghies and supplies to airmen in the water. On 22nd May came a new venture as Pilot Officer Ogilvie and Malezewski, patrolling into France, spotted a Ju.52 transport and after putting two of its three engines out of action, saw it down to tree-top in heavily-wooded country. As they turned for home at the limit of their fuel, two Bf.109s attacked, Ogilvie turning and shooting one down – the other hot footing it for its airfield.

Squadron Leader Whitney Straight, promoted to take over Bader's former unit, No. 242 Squadron, was later forced down into France, from where he escaped following adventures stranger than fiction, returning to England and well-earned leave before further promotion and important appointments overseas. Sergeant Scales was shot down on 10th June and was later reported a prisoner of war. Then, to the dismay of all, the orders came to move to Matlaske, Norfolk, not only for the monotony of East Coast convoy patrols but faced with a change of aircraft, the American-built Bell Airacobra I being issued to 601 Squadron. From Matlaske to Duxford, then to Acaster Malbis near York, the struggle to make something of the unorthodox machine continued, with casualties, including three fatalities, and never more than four aircraft serviceable at one time. Only one operational offensive was possible, Flight Lieutenant J.

Himr (a Czech) taking Sergeant Briggs with him to shoot up a pier at Boulogne and to attack trawlers; Himr was later killed in September 1943 when commanding No. 313 (Czech) Squadron. After Squadron Leader E. J. Jones, Squadron Leader J. D. Bisdee, DFC, from 609 (West Riding) Squadron took control in March 1942 and, on visiting the AOC No. 13 Group, Air Vice-Marshal Saul, asked if the squadron could soon be given a really operational aircraft to fly.

38. The Bell Airacobra, late 1941.

The Air Officer Commanding told John Bisdee that 601 was to get the Hawker Typhoon but Bisdee knowing that although this was a potentially fine machine there were teething troubles, felt that morale had dropped to such a level that another setback would be unfair to the men. So successful was his plea to Air Vice-Marshal Saul that the Typhoon switch was cancelled and, to the joy of all, the Supermarine Spitfire Vb was provided, the Airacobras going to Russia. A move to RAF Digby – a first-class station – helped lift the spirits and just as the squadron was getting into its old form a warning came of a move overseas. When Bisdee was told that he was to hand command to Squadron Leader R. G. A. Barclay, DFC, a 249 Squadron pilot of the Battle of Britain, he again appealed to the AOC and was allowed to stay with 601 for an indefinite time – sharing responsibilities of the move with Barclay.

On 10th April, 1942, the ground personnel left under Squadron Leader Barclay, joining His Majesty's Transport K.6 (the s.s. *Rangitata*) sailing from Liverpool north to the Clyde, giving rise to rumours of Russia. On the 29th, though, they were in Freetown, West Africa, and, after a few happy days in Durban, South Africa, re-embarked in the famous Cunarder *Mauretania* for Port Tewik, Egypt. By 23rd June the ground members were at Landing Ground 12 in North Africa – awaiting their pilots and aircraft. Within hours No. 601's Spitfires touched-down – and they had quite a story to tell. They too had embarked in the Clyde but – in company with No. 603 (City of Edinburgh) Squadron and accompanied by Squadron

Leader Gracie, the one-time Flying Sword leader and veteran of Mediterranean combats, they were soon aboard the U.S.A. aircraft carrier *Wasp*. On 20th April – off Algiers – Squadron Leader Gracie led off the first twelve Spitfires, followed closely by Squadron Leader Bisdee's dozen and again followed by twenty-four others of 603, led by their C.O. Squadron Leader Lord Douglas-Hamilton. Bisdee was first to touch-down in Malta after three hours; forty-one of the forty-eight Spitfires safely landing; two remaining on the carrier owing to technical troubles, one hitting the sea on take-off, one running out of fuel near Malta, two crashing on or off the island.

Within minutes the Luftwaffe and Italian Air Force tried to destroy the reinforcements and 601 pilots were soon in action – seventeen of the precious Spitfires being damaged that first day, mostly on the ground under severe bombing attacks. Next day Squadron Leader Bisdee (who had turned down command of 56 Squadron's Typhoons to stay with 601) destroyed a Ju.88, but was then jumped by several Bf.109s, just managing to bale-out in time and being assisted from his dinghy late that night by a Fleet Air Arm sailor whose courage in braving the mined waters deserved recognition. At this time, though, many acts of heroism went unrewarded and some which were locally recommended failed to reach the Air Ministry for proper attention. One of 601's flight-commanders, Flight Lieutenant Ken Pawson, turned out to sea drawing away a large formation which was about to attack Luqa airfield which was then desperately short of ammunition. Pawson did not return and it is not known if he was overtaken and shot down, or if he drew the enemy away until his fuel ran out, and then gave his life below the waves.

Flight Lieutenant Denis Barnham, a talented artist, led the other flight and Flight Lieutenant 'Pancho' Le Bas, from Argentina, was promoted to replace Ken Pawson. They led their flights from Luqa with rare zeal and in two hectic days when it was believed seventy-four enemy were shot down, 601's share was around ten and by mid-June its score was up to twenty-five Luftwaffe and Italian machines, including some Cantieri Riuniti Cant Z.1007b tri-motored wooden bombers, nicknamed on Malta 'the Bryant & May jobs'. The tail of one of these green-painted machines, with the Arms of the House of Savoy on the fabric, was collected by Bisdee from the grounds of the Naval Hospital, where it had fallen after the C.O.'s burst of fire. Sixty-four replacements for the lost and damaged Spitfires were flown in, from *Wasp* and H.M.S. *Eagle* the Royal Navy carrier, 59 reaching the island to provide relief for battle-weary pilots. Sergeant MacConnell, a new pilot, failed to return from a battle over a convoy and, with Tobruk about to fall to the Afrika Korps, Bisdee was called before the AOC, Malta, and told that 601 was needed in North Africa. On 23rd June, fitted with long-range tanks, the squadron flew off to Landing Ground 07 near Lake Mariut, as part of No. 244 Wing with two other Spitfire units and a Hurricane unit – No. 73 Squadron – formerly under Squadron Leader Aidan Crawley's command as a Curtiss P–40 Kittyhawk outfit. Leading them in July 1941, against Gambut airfield, Crawley had been forced down and was taken prisoner; the news, now passed to his old squadron of pre-war days, was that he had been flown out in a Ju.52 and all hoped that it was not one which the RAF had shot down.

Many of the original ground members, visibly delighted to see squadron aircraft and pilots again, chuckled as they were heard to comment that when they joined the AAF at Hendon they clearly understood that they would never have to serve more than five miles from that airfield! Without exception, though, they would have accompanied aircraft wearing the Sword emblem to the ends of the earth. On 1st July, based now at L.G.154, the Spitfires flew top cover to Nos. 33 and 213 Squadrons, Squadron Leader Bisdee getting in a burst at a new opponent, the Me.210 fast-bomber. On the 6th, Pilot Officer Boyle damaged a Ju.88. On 20th July there was no shortage of volunteers to search for Wing Commander Clive Mayers, the ex-601 Australian who had left also to command a Kittyhawk unit in the Desert Air Force. When one of his pilots was forced down Mayers saved his life – in face of the approaching enemy – by landing and taking him back in his single-seater, a Bar to his DFC was promulgated for this act. Now he had wirelessed that he was forced to land in the Qattara Depression with engine trouble. Bisdee took off with New Zealander Bruce Ingram but although they found the Kittyhawk, there was no sign of Mayers and it was thought that he had been captured. As he was never heard from again, the sad feeling was that he had lost his life in one of the Ju.52 transports en route to Germany.

Four enemy were downed on 24th July and on the 29th came a move to L.G.85 as part of No. 243 Wing, re-equipping there with the Spitfire Vc. Visits of V.I.P.s, including the Prime Minister, called for escort duties and, from E.L.G.219, to Helwan, and on to E.L.G. 154, the squadron supported the Eighth Army in its drive against Rommel. Squadron Leader A. V. Clowes, DFC, DFM, took over from John Bisdee, and the one-time Sergeant Pilot of No. 1 Squadron in Battle of Britain was soon leading the County of London men far into enemy lines, long-range tanks enabling them to destroy Afrika Korps' outposts and transport over a wide area. With the launching of Montgomery's push at El Alamein the squadron provided cover for tank-busting Hurricane IVs of No. 6 Squadron, several enemy machines being shot down as they tried to get at the Hurricanes. On 31st October at Mersa Metruh the docks and enemy troops were ruthlessly gunned and many successes were chalked-up against armoured cars and parked aircraft. Pilot Officer D. E. Llewellyn was forced to land after being hit by flak and Pilot Officer B. R. Terry soon landed beside him, flying Llewellyn back to L.G.172, with Pilot Officer G. Allen-Rowlandson flying above. Although completely out of ammunition they faked dive-bombing attacks on all the enemy vehicles they spotted, to prevent fire from the ground. A well-merited DFC came through for Terry and it is no reflection on the gallant airmen of World War I to recall that a similar act of initiative in those days sometimes brought the Victoria Cross to a squadron pilot. In the Western Desert, though, it was becoming an oft-repeated performance, notwithstanding the undoubted risks involved.

On 7th November, flying from L.G.21, the squadron pummelled the Matruh-Sidi Barrani road, shooting down three Ju.87 dive-bombers, three Bf.109s, and damaging two others. The unlucky Llewellyn was again forced down, this time at L.G.08 which, to his dismay, he found not merely in the hands of the Afrika Korps but of Rommel and his staff. Llewellyn was taken to Rommel but, unattracted by the prospect of remaining in enemy hands until they despatched him to Germany, he made his escape that very night and, helped by friendly natives, was back in allied territory next day with the classic 'There I was with Field Marshal Rommel' for the squadron line-book, though, this time it was no exaggeration.

On 13th November, from Gambut West, the squadron covered the area as the AOC, Air Vice-Marshal Harry Broadhurst (now Air Chief Marshal Sir Harry, of Hawker Siddeley), flew a captured Fieseler Storch observation plane. A week later the squadron command was again changed, this time with Squadron Leader G. H. F. Plinston, who had flown with 607 (County of Durham) in 1940, but who joined 601 from 250 Squadron. Then, with brief sojourns at Zt Msus, El Hasseliate, Melah en Nogra, El Merduma No. 2 (where Christmas was celebrated in traditional style) the squadron escorted Hurribombers and Kittybombers, adding a few enemy aircraft to the total which, at 3rd January, 1943, at El Chel, had reached claims of 175 destroyed, 77 probably-destroyed and 78½ damaged (not allowing for the revised 1940 assessments). A DFC was awarded to Flight Lieutenant Bruce Ingram. Spitfires equipped for bombing – the first in the area – came to 601, at Darragh North, after a brief stay at Hamraiet. Flight Lieutenant J. H. 'Crash' Curry, an American in the Royal Canadian Air Force, who had joined 601 for the flight to Malta got a popular DFC, as did Pilot Officer Ibbotson.

By 7th February, 1943, the squadron was at Castel Benito – Mussolini's great aerodrome of pre-war days – and here the first grass since England was a pleasant change after sand. By 26th February a move had been made to Hazbub Main where, soon after touch-down, five

Bf.109s dived out of the sun and as they opened fire a lone Ju.88 also bombed the field, one squadron armourer being killed and three injured with three airmen of other squadrons killed. Flying Officer W. M. Whitamore took off with others and managed to bring down one fighter and damage another, for which Whitamore got a DFC. The airfield was also shelled by night and although airmen risked their lives to push aircraft to safety the authorities decided to move the squadrons, 601's flights going to Bu Graga and El Hamma respectively. News came from London that Lord Riversdale had accepted appointment as Honorary Air Commodore. This message was followed by a signal announcing a DFC for Squadron Leader Plinston and a move for the squadron into Wing Commander Ian Gleed, DSO, DFC's Wing of Spitfires, flying from Ben Gardane South landing ground. On 20th March, Squadron Leader J. S. Taylor, DFC, moved from 154 Squadron to command and opened his personal account with a Flying Sword machine by getting an enemy fighter on his first squadron sortie.

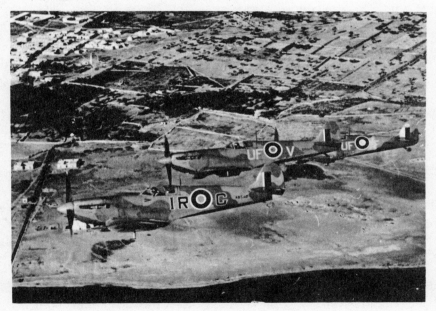

39. 601 Spitfires over North Africa, 1943. Wg Cdr Gleed leading.

On 31st March a squadron lorry hit a concealed mine, Leading Aircraftman Drury losing his life. Moving on with the victorious Eighth Army via the landing grounds at Gabes Main, La Fouconnerie, Bou Goubrine, Hergla and Ben Gardane, the retreating enemy was hit on land and on the evacuation ships. In April twenty Luftwaffe machines were destroyed or damaged and members of the hard-working ground teams received four Mentions in Despatches for

their magnificent efforts on maintenance. As Tripoli was taken, a
Bar to his DFC was awarded to Squadron Leader Taylor and
orders came to return to Malta. A check revealing that in the Western
Desert sixty-three enemy had been destroyed, with sixty-nine either
probably destroyed or damaged – in the air or on the ground. Back
again at Luqa in No. 224 Wing, with Nos. 92, 145, 417 (RCAF)
and 1 and 20 (SAAF) Squadrons, the main role was to escort bombers
– B–25 Mitchells and B–17 Fortresses – for the softening up of
Sicily before allied landings. Squadron Leader Whitamore, DFC,
left on promotion to command No. 81 Squadron and, during the
night of 9th July squadron aircraft helped cover the invasion of
Sicily.

On 12th July, after very little opposition had been encountered,
Ju.87 dive-bombers were sighted and Squadron Leader Taylor, hit
by return fire, lost his life trying to land his disabled Spitfire near
Augusta. In came Squadron Leader Stanislaw Skalski, a Polish
veteran of the Battles of France and Britain where he flew with 501
(County of Gloucester) Squadron and holder of the DFC and two
Bars, the Polish Gold Cross, Polish Silver Cross and Cross of Valour.
He was well-used to the ways of the wild and woolly Auxiliaries
although few were now left in the County of London outfit. On 17th
July the squadron moved to Cassibile for close-escort to bombers
and then to Lentini West. On the next full-moon the enemy bombed
the airfield and three of the longest-serving Auxiliary airmen were
killed, along with two wartime members; five others being wounded.
The Wing Padre, Squadron Leader (Rev) T. E. M. Ashton, conducted
a service attended by every available man and which will never be
forgotten by those present. In true RAF tradition the Flying Swords
concert party put on a first-class show and the squadron pressed on
with the business in hand, grimly determined to avenge their comrades.

By October the base was Tortorella (Foggia No. 2) and Major
M. S. Osler, DFC, a South African, assumed command as Wing
Commander Skalski, on promotion, left to lead the Polish Mustang
Wing, gaining the DSO. After returning to Poland and suffering
imprisonment by the Russians, he wrote his thrilling life-story,
including his time with 501 and 601 Squadrons as highlights of his
career in aviation. From fields at Triolo, Ancona, Canne and Pescara
the squadron built up a high tally of ground targets hit; and Sergeant
Ross, a New Zealander, hit by flak, landed in enemy territory but
evaded capture and came back safely. A fortnight later the squadron's
first successful escaper arrived when Flight Lieutenant R. F. J.
Sherk, who had been shot down in the Quattara area on 29th September, 1942, rejoined after getting away from an Italian P.O.W.
camp. News also came that Flight Sergeant Griffiths, missing since
17th April, 1943, in the Cap Bon area, was back in the United

Kingdom. The long-awaited 200th 'kill' was credited to a Belgian, Flight Sergeant Eid, but, alas, this pilot was killed himself at the end of his operational tour, flight-testing an aircraft as he waited for his next posting.

Almost forgotten in the celebrations for the double-century was a signal of congratulation advising 601 that two trains they had attacked and left in flames contained 240,000 gallons of petrol for the German army, all destroyed just when the enemy needed it most. There was also word of Pancho Le Bas, instructing on Spitfires at Abu Sueir, Egypt, where he was awarded the Air Force Cross and given command of 241 Squadron in Italy.

At Canne L.G. on 1st January, 1944, the squadron converted to the Spitfire Mk.VIII and next day offensive patrols over Avezzano left transports ablaze after which a shipping reconnaissance into Yugoslavia was followed by another strafing mission. Lieutenant D. Cowie, a South African, was hit by flak; he crash-landed but was not seen to leave his aircraft; consequently there was great joy when news came that he was safe, though a prisoner. On 15th January, 1944, members of the squadron received the Africa Star ribbon with 8th Army rosette and next day A party – half the personnel – travelled through mountainous country, camping overnight at a monastery near Grottamindara (where they received much hospitality) arriving at Marcianise airfield by noon next day to prepare for the aircraft. Visits to nearby Pompeii made pleasant interludes for those not on duty as the Spitfires protected the Royal Navy during shelling of the Italian coast. B party, meanwhile, was helping newly-arrived No. 80 Squadron at Madna L.G., their C.O. being Squadron Leader Crash Curry, DFC, old boy of 601. On 24th January, the first of the faster Focke-Wulf 190 fighters was intercepted, two being shot down and one damaged for the loss of a Spitfire, our pilot baling to safety near Anzio.

Then followed the most active period since the Desert, 851 'Ops' hours being flown in February – the most outstanding feature being the 95 per cent serviceability, a Wing record. Liberty Runs were organised into Naples for the San Carlo Opera House and to Caserta for the cinema. March brought news that Captain L. R. S. Waugh, DFC, another South African, missing since New Year's Eve, was safe and a prisoner of war. Over the Anzio beaches on 7th March there was a big air battle as eight of 601's Spitfires, led by Flight Lieutenant Henderson, shot down three of the enemy, with two others damaged. Henderson, though, did not come back. On the 8th came news of a Mention in Despatches for Flight Sergeant R. W. Apps, NCO in charge of A Flight, and for Sergeant Higginson, in charge of transport. On the 11th, an FW.190 was destroyed and on the 13th a DFC came for Flight Lieutenant A. G. Blamer who was at this time in hospital after amputation of two fingers following a determined combat in which he was wounded, bringing down his adversary. This day, too, the C.O. moved to Headquarters, Desert Air Force, at the end of his 'Ops' and was replaced by Squadron Leader J. H. Nicholls, DFC (his decoration had been gained with 601 earlier in the war). Next day another departure as Squadron Leader W. B. Hay left on being promoted to command 417 (RCAF) Squadron.

Over Anzio and Cassino eleven enemy were brought down or damaged and, as if in timely congratulation, a consignment of books arrived from Lord Riversdale to cheer the off-duty hours of all ranks. A Bar to Major Osler's DFC was signalled and a Belgian Croix-de-Guerre for Warrant Officer Eid (decorated and promoted after his regrettable death). Flying now from Venafro serviceability of 99·6 per cent made No. 244 Wing the best in the field, under Wing Commander P. S. Turner, DSO, DFC, a Canadian survivor of the Battle of Britain. Lieutenant P. D. Pote, South African Air Force, was hit by flak and baled into the sea, to be rescued by a U.S.N. destroyer. Soon after this came news of a Bar to Flight Lieutenant Ibbotson's DFC and, with 985 hours flown in May, the County of London established a record for fighter squadrons in this theatre. June opened with well-known Auxiliary Wing Commander H. S. L. 'Cocky' Dundas, DSO, DFC, taking over the Wing. The fall of Rome after a three-week push brought the squadron up to Littorio airfield, close to the capital. On 25th June one of the pre-war members, Group Captain C. P. Paddy Green, DSO, DFC, commanding No. 1 Mobile Operations Room after leading No. 600 (City of London) Squadron, brought his personal Spitfire, MK621, to be cared-for by 601 personnel. During his visit came the news of Roger Bushell's execution, announced in the shocked House of Commons, Roger had been a close friend of Paddy and it was indeed a sad day in squadron history.

H.M.S. *Attacker*, an aircraft carrier, was based within reach of Rome and Lieutenant-Commander Baldwin, DSC, a brilliant pilot, brought Seafires of No. 4 Naval Wing, to be attached to 601 Squadron (their aircraft serials LR640–645). The County of London airmen again assumed the role of Spitbombers, now with 500-pounders, which were neatly deposited on the roads used by the enemy and on any ground targets within range. An off-duty trip into Vatican City was arranged by the Wing Padre and the men were received in audience, irrespective of denomination, by Pope Pius XII; another unforgettable occasion. July saw the move to Fabrica and the acquisition of the Spitfire IX, this coincided with news that, on capture of the airfield at Perugia, the Army had found the grave of 'An Unknown British Airman'. The discovery, close to this, of a tail of an aircraft bearing the Flying Sword helped confirm the casualty as Sergeant Lascelles, lost 16th June in aircraft 'L' serial

MJ389. The bombing of enemy airfields and transportation was briefly interrupted on 25th July when King George VI came to the airfield to thank the squadrons for their splendid work. On 29th July Squadron Leader R. V. Turkington, DFC, ex-241 Squadron, took over command. A happy beginning for August was news from the Army that confirmatory evidence was available of the destruction by 601 of *six* Ju.88 bombers on 12th July, 1943, when claims of only one destroyed, two probably-destroyed and three damaged had been submitted. This unexpected windfall altered the totals to 218 destroyed with 93 probably destroyed or damaged – good reason for an immediate celebration.

40. Squadron Spitfire (flown as HT–B of 601) now at USAF Museum, Ohio.

On 17th August the Prime Minister was escorted in his Dakota on a visit to Marcianise and Venafro and news of a Bar to the C.O.'s DFC was well-received, although it was partly for his work before coming to 601 Squadron. In close support to the advancing armies the squadron wiped out locos and wagons and then participated in one of the war's best-kept secrets. To fool Nazi High Command the squadron moved eastward to Loretto landing ground (designated No. 82 Unit for the move) while creating the impression, by top-secret means, that 601 was still static near Rome. The enemy was taken completely by surprise as, out of nowhere, 601 (82 Unit) bombed and cannoned motor transport and trains, preventing reinforcements getting through to the battle zone. Then, at Fano on 5th September, Spitfire IXbs were received, packing an even more powerful punch. Yet another squadron pilot left to command another squadron (Squadron Leader M. V. Christopherson to be C.O. 185 Squadron). That genial priest the Reverend T. B. 'Tubby' Clayton, CH, MC, founder of Toc H, arrived to chat informally to the men of the County of London's squadron, many of them well acquainted with his church beside the Tower and the Thames and knowing of Tubby's wonderful work in Ypres during World War I. The month was also remarkable for successes against enemy vehicles bringing 'straw-berries' – as congratulatory messages were nicknamed – from Army HQs. The work of 601 cut down casualties amongst 'Pongos' or 'Brown Jobs' as the soldiery were called, and, as the men advanced, the work of the fighters could be assessed from wrecked transportation in the Army's path.

By 30th November it could be reported that 601 had dropped almost 2,000 tons of bombs since taking over the fighter-bomber role in Italy and a personal Thank-you arrived from the 8th Army Commander who said that he was greatly impressed by the accuracy of the squadron's bombing and the magnificent way in which their attacks had been pressed home in difficult conditions. On 4th December a move was made from Fano to Bellaria and a truly typical Christmas was organised for the men by the officers, with turkey and pork served in traditional style to the ground personnel. On 31st December bullock-drawn transports were seen and attacked, evidence of shortage of enemy equipment. Then, on 1st January, as Goering launched his unavailing attacks in Holland and Belgium, 601 Squadron flew twenty-one sorties in their theatre, hitting enemy-occupied houses at Cassiniola. During the strafing runs the C.O.'s machine (PT593) was hit but he managed to land without wheels, riddled with holes.

In the New Year Honours, Flight Sergeant Apps received his second 'Mention' with Leading Aircraftmen Hale and Wylie also the recipients of Mentions in Despatches for their grand work. On 24th January as Wing Commander Turkington, on promotion, moved to 8th Army HQs as RAF Liaison Officer, the B Flight leader – now Squadron Leader C. T. Stimpson – was elevated to the command. From Udine, with Bf.109s making a rare appearance – only to fall to the guns of Flying Officer H. G. Proudman and Warrant Officer Stratton – the squadron moved on to Cortina, then to Treviso. A novel competition was mooted when the NCOs challenged officers to a tourney of indoor and outdoor sports the winners to hold the original cherished Flying Sword in custody. The NCOs scored 61 points to the officer's 60 in a keenly-contested event which would have delighted Roger Bushell and his pre-war chums.

DFC awards were announced for South African Lieutenants Pote and Kruger, both at their homes on leave, although Lieutenant Pote returned to hear the glad tidings at first-hand from the squadron. In the air the pilots were now escorting Vickers Warwicks (a development of the Wellington) on air-sea rescue searches during the final offensives. On 26th March the news came that the sixty-seven married airmen (all with three years' overseas service) were to be returned to the U.K. for leave and for release from the Service if eligible. On 17th April the first Messerschmitt Me.262 jet was sighted over Rimini and during the month an all-time record was set up for strafing barges, motor vehicles, horse-drawn transports, and even motorcycles – a total of more than 300 were destroyed or damaged. Six aircraft were lost, with three pilots missing-believed-killed; three known safe. During the final month of the war in Europe, 601 achieved the record 1,082 operational hours – the first time a fighter squadron had exceeded the thousand-hour mark in this theatre, gaining the Desert Air Force top place. The last operational sortie took place only two days before the cease-fire with a Section led by Flight Lieutenant O'Halloran, accompanied by Flying Officers Hallas and Ross who destroyed four vehicles near Conegliano. The Spitfire flown by Hallas was struck by anti-aircraft fire and although he told the others he might have to bale out, he was not seen to jump – his aircraft crashing east of Rovigo. So the last 601 wartime pilot gave his today, that others might have a tomorrow.

Then came news of disbandment and an Air Ministry press release indicated that 601 had destroyed more than 300 enemy in the air and six on the ground, with 116 damaged in varying degrees, plus 300 vehicles known destroyed and 334 damaged, besides a number of Tiger tanks hit and stopped, if not written-off. By any standard it was a record of which to be proud – even if, along with other fighter squadrons, the Battle of Britain claims have had to be adjusted in the light of post-war research.

41. Gp Cpt the Hon. Max Aitkin,
DSO, DFC and Bar,
returns to command, 1946.

The squadron began to re-form at Hendon in June 1946, Group Captain the Hon Max Aitken, DSO, DFC, MP, reverting to his 1940 rank to lead The Legion and with three other 'scrambled egg' types and two 'three stripers' virtually queuing to rejoin this exclusive band to fly or to serve in any capacity – many ex-officers returning as NCO pilots (a new thing in the Auxiliary Air Force) or as ground airmen. So great was the demand for places that a 'Board' presided over by Squadron Leader Aitken reduced 400 applicants to pilots with 1,500 flying hours or more and such was the enthusiasm that many who failed to qualify, cheerfully asked to be considered for non-flying posts. On 10th July, the North American Harvard FX387 became the new bearer of the Flying Sword emblem, followed later by the Spitfire LF XVIe. In June 1948, pressure of business compelled Squadron Leader (later Sir Maxwell) Aitken to hand over command to Squadron Leader H. S. L. Cocky Dundas, DSO and Bar, DFC, who had been delighted to rejoin as one of the pilots in 1946 when he could so easily have commanded other squadrons. Command in turn passed to Squadron Leader Paul Richey, DFC, in 1950, then to Squadron Leader Christopher McCarthy-Jones who later relinquished command when he became Wing Commander 'Ops' RAuxAF at North Weald – to which airfield the squadron had moved on acquiring the de Havilland Vampire which could not operate from Hendon. Chris McCarthy-Jones persuaded HRH Prince Philip, Duke of Edinburgh, to accept the appointment of Honorary Air Commodore, a most happy move. In 1952 the Gloster Meteor F.8 was received and summer camps at Horsham St Faith; Sylt, Germany; Takali, Malta; safely and successfully undertaken when out of the blue (although some 'rumblings' had been heard, due to the squadron's unique links with Fleet Street) news came that all the flying units of the Royal Auxiliary Air Force were to be disbanded in early 1957.

42. Marshal of the RAF
Sir Dermot Boyle,
GCB, KCVO, KBE, AFC,
one-time adjutant-instructor.

On 6th March, 1957, the final parade was held and Prince Philip (who had presented to the squadron in 1954 The Standard awarded by Her Majesty The Queen) took the salute at Town HQs, Kensington Park Road, the flag designed by Ned Grosvenor, flying at half-mast. Prince Philip, at the party following the parade, was taken to see a typically-601 assessment of the position: a mock lying-in-state designed by the airmen. Wreaths and messages around 'the body of 601 Squadron, RAuxAF, murdered by ignorance' included gems like 'With sincere gratitude to the Air Ministry' – from Bulganin and Khrushchev, the Kremlin; 'Peace – all is Peace'. from the Epping and Ongar District Council; 'In Memory of Happy Nights', from The Young Ladies 'The Egyptian Queen' Malta G.C. The Flying Sword was removed from the archway at Town Headquarters and sent to No. 24 (City of Adelaide) Squadron, an Australian part-time unit, affiliated to the County of London Squadron. It was, perhaps, the one and only regret of The Legion that their many friends in high places, including Marshal of the RAF Sir Dermot Boyle and the then Air Minister, the Hon George Ward (both former members of 601) failed to halt the disbandment of the RAuxAF, after a lengthy battle, more bitter than mild, thanks to these eloquent squadron members.

Prince Philip graciously accepted office as Patron of the 601 Old Comrades Association for which W. J. 'Bill' Kentish has worked so very hard as Hon Secretary, with J. 'Jim' Sharpley as Hon Treasurer. Chairman of the O.C.A. for almost twenty years has been Squadron Leader S. G. 'Vic' Vickers, one of the air-gunners of D.H.9A days, graduating with others to the Hawker Hart. To maintain his pilot rating Vic also flew, concurrently, with the London Air Park Flying Club, Hanworth, and later with the Singapore Flying Club. During World War II he served as Hurricane Liaison Officer between the RAF and the manufacturers. Hit by a piece of doodlebug he was given a week to live but – now over seventy – can chuckle, despite occasional returns to hospital for treatment. Re-unions of the O.C.A., under President Teddy Lanser, MBE, who was an A.C.2 in 1929 but later Equipment Officer right through to disbandment, bring together a splendid mixture of all ranks, including Vice-Presidents Nevil Leyton, former Squadron Medical Officer, now an eminent consultant, and Peter Edelston, who got a well-earned AFC for his ten years' flying with 601. Members of 600 (City of London), deadly rivals before the war, come as honoured guests, in the certain knowledge that 'Air Support' is unlikely to interrupt the gatherings as in days (and nights) of yore.

In his magnificent book *The Flying Sword*, a pilot of post-war days, Tom Moulson, brings much of squadron history to life and of the many true and hilarious tales, one, surely, has general appeal. It is of the visit of Marshal of the RAF Lord Tedder to Town Headquarters when, as was his habit, Tedder left his gold-braided cap behind. His driver returned for it and the cap was handed over, after having been passed around the squadron. Lord Tedder sent a note of thanks which concluded 'Never . . . not even after visiting the Air Training Corps have I collected such a miserly sum as $1/1\frac{1}{2}$d!' From 'that other dispersal' one can visualise the smiles of Michael Peacock, Willie Rhodes-Moorhouse, Roger Bushell and the others who gave their lives for freedom: they could be proud of their post-war counterparts.

43. A post-war dinner of the Old Comrades Association. *Right to left:* Sqdn Ldr Peter Edelston, Wg Cdr Chris McCarthy-Jones, Sqdr Ldr Nevil Leyton, Sqdn Ldr S. G. Vickers.

A full-length book would be needed to tell what has happened to ex-members. As many know, Aidan Crawley, who was awarded the MBE for his great work in Stalag Luft III (his book *Escape From Germany* is a classic), became Under Secretary of State for Air in the 1950s. The three sons of Sir Nigel Norman (killed in a wartime air crash) flew the post-war jets, and Desmond Norman has kept the family name in aviation with the Britten–Norman Islander (and Trislander). Group Captain the Hon Peter Vanneck retains a Service connection as Inspector of the remaining RAuxAF units; Whitney Straight through Rolls-Royce; and Sir Archibald Hope via The Air League, for which he has done a splendid job. J. J. Parkes, the very first Auxiliary to qualify as a pilot, famed as a test pilot, as General Manager de Havilland, Stag Lane, throughout World War II, as a Fellow of the Royal Aeronautical Society and as Chairman and Managing Director of Alvis Ltd – to mention only some of his contributions. Norman Jones, an early Squadron member and founder-member London Aeroplane Club, was a Lieutenant-Commander in the RNVR in World War II, and is now Managing Director of Rollason Aircraft and Chairman of The Tiger Club.

Few stayed in the service but of these one must mention Air Vice-Marshal M. H. Pancho Le Bas, CBE, DSO, AFC, Air Officer Commanding No. 1(B) Group of Strike Command, Group Captain J. A. O'Neill, DFC, and Wing Commander Arthur Gill, a 1937 member who later commanded 84 Squadron in the Far East and more recently was Air Attaché in Oslo. Group Captain J. R. A. Peel, DSO, DFC, was a 1938 member and has been widely credited with firing the first shots in the Battle of Britain on 8th August, 1940, leading 145 Squadron (with Guy Branch as one of his flight-commanders). Squadron Leader F. W. M. Jenson, DFC, AFC, who was commanding No. 183 Squadron of Typhoons in 1945, will be remembered as a pre-war airman who came back to 601 as a Sergeant-Pilot in 1940.

On Tuesday 19th December, 1961, The Standard was laid up during an impressive service at the RAF Church St Clement Dane's, in the presence of Prince Philip; after it was carried in by Desmond Norman, with escort party of Messrs S. G. Vickers, S. Venn, C. Cates and E. Lanser, the Old Comrades Association accepted custody. A note of sadness was the absence of Wing Commander Christopher McCarthy-Jones who had died suddenly in Lagos during February 1960. He, and all who gave their lives, in peace or war, during 601 service, or who have passed on since, were remembered then, as they still are when former members get together. Will there ever be a comparable band of airmen. Many feel it most unlikely.

REPRESENTATIVE SQUADRON AIRCRAFT

de Havilland D.H.9A	E8605 E8627 J7835 J8108 J8478
Avro 504N	J8703 J8706
Westland Wapiti I	J9101 IIA J9612 J9617 J9855 J9856
D.H.60M Gipsy Moth	K1852
Hawker Hart I	K2470 K2976 (Sir Nigel Norman) K2989 K3154 (T) flown by Squadron Leader Sir Philip Sassoon.
Hawker Demon	K4500 K4513 K5713 K5720
Gloster Gauntlet II	K5311 K5334 K7797 K7837 K7888 YN–J
Bristol Blenheim If	L1518 L6603 L8701
Hawker Hurricane I	L2141 P2673 UF–N P3393 P9886 V7601
IIb	Z2918 Z3030 Z3167 Z3355 BD712 UF–Y

Bell Airacobra I	AH585 UF–O AH593 UF–J
	AH601 (C.O.) AH602 UF–W
Vickers-Supermarine Spitfire Vb	BL967 BL991 BL996 EP689
Vc	BR113 *BR175 BR232 (C.O.)
	BR384 BR459 ER340
VIII	JF504 JF754 JF780 JF834
IX	MK551 UF–T MK724 NH297
	SM445
LFXVIe	RW376 SL725 RAH–Y TE330
	HT–B TE473
North American Harvard IIb	FX387
de Havilland D.H. Vampire F.3	VF332 VT812 N VT864 B
	VT869 E VT874
Gloster Meteor T.7	WA620 P WL454 B
F.8	WH471 L WK721 K **WL167
	(C.O.) WL130

  * The 1st 'Spitbomber'
** Black and red diagonal stripes on fin and rudder.

It has been suggested that a Spitfire IX displayed for years at Sabaudia (Nettuno), Italy, at the entrance to the Anti-Aircraft School, may be a 601 machine but correspondence has failed to produce the serial which would confirm this belief. Beautifully restored and on exhibition at the USAF Museum, Wright-Patterson Air Force Base, is Spitfire XVIe TE330, once HT–B of 601's post-war days. At RAF Colerne, Wiltshire, as this is written, is Vampire F.3 VT812/7200M which served with 601 (and other squadrons). It is currently painted in the County of London markings and one hopes it may find its way to the RAF Museum at Hendon in due course.

The Squadron insignia of interlocking red and black triangles were authorised markings on the top wings and fuselage from 1934 with 'Flying Sword' on tail fin. Camouflage came with the Gauntlet and the original code was YN, altered to UF on outbreak of war. During the post-war Reserve Command period RAH was used, changing to HT on transfer into Fighter Command. Red and black triangles returned with Vampire and Meteor; with aircraft letter only.

Badge: A winged sword. The sword commemorates the squadron's link with the County of London.

603
(City of Edinburgh)
Squadron

IT WAS AT Turnhouse on 14th October, 1925, that No. 603 (City of Edinburgh) Squadron began to form under Squadron Leader J. A. McKelvie, AFC, with Flight Lieutenant C. R. Keary, RAF, as his adjutant. A Town Headquarters was established at 26 Learmouth Terrace and there was a brisk response when recruiting started. In April 1926 Lord Trenchard paid a visit with General Peyton, General Officer Commanding, Scottish Command; in July the first annual training camp was held at Leuchars, Fife, using the squadron's initial equipment, the de Havilland D.H.9A and the Avro 504K. Three officers and fifty-five airmen reported for this camp.

In July of 1928 came the first fatality when Pilot Officer J. T. L. Shiells lost his life going solo. He had been the squadron's fencing expert and in his memory his parents donated the Shiells Trophy for competition. By December 1928, the strength had increased to 17 officers and 155 airmen – remarkable progress – and when a new adjutant was required to replace Flight Lieutenant Keary, the Air Ministry wisely sent Flight Lieutenant H. S. P. Walmsley, MC, DFC, a most experienced pilot. In April 1929 came the first public appearance of the squadron pipe band and the following year brought a change of aircraft when 603 Squadron received the Westland Wapiti. Squadron Leader H. R. Murray-Phillips assumed command in 1931, Flight Lieutenant R. H. Legg came in as adjutant and flying instructor and Flying Officer Lord Malcolm Douglas-Hamilton was appointed as assistant-adjutant. The squadron's Honorary Air Commodore was the Earl of Stair who came on a visit with the Prince of Wales.

In July 1931 five Wapitis flew over Edinburgh to greet the King and Queen and by March of 1932 it was possible to put ten Wapitis

into the air for a cross-country flight to Hendon, refuelling at Spital-
gate, Grantham. Summer camp that year was at Manston, Kent,
and the following year during camp, again in Kent, 603 Squadron
logged 613 flying hours – more than any other AAF unit. In 1934
Squadron Leader Lord G. N. Douglas-Hamilton assumed command
with Flight Lieutenant G. F. MacJohnson as adjutant and the diary
for this period shows that such promising pilots as Pilot Officers
I. E. Chalmers-Watson, T. M. McNeil, R. Sorel-Cameron, G. L.
Denholm, I. Kirkpatrick, C. E. R. Tait, and G. I. Wynne-Powell
were making their marks. Then, in March 1934, came the Hawker
Harts and an exhibition for the Empire Air Display in conjunction
with No. 3 Squadron's Bristol Bulldogs was a crowd-thriller. That
summer's Garden Party at Holyrood was attended by the officers
and at the annual camp Manston heard the Air Salute played by
603's pipe band – a stirring occasion.

44. Wapitis of 603 in 1933.

In August the squadron paid a visit to Aldergrove, Belfast, and
in September co-operated with the Hawker Demons of No. 41
Squadron, then commanded by Squadron Leader Boret. Empire
Air Day of 1935 attracted over 4,000 people to Turnhouse and the
splendid flying of the squadron was witnessed by the Duke of Kent,
then Lord High Commissioner (who later lost his life flying from

Invergordon). In September Pilot Officer C. E. R. Tait transferred to the RAF on a short-service commission (rising to the rank of wing commander and gaining the DFC). April 1936 saw Nos. 600 (City of London), 602 (City of Glasgow), 604 (County of Middlesex) and 607 (County of Durham) Squadrons at Turnhouse for a great Easter affiliation programme. In May more than 8,000 spectators attended the year's Empire Air Day, a sum of £323 being sent to the RAF Benevolent Fund. Flight Lieutenant J. L. Jack, MC, was awarded the MBE for his outstanding service to the squadron as the armament officer since 1927.

45. Hawker Hart.

From 1937 to 1939 the adjutant-instructor was Flight Lieutenant F. H. Tyson with Flying Officer E. L. Colbeck-Welch as his assistant, the last-named being promoted later to become adjutant to No. 600 (City of London) Squadron. In 1938 the squadron received the Hawker Hind light-bomber and newcomers G. K. Gilroy and J. A. B. Somerville were followed by Pilot Officers Douglas and G. C. Hunter; Squadron Leader E. H. 'Count' Stevens became C.O. and Flight Lieutenant H. M. Pinfold arrived as adjutant-instructor. In October the squadron was moved into No. 12(F) Group to become a fighter unit after thirteen years with bombers. The Gloster Gladiator biplanes of No. 54(F) Squadron were taken over in time to stage an impressive demonstration when Air Chief Marshal Sir Hugh Dowding, Air Officer Commanding, Fighter Command, came to present the Lord Esher Trophy to 603 as the best all-round AAF squadron of 1938.

In May of 1939, with the public at long last awakening to the importance of the Royal Air Force, more than 17,500 came to

Empire Air Day – the last they were to enjoy, had they but known. During August the squadron was embodied into the RAF, including Squadron Leader (the Reverend) J. Rossie-Brown, the chaplain. On 5th September Flight Lieutenant G. L. Denholm flew the first war patrol and ten days later Spitfires arrived and training commenced at Grangemouth. 1st October brought tragedy when Flying Officer J. A. B. Somerville, a promising pilot, collided with another aircraft when taxying, losing his life so unnecessarily. On the 7th, Pilot Officer G. C. Hunter crashed on landing in bad visibility and was seriously injured. Pilot Officers W. A. Douglas and D. K. A. Mackenzie were then sent to No. 7 Flying Training School, Peterborough, to complete their training and the remaining Gladiators were transferred to Nos. 141 and 152 Squadrons which were just forming.

16th October will ever remain *the* highlight of the squadron history for on this day the first German aircraft to be destroyed since 1918 over British territory fell to the guns of Nos. 603 and 602 Auxiliary Squadrons and it was to 603's Spitfires that the rare honour of being first was credited. Yellow Section (Flight Lieutenant Denholm, with Pilot Officers Gilroy and Morton) was 'scrambled' when, over the Firth of Forth, a German reconnaissance machine was sighted and the RAF's wireless-interception service picked up a message indicating a heavy raid against the Forth Bridge and the Rosyth naval dockyard. Red Section of 603 also took off as did 602 (flying from Drem) and between 2.30 and 2.55 p.m. an He.111 was sighted east of Dalkeith and shot into the sea by the men of the City of Edinburgh Squadron, three men being seen to climb out of the Heinkel near Port Seton.

But the day was not over and, as the diary tells us, another Heinkel was attacked at 3.40 p.m. near Rosyth, the rear-gunner put out of action and one engine stopped by Pilot Officers Morton and Robertson of Red Section. Flying Officer Boulter then fired on a Heinkel east of Aberdour and finally Flight Lieutenant Gifford, with Robertson and Morton, were directed to a convoy which was being bombed near St Abbs Head. Although this Heinkel made off after being hit, the enemy aircraft later turned back, realising it would never reach its base. Three of the four-man crew were found in a collapsible boat which Red Section, after landing and refuelling, directed H.M.S. *Gurkha* to capture, the prisoners being brought to Edinburgh for interrogation. The Spitfires of Robertson and Morton (L1049 and L1050) had bullet-holes from return fire, Norton touching down with only half a gallon of petrol left, his sump punctured by a bullet.

As the world echoed the praises of the Auxiliaries the squadron chaplain, accompanied by the pipe band and off-duty airmen, accorded military honours to the two Luftwaffe airmen killed in action who were buried in Portobello cemetery. Then on 28th October came a shared victory as after the rival-squadron, 602, had scored hits on an He.111, Red Section of 603 finished it off at Kidlaw, six miles south of Haddington; two of the German crew were killed, the pilot was wounded and the observer was unhurt. This, the first enemy aircraft actually to land on Scottish soil drew V.I.P.s and the public from miles around. There followed a brief respite until 18th November when the squadron was sorry to hear that Flight Lieutenant P. Gifford would be leaving – though glad to hear of his promotion to command No. 3 Squadron, RAF. This was a rare tribute to 603 as Gifford was one of the first of the Auxiliaries to take over a regular unit.

A detachment was sent up to Montrose to protect the flying training expansion there and on 7th December Flying Officer J. L. G. Cunningham, Pilot Officer B. J. G. Carbury and Sergeant-Pilot R. Berry sighted a formation of seven Heinkels heading for the airfield. Cunningham immediately singled out one of a formation of three which dived for sea-level as it turned east, the gunner firing wildly at the Spitfire. Meanwhile, on Cunningham's second attack, no fire came from the rear-guns, the gunner had probably been killed. Black smoke then streamed from one engine of this Heinkel as Carbury made a frontal attack on another, seeing white smoke pour from both its engines. Sergeant Berry, at this time, dived on the starboard Heinkel, firing all his ammunition. The enemy machines turned and made off for their bases at top speed and our Spitfires, at the limit of their endurance, had to return, not knowing the ultimate fate of the enemy aircraft. Sergeant Berry was commissioned into the Royal Air Force Volunteer Reserve after this engagement – recruiting for the Auxiliary Air Force having ceased on the outbreak of war.

By mid-December one flight was based at Prestwick with the other at Montrose, for the escorting of convoys. In January 1940, though, the squadron came together at Dyce, Aberdeen's airport. A lone He.111 was intercepted on 19th January and, although many of the Spitfire guns did not fire owing to extreme cold, the enemy machine was later confirmed as being down in the sea. During February and March encounters with the enemy were rare as the occasional reconnaissance aircraft turned back on sighting the Spitfires. By 1st May the squadron was at Drem, SW. of North Berwick, before returning to the home station, Turnhouse. Here Wing Commander Harry Broadhurst and Flight Lieutenant W. F. Blackadder (Auxiliary of 607 (County of Durham) Squadron) came to relate their experiences of the air-fighting over France. The squadron badge, the motto in Deric, translated 'If you Dare' was presented by Air Vice-Marshal Richard Saul, the Air Officer Commanding No. 13(F) Group and then, with the Dunkirk evacuation in full-swing, the pilots 'champed at the bit' at their own inactivity until – on 26th June – came the first raid on Turnhouse. Two of the enemy were shot down and Flying Officer J. E. G. Haig had to crash-land near Harperrigg Reservoir in Spitfire N3190 which ran out of fuel.

On the 3rd, 7th, 12th, 15th and 17th July, the squadron was in action off the East Scottish coast, claiming four Heinkels, a Ju.88 and a Do.215 destroyed, some prisoners being taken. Flying Officer C. D. Peel did not return from the engagement of 17th July, and on the next day three more of the enemy were either destroyed or seriously disabled near Montrose, two of the Spitfires being hit by return fire. During the last ten days of the month two Do.17s and four He.111s were intercepted and shot down or damaged between Aberdeen and Montrose. In August orders came to move down to Hornchurch, Essex, one of the key airfields in the defence of London. At last the squadron was to be tested to the limit and morale was high, tinged with a little regret at departure from Scotland. Already there had been changes from the line-up on embodiment on 23rd August, 1939, when Squadron Leader Stevens had Flight Lieutenants Gifford, Denholm, and Flying Officers H. K. MacDonald, J. A. B. Somerville, Pilot Officers I. S. Ritchie, J. S. Morton and G. K. Gilroy in A Flight and Flight Lieutenant I. Kirkpatrick, Flying Officers F. W. Rushmer, J. L. G. Cunningham, G. T. Wynne-Powell, R. McGregor Waterson, and Pilot Officers C. D. Peel and G. C. Hunter in B Flight.

Somerville had died, tragically; newcomers had arrived including Pilot Officers Richard Hillary of the Oxford University Air Squadron, with his friends Pilot Officers Peter Pease and Colin Pinckney. 'Uncle George' Denholm, 'Sheep' Gilroy, P. Gifford, J. S. Morton, D. Stewart-Clarke, 'Ras' Berry, I. S. Ritchie and Sergeants I. K. Arber and J. R. Caister had seen action. Fighter Command – and the Air Ministry – had no hesitation in putting the squadron into the very front-line especially after the action of 3rd July when three Ju.88s were destroyed and an He.11 damaged by Uncle George Denholm's men – the later evidence from combat films and interrogations of two prisoners being a pointer to things to come as only one Ju.88 had been claimed by pilots whose aircraft recognition had yet to be tested.

Replacing the battle-weary No. 65 Squadron was no easy task and Squadron Leader Denholm – now in command, with Squadron Leader Stevens promoted to become a Controller at No. 11(F) Group – spent 27th August in consultation with the C.O.s of the other squadrons. The next day 603 Squadron fought an uphill battle with a large force of Messerschmitt Bf.109s, four Spitfires were lost and Flight Lieutenant J. L. G. Cunningham and Pilot Officers Don MacDonald and N. J. V. 'Broody' Benson were killed. Next day another Spitfire was lost, Flying Officer J. C. Boulter escaping, slightly wounded. On 30th August Squadron Leader Denholm had to bale out and on 1st September Flying Officer R. McG 'Bubble' Waterson was killed and Sheep Gilroy wounded, two more Spitfires being lost. Next day although two Spitfires were seriously damaged (one was later written-off) three Bf.109s were definitely and one probably destroyed. Sergeant J. Stokoe was wounded but Pilot Officer J. G. E. Haig escaped injury in his forced landing at Hornchurch after combats.

Tuesday 3rd September, the anniversary of the outbreak of war, was a memorable day for the squadron when both Peter Pease and Sergeant Caister destroyed Bf.109s but it was marred by the shooting-down of both Pilot Officers Richard Hillary and D. Stewart-Clarke. It has been said that *The Last Enemy* by Richard Hillary ranks with the very best of the many World War II books and Hillary's death, when re-training to fly night-fighters, was a tremendous blow to all who knew him or who read his book (which is now in its seventh edition). Several of the ground airmen were wounded in the bombings of Hornchurch but morale remained high and the squadron score – although now known to be higher than the actual total with the duplication of claims – was thirty-seven destroyed or damaged in the week 28th August–3rd September.

Sergeant A. R. Sarre successfully landed his damaged Spitfire near Ashford, Kent, on 4th September, when his engine stopped. Next day long-serving member Flight Lieutenant F. W. Rushmer, 'Rusty' to his friends, was killed and newcomer Pilot Officer W. P. H. Rafter was wounded over Kent, the possible claims of Rusty are unknown but this fine pilot, leader of Red Section, would undoubtedly have sold his life dearly. On 5th September, anxious to bring down at least one of many Bf.109s, newly-commissioned Pilot Officer J. R. Caister chased his quarry over the French coast, only to be brought down and taken prisoner. The following day Sergeant Sarre baled-out after combat and Squadron Leader Denholm and Pilot Officer B. G. H. Stapleton made forced landings with damaged Spitfires. Then came a short break but the squadron returned to the fray on 14th September when Brian Carbury brought down a Messerschmitt near London and a second enemy machine was shared by other pilots of 603 in the big battle. On 15th September – with the Prime Minister watching the operations-room table at Headquarters No. 11(F) Group, near Uxbridge – several of the enemy were claimed of which post-war records confirm destruction of Bf.109s by Squadron Leader Denholm and Pilot Officer F. J. MacPhail. During a later engagement George Denholm had to bale out and Richard Hillary's great chum, Peter Pease, lost his life.

Two days of quiet and then on 18th September, Pilot Officer Peter Howes, another friend of Hillary, who had managed to join 603 after flying with 54 Squadron, was killed in combat over Kent. In this engagement Sergeant G. T. Bailey's Spitfire was hit but he managed to nurse it back to Hornchurch. On 23rd September Flight Lieutenant Boulter destroyed a Bf.109 and on the 27th Pilot Officer P. M. 'Pip' Cardell died when his Spitfire fell to a Messerschmitt – his death was quickly avenged in the hectic air-fighting but the following morning another squadron veteran, Flight Lieutenant H. A. J. MacDonald, was killed. 2nd October was a red-letter day in squadron history when Flying Officer Brian Carbury, from New Zealand, brought down a Messerschmitt 109 over the Thames. Seconds later Pilot Officer T. M. Hartas and Pilot Officer P. G. Dexter each destroyed a 109 and although Dexter was afterwards brought down, he managed to bale out, though wounded. On 5th October Pilot Officer J. S. 'Black' Morton had to jump from Spitfire K9807 when it caught fire after combat. He was found, burned, but alive.

46. National Employers Mutual Spitfire, 1941.

Brian Carbury had another success on 7th October, but on Sunday 27th October two pilots recently transferred from 611 (West Lancs) Squadron, Pilot Officers R. B. Dewey and D. A. Maxwell, lost their Spitfires in combat – Dewey being killed and Maxwell baling-out to safety. Flying Officer C. W. Goldsmith, who had left to fly with 54, but who had returned to 603, died from wounds after this same action. It was thought that two Messerschmitts fell to the squadron guns and they were possibly the last to 603's credit in what is known as the Battle of Britain. Distinguished Flying Cross awards were made to Squadron Leader Denholm, Flying Officer Carbury, Pilot Officers Berry and G. K. Gilroy, with a Distinguished Flying Medal for Pilot Officer Caister, then a prisoner of war. A congratulatory signal came from Headquarters No. 11(F) Group on the squadron's fine airmanship and Count Stevens, now commanding RAF Ford, Sussex, came to see his old friends and to add his warm congratulations. Newcomer Pilot Officer David Scott-Malden, who had served with 611 Squadron, made his debut with a fine combat.

The month of November was also notable for a truly amazing

happening. Eight of the squadron Spitfires were patrolling on the 23rd when twenty Italian Air Force Fiat CR.42 fighters were sighted about ten miles SW of Dover, flying westwards after an unsuccessful attempt by Italian Fiat BR.20 bombers against our coastal shipping. Seven of the enemy fighters were shot down, two probably-destroyed and two damaged – for no loss of aircraft or pilots – a splendid 'bag'. From 1st to 12th December the squadron did duty at Rochford and on the 13th, as news came of a DFC for Flight Lieutenant Boulter, the squadron was ordered north to Drem. On the 17th, Sheep Gilroy, earlier mauled by over-zealous Home Guard volunteers who took him for a Luftwaffe pilot after baling-out, was badly hurt in an accident. On Christmas Day, as officers traditionally waited upon their airmen, a lone Ju.88 reached St Abbs Head and was damaged by a quickly-scrambled Spitfire. On 30th December Flight Lieutenant Haig and Flying Officer Carbury moved to No. 58 Operational Training Unit at Grangemouth to instruct new fighter-pilots, after valiant service with 603 Squadron.

In February came a real blow when Flight Lieutenant C. J. Boulter, DFC, was hit by a Hurricane as he was about to take off, this splendid pilot died later in East Fortune Hospital. Squadron Leader Denholm moved to Turnhouse when he was promoted on 1st April and Squadron Leader F. M. Smith from No. 72 Squadron came in to command. An interesting entry in the diary at this period notes that newly-promoted Flight Lieutenant Sheep Gilroy, DFC, was given special leave to superintend the lambing on his farm in the Peeblesshire hills – ninety-score being the tally he reported on re-joining the squadron!

By 16th May the squadron was back at Hornchurch, now on the offensive, and within two days was sweeping the countries of Occupied Europe, sometimes in a wing of three squadrons under Wing Commander Farquhar (ex-602) Squadron or on escorts to our daylight bombers, hitting airfields and other targets to force the Luftwaffe into the air. In fact the enemy rarely intervened except to try and pick off lame-ducks stragglers and combats were very few. Detached again into Rochford, the squadron pipe-band was flown down from Turnhouse for Southend's War Weapons Week, creating an unforgettable impression in the district. Pilot Officer K. J. McKelvie, after a tussle with two Bf.109s, returned with his rudder shot away and tailplane badly damaged, yet made a good landing. Unluckily, a month later he collided with Pilot Officer Fawkes over France and although Fawkes brought his battered machine back for a crash-landing in Kent, McKelvie was seen to bale out but did not return, as had been hoped, via the Pyrenees, and it was assumed he was en route to a German P.O.W. Camp. Flying Officer Douglas was wounded by return cannon-fire, making a forced landing at Hawkinge, Kent. 'Lord Haw-Haw' gleefully broadcast that Flying

Officer Harry Prowse was a prisoner but he did not add that Harry had been seen to shoot down two Bf.109s before going down himself!

Squadron Leader M. J. Louden (ex-242 Squadron) assumed command in July 1941 as the squadron moved back from Rochford into Hornchurch and Sheep Gilroy was promoted to take command of No. 609 (West Riding) Squadron, adding a Bar to his DFC, and the DSO, for leadership and combat. Flight Lieutenant G. D. Duncan Smith came in as a flight-commander as Flight Lieutenant J. S. Morton, DFC, left to be trained as a fighter controller – his personal score being fourteen enemy destroyed or damaged. On 21st August Pilot Officer Falconer, hit by flak over France, dived over the Channel to try and make the distance, getting to within two miles of our shore before he had to ditch the Spitfire in the sea. Soldiers swam out to him and all were picked up by the rescue launch which had arrived in response to the wireless 'Mayday' (the standard call for help – from the French *m'aidez*).

On Squadron Leader Louden's departure for North Africa, he was replaced by Squadron Leader T. H. T. Forshaw, formerly of 616 and 609 Squadrons; and 603 moved into Fairlop, nearer to London, the site purchased to be London's airport but, at this stage, a sea of mud. Flight Lieutenant Lord David Douglas-Hamilton kept the pipers well-occupied entertaining local RAF and Army units, and, finding Lieutenant Lord Clonmore serving nearby, managed to arrange liaison visits as a break for the pilots. The airport committee for Fairlop invited squadron representatives to the Mansion House, London, for luncheon to commemorate the sinking of two flakships, by 603's cannon-fire, which enabled our Hurribombers to attack enemy ships in comparative ease. On 15th December the squadron again returned to Dyce, near Aberdeen, revelling in the clean cold air after the Essex smog. Sadly, soon after this move, Squadron Leader Forshaw scrambled after a suspected raider and crashed into the sea SE. of Newburgh. Thus was lost a much-loved C.O. and in his stead, Squadron Leader Lord David Douglas-Hamilton was promoted to command. With only one further combat, a Ju.88 destroyed off Kinnairds Head, warning came for the squadron to prepare for a move overseas.

47. Spitfires, Malta, 1942.

The groundcrews embarked in their troopship on 13th April, 1942, and, via the Cape of Good Hope, were in Egypt on 4th June, and off Cyprus on 26th June, via the Suez Canal. Off-loaded at Famagusta they moved to the airfield at Nicosia and in the absence of their squadron Spitfires, serviced the aircraft of No. 451 (RAAF) Squadron and the P–40 Kittyhawks of the 65th United States Air Force Squadron. Meanwhile, unbeknown to these airmen, the pilots of 603 had assembled at Greenock, watching as their Spitfires were hoisted aboard the US aircraft carrier *Wasp*, along with the aircraft of No. 601 (County of London) Squadron. At dawn on 20th April, a total of forty-six Spitfires flew from the carrier's deck for the four-hour Mediterranean flight into Malta, touching-down at Luqa (now Malta's civil airport), from where 603 moved into the airfield at Takali. Here the squadron was strengthened by Flying Officer Wally McLeod who had flown with 411 (Canadian) Squadron but, anxious for action, had volunteered for Malta. He had only been on the island twenty-four hours when he and Squadron Leader Lord Douglas-Hamilton chased and caught an Italian Cant 1007 bomber which began to smoke as their fire went home.

48. Beaufighter launching rockets against shipping.

Overwhelming fighters then drove off the two Spitfires damaging McLeod's machine in which he only just got back to base. This was a lesson the young Canadian-Scot never forgot and he soon destroyed a Macchi 202 fighter then a Bf.109. When the merchantman *Welshman* finally limped into harbour with Spitfire Vc aircraft aboard, McLeod left the squadron, taking some 603 pilots, to form No. 1435 Flight and, in five weeks, gained the DFC and Bar for his magnificent combats. Returning to England Wally McLeod later led a Canadian Squadron, gaining the DSO but, after his twenty-first victory, was brought down; the Royal Canadian Air Force stated that it was the greatest loss they had ever suffered. Members of 603 Squadron should remember that this great pilot, from a Scottish family, never forgot his association with the City of Edinburgh men. After McLeod's departure from 603, the other Spitfire Vc reinforcements from *Welshman* replaced aircraft flown off the carrier and, in three months, claimed some sixty victories over the Italian and Luftwaffe machines which were constantly attacking the George Cross island; accurate records were lost in the many bombings by the enemy.

Some of the survivors of the squadron – for there were many casualties alas – joined other units to make up composite squadrons, whilst at Port Said, on 19th December, 1942, the original ground-crews gathered together and moved under the auspices of No. 201 Group's No. 238 Wing to Edku where Wing Commander H. A. Chater, the new C.O., explained that the new role of 603 Squadron was to be as a Naval Co-operation Unit and that they would shortly be equipped with the Bristol Beaufighters Mk.I and Mk.VI. As the Desert War progressed the squadron moved from Mersa Matruh to Buq Buq, then to El Adem, Martuba, Benghazi, and Misurata, covering the allied convoys and landings in North Africa with little excitement apart from the successful ditching in the Mediterranean of 'J' for Johnny, the pilot and navigator being picked up by our ships.

In August 1943 the aircraft were fitted to carry 250 lb bombs and attacked Kalamata landing ground and the harbours, also visiting Western Greece in search of targets, flying from Berka III with No. 252 Squadron. By 4th September, 1943, the squadron was in Sicily, at Borizzo, and, during the Salerno fighting, scored its first Beaufighter victory when on 24th September three of the squadron's aircraft sighted six Ju.52 transports, destroying three and probably destroying a fourth, all, it was thought, laden with troops for Rommel. Pilot Officer Megone's aircraft was hit and he landed it, on fire, on Pianosa Island. He and his navigator put out the blaze, took off again – for which Megone was deservedly awarded the DFC. On 5th October at Landing Ground 91, the latest Mark X Beaufighters were received and, from the 12th, the squadron was transferred to the Aegean, escorting B–25 Mitchell bombers of the USAF 310th Bomber Group – equipped with 75 mm cannon!

A Do.24 flying boat and an Arado 196 floatplane were destroyed by the Beaufighters, together with aircraft on Luftwaffe airfields and schooners in use by the Nazis, in their harbours. On 6th November the squadron moved into El Adem, Libya, for low-flying raids against barges and caiques in Port Naussa, followed by the destruction of two Arado 196s. When 'Y' had to ditch, with pilot and navigator, Pilot Officer Hopkins and Warrant Officer Roger, the pair had an unexpected pick-up in the form of one of our submarines which took them to Malta. Escorting the Torpedo-Beaus of No. 47 Squadron, the Siebel Ferry at Leros was destroyed by 603 and DFC awards came to Squadron Leader G. B. Atkinson, Pilot Officer

R. H. Giles and Pilot Officer K. I. E. Hopkins. The aircraft were fitted with rails to take eight 60 lb rockets – the first in the Mediterranean theatre – and from airfield Gambut III, under Wing Commander Ronaldson Lewis, DFC (ex-504 County of Nottingham Squadron), a daily barrage against enemy hideouts in Crete and Greece was kept up.

49. Airmen fitting rocket projectiles to Beaufighters.

Christmas Day of 1943 was voted the best ever by squadron airmen, the officers and NCOs giving up their stored 'goodies' to give their hard-working groundcrews a treat. Then, on 27th January, 1944, near Mykonos, the Beaufighters fell upon three Ju.52s, escorted by four Arado 196s. Three of the Junkers and two Arados fell in flames – the Ju.52s obviously carrying petrol for the Afrika Korps. The Air Officer Commanding, Middle East, Air Marshal Sir Keith Park (in whose No. 11 Group the squadron fought in 1940) flew his Hurricane in from Cairo to thank the squadron for their fine work. As he spoke, aircraft of 603 were destroying the fuel dump at Cape Parthinos, denying the Nazis yet another source of petrol. During April seven vessels, totalling about 990 tons, were destroyed and another 300 tons of shipping damaged. The Beaufighters, fitted with overload tanks, now had the fantastic endurance of eight hours, making possible a visit to every port and airfield in Northern Greece in search of likely targets. In May 570 tons of shipping was destroyed or damaged and one Arado shot down, with two others left disabled.

In six months, the squadron had attacked 16,000 tons of shipping with varying successes and had added 19 enemy aircraft destroyed or damaged to the astronomical tally of 535 machines hit by squadron pilots since 16th October, 1939. This did not include combats for which no claim at all was made, nor the machine shared between 603 and two other squadrons, for which a claim of one-third was approved!

50. 603 leave a ship to sink after a rocket attack.

On 1st June, incorporating aircraft from Nos. 16 (SAAF) plus 227 and 252 Squadrons, 603's crews joined in an attack on a convoy north of Candia, excellent pictures being recorded of the burning vessels, a 950-tonner being credited to the City of Edinburgh contingent. Wing Commander J. D. T. Revell came in to command, having earlier commanded Nos. 209 and 221 Squadrons, and awards were made of a DFC to Flying Officer Ross and Distinguished Flying Medals to Flight Sergeants Yates, Edgar and Pennie. On 28th August a wonderful piece of news was that Flying Officer Jenkinson had been picked up by H.M.S. *Lauderdale* after being reported missing: he had spent 6 days $9\frac{1}{2}$ hours in his single-seat dinghy – one of the war's records. On 23rd September command of the squadron was handed over to Wing Commander Christopher Foxley-Norris who had earlier flown Lysanders with 13 Squadron and Hurricanes in the Battle of Britain with 3 Squadron, later with 615 (County of Surrey) Squadron. He came to 603 from neighbouring 252 Squadron in which he had commanded a flight and now led the

City of Edinburgh crews on intruder sorties over enemy-held territory, and on pinpoint raids on radar stations to disrupt the Luftwaffe's detecting system.

During September five vessels were sunk or left on fire, a total of 2,350 tons, and during these raids five more enemy machines were either shot down or damaged. A change from routine was the flying of 'intimidation' patrols over odd Italian garrisons which were still showing resistance. On 25th October the squadron escorted the Rt. Hon Anthony Eden to Athens for talks with the Greeks and then – in November – came warning that the squadron was wanted back in the United Kingdom to take over another vital role. Just over a hundred bachelor airmen who had joined the squadron in Scotland before or during the war stayed overseas to service the Beaufighters of other units, some of them from 603 Squadron, and on 10th January, 1945, at Peterhead, on the coast north of Aberdeen, the squadron came together again, taking over the Spitfire XVIs of No. 229 Squadron, with Squadron Leader A. Patterson, DFC, in command, flying as part of a 'clutch' of squadrons under Group Captain A. H. Donaldson, DSO, DFC, AFC, one of the RAF's great leaders.

51. Air Chief Marshal
Sir Christopher Foxley-Norris
in 1969.

Armed reconnaissance sorties were flown over Holland by the pilots who represented not only Scotland's cities and towns, but the rest of the British Isles, Australia, Canada, India, and New Zealand. It was of interest that at this period pilots named McAndrew, McConochie and McGinn came from three different countries – including India and New Zealand. A former prisoner of war now joined the squadron – Flight Lieutenant Kirkman – who had slipped quietly out of an Italian P.O.W. camp, and another newcomer was Flight Sergeant Webb who had got back to England with the aid of patriots after being shot down over France. In February the command was handed on to Squadron Leader T. C. Rigler, DFC, DFM, who had flown with the squadron as a Sergeant-Pilot. The old squadron code letters of XT were back in use and the Spitfires were fitted to take either two 250 lb or one 500 lb bomb, plus the cannons. The month concluded with a log of 277 'Ops' and the dropping of 120,000 lbs of bombs in the days when flying was possible.

In March came a move to Ludham, Norfolk, with instructions that dive-bombing was to be the squadron's task – particularly against the sites from which the V.2 rockets were being launched. The pilots were only too keen to try to halt this rain of terror reaching England and Antwerp. Squadron Leader P. G. Ottewill, who had won the George Medal as a Sergeant-Pilot, took over and with 602 (City of Glasgow) now based close by at Coltishall, the old rivalry restarted, this time to see which squadron could claim the most locomotives or road vehicles hit. On 21st March, off Ijmuiden, Holland, the squadron, out on reconnaissance, saw enemy shore batteries firing on a Catalina flying-boat and, investigating, found that it was trying to pick up aircrews from their dinghies, after they had been forced down following the night's bombing raids. Diving down from 7,000 to 1,500 feet, six of the squadron's Spitfires placed their bombs squarely on the gun-positions and the Catalina was thus enabled to complete its errand of mercy. 'The Salvation Navy' was the nickname given to the aircraft and launches of the air-sea rescue services.

Looking at the squadron Line Book, the account of (sometimes) exaggerated statements, we note that at this time there is an entry 'Flight Lieutenant Welch says he only took a day off to make up his flying log book'. To the uninitiated it implies that this pilot was so busy on operations that a 24-hour day did not permit even the recording of his flying times! On 30th March, at the end of a busy month, a DFC came for Squadron Leader Ottewill, GM, and the notes add that the incredible figure of 1,008 hours had been flown in that month, with 420,000 lbs of bombs dropped on the enemy. On departure of the C.O. for higher appointment in came Squadron Leader H. R. P. Pertwee, DFC, who had led a flight in neighbouring 602 Squadron. A DFC was awarded to Flight Lieutenant G. Batchelor for his fine work and, from Coltishall, the squadron escorted Bomber Command's Lancasters on their day missions; the Wing, including 602 Squadron, led by Wing Commander 'Bill' Douglas, a former squadron pilot. When the V.1. and V.2 menace ended, the Air Officer Commanding-in-Chief signalled his thanks and added 'Much of the peace London is now enjoying is due to the efforts of 603 Squadron'. A tribute indeed.

On 29th April, with the end of the war in Europe in sight, the squadron returned to Turnhouse, their home airfield, and on VE Day, flying from Drem, had the unusual experience of taking off over the North Sea to escort Luftwaffe machines flying in from Norway after surrender. A few days to celebrate victory and then, out of the blue, a move to Skeabrae, Orkneys ('overseas again' quipped the airmen). However, it was only a brief stay to cover arrival of German vessels into Scapa Flow and then, in July, return to Turnhouse and, on VJ Day, 15th August, as news came of Japan's defeat, the squadron was told to disband. A magnificent party was organised at the Balmoral Restaurant, Princes Street, Edinburgh, the squadron welcoming many old members including Group Captains George Denholm, DFC, and Count Stevens, Wing Commanders Sheep Gilroy, DSO, DFC and Bar, and Bill Douglas, DFC and Bar – men who had commanded 603 and other units during the six years of war. Sadly the diary does not quote the names of the valiant ground personnel whose loyal service had maintained the aircraft on the top-line or whose diligence in the orderly room had ensured leaves and other benefits of smooth administration.

In May of 1946 the squadron began recruiting to re-form in the post-war Auxiliary Air Force and by 1947 Spitfires F.22 replaced the 1946 issue of the LF.XVIe, with which 603 had ended hostilities. Squadron Leader G. K. Sheep Gilroy returned to command, happy, as were so many, to serve again in a lower rank. In 1949 Sheep handed on the torch to Squadron Leader J. W. E. Holmes, DFC, AFC, who in turn passed the command to Squadron Leader P. J. Anson, DFC, who had commanded 615 (County of Surrey) in Burma in 1945. In May 1951 the squadron received the de Havilland Vampire FB.5 (with the Gloster Meteor T.7 trainer for communications

52. 'At home', Turnhouse, post-war.

duties, etc). Leuchars in Fife was used as Turnhouse runways were extended. The then Princess Elizabeth, as the squadron's Honorary Air Commodore, presented the Esher Trophy and the summer camp of that year – 1952 – was held in Germany, at RAF Celle. In March 1953 Squadron Leader R. Lloyd-Davies, DFC, became C.O. but after five months this ex-25 Squadron and BOAC pilot was killed, and the post was filled by Squadron Leader R. A. Schofield who held the reins until early in 1957 when orders came for all the Royal Auxiliary Air Force squadrons to disband.

When all the commanding officers were invited, with squadron representatives, to meet Her Majesty The Queen at Buckingham Palace, to receive her personally-signed letter of thanks to be read out to all ranks, the squadron was singled-out for special mention as Her Majesty wrote 'The association of the force with my family has always been close. I was proud to become Honorary Air Commodore of Nos. 603, 2603 and 3603 (City of Edinburgh) Squadrons in 1951, and to succeed my father as Honorary Air Commodore-in-Chief of the Royal Auxiliary Air Force in 1952.' There could be no more fitting end to the undying record of the squadron which dared all until the defeat of evil. The men came together again once more, for the receiving of The Standard, presented by Her Majesty The Queen at Holyrood House and to reminisce of days past and comrades no longer present. They were glad to hear of the promotions of Old Boys like Air Chief Marshal Sir Christopher Foxley-Norris, KCB, DSO, OBE, MA (currently Chief of Personnel & Logistics, Ministry of Defence), and of Air Marshal Sir Hugh Walmsley, KCB, KCIE, CBE, MC, DFC, of Air Vice Marshals E. L. Colbeck-Welch, CBE, DFC, and David Scott-Malden, DSO, DFC, of Air Commodore Ronald 'Ras' Berry, CBE, DSO, DFC and Bar, who walked in Sir Winston Churchill's funeral procession as a Battle of Britain pilot of 603 Squadron, of Air Commodore Archie Winskill, CBE, DFC and Bar, who commanded Turnhouse post-war. They remembered the interest shown by the people of Edinburgh, not least by their first post-war Honorary Air Commodore, Sir William Young Darling, CBE, MC, DL, JP, FRSE, MP, and were glad that steps had been taken to honour the squadron at the Edinburgh RAF Association premises and in the positioning, at Turnhouse, of a Spitfire rescued from the Edzell Maintenance Unit, in memory of those of 603 killed in action. The squadron silver went to the Scottish United Services Museum and the squadron association's benevolent fund was in the capable hands of Wing Commander T. Menzies McNeil, Chairman of Homes endowed by the fund. A firm link had been formed with No. 4. (Otago) Squadron, a Territorial Unit of the Royal New Zealand Air Force and there are many, in many countries, who are glad that they once served in or were associated with the City of Edinburgh Squadron, in peace or in war.

REPRESENTATIVE SQUADRON AIRCRAFT

de Havilland D.H.9a	
Avro 504K	
Westland Wapiti IIa	J9858 J9859 K1136 K1144
Hawker Hart I	K2996 K3052 K3861 K3872 K3750 (Trainer)
Hawker Hind	K4642 K5498 K6809
Gloster Gladiator I	K7917 K7924 K7928 K7935 K7972
Bristol Beaufighter I	X7772
If	V8321
VIc	JL588 JL626
X	NE610 TFX KW346
Vickers-Supermarine Spitfire I	L1007 L1076 N3196 P9553 R7019 X4271 X4277 (Hillary)
IIa	P7742 P7750
Va	W3369 X4665 X4669
Vb	AB134 BL478 BL634
LFXVIe	SM348 TE347 (post-war RAJ–O) TE384 TE477
F.22	PK342 XT–N PK354 XT–L PK525 XT–M PK570 XT–F
Gloster Meteor T.7	WF838 Y WG949 Z
de Havilland DH Vampire FB5	VZ864 G WA430 J WA440 N

53. Post-war Spitfire XVI TE384, preserved.

Former squadron machines now preserved include Spitfire IIa P7350, flying in the Historic Aircraft Flight at RAF Coltishall, Norfolk, painted in the code of No. 266 (Rhodesia) Squadron with which it flew in the Battle of Britain. Currently at RAF Henlow, Bedfordshire, perhaps earmarked for the RAF Museum, is Spitfire

LFXVIe TE184 XT–C which became instructional airframe 7027M, later the gate guardian at RAF Syerston, Nottinghamshire. As a genuine aircraft, thought might be given to having it at Turnhouse at some future date. Another interesting Spitfire was P7742, issued to 603 as a Mk.IIa on 17th May, 1941, as a gift from the National Employers Mutual General Assurance, hence the initials N.E.M. near the cockpit. This aircraft later flew with Nos. 111 and 145 Squadrons, 61, 53 Operational Training Units, surviving until 21st November, 1944, when struck off charge as no longer needed – one of the longest-lived donated Spitfires. At RAF Lyneham, for the use of the local Air Training Corps' cadets, is Meteor T.7 WF825 which was once 'Z' of 603 Squadron and was later with 33 Squadron.

Prior to becoming a fighter squadron in 1938 the squadron aircraft merely carried the figures 603 on either side of the fuselages but on acquiring the Gladiators – and a camouflage system – the code RL was allotted. On the outbreak of hostilities in 1939 the code became XT which was used until departure for Malta. On taking over 229 Squadron's machines in 1945 the code XT returned but on re-forming in the post-war Auxiliary Air Force letters RAJ were allocated by Reserve Command. On returning to Fighter Command XT was re-issued but from 1951 the insignia of light blue/dark blue check band along the fuselage was bordered above and below by a black band. This was continued on the Vampires' tail booms, the squadron badge being painted on the noses on a black background.

Badge: On a rock a triple-towered castle, flying therefrom to the sinister a pennon. The castle is similar to that in the City of Edinburgh arms.

Motto (translated): 'If you dare.'

605
(County of Warwick)
Squadron

ON 5TH OCTOBER, 1926, at Castle Bromwich, Birmingham, the County of Warwick Bombing Squadron came into being with Squadron Leader J. A. C. Wright appointed to command, with Flight Lieutenant F. O. Soden, DFC, adjutant and flying instructor. A few days later de Havilland D.H.9A serial E8686, equipped for dual-control, came from RAF Henlow, Bedfordshire, followed next day, 26th October, by Avro 504K serial F9828 and a second D.H.9A and Avro 504K. On 23rd November the appointment of Pilot Officer C. L. Knox, VC, was gazetted; a one-time Second-Lieutenant, Royal Engineers, whose Victoria Cross was gained with No. 150 Field Regiment at Tugny, France, on 22nd March, 1918. Recruiting of pilots, air-gunners, and ground personnel was a priority and by 21st December, with the arrival of the Avro 504N, popularly known as the Lynx-Avro, the strength increased and the first squadron guest night was held.

On 9th April, 1927, Pilot Officer Knox, VC, taking off in Avro 504N J738, fouled telegraph-wires and crashed, the Lynx-Avro being a write-off. On 12th May Flight Lieutenant W. R. Cox, MC, AFC, was posted-in from No. 503 (County of Lincoln) Squadron as adjutant-instructor, the squadron parading for a colour-hoisting on the 15th, on which date the diary records that all officers had now flown solo and that more and more airmen could be given air-experience flights. During June the first weekend camp was held and Squadron Leader (later Air Marshal Sir Robert) Saundby brought a Vickers Virginia to demonstrate the art of army co-operation. Visits by Fairey Fox and Hawker Horsley aircraft provided interest and for the Birmingham Air Display of 16th July, the Commander-in-Chief, Air Defence of Great Britain, Air Marshal Salmond, Air Vice-

Marshal Brooke-Popham and General Sir Sefton Brancker, came as
V.I.P.s.

Liaison was established with Birmingham University and Dr
Johnson brought students from the Metallurgy Department to hear a
talk on aero-engines from the squadron's technical personnel. On
31st July the squadron left for Manston (Ramsgate Airport) for
annual camp, the D.H.9As flying direct, with the four Lynx-Avros
refuelling at RAF Henlow. During parachuting exercises Pilot
Officer Knox, VC, cracked his pelvis and Pilot Officer Mahoney
sprained his ankle. A visit to Lympe was made to meet Nos. 600 and
601 Squadrons and on 13th August came the great news that the
squadron was to re-equip as soon as suitable replacement aircraft
could be allotted. Even more exciting was the announcement on 22nd
August of the award of the coveted Esher Trophy to 605 Squadron
after only one full year of existence. Towards the end of the month
Fairey Fawns were flown up to 602 (City of Glasgow) Squadron at
Renfrew as a navigational sortie; and an unusual diary note was that
Sir Oswald Mosley lunched with the squadron.

54. Westland Wapitis.

On 1st October squadron aircraft flew to Kenley, Surrey, to take
part in a welcome to the Schneider Trophy team; and on the 20th
the Secretary of State for Air, Sir Samuel Hoare, came to present the
Esher Trophy in the presence of the Lord Mayor of Birmingham
and many RAF notabilities. During 1928 a trumpet band and then
a dance band were formed and on 30th June three squadron machines
participated in the Hendon Pageant. 4th July was a very busy day
as squadron personnel co-operated in the refuelling of 32 RAF
aircraft en route to displays at Blackpool and Aldergrove, Northern
Ireland. Another unusual note is that Squadron Leader (Reverend)
H. N. Forbes, Auxiliary Chaplain, preached from the cockpit of a
D.H.9A.

Mock raids were staged against Manston and Eastchurch and Air Commodore Hugh Dowding, then Director of Training, inspected the squadron. During 1929 the squadron band was proficient enough to play on special occasions and other noteworthy items were the arrivals of Flight Lieutenant S. D. Macdonald, DFC, as adjutant and Flying Officer G. W. Tuttle as assistant adjutant, two very competent officers to instruct and advise. During February 1930 there was a voluntary weekend camp and Flight Lieutenant R. L. R. Atcherley – known throughout the Service as 'Batchy' for his practical jokes – came with C Flight of 23 Squadron. On 20th February came the first Westland Wapitis and a record total of 294 flying hours was logged as the squadron joined Nos. 600 (City of London) and 601 (County of London) to become No. 53 (Day Bomber) Wing. To the delight of all, the Esher Trophy was again won by 605 Squadron.

55. The 605 Mess, Castle Bromwich, 1929.

During 1931, Squadron Leader J. A. C. Wright, was awarded the Air Force Cross and also qualified for the Territorial Decoration. May was a memorable month, marked by the visits of HRH the Prince of Wales and HRH the Duke of York, who were flown in a Lynx-Avro by Flight Lieutenant Macdonald. Following the squadron's third award of the Esher Trophy, the Prince of Wales honoured the unit by coming to Castle Bromwich to present the trophy, after which he was entertained in the new drill hall. The year 1932 seems to have been one of steady consolidation and training, for in 1933 it was again announced that 605 had gained the Esher Trophy. On 27th February, 1934, the Prince of Wales came in his own aircraft to visit the British Industries Fair and Prime Minister Ramsay MacDonald also called en route to Speke (Liverpool) where he inaugurated the Midland and Scottish Air Ferries.

On 25th May, 1935, more than 10,000 people attended the Empire Air Day display. On 1st March, 1936, Lord Willoughby de Broke, MC, was commissioned in the Auxiliary Air Force and, as the new commanding officer, left for the RAF Central Flying School for an intensive refresher flying course. Flying Officers G. A. L. Manton and J. L. Rotherham, both RAF, came in to replace departing officers and during 1936 another change was the arrival of Hawker Hart day bombers in time for the camp at Aldergrove, for which 187 members of the squadron reported. The Hawker Hind replaced the Hart as the adjutant, then Flight Lieutenant R. E. Bain, was promoted to command No. 43 Squadron.

56. Squadron at Bournemouth camp, 1937.

For the 1937 Empire Air Day 12,000 people came to watch the display and in 1938 Viscount Bearsted, MC, the Honorary Air Commodore, presented the squadron with a silver replica of the Bear and Ragged Staff county badge. Flying Officer D. G. Smallwood came in as assistant-adjutant and the Hon Air Commodore role was taken over Sir Lindsay Everard, MP, well-known patron of light aviation in the Midlands. On 1st January, 1939, came an historic moment when 605 was re-categorised as a fighter unit and began to receive the Gloster Gladiator biplane, the one sad aspect being the departure of the loyal air-gunners, although some opted for pilot-training in the RAF Volunteer Reserve and a few stayed as non-flying ground crew. During August Air Vice-Marshal Leslie Gossage, the Air Officer Commanding No. 11 (Fighter) Group, told the squadron that it was to get the Hawker Hurricane and during the hurried conversion period, when both Gladiators and Hurricanes were being flown, exercises to intercept the French Air Force's bombers were valuable occasions for pilots.

A few days before war was declared the squadron was embodied into the RAF, and on 27th August a mixed force of six Hurricanes, ten Gladiators and two dual-control Fairey Battles left for Tangmere, Sussex, the squadron's war station. No. 1 (F) Squadron left for France leaving No. 43 Squadron to defend the area until 605 could take over completely with Hurricanes. On 20th September tragedy came when Flying Officer Warren lost his life in collision with another Gladiator – Flying Officer Forbes baling-out safely. A few days later the remaining Gladiators were transferred to 615 (County of Surrey) Squadron.

On 12th November the Crazy Gang delighted the RAF audience with an afternoon performance; rushing down from London specially. As No. 43 Squadron was moved up to Acklington for defence of NE. England, a new squadron – No. 92 – began forming at Tangmere with the Bristol Blenheim and their Auxiliary C.O., Squadron Leader Roger Bushell, paid tribute later to the fine co-operation he received from Squadron Leader Lord Willoughby de Broke and other members of the County of Warwick Squadron. Now, sadly for many, but fitting tribute to the Auxiliaries, pilots of experience were needed to command and serve as flight-commanders in old and newly-formed RAF units, Flight Lieutenant W. M. Churchill moving to No. 3 Squadron to take over a flight and Squadron Leader M. T. Avent was promoted to command 609 (West Riding) Squadron. On 29th November No. 601 Squadron replaced 92 Squadron and on 20th December there were mixed feelings at the news of the C.O.'s promotion. At the farewell party to Wing Commander Lord Willoughby de Broke, MC (who received the Air Force Cross soon afterwards for his sterling work with the squadron), Flight Lieutenant R. G. Grant-Ferris, MP, voiced the sentiments of all in his well-chosen speech and toast. What Lord Willoughby de Broke contributed as Senior Controller at No. 11(F) Group in the Battle of Britain has never properly been told but ask any Sector Controller what that calm almost nonchalant word of command meant – it has been said that Lord Willoughby's 'cool' was worth another squadron of fighters and Air Chief Marshal Sir Keith Park, at that time AOC 11 Group, would be first to agree.

Squadron Leader G. V. Perry was appointed to command the

squadron and in February 1940 the orders came for a move north, to
Leuchars, near Dundee, with a refuelling call at Acklington. On the
27th a move even further north, to Wick just short of John O'Groats,
there to join forces again with 43 Squadron with which unit 605
had affiliated. On 28th March came a moment of history when
Flying Officer P. G. Leeson, leading Yellow Section, with Pilot
Officer K. S. Law and Sergeant Stephen, saw an He.111 entering
cloud at 6,000 feet, flying at about 250 m.p.h. Leeson got in two short
bursts and saw the Heinkel burst into flames. On landing, Yellow
Section learned that 43 Squadron had also attacked the same aircraft when it was down to 1,000 feet. So the claim was divided into
half-destroyed each, the main thing being that the squadron's first
sighting had brought the first kill.

57. Lord Willoughby de Broke, MC, AFC, with Viscount Trenchard.

April brought sadness when it was learned that A.C.2 H. V.
Taylor (645484) had been killed in Southend-on-Sea. On 8th April,
when 605 was off duty, 43 Squadron had another combat, the enemy
machine actually landing at Wick, with two crew-members dead,
the other two being taken prisoner. The next day the Nazis entered
Denmark, and Norway declared war, bringing the threat of action
to Scotland, Orkneys and Shetlands. On the 10th Pilot Officer I. J.
Muirhead intercepted an enemy aircraft but could not confirm
the result of his firing as the reconnaissance machine disappeared
into cloud. Flying Officer Leeson, however, brought down a raider,

seeing two airmen bale out as the aircraft fell. That night there was an attack on Scapa Flow and although four squadron pilots were engaged in combats and seven enemy aircraft were shot down, it was impossible to allocate them as the Fleet Air Arm put up a squadron of Blackburn Skuas and their aircraft fired on machines earlier hit by 605 and also by the ack-ack.

On 9th May, though, there was no doubt about the Do.17 which fell to the shooting of Flying Officers G. R. Edge, G. W. B. Austin, and R. Hope, off Dunnet Head. Next day came the Nazi invasion of Holland and Belgium and Flying Officer H. B. L. Hillcoat, AAF, with Pilot Officers Carter and Hawken, plus Sergeant Lewis, all RAF, were ordered to join squadrons in France. On 21st May 605 was instructed to fly down to Hawkinge, near Folkestone; next day ordered out to patrol near Arras where, in a skirmish with the Luftwaffe, Flying Officer Austin and Sergeant Moffatt were reported missing. Six Messerschmitt 109 fighters were claimed and in a later engagement with a Heinkel formation, of which four were claimed, Flying Officer Wright was lost. Joining up with 79 Squadron to make a composite unit Flight Lieutenant Leeson failed to come back and the German radio announced that he was a casualty. On 23rd and 24th May 605 joined with Nos. 253 and 229 Squadrons to patrol Courtrai-Tournai-Lille areas but the enemy refused battle. Next day, though, Pilot Officer Muirhead shot down a Henschel Hs.126 near Gravelines and then the squadron made up a composite force with Nos. 17 and 79 Squadrons, bringing down Ju.87 dive-bombers as they tried to attack the British Army in the Calais-Gravelines sector. Three destroyed and three probably-destroyed Stukas were allocated to the County of Warwick pilots.

On the 26th, joining with 32 and 245 Squadrons over Dunkirk, one Ju.87 was destroyed and Pilot Officer Muirhead was picked up from the sea – believed shot down by the Royal Navy whose gunners were, understandably, at this period 'trigger-happy'. Next day Lord Willoughby de Broke paid a welcome visit which was clouded by the non-return from patrol of Squadron Leader G. V. Perry and Flying Officer P. J. Danielson. The following morning the squadron was sent to Drem, south of Edinburgh, for a rest period. Squadron Leader Walter Churchill, DFC, an old member from the AAF Reserve, had returned and was given command, another piece of good news being that Flying Officer Forbes, earlier posted as missing, was known to be a prisoner of war. On 19th June a large force was reported approaching the Firth of Forth, ostensibly to attack the Forth Bridge and the Naval establishment – the squadron engaged the leading aircraft and claimed seven destroyed or disabled in company with other defensive fighters.

On 21st June Flight Lieutenant A. A. McKellar arrived from 602 (City of Glasgow) who were sharing the airfield; and on the

25th came the squadron's first war decoration, a Distinguished Flying Cross for Pilot Officer I. J. Muirhead. The squadron was now back to full-strength and declared operational on 31st July, anxious to see action. Squadron Leader G. R. Edge, on promotion, was sent to command 253 Squadron. On 15th August, when defending Newcastle against a large enemy force from Scandinavia, B Flight claimed four confirmed, four probably-destroyed and three damaged, for the loss of Pilot Officer K. S. Law's Hurricane, shot down near Newcastle, the pilot wounded. Flight Lieutenant McKellar had three successful combats, Pilot Officer Passy one, and Pilot Officer Currant one and another shared with Pilot Officer Muirhead. In the confusion with other units also firing at the same machines, the tally was possibly over-stated.

On 29th August Squadron Leader D. R. Scott left to command No. 306 (Polish) Squadron, after five happy years with 605, who were sorry at his going, though delighted at his promotion. The DFC was promulgated for Flight Lieutenant Archie McKellar for his sorties with 605 and 602 Squadrons and then, on 7th September, at long last, came a move south to Croydon, London's pre-war airport, under control of RAF Kenley, Surrey. Twelve aircraft were ordered off at 1150 hours on the 8th, joining 253 Squadron under former-member, Gerry Edge. The two squadrons met a mixed crowd of Dorniers, Junkers 88s and Bf.109s near Tunbridge Wells, claiming one destroyed and others damaged but Pilot Officer J. Fleming was brought down by a Bf.109 and he baled out, badly burned. Next afternoon, in the Aldershot area, there was a tremendous battle and although McKellar, Currant and Sergeant Wright claimed a total of five enemy destroyed, it is likely that another squadron finished off some of these, as only one can be credited to 605 from post-war research. Sadly Pilot Officer G. M. Forrester was killed and Pilot Officer Humphreys wounded when he baled out, two Hurricanes being lost.

10th September was a blank day owing to the weather but next afternoon and evening saw action when five more Luftwaffe machines were claimed, one of them frightened into diving and hitting the sea before our Hurricane had opened fire. That night a squadron dinner was held at The Greyhound Hotel, Croydon and the following day there was no argument when a Ju.88 was caught by three Hurricanes flown by Pilot Officers Currant and Cooper-Slipper accompanied by Sergeant E. W. Wright, and brought down just short of the French coast after a long chase. Next day a Ju.88 was claimed as damaged in combat but on post-war evidence is now thought to have crashed on landing at Rouen. There were no interceptions on the 14th but great celebrations for Squadron Leader Edge's DFC, even though Gerry was now commanding 253 Squadron. Newly-promoted Flight Lieutenant C. F. 'Bunny' Currant claimed two Do.17s and a

Bf.109 in the hectic fighting of 15th September, with McKellar claiming two 109s and Cooper-Slipper a damaged Dornier which he hit amidships. That night McKellar had an inconclusive combat with an He.111. Pilot Officer R. E. Jones had been the squadron's only casualty that day, his Hurricane being lost when he baled out slightly wounded. Tom Cooper-Slipper's aircraft was also lost in a collision but he managed to jump to safety over Kent. To cap a busy day, bombs fell near to the airmen's sleeping quarters, luckily with no injuries to personnel.

A very quiet week followed with many feeling that the Nazis were now preparing for their invasion. A Bar to the DFC was announced for McKellar and a Hurricane was lost when Pilot Officer Watson was jumped during an early-morning patrol and wounded. On 24th September Pilot Officers Muirhead and W. J. Glowacki (Polish) chased a Dornier to the French coast where three Bf.109s intercepted the Hurricanes, Glowacki's aircraft failing to return. On the 27th the squadron claimed three enemy destroyed, two as probables and three more as damaged, without loss. Two days later Squadron Leader W. M. Churchill was posted to command the first of the American units, No. 71 'Eagle' Squadron, RAF; McKellar was promoted to take over 605 Squadron. Unhappily this memorable month closed with the loss of two more Hurricanes and the death of Flying Officer P. G. Crofts, a newcomer, Flying Officer R. Hope had baled-out unhurt.

On 4th October, with the Luftwaffe attacks now few and far between, A section led by Flight Lieutenant Currant overtook a Heinkel, seen with a lengthy bomb or mine hanging below the fuselage. It dropped the missile near Rye and made off but Currant and Pilot Officer J. A. Milne found two Ju.88s off Dungeness and promptly shot one down, the second making off for France where post-war research shows that it landed in a damaged state, with a wounded crew-member. Later that day Pilot Officer C. E. English had to make a forced landing in Surrey after an inconclusive combat, his Hurricane being repairable. On 7th October, in better weather, the Luftwaffe sent over a great many Messerschmitt Bf.109s during the morning. Archie McKellar destroyed two between Maidstone and Biggin Hill and Pilot Officer R. W. Foster got a third. Pilot Officers English and Muirhead were brought down, English losing his life as Muirhead baled out unhurt. Later that day McKellar claimed another Bf.109 with other pilots sharing a second.

On 8th October a Ju.88 was intercepted and damaged near Gatwick and the diary notes that a 32-seater single-decker London bus was the squadron's new transport. On the 12th two Bf.109s were damaged but Sergeant P. R. C. McIntosh was lost, only two days after joining the squadron. On the 14th came another blow when Flying Officer R. Hope, chasing an He.111 into London, was killed, possibly by return fire from the enemy machine. Next day yet another stalwart, Flight Lieutenant I. J. Muirhead, DFC, died when he was shot down by a Bf.109 over Kent. On 20th October McKellar destroyed a Bf.109 in a battle over Ashford, but two Hurricanes were damaged, their pilots luckily unhurt. Two days later Pilot Officer J. A. Milne was hurt when he had to make a forced landing after combat, the Hurricane being a write-off. As a break the pilots were allowed to visit a dump of Luftwaffe wrecks and to collect 'trophies' for the dispersal huts. On the 26th two Bf.109s were damaged over Tonbridge; two Hurricanes were lost although their pilots, Flying Officer C. W. Passy and Pilot Officer J. C. F. Hayter, were uninjured. On this day the squadron learned that 605 were to be the first to get the more powerful Hurricane II.

Next Day McKellar scored his 20th success with 605 – a Bf.109 – but on 1st November, taking off alone at the report of enemy activity, he failed to return and enquiries revealed that his Hurricane had been found, eyewitnesses stating it had emerged from the clouds in an inverted spin. Nearby was found the wreckage of a Bf.109 and, as this was not claimed, it was thought that it was Archie McKellar's last victory. On 6th November Squadron Leader McKellar was buried in Glasgow and two days later the award of a Distinguished Service Order – for which he had been recommended some time before his death – was announced. On this day the squadron was visited by HRH the Duke of Kent who expressed his sympathy at the loss of McKellar. Flight Lieutenant C. F. Currant assumed temporary command and news came that he had been awarded a Bar to his DFC, also that Tom Cooper-Slipper had the DFC, and Sergeant E. W. Wright the Distinguished Flying Medal.

On 15th November, after a quiet period, the Luftwaffe tried a large hit-and-run sortie with about fifty Messerschmitts, 605 getting three destroyed and two others severely damaged, though a new pilot, Pilot Officer Gauze, was lost. A week later Air Vice-Marshal Keith Park flew down in his Hurricane to congratulate the squadron on their successes and the day was completed by the landing of a Luftwaffe fighter, the pilot claiming he was unaware that the airfield was in England! Squadron Leader G. R. Edge, DFC, who had been wounded in September leading 253 Squadron, arrived to take command of 605, a popular appointment. He was soon faced with problems when, on 1st December, during air-battles over Canterbury, three Hurricanes were lost, all the pilots parachuting to safety. Added to the loss of the aircraft, though, several experienced pilots were moved away to instruct and Gerry Edge was left to re-build the squadron. On 29th December 'Timothy' the goat was officially enrolled as squadron mascot, the instructions issued for his care noting that he was always to be tethered down-wind and kept constantly on the move!

On 30th December, Air Marshal Sholto Douglas, the new Commander-in-Chief, Fighter Command, came to talk about the new role of the squadron with the Hurricane II, the first operation being on 10th February as escort to Blenheims of No. 2(B) Group bombing Boulogne, the Hurricanes attacking ground guns as no enemy aircraft intervened. On 26th February came a move to Martlesham, Suffolk, for a rest and to patrol the shipping lanes. On 24th March a lone raider bombed the airfield and was overtaken by Flying Officer Foster and damaged before disappearing into low cloud. On the 26th a Do.17 was intercepted over a British convoy and, to quote the combat report, 'was rapidly turned into a speedboat and then into a submarine which did not re-surface'. In other words, the Dornier was shot into the sea. At the end of that month another move was made, this time to Tern Hill, Shropshire; here tests were carried out at heights of up to 36,000 feet, with the Station Commander, Wing Commander Isherwood, AFC (later to go to Russia in charge of the RAF Hurricane Wing).

Group Captain Lord Willoughby de Broke and the Honorary Air Commodore, Sir Lindsay Everard, came to visit as the squadron moved yet again, this time to Baginton, Coventry, for intensive training in both day and night operations, with attachments to both Bramcote and Honiley airfields. No. 457 Squadron – of Australian pilots, with mixed groundcrews – was forming and 605 provided much assistance, especially in experience, also co-operating with the Spitfires of 266 (Rhodesia) Squadron. On 4th August a sweep was flown over Birmingham, Walsall, Wolverhampton, to give 457 Squadron interception training and to let the County of Warwick residents see their own squadron in the air. A display was also flown for boy scouts camping at Warwick Castle and on the 30th a lone Ju.88 carrying out a reconnaissance over Birmingham was driven off and damaged, news being received later that it had made a forced-landing in Eire. On 2nd September the last pre-war Auxiliary pilot, Squadron Leader Gerry Edge, was promoted, leaving to command a unit in the Middle East, Squadron Leader R. Reid taking over and leading the squadron in a dive-bombing exercise

58. W/O Cornish and Officers, before leaving for the Far East, November 1941.

against the Standard Motor Works, after escorting a V.I.P. into Castle Bromwich. It was later said that the V.I.P. was the Prime Minister who had come to watch the exercise.

Rumours were spreading that the squadron was going to Russia and on 24th October a farewell parade was held, Group Captain Lord Willoughby de Broke remarking that 'the marching could not be bettered in Birdcage Walk by the Brigade of Guards'. A short spell at Kenley, Surrey, lulled some of the rumour-mongers into silence, but on 1st December, the ground personnel embarked in H.M.S. *Indomitable* for the Far East. The pilots, meantime, arrived at Hal Far, Malta, on 1st January, 1942, under Squadron Leader S. E. Andrews, and flew over the island for some time. As Singapore was in danger of falling when *Indomitable* approached, the 605 personnel were taken on to Palembang, Dutch East Indies, some aircraft moving back for a short period to Seletar on Singapore Island, before retreating to Tjililitan, Andir, and Tasik Majala, in the unavailing effort to save Java and Sumatra from Japanese occupation. Eventually the entire surviving personnel were captured and the squadron was presumed disbanded about 6th March, 1942, with very little official news of where the airmen were, and how many were alive.

59. Wg Cdr Peter Townsend re-forms the squadron, 1942.

The Air Ministry immediately decided to revive the nameplate of the County of Warwick Squadron and in June 1942 a new 605 Squadron re-formed at Ford, Sussex, under the leadership of Wing Commander Peter Townsend, DSO, DFC, a pre-war RAF pilot with combat experience in France and throughout the Battle of Britain. The new aircraft was the Douglas Boston III, with a Douglas Havoc night-fighter and an impressed civilian machine with a tricycle undercarriage, the General Aircraft Owlet, for the pilots to gain experience before flying the low-level fighter-bombers. On 14th July the aircraft attacked the marshalling yards at Caen and, during operations of 2nd August, over Beauvais, the A Flight leader was lost. On 7th August Wing Commander George Denholm, DFC, who had led 603 (City of Edinburgh) Squadron in 1940, came to command on the appointment of Wing Commander Townsend to be Air Equerry to King George VI. Moves were made to Hunsdon, Hertfordshire, for training, and on 19th August for the Dieppe landings the squadron attacked gun emplacements, aircrews of several nationalities, including Colonel Kratz, U.S.A., with Czech and Uruguay pilots, gaining experience. Leaflets were dropped (codename 'Nickelling') over Europe during November and, after further operational missions with 605, Colonel Kratz returned to the U.S.A. to take charge of their night-fighter school. On 24th November the squadron badge, approved by King George VI, was presented to the C.O. by Air Marshal Sir Trafford Leigh-Mallory and he gave the great news that the squadron would soon be getting the de Havilland Mosquito night-intruder version.

60. Reunion in 1943.

In March 1943 the move began to Castle Camps, Cambridgeshire, after the Mosquito II arrived for training. The wireless-operator/air-gunner crews were now redundant, with the navigator being responsible for the wireless. It was decided to try and train as many squadron personnel as possible for navigation duties to retain them after their air-gunnery tasks ended. A DFC, was announced for

Flight Lieutenant M. H. Maggs who had flown in 96 Squadron, Royal Flying Corps, in 1917, and had joined the RAF Volunteer Reserve in June 1939 serving in the Operations Room at 11(F) Group HQs, until he volunteered for aircrew duties in November 1939, flying first with 78 Squadron's Whitley bombers, then with 264 Squadron's Defiant two-seat fighters. Commissioned in May 1940, he had flown 83 'Ops' and had survived a crash in a Defiant when his pilot was killed. He had two confirmed successes and one probable.

On 10th March, 1943, the first operations were flown in the Mosquitos and one aircraft failed to return. Photographs were taken for propaganda in the Birmingham area and on 30th April Wing Commander C. D. Tomalin, AFC, was promoted from flight-commander duties to take over the squadron, his DFC, being announced soon afterwards. On 23rd August the squadron visited Berlin for the first time and in September, at the end of his operational tour, the C.O. was appointed Intruder Controller at HQs, Fighter Command. To command 605 came Wing Commander B. R. O'B. Hoare, DSO, DFC and Bar, a most experienced intruder pilot, now on his third tour of operations with his navigator, Flying Officer Potter, DFC, both from No. 23 Squadron. On 19th January, 1944, following a most successful period at Bradwell Bay, Essex, since October, the squadron's hundredth victory was celebrated; the C.O. getting the much-wanted century, by shooting down a Ju.188 at Chievres. A Bar to his DSO was promulgated and a record period including three ammunition trains, locomotives, barges, and thirty-three aircraft destroyed in the air and on the ground, plus many others damaged, was marked by a party at the Dorchester Hotel on 15th April when seven former commanding officers attended and Sir Lindsay Everard presented the squadron with a silver model of a Mosquito. During this month the

61. Mosquito FB.VI formation of 605, 1943.

squadron was moved to Manston in Kent for the intensive attacks on enemy airfields prior to the invasion of Europe.

As Wing Commander Hoare came to the end of his tour he was replaced by Wing Commander N. J. Starr, DFC, a veteran of Malta, with navigator Flight Lieutenant G. C. Wright, AFC. For D-Day, 6th June, eighteen aircraft were airborne and Flying Officer Roy Lelong, a New Zealand pilot, scored the day's first victory, an Me.410 near Evreux. On this day, sad to relate, Flight Lieutenant A. Whitten Brown, son of the great Sir Arthur Whitten Brown, who flew with Sir John Alcock in the first Atlantic direct flight, was reported missing. On 13th June Mosquito 'Z' blew up with a 500-pounder and eight 20 pounders aboard, during maintenance by 6605 Servicing Echelon, Flight Lieutenant Rebbeck, MBE, the squadron engineering officer, being injured. With the arrival of the V.1 flying bombs, the 'Noball' sites in France were priority targets, but on the night of 14/15th June history was made when Flight Lieutenant J. G. Musgrave and Flight Sergeant Samwell destroyed the first 'Diver', codeword for the flying bomb nicknamed 'doodlebug'. By the end of June the squadron had destroyed thirty-six and added another twenty-nine in July, in addition to the normal anti-airfield sorties over Europe.

In September 1944 Wing Commander R. A. Mitchell, DFC and Bar, assumed command (Wing Commander Starr took over No. 142 Wing in Belgium, only to lose his life en route to his wedding, in an Anson, shot down over Dunkirk). Manston's C.O., Group Captain G. L. Raphael, DSO, DFC, flew a squadron aircraft on night sorties taking Flight Lieutenant L. R. Page, DFM, as navigator. One aircraft, returning from Norway saw a V.1 air-launched from an He.111 and, chasing the pilotless bomb, promptly shot it down. On 20th September squadron aircraft landed in France, at St Dizier, and after a few nights of routine patrols, Flying Officer Roy Lelong left on 2nd October for a daylight 'Ranger' to the Baltic. Finding a group of Do.24 flying-boats in Jasmunder Bay he dived down and destroyed five of them, claiming two others as damaged. On the flight home he sighted a Blohm & Voss BV.138 below him and, using up his remaining ammunition, left it on fire. When his combat film was processed and assessed by Headquarters Fighter Command, the pilot's claims were upgraded to six destroyed (including the BV.138), one probable and five damaged, one of the most remarkable sorties of World War II, particularly as the Mosquito returned on one engine from Northern Germany to base.

On 7th October, flying from St Dizier out as far as Vienna, squadron aircraft returned with claims of two Ju.52s, one Ju.87, two Fieseler Storchs, four unidentified machines all destroyed and others damaged, the greater part of the credit going to Flight Lieutenant A. J. Craven whose tally was now eleven destroyed or damaged.

Alas he was posted missing on the last day of October, awards of the DFM, and DFC, being promulgated later, also a Bar to the DFC for Wing Commander Starr, for his work with 605 prior to moving away. During November the squadron severed a long association with Fighter Command (at this time known as Air Defence of Great Britain) and transferred to No. 2 (Bomber) Group of the 2nd Tactical Air Force, moving to Hartford Bridge, near Camberley, Surrey (now Blackbushe Airport), as part of No. 136 Wing, with No. 418 (Canadian) Squadron. During December it was learned that Warrant Officer Harris, missing on 1st September, was a prisoner of war, the first since the squadron operated Mosquitos. In January, despite atrocious weather, attacks were made to assist the Americans during the Battle of the Bulge in the Ardennes. In February although 173 sorties were flown, there was an absence of Luftwaffe aircraft and the squadron total of ninety-seven destroyed since re-forming at Ford was unaltered, with every pilot itching to get the century as an intruder unit. On 15th March the squadron moved over to Coxyde, Belgium, to bomb enemy positions in support of Montgomery's push into Germany.

During the night of 17th/18th March the C.O. was reported missing and Wing Commander A. W. Horne, DFC, AFC, came to take over. On 28th April came another move, this time into Volkel, Holland, and although in early May an FW.190 was destroyed and another claimed as damaged, the total of destroyed was still only ninety-eight and, when operations finally ceased before VE Day, the intruder figures read: 98 destroyed, 8 probably-destroyed, 79 damaged; plus 75 flying bombs, 19 locomotives destroyed and 306 damaged to varying degrees, and 184 barges disabled. Casualties since re-forming were 38 aircraft and their crews, of which 34 were during operations. After VE Day it was possible to fly groundcrews on Cook's Tours of the former targets whilst on 10th June, 1945, twelve aircraft put on a show for Marshal Zhukov, at Frankfurt, A similar display was flown at Copenhagen on 1st July and from 9th July a ferry was started to Berlin with couriers and mail.

For VJ Day on 15th August there was a party in Helmond but, despite the efforts of the acting C.O. Squadron Leader I. F. McCall, a returned prisoner of war, there was a lack of enthusiasm at the gathering, mainly due to the departures of so many stalwarts released from the Service. On 31st August it was announced that the number-plate of 605 was to disappear and that the squadron would hence-forth be known as No. 4(B) Squadron, to allow the County of Warwick Squadron to re-form in the post-war Auxiliary Air Force.

On 9th October, 1945, a cable was received from HRH the Duke of Gloucester who had met thirty released prisoners of war from Japan, including 605 members Flight Sergeant Price, Sergeant Broadiss, Sergeant Ravenscroft and Sergeant Thompson, all said to be well. The squadron re-formed officially in June 1946, at Honiley, equipped with the Mosquito NF.30 and with Squadron Leader R. J. Walker in command. A reunion dinner was held, attended by pre-war wartime and post-war members, including former adjutant, now Air Vice-Marshal, S. D. Macdonald, Air Officer Commanding No. 11(F) Group; Air Commodore Lord Willoughby de Broke; Group Captain Gerry Edge; Wing Commander R. Grant-Ferris, M.P.;

62. Reunion dinner, 1949. *Left to right:* Rev. unknown, Wg Cdr Mitchell, Flt Lt Wood, Wg Cdr Grant-Ferris, unknown, Wg Cdr Huins, unknown, AV-M Macdonald, Sir Lindsay Everard, Lord Willoughby de Broke, Chairman Warwicks TA Assn., Gp Cpt Edge, Wg Cdr Longsdon, Col Masterson.

63. Menu and autographs for the dinner.

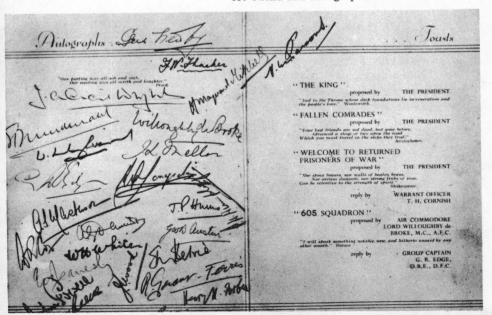

and Sir Lindsay Everard, DL, JP, who, in 1947, was succeeded as Honorary Air Commodore by Air Commodore J. A. Cecil Wright, AFC, TD, the squadron's first C.O. Warrant Officer Tom Cornish, who had marched off the airmen at the farewell parade before embarkation in 1942, responded to the toast 'Welcome to Returned Prisoners of War'.

During 1948 the squadron became one of the first two squadrons of the Royal Auxiliary Air Force to be equipped with jets and the first to get the de Havilland Vampire, the F.1 arriving in July with Flight Lieutenant P. J. Anson, DFC, as training officer (he had commanded 615 in Burma). Squadron Leader Sing had relieved Squadron Leader Walker and following a summer camp at Tangmere, the first camp overseas was held at Sylt in Germany. In 1950 Squadron Leader Anson left on promotion to command No. 603 (City of Edinburgh) Squadron and Squadron Leader R. T. C. Goodwin took over 605, to be relieved later by Squadron Leader J. A. Timmis and finally by Squadron Leader P. M. R. Walton, B.Sc, who had joined the squadron in 1948.

64. Vampire F.1 of 605 at the gates of RAF Credenhill.

During 1952 the Vampire F.B.5 was received and summer camp was held in Malta. The year's most memorable event, though, was the Freedom of Entry into Coventry, an impressive parade including a flypast tribute by aircraft of Nos. 504 (County of Nottingham) and 613 (City of Manchester) Squadrons. A Standard, awarded for the squadron's meritorious service, was presented by HRH Princess Margaret, attended by Air Commodore J. A. Cecil Wright, and then, in company with the other flying units of the RAuxAF, came the blow of disbandment in March 1957. It was a sad moment but now, at last, one could look back at the squadron's achievements and be truly proud of the 2 DSO awards and the Bar to the DSO, the 36 DFCs and the 8 Bars to DFCs, the 4 DFMs and the 3 AFCs, plus the many Mentions in Despatches. Also of what had happened to some former members, i.e., Air Marshal Sir Geoffrey Tuttle, KBE,

CB, DFC, FRAeS (Retd); Air Marshal Sir Denis Smallwood, KCB, CBE, DSO, DFC (Vice Chief of the Air Staff, 1971); Air Vice-Marshal Rotherham, CB, CBE, BA, DIC, AFRAeS; Air Commodore C. D. Tomalin, OBE, DFC, AFC (manager of the British diving team at the 1948 Olympics, after diving for Great Britain in the 1936 Berlin Olympic Games). Group Captains Alec Ingle, DFC, AFC, and E. W. 'Ricky' Wright, CBE, DFC, DFM, who remained in the post-war RAF and, with other Battle of Britain pilots, walked in Sir Winston Churchill's funeral procession.

How many remember that Bill Bedford, OBE, AFC, FRAeS, chief test pilot for Hawker Siddeley, who flew the P.1127, the world's first operational V/STOL (vertical short take off and landing) aircraft on its maiden flight, and who has done such magnificent work with the Harrier, its successor, was a 605 pilot in 1941, before transferring to 135 Squadron in Burma; or that Wing Commander H. M. Stephen, DSO, DFC and Bar, scored his first success with 605? Several former members have worked hard to maintain contact with those who flew and serviced squadron machines, notably Graham W. B. Austin, OBE, AFC, and Messrs G. Greenwood and Hugh Louden. It was a tragedy when, after years on display at RAF Credenhill, Hereford, one of the squadron's Vampire F.1's, TG349/7203M, was not earmarked for preservation. It seems that the only existing relic is the fuselage of Mosquito VI serial TA122 bearing the squadron code, now at the Royal Netherlands Air Force Museum, Soesterberg, after being at the Delft Technical School for years. Perhaps it is still not too late to exhibit – in Birmingham or Coventry – a former squadron aircraft, or one restored in 605's markings? A unit with such a glorious history must never, ever, be forgotten – particularly in Warwickshire.

REPRESENTATIVE SQUADRON AIRCRAFT

de Havilland D.H.9A		E8686 J7814
Avro 504K		F9828 504N J738
Avro Tutor		K3309 K3311
Westland Wapiti IIa		J9864 J9865 J9866 K1147 K1156 K1343 K2237 (Mk. VI Dual)
Hawker Hart I		K2435 K2452 K3861 K3888 K3890 K3891 K3892
Hawker Hind		K5431 K5531
Gloster Gladiator I		K7942 HE–H K7961 K8044
	II	N2308 N2312 N5586 HE–K
Hawker Hurricane I		N2349 N2546 P3737 V6783 V6943
	IIa	Z4969 IIb BD742 BD855 BG753
Douglas Havoc I		BB895
Boston III		W8305 Z2188 Z2232

de Havilland Mosquito II	DZ657 DZ714 DZ760 UP–K
FB.VI	HJ778 UP–A HJ790 NS876 NT114
NF.30	MM790 RAL–F NT291 NT479 NT590
de Havilland Vampire F.1	TG381 RAL–A(NR–A) TG420 TG427 VF279 RAL–Q
FB.5	WA358 NR–B WA360 H WA364 L WG844 T
Gloster Meteor T.7	WA682

Up to outbreak of war on 3rd September, 1939, the Gladiators carried the code 'HE' and were transferred to 263 Squadron who flew them in Norway in this code. The letters 'UP' carried on the Hurricanes, Bostons and Mosquitoes II and VI were probably restricted to the U.K. and Northern Europe. Post-war, in Reserve Command, the code 'RAL' was used until 1949 on transfer to Fighter Command when 'NR' was allotted until the Vampires FB.5 bore a coloured insignia of pale blue rectangle outlined in red on the tail boom.

Badge: On a mount a bear supporting a ragged staff. The device long associated with the County of Warwick.

Motto (translated): 'I never sleep'.

604
(County of Middlesex)
Squadron

NUMBER 604 (County of Middlesex) Squadron came into being at Hendon on 17th March, 1930, and Flight Lieutenant F. J. Fogarty, DFC, RAF, was posted in as adjutant and flying instructor, with a warrant officer and nineteen airmen forming the Royal Air Force hard core on which the new squadron of part-timers would be built. Lieutenant-Colonel A. S. W. Dore, DSO, TD, became the commanding officer and although appointed an honorary wing commander, wore the badges of rank of squadron leader. From H.M.S. *Eagle* came Flying Officer W. H. Bowden, RAF, and the first civilian to volunteer was Mr A. E. Chatterton. On 2nd April, 1930, a de Havilland DH.9A arrived from No. 600 (City of London) Squadron, followed a week later by an Avro 504K from No. 605 (County of Warwick) Squadron and by a second DH.9A, from No. 601 (County of London) Squadron. From the Home Aircraft Depot at Henlow, Bedfordshire, came two Avro 504N's having been in use to Nos. 3 and 5 Training Schools.

Flying Officer D. H. Back, who had flown with 602 (City of Glasgow) Squadron, transferred to 604 on moving into London and Flying Officer R. J. Legg, RAF, arrived from Cranwell. The next batch of civilian volunteers included Messrs C. P. Gabriel, L. E. A. Healey, R. S. Smallman-Tew and I. G. Statham; after their ab-initio flying training they were appointed pilot officers in the Auxiliary Air Force. A total of 119 flying hours was recorded for June and a Gipsy Moth was acquired from 601 Squadron, plus another Avro 504N from Henlow, as Messrs J. Cherry and C. D. Griffiths joined and after initial training were commissioned.

On 11th September the squadron received its first operational aircraft, Westland Wapitis. Pilot Officers Chatterton, Gabriel, and

Statham made history by being the first to obtain the coveted Royal Air Force flying badge and with the Auxiliary Air Force recruiting figures now nine officers and forty-two airmen by September, 206 flying hours were logged. Messrs M. F. Anderson and R. A. Chisholm commenced training in October and a de Havilland D.H.60M Gipsy Moth came from Stag Lane to help speed up flying training.

On 17th February, 1931, Flight Lieutenant Fogarty took off from Hampstead Heath in Wapiti J9096 which had been force-landed there the previous day by a 605 Squadron pilot. The aircraft stalled and crashed on to a house, becoming a total wreck. Happily the pilot was uninjured otherwise the Royal Air Force would have lost an officer who was destined for great things. May saw the squadron putting on an impressive flying demonstration at Hendon and the following month nine aircraft took part in the Air Pageant, one of the country's great pre-war aviation events. Affiliation with No. 32(F) Squadron, RAF, was followed by annual camp at Tangmere, Sussex, during which 604 became a 'Blueband' bombing squadron.

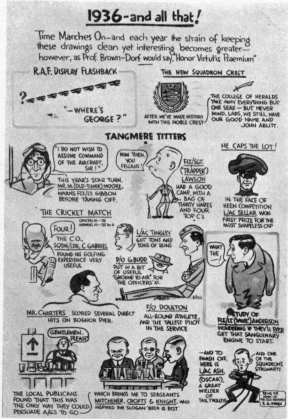

65. Chris Wren cartoon of the squadron in 1936.

The year 1932 was memorable for the visit, in June, of Air Marshal HRH The Prince of Wales, the Honorary Air Commodore-in-Chief, Auxiliary Air Force, accompanied by the Rt. Hon Sir Samuel Hoare, appointed as 604 Squadron's first Honorary Air Commodore. The occasion was the presentation to the squadron of the Esher Trophy, for the best all-round AAF unit, a tremendous achievement for a newly-formed squadron. As training proceeded the squadron was further honoured when, in May 1933, the Chief of the Air Staff, Marshal of the RAF Sir John Salmond, called, with the Mayors of Hampstead and Hendon, after which the boys of Mill Hill School were taken for flights.

During 1934, Town Headquarters were opened by Viscount Trenchard, at Heath Brow, Hampstead, and during that summer the squadron role was changed to that of a fighter unit; most popular with personnel. After his five-year tour of duty Squadron Leader Dore handed over command to Squadron Leader Gabriel, one of the first weekenders to qualify as a pilot. In June 1935 Hawker Demon fighters, with the Kestrel V (de-rated) engine, arrived and four of the aircraft took part in the Mildenhall Royal Review to commemorate the Silver Jubilee of King George V and Queen Mary. On 4th August came tragedy when Flying Officer R. L. Nimmo and A.C.2 S. T. Mabbutt lost their lives as Demon K4502 crashed on to the railway lines near Colindale underground station.

Early in 1936, Flying Officer John Grandy, RAF, left the squadron to the regret of all after serving as instructor. Following his move to No. 9 Flying Training School he was promoted to command No. 249(F) Squadron, in which Flight Lieutenant J. B. Nicolson gained Fighter Command's only Victoria Cross. Squadron Leader Grandy was awarded the Distinguished Service Order for his leadership of 249 and other units and, in post-war years, held high posts culminating in the office of Chief of the Air Staff; ex-members of 604 Squadron following his rise to the top with keen interest. As Flying Officer Grandy left the squadron another historic page was turned as Mr John Cunningham was commissioned. Avro Tutors replaced the Avro 504s as trainers and further evidence of the squadron's efficiency was the winning of the Esher Trophy for the years

66. Hawker Demon, 1938.

1935/36, presented in 1937 by Lord Swinton and in 1938 by Air Chief Marshal Sir Hugh Dowding, Air Officer Commanding-in-Chief of Fighter Command.

At the 1938 Hendon Pageant the dive-bombing event was entrusted to 604 Squadron and following summer camp at Hawkinge, Kent, the squadron was called-up and based at its war station, North Weald, Essex, for the period of the Munich crisis. The 1939 camp was held at Ford, Sussex, and on 24th August the squadron was embodied into the Royal Air Force, not one officer or airman being absent!

On 1st September the squadron flew into North Weald, equipped now with the Bristol Blenheim Mk.I two-seater fighter, fitted with one Browning Mk.II in the port wing's leading edge and four Brownings beneath the pilot's cockpit – with a lone Vickers K in the Daimler turret. Squadron Leader John Cherry, AAF, former squadron pilot, was in charge of North Weald's operations room and commanding the squadron at this time was Squadron Leader R. A. Budd. During the month the first Sergeant-Pilots, Havercroft, Woolley, Forest and Jackson, were instructed on Blenheims by Flight Lieutenant M. F. Anderson and Flying Officer John Cunningham and the first members of the Women's Auxiliary Air Force reported to North Weald, some to work with the squadron. Co-operation with anti-aircraft batteries and searchlights occupied the waiting hours; and on 4th October the first squadron shots were fired, but only at drifting barrage balloons which were a menace to civil as well as military aircraft.

On 10th October Flying Officer Cunningham, with his air-gunner, 'Jimmy' Rawnsley, taxied out on the controller's orders but were recalled when the unidentified machine for which they were about to be scrambled was found to be friendly. After a session of reconnaissance flights over factories to check camouflage or blackouts the squadron was officially designated night-fighter and in December 1939 was equipped with the first Blenheim Mk.IV fitted with A/I (airborne interception) equipment, the aircraft being P4847.

67. Line-up of Blenheim Ifs at Northolt, April 1940.

Moving to Martlesham Heath, Suffolk, in January 1940, for intensive training, the aircraft had to be dispersed so that their gun turrets could be ready to provide airfield defence when the machines were not flying. When airborne it was mainly to escort convoys in weather too bad for the single-engined fighters, or to patrol over the vital train-ferries from Harwich to the Continent. Then came a move back to Middlesex, this time to Northolt, to share the airfield with No. 65(F) Squadron, a unit commanded by one of the war's first Auxiliary combatants, Squadron Leader G. C. Pinkerton, DFC, who, flying with 602 (City of Glasgow) Squadron, had shared in the destruction of some of the first Luftwaffe raiders when they tried to attack the Forth Bridge and Rosyth Naval Base in October 1939 (see Chapter I).

Flight Lieutenant L .E. A. Healey moved to No. 11(F) Group at Hillingdon, to become Armament Officer and to play a vital role in the air war of 1940. Then, with lectures on tropical diseases and the squadron vehicles hurriedly fitted with chains and tracks, four days' embarkation leave was granted and rumours circulated, each one contradicting the next. The blue and white swastikas (not the Nazi version) applied to the Blenheims of 604 and 23 Squadrons gave a clue to the answer, but the signing of the Russo–Finnish armistice cancelled the planned move. Headquarters, Fighter Command, sent congratulations to the squadron for their speedy compliance with orders and today, coincidentally, one can find in Finland the only genuine Blenheim preserved in Europe (the one at Hendon for the RAF Museum is a Canadian Bolingbroke). Chris Wren, who returned from Finland in 1970, was certainly reminded, when looking at the Blenheim, of that hectic time for his old squadron during March 1940.

On 25th March B Flight was moved to Kenley, Surrey, to fly cover for the British Expeditionary Force leave boats from France. As the squadron's Honorary Air Commodore, Sir Samuel Hoare, was appointed to the Air Ministry as Secretary of State for Air, a diary note records that Air Ministry refused press photographers permission to photograph the 604 Squadron Blenheims as the fighter version was top secret. On 10th May B Flight escorted twelve long-nosed Blenheims on a raid against the beaches near The Hague, where the enemy were landing from troop-transports. The squadron's Blenheims dived down and front guns destroyed four Ju.52 transports damaging three others. It was first blood to the County of Middlesex airmen.

Pilot Officer I. K. S. Joll and his air-gunner managed to make their getaway after crash-landing on the beaches; being helped by the Dutch. The other aircraft landed back at Wattisham, Suffolk, unharmed. On 14th May B Flight moved forward to Manston, Kent, and A Flight into Hawkinge to carry out standing-patrols as far into France and Belgium as fuel allowed (unseen by the soldiers who complained that the RAF were absent at this time when they needed protection, whereas our aircraft were keeping many Luftwaffe attacks away from the Dunkirk and Calais areas). On 18th May Air Vice-Marshal Keith Park, the Air Officer Commanding No. 11(F) Group, flew down in his Hurricane to talk to the squadron. Flying Officer A. S. Hunter took the AOC's words so much to heart that he became airborne that evening and shot an enemy machine (a Heinkel He.115) into the sea near Dunkirk; the first night victory to the squadron. On the 19th Flying Officer G. O. Budd damaged an enemy aircraft as it was landing at Merville: Flying Officer Gillies did not return from this day's fighting and was entered as the squadron's first war casualty, pending further information.

On 22nd May, Green Section, over Dunkirk, damaged an He.111 and then escorted Naval torpedo boats from Sheerness on attacks against enemy shipping in Ostend. On the 23rd, pilots of No. 615 (County of Surrey 'Churchill's Own') were attached as they returned from France minus their aircraft; and Air Vice-Marshal Sir Quintin Brand, an Ace of the Royal Flying Corps, came to chat about night-fighting tactics of the two wars. On 30th May, Gladiators flown by 615 pilots, were added to the 604 Squadron strength for patrols over base. The return visit of Air Vice-Marshal Park in his Hurricane, after a final flight over Dunkirk, brought 'Operation Dynamo' to a close and Winston Churchill, now Prime Minister, was quick to remind the country that wars were not won by evacuations – however impressive and miraculous the achievements of the previous weeks.

All the air-gunners were now promoted to sergeant and allowed a flying badge instead of the old sleeve-bullet. The squadron moved into Gravesend and here was joined by Pilot Officers E. D. Crew and K. Geddes and Sergeant Pilot P. P. Jackson, plus air-gunners. After an uneventful month the squadron again moved, this time to Middle Wallop, Hampshire, on 27th July. On 11th August, as Luftwaffe raids increased prior to Hitler's planned invasion, two Blenheims took off to search for RAF pilots in dinghies and to investigate an enemy seaplane in the Channel. An He.59 carrying Red Cross markings was spotting for German guns on the French coast. After the Blenheims had set the seaplane ablaze two enemy rescue ships arrived escorted by six Messerschmitt Bf.109s which attacked the three Spitfires covering the Blenheims: two of the enemy fighters were probably destroyed and the Blenheims returned safely to base. On the 13th the squadron was ordered to carry out daylight patrols, though known to be no match for the Bf.109s. On 15th August Luftwaffe attacks on Middle Wallop destroyed three of the Blenheims and damaged a fourth.

On the last night of August Flight Lieutenant Cunningham was ordered off in 'Q', with Sergeant Rawnsley and one of several 'operators' attached to the squadron to work what was then top-secret equipment installed in some of the Blenheims. Called 'The Black Box' by some, 'The Gubbins' by others, the airmen who had to supervise the A.I. gear – Air Interception radar – had served as ground radar operators, some of them had been lucky to get out of France. Now they had to cope with all manner of faults in the teething stages of this new invention and to bear the criticisms, often undeserved, of pilots and air-gunners. On this night, unluckily, the enemy got away and the A.I. operator was fortunate in that he flew with that most patient of pilots, John Cunningham, who knew the results would come when the squadron got a more suitable aircraft.

In September, to the great delight of all, the first Bristol Beaufighter Mk. If, arrived and enthusiasm rose. Air-gunners, disappointed at the absence of a gun-turret in the Beaufighter (which had four 20 mm cannons controlled by the pilot), were given the opportunity of transfer to other squadrons or to qualify as Radio Operators (Air) for which a new aircrew category was later introduced with the R.O. badge. The first operational patrol in a Beaufighter was flown by the C.O., Squadron Leader Michael Anderson, his operator Bernard Cannon, on 30th October. Newcomer Pilot Officer K. A. B. Gilfillan, posted-in as Special Signals Officer, worked tremendously hard to ensure that the A.I. equipment did not fail in the air and a Civilian Scientific Officer, Mr Donald Parry, came to convert the air-gunners into Radio Operators (Air).

On 19th November, Flight Lieutenant Cunningham with John Phillipson as his operator destroyed a Ju.88 and in order to conceal from the enemy the use of airborne radar equipment the newspapers were allowed to think that John Cunningham had exceptional night vision. The nickname 'Catseyes' was immediately headlined and caused John very considerable embarrassment for the rest of the war and for many years afterwards. On 6th December Sergeant Peter Jackson damaged a Ju.88 which was held in the searchlights and on the 12th John Cunningham destroyed his second Ju.88. On 22nd December Sergeant Jackson was about to open fire when a Ju.88 saw the Beaufighter and opened up, injuring Peter Jackson who had to break off the encounter. The next night John Cunningham took off at dusk and fifty miles out to sea sighted the first of several He.111s coming in to attack English targets. Hitting it after a careful pursuit, Flight Lieutenant Cunningham had the great satisfaction of seeing it explode in mid-air.

In the first week of January 1941 after a Heinkel probable, John Cunningham was awarded the Distinguished Flying Cross and Sergeant Jackson the Distinguished Flying Medal for, after ordering his A.I. Operator to bale out on 22nd December, Peter Jackson, in great pain from his injuries, had landed his precious Beaufighter back at base. During February John Cunningham had his first successful combat with Jimmy Rawnsley as his operator; and Squadron Leader Anderson, after a successful encounter with the enemy, received the DFC, for this and earlier combats. March was a memorable month with five enemy destroyed, one probably destroyed and four claimed as damaged. The DFM was awarded to Sergeant Jimmy Rawnsley; and Squadron Leader Anderson Flight Lieutenant P. C. F. Lawton and H. Speke were Mentioned in Despatches. On the 26th John Cunningham was promoted and became flight-commander; on 1st April Flight Lieutenant R. A. Chisholm got the DFC. Then came the night of 4th April, long-remembered, for from six patrols there were four contacts leading to the destruction of three of the enemy. The weather, however, clamped down and Flight Lieutenant Lawton and his operator Sergeant Patson had to abandon their Beaufighter when no airfield within range was left open for landings, both landing successfully to fly and fight again.

68. John Cunningham.

April was a most hectic month with 25 enemy machines either destroyed or seriously disabled, including a hat trick on 15th April for John Cunningham. The Distinguished Service Order was promulgated for this feat and the Air Officer Commanding-in-Chief, Fighter Command, Air Marshal Sir Sholto Douglas, came down specially to congratulate John and the squadron, with signals arriving from the Secretary of State for Air, Sir Archibald Sinclair, and from Chief of the Air Staff. Flight Lieutenant C. K. Gomm was awarded the DFC. Middle Wallop was raided by the Luftwaffe but neither aircraft nor personnel were affected. Squadron Leader Michael Anderson, DFC, left to command High Ercall, Shropshire, a night-fighter training airfield and the month ended with the DFM for Sergeant Ripley. On 1st May Flying Officer Joll, survivor of the Dutch beach landing, damaged a Heinkel, his operator, Sergeant O'Leary being wounded by return fire.

May saw further activity and success, the squadron bag totalling fourteen; practically all destroyed over the U.K. with the odd machine limping back but not necessarily to reach its base. During this month several prisoners were taken from the crashed enemy machines, yielding vital information to Air Ministry. Flight Lieutenant Chisholm, although somewhat frustrated when his guns seized as he began to hit a Heinkel, had the partial satisfaction of seeing his target fall to anti-aircraft guns. The C.O., Wing Commander Appleton, had his hydraulics shot-up by return fire after he had attacked a Heinkel (which crashed later). The C.O. then made a fine belly-landing in the dark – no mean performance. HM King George VI came down to observe a typical night's work and moved on to 'Starlight' the G.C.I. (Ground Control Interception) station at Sopley near Christchurch which controlled the night-fighters. Meanwhile Squadron Leader Cunningham and Jimmy Rawnsley had taken off and, for this Command Performance, shot down an He.111. After watching with interest the converging 'plots' at the G.C.I. station, the King went outside to watch John Cunningham's interception and attack and saw the Heinkel falling in flames.

Sergeant Wright scored a success this same night but was so badly shot-up that he and his operator had to bale out when their port engine burst into flames. A Bar to the Distinguished Flying Medal was approved for Jimmy Rawnsley and a DFM awarded to Sergeant O'Leary. Early in June, Peter Jackson, now commissioned, added the DFC to his DFM and the C.O.'s operator, Pilot Officer D. A. Jackson (no relation), was also awarded the DFC. Eleven kills were added in June, including one Cunningham combat when only 28 rounds of fire destroyed a Heinkel. Another highlight was the heroic action of Sergeant Phillips who pulled his unconscious pilot from their blazing Beaufighter after Pilot Officer Gossland had touched-down eight miles SE of base with engine trouble. Distinguished Flying Crosses were announced for Squadron Leader Budd, Flying Officer Geddes and Flying Officer Crew, with DFM awards to Sergeants Cannon, Evans, and Guthrie, operators whose efforts had contributed in no small way to the run of successes.

July opened with the unusual role, for 604, of providing close escort to bombers, during which operations Flying Officers Joll and Patten each destroyed an He.111. Then, on the 7th, the Luftwaffe again retaliated and bombed Middle Wallop in moonlight, losing four of their small force to the accurate interceptions and gunfire of Flight Lieutenant Speke and Flying Officer Crew, who with their skilful operators claimed a couple apiece. On the night of the 8th Wing Commander Appleton, Flight Lieutenant Speke, and Flying

Officer Chisholm each scored a victory and the fifteenth success was recorded 'with the present night-fighting and detecting machinery' to quote a contemporary report. On the 9th the only enemy machine to venture into the area was destroyed by Squadron Leader Skinner, a new flight-commander. On the 15th the entire strength of 400 officers and airmen attended a smoking party to say Goodbye to the adjutant, Flight Lieutenant Olliff-Lee. The Air Officer Commanding, wisely considering that flying might not be everyone's priority the next day, stood the squadron down! A visit was, instead, paid to the Sopley G.C.I. station which had helped the squadron to make the most of Middle Wallop's successes. This day also marked a DFC for Flight Lieutenant Speke.

On 20th July there was universal pleasure at the award of the DSO to Wing Commander Charles Appleton. But the 25th was a very sad occasion when Flight Lieutenant Speke and Sergeant Dawson, his Australian operator, were killed near Upavon, Wiltshire; a crew very deeply mourned by all members of the squadron. On 10th August one flight was detached to Coltishall near Norwich under Wing Commander Cunningham, promoted to command 604 Squadron. John destroyed an He.111 and damaged another, crowning the eventful sortie under the control of the Neatishead G.C.I. station by making a single-engined landing.

On 20th October Flight Lieutenant C. H. Hartley, with Sergeant Croysdill, chased a Dornier from Bath to Ostend, leaving it as a 'damaged' in their combat report. The month ended with Flight Lieutenant J. B. Selway, flying with operator Flight Lieutenant Derek Jackson, DFC, getting a Dornier off the French coast one night and another Dornier claimed damaged off Plymouth four nights later. The month of November began well: Flying Officer Crew was carrying out a searchlight exercise when the enemy suddenly put in an appearance, the intruding aircraft was promptly shot into the sea. After quite a dog-fight another Dornier also turned for France in a disabled state. At this time Lieutenant Per Bugge, a Norwegian, joined the squadron, little knowing that more than twenty years later he would still be associated with John Cunningham, in the de Havilland team at Hatfield.

Flight Lieutenant M. H. Constable-Maxwell, DFC, a Battle of Britain Hurricane pilot, arrived with Sergeant John Quinton as operator. The year's review noted 5,800 hours' flying, 56 enemy destroyed with 40 others 'probably destroyed or damaged'. Two DSO awards, ten DFCs, one Bar to the DFC, eight DFMs and one Bar to the DFM, three British Empire Medals to the hard-working groundcrews, plus four Mentions in Despatches, with the MBE for Squadron Leader J. L. Brown of Sopley G.C.I., for his part in the successes of 604 Squadron. Four crashes, though, had cost eight men their lives and their sacrifices would not be forgotten.

On 2nd February, 1942, Squadron Leader R. A. Chisholm was awarded a Bar to his DFC, and St Valentine's Day was enlivened by the rescue of five bomber airmen after 604 had found their dinghy off Bournemouth and directed a launch to the spot. March was a quiet period and it was 1st April when Flight Lieutenant Edward Crew, with Pilot Officer Pacey, intercepted and destroyed a Heinkel off the Dorset coast. On the 27th came an accident when Lieutenant Räd, a Norwegian, had to crash-land short of Colerne, near Chippenham. His operator was killed instantly but Lieutenant Lövestad, another Norwegian, travelling as a passenger in the pilot's cockpit, managed to pull Lieutenant Räd clear just in time, saving his life.

Pilot Officer Tharp opened his account by bringing down a Dornier 217 near Seaton, Devon; four prisoners being taken. Then on the nights of the 'Baedeker' raids on Bath, 25th and 26th April (Hitler's reprisals for Bomber Command's raids), Flight Lieutenant Crew attacked two enemy bombers, claiming only a probable and a damaged as he did not see their end. On 1st May, Pilot Officer Howard-Williams and his operator Sergeant Nordberg had to bale into the sea twelve miles SW of St Catherine's Point and were saved by the prompt action of John Cunningham and other pilots who dropped flares, enabling the Navy to find them after $2\frac{1}{2}$ hours in their dinghies.

On 3rd May the squadron moved to Exeter and quickly shared a success with No. 307 (Polish) Squadron. Over Cowes, Isle of Wight, Flight Lieutenant Crew scored his eighth victory: a Do.217, and on the 24th May, after nights of inactivity, Squadron Leader Skinner got an He.111 over Studland Bay. Then almost a month elapsed until, on 21st June, a new crew in Pilot Officer Foster and Flight Sergeant Newton opened their account with an He.111 over Ventnor. July saw the departure, for a rest period, of Wing Commander John Cunningham, DSO and Bar, DFC and Bar, with Flight Lieutenant Jimmy Rawnsley, DFC, DFM and Bar, after six years with the squadron and undoubtedly at that time the greatest night-fighting team in the world. As they left for staff appointments at No. 81 Group, Training Command, only Squadron Leader J. B. Selway remained of the pre-war Auxiliary officers, though happily the ground personnel still had a stiffening of volunteer airmen. This happy blending of part-timers and regulars was without question the main reason for the outstanding morale of the County squadrons, for even when they lost all their pre-war aircrew members, many promoted to high ranks, the unorthodox spirit somehow remained. Personnel of all ranks worked harmoniously when on duty and, whenever they could relax, one of the clues to the AAF influence was that the inevitable and traditional sing-songs included not only the forces' favourites such as 'They say there's a troopship just leaving Bombay' but the classical rugby anthems like 'Cats on the rooftops'. The farewell party for John Cunningham and Jimmy Rawnsley was one of the historic nights in 604's history.

Two aircraft were detached to Predannack in Cornwall to cope with odd raiders entering the Irish Sea from the Cherbourg Peninsula bases. On 29th July, Flight Lieutenant Hoy took along the Signals Officer, Pilot Officer Anthony, in addition to his operator Pilot Officer Dalton, and when the A.I. failed Anthony provided another pair of eyes which helped lead to the interception and destruction of an He.111 over the sea. On the next night Pilot Officer Keele and Pilot Officer Cowles shot down two enemy machines, prisoners being taken from one and return fire from the second fortunately missing the Beaufighter. On 4th August, though, as Pilot Officer Stephen Spencer and Sergeant Pottage shot a bomber into the sea, the enemy rear-gunner scored hits on the Beaufighter and Spencer was ordered to head for Hurn near Bournemouth to land. Delay occurred in bringing the damaged aircraft in to land and Spencer ordered Pottage to bale out; which he did successfully. Spencer, alas, was unable to get out in time and died as the Beaufighter crashed at Branksome Park, this tragedy costing the RAF a pilot who would have ranked with the best.

Admiral Risen, the Norwegian Commander-in-Chief, came to decorate Lieutenant Leif Lövestad for his courageous rescue of Johan Räd and it was a timely reminder for many of what these gallant Norwegians had experienced before joining the squadron. Per Bugge and Johan Räd took nine days in a small fishing boat to reach Scotland from Norway, knowing that the Luftwaffe might at any time send a bomber to blow them to bits. Leif Lövestad had crossed in another small boat and Claus Björn, who flew as Bugge's operator, had made the long journey through Sweden, Russia, Japan and the U.S.A., to train in Canada before coming to England. Group Captain A. S. W. Dore, the squadron's first C.O., accompanied Admiral Risen to see again the handful of pre-war members and to meet the wartime newcomers. The complete squadron was now at Predannack engaged in Bay of Biscay patrols, many leading to the rescue of allied airmen found in their dinghies far from land and often being fired on by Luftwaffe aircraft. Squadron Leader Rory Chisholm and Flight Lieutenant Edward Crew were awarded Bars to their DFCs. Soon afterwards came a move into Ford, Sussex, and the chance to have a crack at any Luftwaffe aircraft trying hit and run sorties in the South East of England.

3rd March, 1943, saw the start of a new shooting season when Wing Commander Wood, AFC, the new C.O., and Flight Lieutenant Hoy, each got enemy aircraft near Beachy Head. Then came a lull until the 27th when Flight Lieutenant J. R. Wood and operator Flying Officer Ellis were carrying out their N.F.T. (night flying test) in the afternoon and were vectored (directed) to an enemy aircraft which was engaged in a quick sortie over Worthing, either for reconnaissance before that night's bombing, or for a hit and run attack. Whatever the Luftwaffe intention it cost them an aircraft as at 2.17 p.m. Flight Lieutenant Wood shot it into the Channel with a well-placed burst of cannon-fire.

On the night of 15th/16th April the squadron lost Wing Commander Wood, the C.O. (with operator Flying Officer Larcey), last positioned at fourteen miles south of Beachy Head. Whether jumped by an FW.190 fighter or lost through mechanical trouble, was not known and intensive searches failed to find them. The decision by Fighter Command to allow 604 to carry out 'Rangers' long offensive patrols into Europe against Luftwaffe airfields, to catch the enemy taking off or landing, or to hit other targets of opportunity, dispelled some of the gloom felt at the loss of their commanding officer just as he was settling-in. Then came a move up to Scorton, Yorkshire, and here, after taking over No. 219 Squadron's Beaufighters Mk.VI, with their Mk.VIII radar, Wing Commander Michael Constable Maxwell, DFC (who had served earlier with the squadron), came in from No. 256 Squadron to command the County of Middlesex team.

69. Wg Cdr Maxwell and Flt Lt Quinton.

On 6th May came another feat of heroism when Lieutenant Ree, a Norwegian pilot, had the misfortune to suffer failure of both engines during a practice flight. The Beaufighter caught fire on crash-landing a mile from base and the pilot bravely stayed to drag out his operator, Lieutenant Aagaard, from the blazing wreckage. On 15th May Sunderland was raided by six enemy aircraft; Flying Officer Keele, with Flying Officer Cowles, shot one down but when Flying Officers Hamilton and Coates failed to return it was feared they had been brought down by a raider, for they had announced sighting the enemy.

In June Flight Lieutenant Jeremy Howard-Williams, taking Flight Lieutenant John Quinton as his operator, went on loan to No. 68 Squadron at Coltishall, a mixed unit with one flight entirely Czech aircrew. The 604 pair damaged a Ju.88 and, by coincidence, a former 604 Squadron crew, Flying Officer D. B. Wills and Flying Officer Ledeboer, now with 68, destroyed a second night raider, then No. 417 Squadron, United States Air Force, equipped with Beaufighters, came to Scorton to liaise with and benefit from 604's experiences. Flying Officers Wills and Ledeboer of 68, attached to their old unit, 604, for a time, had the unique distinction of shooting down the first Heinkel He.177 four-engined bomber (the engines placed in pairs in two nacelles) met in the North East of England. On 13th July, over the River Humber, Warrant Officers Ray and Waller destroyed a Dornier and Squadron Leader Hoy, with Warrant Officer Le Conte, damaged another. Standing patrols were now flown so that at least two aircraft were already airborne should the enemy appear. On the 25th July this policy paid dividends when Squadron Leader Hoy got one Dornier, Flying Officer Keele shot down two more and the C.O. ('Maxie' to his officers) damaged a fifth in that memorable night's attacks.

At daybreak on 27th July Squadron Leader Hoy and Warrant Officer Ray, with their operators, were waiting in the air for the Luftwaffe's 'Weather Willie', a fast-moving Ju.88 which radioed reports for the U-boats and for Lord Haw-Haw's broadcasts. This time, though, the enemy was forced to wireless to his base that he was not returning, as he hit the sea! Then, on the night of 17th August four enemy aircraft were intercepted, two being shot down and two probably destroyed, one of our aircraft having to crash-land with injuries to the crew after return fire. On 22nd August Wing Commander Maxwell shot down another 'Weather Willie', the month ending with well-earned DFCs for Flying Officers Keele and Cowles.

It was not until 21st September that another combat ensued when Squadron Leader Joll (with Flying Officer Thomas) got a Do.217 – a detachment now operating from Peterhead, beyond Aberdeen. A DFC for Squadron Leader Hoy was a most popular event, as was a move into RAF Church Fenton near Leeds, a peace-time station with many amenities. Here the squadron re-equipped with 'The Wooden Wonder', the sleek de Havilland Mosquito Mk.XII and XIII, the nose well-stocked with airborne radar and with four 20 mm cannons. The observer radio was now seated beside the pilot with the radar set in front of him and when 604 learned, to its delight, that it was to be the first night-fighter squadron to be sent overseas with the Allied Expeditionary Air Force, the R.O. badges were withdrawn and 'N' for navigator badges issued. This was so that any operator unlucky enough to come down in Europe would, it was hoped, be spared unnecessary force during interrogation as it was well known that the enemy wanted details of our airborne radar. Aircrews were instructed not to chase enemy machines over the Occupied Europe coastline at this time.

On 14th May, 1944, Flight Lieutenant Surman scored the first Mosquito kill for the squadron after a real tussle with a Dornier 217 over the Isle of Wight. Flying Officer Macdonald damaged a Ju.88 which limped off before our pilot could confirm destruction and the following night Wing Commander Maxwell, with Flight Lieutenant Quinton, had another successful encounter and an indication of John Quinton's make-up was that although he was under no obligation he took his duties as squadron navigation officer so seriously that he actually qualified as a 'straight' navigator in addition to the nav-radar role for which he was detailed.

70. Aircrews, Normandy, July 1944. Sqdn Ldr Furze centre.

On 27th May Flying Officer 'Dusty' Miller, with Warrant Officer Catchpole, spotted an E-boat in the Channel, raking it with cannon-fire. He followed this with an He.177 in July, his DFC being awarded after this combat. Flight Lieutenant Hooper, DFC, flying with Flying

Officer Hubbard, DFM, got a Ju.88 off Cherbourg, and as the great invasion armada crossed to the Normandy beaches the squadron flew overhead to ward off the expected Luftwaffe bombers. To 604's regret, the enemy was conspicuous by its absence and it was not until 13th June that Flight Lieutenant Ellis, with Flying Officer Williams, got an He.177. The following night the squadron's first Focke-Wulf 190s were met and Flying Officer Wood, with Flight Lieutenant Elliot, caught up with two near Carentan, shooting down the first and seeing the second one disappear after being hit. On 22nd/23rd June Flight Lieutenant Sandeman, with Flying Officer Coates, claimed the first Ju.188, the new faster version of the Ju.88. Flying Officer Smith, with Flying Officer Roberts, shot down a Ju.88, the squadron now based at Hurn, Hampshire, awaiting the move to a suitable airstrip in France.

The first nights of July saw the enemy, presumably reinforced from other fronts, staging a come-back, only to meet the impenetrable defence of the night-fighters. Wing Commander Maxwell and Flight Lieutenant Quinton got two Ju.88s, the second counting as the squadron's 100th victory with A.I. This team added a Do.217 claimed as probable for good measure. Warrant Officers Moore and Hogg got the squadron's first Messerschmitt Me.410 fighter-bomber and Squadron Leader Denis Furze with Flight Lieutenant Downes, and Flying Officer Miller with Warrant Officer Catchpole, added Junkers 188 and 88s. Into the squadron to command came Wing Commander Desmond Hughes, Battle of Britain Defiant pilot with the DFC for 1940 combats and two Bars for night-fighting with 125 (Newfoundland) and 600 (City of London) Squadrons. His navigator was Flight Lieutenant Laurie Dixon, DFC and Bar, from 125 and 600 Squadrons; a very operational team anxious to compare the night skies over France with those of North Africa and Italy.

Wing Commander Maxwell left for a staff post, a DSO being promulgated for his 604 leadership. John Quinton, wishing to stay with 'the action', was appointed Navigation Officer to No. 142 Wing, the parent-body for the first night-fighters earmarked for France. The squadron now moved to Colerne, Wiltshire, for a brief spell, claiming a Ju.88 and an FW.190 before the first aircraft flew out, on 24th July, 1944, to A.15 (A for American airfield) the allied tag for the captured Cherbourg-Maupertus aerodrome. Six machines crossed to Cherbourg, the others moving to Zeals, Wiltshire, guarding the vast concentration of personnel and stores being moved towards France. The echelon which now served the squadron aircraft moved into Hartford Bridge (Blackbushe Airport), Surrey. Three Ju.88s were downed in the last days and nights of July and one on 1st August by an aircraft operating from Colerne. On this day Squadron Leader A. H. B. Friendship, DFM, left on promotion to become instructor at the Central Gunnery School, Catfoss.

On 3rd August the detachment at A.15 opened their score with a Do.217 and Flight Lieutenant A. H. Drummond arrived with navigator Flight Lieutenant R. J. Gillies, DFC and Bar, after flying with 600 Squadron in Middle East. On 4th August Flight Lieutenant Jack Haddon, with Flying Officer McIlvenny, got a pair of bombers, Junkers 188 and 88, near Rennes, and on 6th August the entire squadron at last came together at A.8, an airstrip near Picauville, close to the Arromanches beaches.

71. Mosquito XIII and groundcrew at A.8, Picauville, France.

Seven aircraft took off that night from the prefabricated runway laid on an orchard-site and four had combats, a total of four enemy aircraft destroyed. A damaged Me.410 was credited to Flight Lieutenant Hooper, DFC, who, with navigator Flying Officer Hubbard, DFM, did not return from their patrol after giving the 'Tally-ho' over their radio, firing was actually heard over the position where they were last plotted by the mobile operations room in Normandy. The next day an intensive air-sea rescue search took place, backed up by squadron machines, but failed to trace the aircraft or crew, thought later to have fallen either to the enemy aircraft they attacked, or to some unfortunate allied error by aircraft or Naval guns. It was a sad loss to the squadron and to the Royal Air Force of a most experienced and well-liked team.

On the nights of 7th and 8th August the squadron added six enemy machines to its tally, the AOC No. 185 Group sending his congratulations, for these successes were saving thousands of allied lives as British and American ground forces, with Polish and other troops, pushed on to take Caen. Every bomber intercepted and forced to jettison its bombs before attack spared lives in our front-line encampments. On the night of 11th August, though, came a tragic accident as Flight Lieutenant Miller and Warrant Officer

Catchpole, landing after claiming a Dornier probably destroyed, came into collision with a Mosquito of 264 Squadron which was taxying out for take-off; the navigator of the 264 aircraft, alas, lost his life.

The next day a DFC was announced for Warrant Officer Gosling and on 28th August another unusual happening occurred when Flight Lieutenant Sandeman and Flying Officer Coates, in pursuit of a Ju.88 near Paris, opened fire and were then struck by some unknown object at 10,000 feet. Sandeman, recovering consciousness when at about 3,000 feet, pulled the ripcord and landed at Corbeil. Flying Officer Coates, though, died in the Mosquito; the cause of this disaster was never established. By 1st September the airstrip at A.8 had deteriorated so badly that it was unsafe and the squadrons moved; first to B.6 (in the British area) then to B.17 at Carpiquet near Caen. A DFC came for Flight Lieutenant John Quinton, one of the most popular officers ever to wear the RAF-blue. When he learned that Wing Commander Maxwell had been appointed to command No. 84 Squadron of fighter-bomber Mosquitos, earmarked for the Far East, Quinton wangled his way to rejoin Maxwell and, in Malaya and Indonesia, became the first navigator to command a flight in a fighter-bomber squadron. His thoroughness in qualifying as a straight navigator bringing the reward he so justly earned.

A DFC was also promulgated for Flying Officer Waller, and Flight Lieutenant Jack Meadows left to take over a flight in 219 Squadron, where his DFC was announced later (partly for 604 combats). On 20th September Flight Lieutenant Miller cannoned two armed trawlers off Jersey and despite accurate flak left one ablaze. On the 24th the squadron moved back to Predannack in Cornwall, there to re-equip with the newest type of Mosquito, with its advanced type of radar. In October more awards were announced, including a Bar to his DFC for Dusty Miller and DFCs for Surman, Weston and Catchpole (the last-named now commissioned). To relieve the monotony an all-aircrew revue was written, produced and staged within nine days, to the delight of Predannack personnel. A small detachment of aircraft moved to Ford, to prevent isolated raiders reaching London and to try and help combat the flying bomb menace. Squadron Leader Hugh Drummond left for Middle East, there to take command of 600 Squadron.

Group Captain Cunningham, leaving his chairborne post, flew down to Odiham, Hants, where the squadron was anxiously waiting a return to France. Under the control now of No. 147 Wing the Mosquitos were, however, able to patrol over Belgium and Holland and, in emergencies, land at Brussels-Melsbroek for refuelling or technical help. Flight Lieutenants Foster and Newton tangling with a Luftwaffe night-fighter, hit it, then suffered engine-failure, but managed to land safely. Then Captain O. Kristiansen (Norwegian) restored morale with a Ju.88 over our front-lines and, to the joy of all, on 31st December the squadron moved into Lille-Vendreville (B.51) Flight Lieutenant Cross, with Flying Officer Beaumont, getting two Ju.87 dive-bombers that same night.

72. Wg Cdr Desmond Hughes and Flt Lt Dixon.

On 1st January, 1945, Goering staged his last fling against allied air-fields in Belgium and Holland. The squadron aircraft were not affected, but that night Squadron Leader Furze claimed an He.219 over Munchen-Gladbach and, in three quick combats in the same sortie, Flight Lieutenant Foster, with Flight Lieutenant Newton, shot down a trio of Ju.88s, both airmen getting Bars to their DFCs. Pilot Officer Nicholas, with Flying Officer Irvine, added another Ju.88 near Hortsmar on the 4th January and on the 14th Wing Commander Hughes, with Flight Lieutenant Dixon, shot down a Ju.188 over Rotterdam. Very bad weather then curtailed operational flying and combats were few and far between with only occasional sightings of Luftwaffe machines. A DSO was awarded to Wing Commander Desmond Hughes, his tally now eighteen confirmed plus others damaged. Flight Lieutenant Wheeler, with Flying Officer Phillips, caught a Ju.88 near Dunkirk but most nights were now spent trying to bring down the 'Divers' – V.1. flying bombs – heading for Antwerp or the U.K. and in aiding the air-sea rescue operations as the great bombing forces returned over the Channel from Germany.

On 24th March, Flight Lieutenant Leppard, with navigator Flight Lieutenant Houghton, got a Bf.109 near Haltern. With aircraft diverted to land in England owing to poor visibility over the

Continent, it was some time before it was known that Flying Officer T. R. Wood, with Flying Officer Leafe, had destroyed a Ju.88 in the early hours of 27th March; destined to be the last 604 Squadron combat of the war as a run of poor weather prevented further March sorties. This, though, allowed the aircrews to stage a mammoth Thank-you party for their ground airmen in University Hall, Lille. Patrols were flown whenever possible in April, mainly over the Scheldt Estuary, but no enemy aircraft were ever sighted. On 18th April came orders for the squadron to disband and for their aircraft to go to Nos. 264 and 409 Squadrons, the latter a Canadian unit. Thus ended the wartime story of the County of Middlesex Squadron with a record second to none.

73. Post-war Spitfire XVIe at RAF Halton.

On 1st June, 1946, recruiting re-opened at Hendon and Group Captain Cunningham, back at de Havilland's Hatfield factories, became commanding officer, reverting to the rank of squadron leader to head 604, equipped with Spitfire LFXVIe aircraft as from 31st July, 1946. The Rt. Hon Viscount Templewood, GCSI, GBE, CMG, DL, JP (formerly Sir Samuel Hoare), resumed office as Honorary Air Commodore. In 1948 an Essex Flight was established at RAF North Weald, 604 moving there as a squadron on 27th March, 1949, with Hendon becoming increasingly unsuitable for fighter aircraft. John Cunningham's commitments as test pilot for the Comet demanded so much time that command was handed over to Squadron Leader K. T. Lofts, DFC and Bar, a pre-war Auxiliary of 615 (County of Surrey) Squadron and wartime C.O. of Nos. 340, 134 and 66 Squadrons, finally Wing Commander Flying at Hornchurch. The squadron regained the coveted Esher Trophy in 1949 but suffered a severe blow when Keith Lofts was killed in a flying accident, the command passing to Squadron Leader A. Deytrikh, a wartime pilot with 66 Squadron and later employed on testing duties. He had joined 604 in 1947 and now saw his squadron change-over from Spitfires to the jets: de Havilland Vampire F.3 being received in 1951.

Summer camps were held at Thorney Island and Malta and on 27th February, 1952, in the Middlesex Guildhall, Westminster, the Middlesex County Council publicly congratulated the squadron on its great achievements and, in turn, the County Council was thanked for its encouragement over the years, especially at Hendon and Northolt. During August 1952 the Gloster Meteor F.8 was received and in September 1953 Squadron Leader T. P. Turnbull, DFC, a photo-reconnaissance wartime pilot with 542 Squadron and the USAF PRU, assumed command, having joined the Royal Auxiliary Air Force in 1949. The squadron was still operating Meteors in the front line of the country's defences when, in March 1957 came the decision to disband the flying units of the RAuxAF, the Queen inviting representatives to Buckingham Palace so that, as Honorary Air Commodore-in-Chief, with HRH Prince Philip at her side, she could personally thank all ranks for their epic contributions as volunteers.

74. Squadron personnel and Meteors, Tangmere, 1956.

On 28th May, 1960, in Richmond Terrace, Whitehall, facing the then Air Ministry (now Ministry of Defence), Sir Frederick Handley Page, the Lord Lieutenant of Middlesex, presented The Standard awarded by Her Majesty to Flight Lieutenant J. N. G. Buckley, former 604 pilot, serving at this time with 33 Squadron, RAF; Group Captain John Cunningham replied to Sir Frederick's eloquent address and afterwards The Standard was laid-up in the RAF Church of St Clement Danes, received by the Resident Chaplain, Reverend H. L. O. Rees, who had earlier consecrated it. So, with the squadron's last formal parade, a glorious chapter of aviation history came to a close, though some were determined not to allow the County of Middlesex Squadron to disappear as a flying unit. With the loan of £250 from the Kemsley Flying Trust – which was soon repaid – a Percival Proctor III G–ALOK (LZ589 during RAF service) appeared as the mount of the County of Middlesex Fighter Squadron Flying

Group, the balance of the £525 cost-price subscribed by members, and for some time 'Oscar Kilo' gave tremendous pleasure to squadron types.

Only now is it possible to look back objectively at what 604 Squadron contributed in peace and war and although some will regard a score of 132 enemy aircraft destroyed or damaged, and the accompanying 4 DSO awards (and one Bar) the 37 DFCs or Bars, 9 DFMs, 4 BEMs, 3 Norwegian War Medals and countless Mentions in Despatches, as important others will think of the airmen whose names do not appear in the squadron diary and consequently are not available for this chapter, yet whose efforts made possible the successes and decorations. Some officers, and other ranks, served in the post-war Royal Air Force and one thinks of Marshal of the RAF Sir John Grandy, KCB, KBE, DSO, who recently retired as Chief of Air Staff; of Air Chief Marshal Sir Francis Fogarty, GBE, KCB, DFC, AFC; of Air Marshal Sir Christopher Hartley, KCB, CBE, DFC, AFC; of Air Vive-Marshal Desmond Hughes, CB, CBE, DSO, DFC, AFC, MA, Commandant of the RAF College, Cranwell, as this is written; of Air Commodore E. D. Crew, DSO, DFC; of Group Captain P. C. F. Lawton, DFC, LL.B, MInstT, a British European Airways executive; and of Flight Lieutenant E. A. Chris Wren, ARAeS, a squadron airman 1932–41, whose cartoons and writings have enlivened aeronautical journals for many years. Roderick Chisholm's book *Cover of Darkness*, and *Night Fighter* by C. F. Rawnsley ('Jimmy'), and Robert Wright – who served as Observer Radio in the squadron and whose classic on Air Chief Marshal Lord Dowding and contribution to the Battle of Britain film deserve mention – have also placed 604 high in the literary field.

Yet there are still those whose deeds may be unknown even to their comrades; the service of Flight Lieutenant S. H. J. Elliott (of Radlett) who was navigator to Dusty Miller despite amputation of a leg when a boy; or of Squadron Leader Gordon Hayhurst who broke his spine in an air crash and was told he would never fly again: he insisted on returning to pilot Hurricanes and was operating over the Dieppe landing a year after his crash; joining 604 in 1943 to end with a bag of six enemy aircraft. Let us not forget the work of 'Chiefy' Wheadon, of Flight Sergeant Fred Willis, of Sergeant K. Abbs, of Fred Beagle and Bernard Cornthwaite, and of 804385 A. A. Yerrell, now a hard worker for the British Legion in Kenton, Middlesex; finally Bob Batt, CEng, AFRAeS, a director of Aviation Traders.

Some may not know that Flight Lieutenant John Quinton, DFC, finding no flying opportunities with post-war 604, rejoined the Royal Air Force and, undergoing a refresher course, was asked to take a fifteen-year-old ATC cadet under his wing for a flight in a Wellington over Yorkshire. The Miles Martinet target collided with

the bomber and as the Wellington began to break up Quinton picked
up the only parachute within reach, clipped it to the cadet's harness,
putting the boy's fingers on the ripcord as he pushed him through a
gaping hole in the aircraft. The cadet was the only survivor, seven
officers and another cadet (a passenger in the Martinet) losing their
lives. When the full facts were revealed, a posthumous George Cross
was awarded to John Quinton in October 1951; so exacting are the
conditions for this award, second only to the Victoria Cross, that
twenty years later, no further GC has been gained by the RAF.

75. Air Marshal Sir Francis Fogarty (once adjutant 604 Sqdn) receives
the Quinton Trophy from the Air Training Corps (awarded to the best
ex-ATC apprentice at Halton each entry). The young airman second from
left is Derek Coates, whose life was saved by Flt Lt Quinton's self-sacrifice.
On Sir Francis Fogarty's right is the Hon. George Ward, then Under
Secretary of State for Air, a former pilot of 601 Sqdn.

Few will be unaware of what Group Captain John Cunningham
has meant to our aircraft industry with his epic flights in the de
Havilland Comet and Trident. Adding a second Bar to his DSO,
with 85 Squadron after leaving 604 (Jimmy Rawnsley got a DSO at
this time) John Cunningham was later made a Commander of the
order of the British Empire and appointed a Deputy Lieutenant for
the County of Middlesex. Peter Bugge, who flew Douglas DC–4s

with Scandinavian Air Services after the war, joined John Cunningham as a Comet test pilot in 1949 and has also played a vital part in the de Havilland (now Hawker Siddeley) developments.

Captain 'Bill' Hart, searchlight liaison officer with the squadron, co-operated in more ways than one, especially in regard to the welfare of the aircrews during the stint in France, moving twenty-seven hens across the Channel to ensure a supply of new-laid eggs! Corporal Edwin Priestnall, the senior safety equipment NCO, also played his part and before joining the squadron had the rare distinction of having packed parachutes for eighty bomber aircrew who baled out successfully – including four VC winners. Let former Flight Sergeant J. 'Doughey' Baker, squadron aircraft fitter, speak for all former members, as he did at the 1960 Standard parade when he said 'If I had my life over again, I would do exactly as I did in 1935. The years I've spent with the squadron have been the happiest and most exciting of my life'. That, in a nutshell, reflects the true spirit of the AAF and RAuxAF volunteers.

One hopes that when the Royal Air Force Museum opens at Hendon the Auxiliary Air Force will have adequate coverage, and as this chapter is closed, in August 1972, there are one-time 604 Squadron machines to be seen at RAF Halton (Spitfire RW386/6944M); RAF Leconfield (Spitfire RW382/7245M, in 234 Squadron markings); and at RAF Finningley (Meteor WL168 [ex 604] is now repainted as WH456 of 616 [South Yorkshire] Squadron). Outside *The Spitfire* public house, formerly *The Red Lion*, Upperhill, Herefordshire, stands Spitfire TD135 (once NG–U of 604 Squadron) allegedly bought for £25 after being used and neglected by an ATC unit in NE England. It now does a useful job in that a coin in a collecting box for the Old Age Pensioners starts the battery-operated airscrew.

REPRESENTATIVE SQUADRON AIRCRAFT

de Havilland D.H.9A	J7319 J8472
Avro 504K	H3015
Avro 504N	J8541 K1043 K1045
de Havilland D.H.60M Gipsy Moth	K1103 K1831
Westland Wapiti I	J9095/96
Wapiti IIa	K1325 K1326 K1327 K1328 K1379
Hawker Demon	K4496 K4499 K4504 K5715 K5721 K5727 K8192
Bristol Blenheim If	L4908 O L6615 L8607 NG–A L8674 C L8680 O
Bristol Blenheim IV	P4847 (A.I. equipped) Gloster Gladiator I K7970 K8033

Bristol Beaufighter If		R2054 (prototype) R2073 R2098 H R2101 R R2203
	VIf	V8556 V8557 R (Wg Cdr Cunningham) V8738
de Havilland D.H. Mosquito XII		XK183 NG–L
	XIII	HK 527 MM449 MM465 MM517 MM528 NG–H
Vickers Supermarine Spitfire LF XVIe		SL681 RAK–W TE275 NG–W TE439 NG–R
North American Harvard IIB		KF709
de Havilland D.H. Vampire F.3		VF321 VF344 C VT816 F VV194 H
Gloster Meteor	F.8	WE867 C WH408 D WL127 B WL132 WL168
	T.7	VZ630 WA620 WG938 WG939

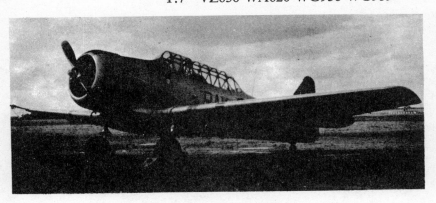

76. Squadron Harvard at Acklington, 1951.

When the Hawker Demons were received, the Air Ministry allocated to 604 Squadron their first official markings of red and yellow interlocking triangles, carried across the top wings and along the aircraft fuselage with the armorial bearings of the County of Middlesex on the tail (prior to the approval of a squadron badge in May 1936). On receipt of the Blenheims the squadron was allotted the code WQ but this was changed on the outbreak of war to NG. Post-war, in Reserve Command the code RAK was carried but from 1949, back in Fighter Command, the Spitfires bore NG again. The Vampires and Meteors carried the pre-war red and yellow interlocking triangles.

Badge: A seax; part of the armorial bearings of the county.

Motto (translated): 'If you want peace, prepare for war.'

607
(County of Durham)
Squadron

ON 17TH MARCH, 1930, No. 607 (County of Durham) Squadron came into being at Usworth near the site of the World War I aerodrome known as North Hylton. Progress in constructing a hutted camp was very slow and although a C.O. had been appointed in Squadron Leader W. L. Runciman and enthusiastic volunteers were enrolling for part-time service, it was not until 25th October, 1932, that the first squadron aircraft appeared in the shape of a de Havilland Gipsy Moth for initial training. It was followed, appropriately, perhaps, by a Westland Wapiti from Hendon, and by two Avro 504s, so that three of the country's great aircraft manufacturers were represented. During the summer of 1933 Messrs L. E. Smith and J. A. Vick obtained their A licences and commissions as Royal Air Force Pilot Officers on the Auxiliary List. In July 1933 recruiting was stepped up and 150 applications were received for the 50 vacancies for ground-crew personnel.

Early in 1934 Messrs J. R. Kayll and M. M. Irving secured their A licences and on 2nd June, 1934, it was possible to demonstrate nine Wapitis before the squadron's first Honorary Air Commodore, the Most Honourable the Marquess of Londonderry, KG, MVO. At the summer camp, held at Leuchars, Scotland, Messrs J. Sample, T. R. T. Carr Ellison, W. E. Gore and S. W. Kaye strengthened the potential officer-pilot numbers and by 20th July, 1935, the thirteen officers and ninety-seven airmen were able to parade for King George's Jubilee, Squadron Leader Runciman and Leading Aircraftman Galbraith receiving the special medal struck for this occasion. The first air-gunners had successfully passed their tests – 607 being then designated a bomber squadron – and Messrs J. M. Bazin and W. F. Blackadder had been commissioned to serve as pilots. In May 1936

77. Westland Wapitis of 607 Squadron.

the first Empire Air Day at Usworth attracted 3,484 paying spectators after which eight aircraft flew to Aldergrove in Northern Ireland to visit the Marquess of Londonderry at Newtownards. A month later the squadron surprised the pundits by winning the Brooke-Popham inter-squadron trophy challenge cup at Bisley, and in July Flight Lieutenant G. A. L. Manton, RAF, became adjutant and the squadron was told it was to become a fighter unit, equipped with the Hawker Demon.

78. Hawker Demons.

A new drill hall was opened and training included co-operation with the 7th Durham Light Infantry (Searchlight) Brigade. A squadron badge was approved and on 11th May, 1937, the commanding officer, Squadron Leader Runciman, was awarded the Air Force Cross in the Coronation Honours List of King George VI, for his sterling work with 607 Squadron. Empire Air Day drew over 15,000 visitors, indicating that at last the country was awakening to the possible treaty-breaking ahead. Nos. 103 (Bomber) and 226 (Army Co-operation) Squadrons flew in to exercise with 607 and in

August the Demons flew down to Rochford, Essex (now Southend Municipal Airport), for a fifteen-day camp which included visits to many famous airfields and inspections by V.I.P.s including Air Marshal Sir Hugh Dowding, Air Officer Commanding-in-Chief, Fighter Command. In 1938 the summer camp was held at Warmwell, Dorset, in company with Nos. 504 (County of Nottingham) and 605 (County of Warwick) Squadrons and, during the Munich crisis which followed, no fewer than 21 pilots and 145 ground personnel reported on call-up; a splendid turnout.

79. Summer camp, Rochford, 1937. *Officers left to right:* Dixon, Bazin, Bedington, White, Smith, Gore, Vick, Wardale, Runciman (sports shirt, arms folded).

In December the squadron was re-equipped with the Gloster Gladiator biplane fighter and as this was a single-seater the squadron air-gunners were offered the alternatives of release from the Auxiliary Air Force, pilot-training, or transfer to ground duties. Many volunteered immediately for pilot-training and three at least are known to have qualified for the RAF flying badge. Some who opted for release returned to fly as air-gunners in Bomber and Coastal Command when war came.

On the posting-away of Squadron Leader Runciman and his promotion, Squadron Leader L. E. Smith, the first to gain his A licence, was appointed to command with Flight Lieutenants J. Sample and J. R. Kayll as the two flight-commanders. A happy thought, on the expiration of the Marquess of Londonderry's five-year term of office, was the announcement that Wing Commander the Hon W. L. Runciman, AFC, was to become the Honorary Air Commodore. The August camp was at Abbotsinch, Scotland, but on 24th August, 1939, came orders for premature return to Usworth as all Auxiliaries were embodied into the Royal Air Force for full-time duty. By 10th October the squadron was at Acklington and with the newly-formed No. 152 Squadron not yet operational and with 609 (West Riding) Squadron only operational by day, it fell to 607 to bear the brunt of the initial defensive patrols. On 16th October, after a Scapa Flow raid warning had been picked-up, the squadron flew up to Drem near Berwick but, owing to a breakdown in the radar plotting system, did not share in the jubilation of Nos. 602 (City of Glasgow) and 603 (City of Edinburgh) Squadrons, who brought down the first enemy aircraft over the British Isles in World War II.

80. Summer camp, Abbotsinch, August 1939.

The following day, however, B Flight was ordered off and the Section led by Flight Lieutenant Sample (Flying Officer Craig and Pilot Officer Whitty were his No. 2 and No. 3) sighted a Do.18 flying-boat, twenty-five miles out to sea. All three Gladiator pilots attacked in turn from astern and although the enemy machine limped away, news came later that it had crashed into the sea some fifty miles out, the crew of four being taken prisoner by a trawler's crew. Thus the first combat had brought the squadron's first victory. Meantime the other airborne Gladiator pilots, Flying Officers Bazin, Pumphrey, and Thompson, had also sighted not one but four sea-planes, just below cloud. They gave chase and opened fire at a 'Vic' of three at extreme range, the enemy machines making for cloud-cover as the Gladiators were ordered back to base.

On 13th November came the first rumours of a move overseas, and then in seven civil airlines, a mixture of Imperial Airways' types including an impressed Fokker, the airmen left, via Croydon, for Merville, France, the sixteen Gladiators following. They were now part of the Allied Expeditionary Air Force's No. 60/61 Wings, some eight miles from Bethune. A solitary He.111 was chased during November and in December the only excitement was the visit of King George VI to Seclin where the C.O. and Flight Lieutenant Sample were presented to him. Then, with Merville waterlogged, a move was made to Vitry-en-Artois, and daily stooging was interspersed with escorts over the English Channel for the first leave-boats taking personnel to the U.K. On 1st January, 1940, the Under-Secretary of State for Air, Captain Balfour, came with the Assistant Chief of Air Staff, Air Vice-Marshal Sholto Douglas. On 9th January Winston Churchill came and delighted the men with his morale-lifting chat.

81. W. F. Blackadder with Gladiator.

It was something of a shock – despite the 'buzz', a growing rumour of previous days – when, at 4.12 a.m. on 10th May, the air-raid alarm sounded and the squadron was ordered into the air. By 7.0 a.m. the first refuellings had taken place and claims for seven enemy aircraft destroyed or damaged were submitted. The Squadron's first Hawker Hurricanes had recently been allocated and the Luftwaffe attacking Vitry must have had a shock when they were intercepted not only by the sturdy Gladiator biplanes but also by the more powerful Hurricanes. The aerodrome was repeatedly bombed and aircraft had to divert to any serviceable airfield for refuelling and to be re-armed, causing chaos in the reporting of claims which became tagged on to whichever units were sharing the bases used. Then, by 18th May, with the squadron's tally of victories rising every day, orders came for personnel to move towards the coast, taking only minimum kit. Records were burned and, as the men moved slowly forward in whatever vehicles became available, hampered by refugees and by troops going in the opposite direction, all kit was abandoned, except for rifles and revolvers, and the men were ordered to make for Boulogne.

On 21st May the remnants of the squadron boarded the *Biarritz*, a cross-channel steamer, reaching Dover safely. From there they entrained first for Tidworth, then headed for Croydon, eventually reaching Usworth again, to re-fit. When the sad checks were made it seemed that the C.O., Squadron Leader L. E. Smith, was missing, as was Flying Officer Weatherill. Flying Officers M. H. B. Thompson and le Brulle were believed killed and Flight Lieutenant Fidler, Flying Officer Pumphrey, and Sergeant-Pilot Thomas were thought to be prisoners of war. To this sad news the adjutant was compelled to add the names of Flight Lieutenant Sullivan and Flying Officers G. I. Cuthbert and J. B. Russell, though whether these officers were prisoners or dead could not be established in the terrible confusion then existing. The award of the Distinguished Service Order to Flight Lieutenant W. F. Blackadder; with DFCs to Flight Lieutenants J. Sample and J. R. Kayll (who had left the squadron on promotion, to take command of 615 [County of Surrey] with which unit 607 had gone to France) and also to Flying Officer W. E. Gore who was wounded and recovering in a Torquay hospital pleased all.

82. Hurricane in France, April 1940.

Squadron Leader J. A. Vick became C.O. and by August the squadron was again ready for operations. A check, insofar as it was possible, of Allied Expeditionary Air Force and Air Ministry records, indicated that during the fighting in France No. 607 Squadron had probably destroyed 72 enemy aircraft with another 56 unconfirmed and either damaged or possibly destroyed. It was a fine contribution from the County of Durham's airmen and it was on the 15th August, when the Luftwaffe High Command made the fatal mistake of assuming their pressure on SE England had left the North East undefended, that 607 Squadron – with so many replacement pilots – struck again. The Operations Room at No. 13(F) Group Headquarters near Newcastle picked up radar plots of enemy machines a hundred miles out to sea, heading on a south-westerly course from Scandinavia towards Newcastle and Tyneside.

Heinkel 115 seaplanes had earlier taken off to head for the Scottish coast to try and lure away fighter squadrons based in the North of England but a vital merchant convoy was due to sail from Hull at noon and our defences were on the top-line against attacks on these ships. The first squadrons ordered out to sea to meet the incoming raiders reported that instead of the expected thirty Luftwaffe aircraft there were more than a hundred sighted off the Farne Islands. 607 Squadron's pilots, to their dismay, were held back to defend Tyneside instead of going out over the sea but – in company with Nos. 41, and 605 (County of Warwick) Squadrons – managed to attack a few He.111 bombers which got past other fighters. Not one major factory or airfield was seriously affected by this massive raid, though some houses in Sunderland were hit; the squadron claimed eight enemy destroyed and eleven probably destroyed or seriously damaged. The post-war analysis of Luftwaffe records reduced the RAF's overall claims of 182 enemy aircraft destroyed to 75 Luftwaffe machines lost for only 34 RAF machines (17 pilots killed and 16 wounded, indicating the fierce combats involved). The County of Durham's new and inexperienced pilots may have claimed enemy destroyed which in fact limped home but during this epic air battle no aircraft or pilot of the squadron suffered injury – a remarkable achievement with our own anti-aircraft guns blazing away over Sunderland. Luftwaffe claims of 101 RAF aircraft brought down were far more exaggerated than our own.

A period of comparative quiet followed, interspersed with some coastal patrolling and convoy escorting, enabling the squadron to build up confidence for a move south which all felt must come as hard-pressed squadrons around London badly needed resting. It was on 1st September that orders arrived for the squadron to fly down to Tangmere, Sussex. Held in reserve for the first few days as pilots flew around the area to accustom themselves to the hazards of balloons and our gun-sites, it was not until 9th September that they saw action. It was a tragic day for 607 as during a life-or-death fight over Mayfield, six Hurricanes were brought down, Pilot Officers S. B. Parnall, G. J. Drake and J. D. Lanahan being killed with Sergeants P. A. Burnell-Phillips and R. A. Spyer wounded. Two of the enemy's Bf.109 fighters were shot down for certain and it is possible others fell to the guns of the dead men. Reinforced by three Polish pilots the squadron was in the thick of the great battles of 15th September, claiming three enemy destroyed during six separate sorties and losing the Hurricane of Pilot Officer P. J. T. Stephenson who baled out wounded, after return fire from a Dornier which, it is thought, later fell into the English Channel.

In a dog-fight near Gravesend on 17th September, Sergeant J.

Lansdell was killed and another squadron Hurricane lost when our own anti-aircraft fire hit Pilot Officer G. H. E. Welford's machine – he happily, escaped with minor injuries. On 25th September two Messerschmitt Bf.109s were shot down off the Isle of Wight for the loss of one Hurricane, Flight Lieutenant C. E. Bowen parachuting to safety on the island. 27th September saw the squadron adding to its score, although confusion was still arising when one pilot attacked at 20,000 feet, seeing the enemy falling – seemingly to destruction. Then, at, say, 10,000 feet, the Luftwaffe machine would be attacked again, causing a duplicated claim. On 28th September Flight Lieutenant W. E. Gore, DFC, and Flight Lieutenant M. M. Irving lost their lives off Selsey Bill – a severe blow to the squadron which later lost Flight Lieutenant C. E. Bowen and Sergeant N. Brumby over Swanage on 1st October.

On 5th October, again near Swanage, four more Hurricanes were lost, although one was later repaired and used for training. The relentless pressure of the air fighting was making itself felt more and more and on 7th October Flying Officer I. B. Difford collided with Pilot Officer A. M. W. Scott in the air, Difford losing his life as Scott baled out to safety. The depleted squadron was now given a well-earned break and moved to Turnhouse near Edinburgh – a Distinguished Flying Cross being promulgated for Flight Lieutenant J. M. Bazin with Distinguished Flying Medals for Flight-Sergeants Townsend and Burnett-Phillips. Twenty new pilots reported for duty, eight of them British or Commonwealth – the other dozen all Polish, with Squadron Leader A. W. Vincent arriving to command. On 12th December the squadron pilots returned to Usworth and were joined by Pilot Officer W. H. Ireson.

Attachments of aircraft and pilots were sent to places as far apart as Macmerry, Castletown (Caithness) and Skitten near Wick, and there were rumours of a new assignment when Squadron Leader G. D. Craig came in as C.O. With the Prime Minister's edict that Europe was to be 'set ablaze' No. 607 Squadron was selected to be the first Hurricane fighter-bomber unit of the Royal Air Force. Training at Martlesham Heath, Suffolk, with aircraft fitted either for eight 40 lb or two 250 lb bombs, the squadron commenced 'sweeping' Europe, getting in useful practice first by escorting our first daylight offensives operated by the Blenheim light-bombers and by the Handley Page Hampdens of RAF Bomber Command. Then, with a move to Manston, Kent, Squadron Leader Craig had the distinction of dropping the first 607 Squadron bombs when, in company with Sergeant Lees, transformers near Tingry were hit by four 250-pounders on 30th October, 1941.

General de Gaulle visited the squadron and told the men that the French would understand the necessity for attacking targets in their occupied country. On 4th November Squadron Leader Craig, attacking Le Touquet airfield at low level, did not return. At the end of that month the record said 'Despite inevitable losses, we have flown 110 bomber hours and morale has never been higher'. Ground personnel (almost the only pre-war Auxiliaries left at this stage) toiled unceasingly to help avenge the deaths of their pilots and the losses of Hurricanes. The variety of tasks entrusted to 607 Squadron was incredible. One night they would be escorting a Commando Force raiding the French Coast, the next day attacking a submarine. commandeered by the Nazis from the French Navy, later that same day the Hurricanes would be bombing enemy barges still in the canals and estuaries from Bruges to Boulogne.

Squadron Leader N. J. Mowat was appointed to command and when eight of the Hurribombers (as they were quickly nicknamed) took off on 8th December, 1941, English, Scots, Australian, Canadian, South African, Free French, Polish, and American pilots were in the cockpits, a far cry from 1930 when Durham men were taking the first A licences. Yet the spirit of the squadron was unchanged and these men from so many lands were proud of the badge on the nose of their aircraft and the fact that it was an Auxiliary Squadron, even if few of them qualified for the brass A lapel-badge. In February 1942 a warning came for a second move overseas and, at about the same time, a DSO came for Squadron Leader Mowat and a DFM for Flight-Sergeant Gill.

On 21st March the troopship *Empress of Russia* sailed in convoy from Liverpool with the groundcrews of 607 Squadron and with some of the pilots. On 6th April the ship docked for a few hours at Freetown, West Africa, where Squadron Leader Mowat took advantage of being ashore to fly a Hurricane just assembled for flight to the Middle East, instead of spending the time shopping for souvenirs: 'Just keeping my hand in,' he commented. On 22nd April the airmen Crossed the Line with traditional ceremony by Father Neptune and four days later they were being royally entertained in Durban, South Africa. Transferring to the liner *Ile de France* they reached Bombay and there entrained for Calcutta, hospitality being lavished upon them en route by pro-British residents at wayside halts.

By 20th June, 1942, the squadron was at Alipore, the Hurricanes, flown from Karachi by disembarked and air-lifted pilots, started to arrive at the new base and on 14th July the Air Officer Commanding No. 224 Group congratulated 607 Squadron on being ready to operate after so short a time. As the Japanese were raiding our forces from bases in Burma the squadron moved to Jessore, then to Feni, escorting Blenheim bombers or a Hudson on photo-reconnaissance, or intercepting the occasional Japanese aircraft which ventured into range. Flight-Sergeant Bates, who had to force-land during a 'Rhubarb' against a Japanese steamer (which was sunk) made his way back after a perilous 21-day trek through the jungle – a magnificent effort. Then came tragedy as Flight-Sergeant Gill, DFM, a great pilot, was jumped by four Japanese Zero fighters and killed, but only after a terrific tussle witnessed from the ground. He was buried where he fell with full military honours at the satellite field called Manston, after the Kent base from which this pilot had gained his decoration.

On promotion, the C.O., Wing Commander Mowat, DSO, DFC, was relieved by Squadron Leader R. H. Holland, DFC, who welcomed His Excellency the Viceroy of India, Lord Linlithgow, on a visit to the squadron. For his gallantry in rescuing the crew from a blazing Hudson at Feni, Corporal T. W. Chellew was awarded the George Medal. He had extricated an injured airman, recovered two bodies, despite exploding ammunition and the two bombs on board, then continued his search for the fourth airman, who was found pinned beneath the bent propeller: a display of high courage which richly deserved the decoration.

In March 1943 Wing Commander Mowat returned to command, reverting, as so many did, to a lower rank, to continue on operations, but a month later he was relieved by Squadron Leader P. J. T. Stephenson, DFC, an 'old boy' of 1940 days. The squadron diary at this period notes 'The weather is more suitable for underwater craft'. When an officer came to talk on 'Escape from Burma' it was noted that 607 pilots and groundcrews only wanted to get out of India and nearer the action. The Hurricane IIb which had served the squadron well since February was exchanged, with mixed feelings, for the Spitfire Vc in September–December 1943, but only a limited number of the sleeker, if less sturdy aircraft, arrived on the promise of 'a much faster type' soon! Coinciding with the departure of Squadron Leader Stephenson and arrival of Squadron Leader G. G. A. Davies in March 1944 the first Spitfire Mark VIII was received – specially designed with Burma in mind – built for high and low operations, with a Rolls-Royce Merlin engine of 1,520 h.p. and top speed of 400 m.p.h.

83. Servicing squadron Spitfires in Burma.

In May of 1944 the tide at last turned and 607 Squadron began a new run of successes in the air as Japanese bombers and fighters were met and accounted-for almost daily. The battle for the Imphal Valley was on and by the end of the month the squadron could confirm 28 Japanese aircraft destroyed, 14 probables, and 69 others damaged. From Wangjing airfield the squadron moved to Imphal: in July on to Baigachi, after a record bag on 17th June of 4 Oscars shot down with seven others either destroyed or damaged. Air Commodore Stanley Vincent, who had flown fighters in both world wars, signalled to the squadron:

'Many thanks for the good work with 221 Group. During 3 months 12 e/a destroyed, 9 probables and 26 damaged is a very satisfactory record when it is particularly borne out that the enemy's main object seems to have been to avoid combat with 607. Very good luck, hunting and shooting in the future.'

On 15th September, 1944, Group Captain R. F. Boyd, DSO, DFC, a 602 Squadron Battle of Britain pilot, led 607 Squadron over Calcutta in proud memory of those County of Durham men who laid down their lives. Then, with 45-gallon long-range tanks fitted to a new batch of Spitfire VIIIs the squadron was able to press on even further into enemy-held territory, escorting the Douglas Dakotas dropping supplies to the 14th Army. The squadron's old machines passed on to their 1939–40 comrades in France, No. 615 (County of Surrey) Squadron. In January 1945 moving on from Sapan and then from Tulihall, the squadron's great wish was realised: a move actually into Burma itself. Flying from Tabingaung in January–February a record thirty-day total of operational hours, 1051 in all, were flown. In February an ENSA concert party, headed by Frances Day, included her famous number 'Won't some kind gentleman see me home' and although she did not specifically mention Durham, there was no lack of volunteers to respond to her invitation.

In May, Squadron Leader C. M. Humphreys took over command. News of the end of the war in Europe brought morale to a very high peak, coupled with a determination to finish off the fight in SE Asia. Leaflets were dropped warning the Japanese soldiers that defeat was only a matter of time. There was yet another change in command, with Squadron Leader C. O. J. Pegge, DFC, a veteran of 610 (County of Chester) Squadron in the Battle of Britain, coming in. A few final offensive sorties left enemy targets ablaze and on 31st July news came that 607 Squadron was to disband, the final official message including the wish that the County of Durham Squadron would soon be flying again in the post-war Auxiliary Air Force. Personnel with time still to serve were drafted elsewhere for the remaining days of war and then to the forces occupying Japanese-held areas as they were liberated.

Meetings with prisoners of war released from captivity were moving moments, some had to be despatched with all speed to Ceylon for convalescence, so badly had they fared in enemy hands. The last weeks of operations had taken the squadron to Dwehla, Kwetnge, Kaleywa and Mingaladon and the final date entered in the squadron war diary was 19th August when the last member departed.

It was in June of 1946 that the volunteers began to re-gather at Ouston, an RAF airfield between Gateshead and Chester-le-Street; Usworth, the pre-war base having been earmarked to be Sunderland's civil airport. The first post-war C.O. was Squadron Leader J. R. Kayll, DSO, OBE, DFC, a pre-war member who had left 607 in early 1940 to command 615 and, on further promotion, to lead the Hornchurch Wing. He had been forced down into enemy territory on a mission in 1941 and spent the rest of the war as a prisoner of the Germans.

There were three other originals; Flight Lieutenant W. F. Blackadder, DSO, OBE, Edinburgh University, Cambridge, and Scottish rugby player, renowned for his organisation of the Auxiliary Air Force versus Royal Air Force rugby challenge in 1938, as well as for his solo reconnaissance of the roads and bridges during the German advances into France in May 1940. He was credited with seven enemy aircraft brought down and left 607 in November 1940 to command No. 245 (Northern Rhodesia) Squadron. He cheerfully dropped two rings to fly again, as did Flight Lieutenant J. M. Bazin, DSO, DFC, who had achieved the rare distinction for a fighter pilot of commanding No. 9 (Bomber) Squadron after leaving 607 and spending a time as a Controller in the No. 14(F) Group Operations Room near Inverness. Leading his Lancasters against the *Tirpitz* and other heavily-defended targets, Wing Commander Bazin's personal knowledge of fighter tactics was invaluable to his crews. The fourth pre-war pilot, was Flying Officer R. E. W. Pumphrey, reported missing in May 1940 and a prisoner of war for five years. The Hon W. L. Runciman, OBE, AFC – first squadron commander, who had later commanded the Bristol University Air Squadron and had been Group Captain, Air Attaché Teheran later in World War II – resumed as Honorary Air Commodore (he later became Viscount Runciman of Doxford).

The initial machines received in 1946 were the Spitfire Mk.XIV, a fighter-reconnaissance version, and these were exchanged in 1948 for the Spitfire F.22. In this year the first overseas summer camp was held at Lübeck, Germany; the previous year Leuchars, Scotland, was the venue. In 1949 Squadron Leader J. M. Bazin assumed command and on 4th December Air Marshal R. M. Foster, CB, CBE, DFC, unveiled a 607 Squadron Memorial Tablet in Durham Cathedral, with the Rt Hon Viscount Runciman reading a Lesson. In 1951 the squadron was re-equipped with the de Havilland jet Vampire FB.5

and Squadron Leader A. B. Dunford, DFC, became C.O.; he had been a pre-war Territorial Army volunteer who transferred to the RAF, getting his DFC in Burma with No. 155 Squadron, before ending the war with 683 Squadron. Two Gloster Meteor two-seat T.7 trainers

84. Squadron camp, Lübeck, 1948.

were received to speed-up the pilot-training programme and successful camps were held at Horsham St Faith, Norfolk, and at Sylt in Germany. In September 1953 Squadron Leader J. A. Stephen, RAF, who had been a wartime instructor in Rhodesia before flying with Nos. 137 and 19 Squadrons, was appointed C.O., handing over his command in June 1956 to Squadron Leader G. Gray who had been taken prisoner in February 1945 when flying with No. 111 Squadron and who after the war had flown in Nos. 1, 66, and 502 (County of Ulster) Squadrons, serving as adjutant to the Northern Ireland Auxiliaries.

85. Spitfire F.22 in the Cooper Trophy Race, 1948.

The rumours which had been prevalent from 1954 when the Javelin and the Hunter aircraft did not come to the Royal Auxiliary Air Force, culminated in disbandment of all the twenty squadrons in March 1957, at which time plans were set in motion to ensure that the contribution in peace and war of the County of Durham's Squadron would not be forgotten. Reunions were organised by Messrs R. E. Gibson of James Street, Gateshead, and C. Kenny of Darras Road, Ponteland. On 22nd May, 1960, thanks to the efforts of a hard-working committee under Viscount Runciman and including W. F. Blackadder, G. D. Craig, A. B. Dunford, M. Butcher and J. R. Kayll, The Standard awarded by Her Majesty the Queen was presented to 607 Squadron on Palace Green, Durham, by Marshal of the RAF Sir Dermot Boyle, who handed it to Flight Lieutenant M. C. Butcher, a former squadron pilot. The Standard was marched to the cathedral, received by the Dean and laid-up during Evensong the same day, to hang over the squadron's memorial tablet.

A Dinner had been held on the evening before the ceremony, in the Old Assembly Rooms, Newcastle-on-Tyne, and, other than this nostalgic gathering, two other things will long be remembered. One: that on Palace Green, Durham, stood a genuine 607 Squadron Hurricane I serial P2617, believed earmarked for the Royal Air Force Museum at Hendon. The other the words of Viscount Runciman, in responding to Sir Dermot Boyle's tribute to the squadron, when he said – speaking as an original member rather than as Honorary Air Commodore:

'Sir, There stand here today not the officers and airmen of a squadron in being, but only some remainder of those who in peace and war served with 607 during 25 years. That is our misfortune, not our fault. If, in the years to come, Her Majesty should again require of this squadron that service for which she has been pleased to award us this Standard, our successors will, I am confident, be found worthy of it.

We who have served in No. 607 (County of Durham) Squadron are proud and grateful for the honour conferred on the squadron by Her Majesty in the award of this Standard and we thank you, Sir, for coming here today to present it. We thank you not only as a former Chief of the Air Staff, as a distinguished airman and fighter, but also because you have yourself served with an Auxiliary Squadron, and we make bold to claim you as in some sense one of ourselves.'

The thoughts of all present (and of those unable to be there in person) must have gone back over the years – to the fighting in France and the battles over Tyneside in 1940, the contribution it made when *Scharnhorst* and *Gneisenau* sailed from Brest in 1942, when the Hurribombers destroyed an E-boat and hit two other vessels. Some, though, would recall the Army Commander in Burma who wrote: 'I would like you to make it known to every pilot just how much the brilliant offensive action of your fighter-bombers was appreciated. You have killed hundreds of Jap soldiers and have saved the lives of thousands of defenceless civilians.'

Many who first served in the squadron, left to strengthen other newly-formed units, bringing great credit upon themselves and upon 607's influence and training. One cannot trace them all, alas, but Group Captain Alexander Gabszewicz, who left 607 to join No. 316 (Polish) Squadron, later gained the DSO and Bar, and DFC leading both Polish and USAAF squadrons. Another Polish pilot in 607, Flying Officer Franek Surma, served with several RAF squadrons before joining 308 (Polish) Squadron, having six enemy to his credit when he was finally killed in action. A third ex-607 Pole, Squadron Leader Wlasnowalski, moved to 213 Squadron and brought his final score to five before he, too, was killed in combat. Flying Officer

86. Ex-members with Hurricane P2617, Palace Green, Durham, May 1960. *Left to right:* unknown, Sgt Brown, unknown, Sgt Metcalf, unknown, Viscount Runciman, Cpl Lote, Sqdn Ldr Smith, Sgt Anderson, Flt Lt Thompson, Flt Lt Hope Pool, Sgt Greenfield, L.A.C. Crowe, Wg Cdr Blackadder.

J. B. W. Humpherson, DFC, who flew the squadron Gladiators in France and was awarded the DFC later in 1940 with No. 32 Squadron was credited with six enemy machines before he gave his life in his country's service. Squadron Leader John Sample, DFC, who left to command 504 (County of Nottingham) also lost his life after the 1940 fighting.

The Spitfire which stood for many years at Ouston in 607's post-war markings (though never with the squadron) has now gone temporarily to East Fortune, a wartime training airfield acting as store for the Royal Scottish Museum in Edinburgh. Here the Spitfire will later be displayed in markings yet to be decided. In addition to the Hurricane already mentioned, one 607 aircraft still to be seen is Spitfire XVI TE184 (used at Ouston for ground instructional purposes) now earmarked for the Belfast Transport Museum. It is a pity that others are not available.

87. The C.O.'s Vampire F.B.9.

REPRESENTATIVE SQUADRON AIRCRAFT

Aircraft	Mark	Serials
Avro 504N		K1807
Westland Wapiti	IIa	J9869 K1145 K1327 K1336 K1378 K2243
Hawker Demon		K5683 K5684 K5685 K5687
Hawker Hart (Trainer)		K5863 K5864
Gloster Gladiator		K6137 K7983 K7999 K8020 K8030
Miles Master		N7578
Hawker Hurricane	I	P2571 P2874 P2900 P2901
	IIb	HV652 BE475 BM948
	IIc	BN581 BN676 BN906 BP240
Vickers-Supermarine Spitfire	Vc	MA341 MA688 MA857
	VIII	MD274 MT941 MV367 AF–B
	XVI	RM740 SM928 RAN–E TZ116 RAN–D
	F.22	PK384 LA–F PK557 LA–G PK603 LA–Q
North American Harvard	IIb	KF379 RAN–A KF737 RAN–A KF193 LA–C
Gloster Meteor T.7.		WH225 N VW439 R VW489 Q
de Havilland Vampire	FB.5	VV617 A WA377 B (CO's aircraft) WA448 C WA522 D WA419 E VX472 F
	FB.9	WR266 B (C.O.'s aircraft 1957)

The squadron's first code appears to have been LW and this was changed to AF on outbreak of war; being retained until disbandment in 1945. On re-forming in Reserve Command in 1946 the letters RAN were allotted, changing to LA on transfer into Fighter Command. With arrival of the Vampires, however, the code disappeared and a squadron design of interlocking triangles of mauve and stone-colours came into use with the individual aircraft letter carried on the nose.

Badge: A winged lion salient, the hind legs also winged. Official authorisation of an unofficial squadron badge.

608
(North Riding)
Squadron

ON 17TH MARCH, 1930, No. 608 (North Riding) Squadron was formed at Thornaby; long before the Royal Air Force station was established there in 1937. Squadron Leader W. Howard-Davies became C.O. and early entrants for pilot-training included Messrs G. Shaw, G. H. Ambler, I. W. W. Thomson and W. V. Hodson. Flight Lieutenant C. L. Falconer was the first adjutant with Pilot Officer G. Bearne as his assistant. Dr J. Howell was appointed squadron medical officer and K. Pyman, MC, became the accountant with Messrs J. L. Clayton, A. N. Wilson and J. Newhouse swelling the officer-entry. Recruiting for suitable airmen for ground trades commenced and – designated as a bombing squadron – the first aircraft received were the Avro 504N and the Westland Wapiti.

In 1932 Squadron Leader I. W. Thomson was appointed to command and by 1934 the squadron was participating in the annual exercises at Manston, Kent. A notable happening this year was the entry of Flight Lieutenant G. Shaw's British Klemm Eagle monoplane in the MacRobertson England to Australia Air Race, which started from Mildenhall, Suffolk, on 20th October. This was the only Auxiliary Air Force entry and, alas, Flight Lieutenant Shaw had to pull out of the race at Bushire, a seaport, in Persia (now Iran), with a damaged undercarriage. This was a tremendous disappointment to all members of the squadron who had taken great interest in the preparation of the aircraft for this record-breaking attempt.

On 30th December, 1934, Squadron Leader G. H. Ambler took command and J. G. Considine joined about this time. The Rt. Hon Viscount Swinton, GBE, MC (formerly Sir Philip Cunliffe Lister), who had become Secretary of State for Air in June 1935, honoured the squadron by accepting appointment as the first Honorary Air

Commodore. On 14th January, 1937, re-equipment with the Hawker Demon two-seater interceptor began and the squadron was transferred into No. 12 (Fighter) Group. This type of aircraft and commitment did not long remain. On 20th March, 1939 – with the Air Ministry appreciating the Nazi threat to the North East of England ports – No. 608 (Fighter) Squadron, whose badge had been approved in this role, was again re-designated, this time to become a General Reconnaissance unit within No. 18(R) Group. The Avro Anson began to arrive and for the summer camp of 1939 there were 21 officers and 234 airmen on strength including newcomers A. D. Braithwaite and J. Robinson for aircrew training.

88. Flt Lt Shaw's British Klemm Eagle, 1934.

On 24th August, 1939, the squadron was embodied into the Royal Air Force for full-time duties and an early assignment of considerable value was the photographing of the I.C.I. plant's camouflage schemes using colour-film over and around Billingham. Low-level bombing practice was another priority and Squadron Leader G. Shaw took command on being promoted. Convoy escorts were flown in conjunction with No. 220 Squadron, RAF, and Acting/Pilot Officer Cunliffe Lister reported for duty. On 21st September the squadron's first war operational mission was logged when Squadron Leader Shaw, with Flying Officer Woolcock, Leading Aircraftman Kelly and Corporal Knott, flew a photographic sortie of 'likely targets' – the records do not say what they were. A total of $226\frac{1}{2}$ flying hours was recorded for September; a proud achievement.

27th October, though, brought stark tragedy to the squadron, and to the pilot of a Hurricane fighter who mistook Anson N5204 for an enemy raider near the Humber Lightship. The Anson, crewed by Flight Lieutenant Garnett (missing believed killed), Acting/Pilot Officer Baird (missing believed killed), Corporal Wilson (killed) and Aircraftman Smith (wounded), fell into the North Sea, Wilson and

Smith being picked up by HMS *Ganges*. As a result of this terrible mistake instructions were received from Air Ministry that all the roundels (the red, white and blue disc-markings) on fuselages and wings be repainted and that undercarriages were to be left down when near our shipping, which our fighters were also protecting, often in very poor visibility. The funeral at St Cuthbert's Church, Yarm Road, Stockton, on 1st November brought home to all who witnessed it the grim reality of war.

On 19th November came another tragedy when Pilot Officer J. W. C. Robertson, during release from duty, was so keen to fly that he joined a crew of No. 220 Squadron for an air-firing exercise, only to lose his life off the coast of Scotland. A week later came the squadron's first night operations in support of a convoy with HMS *Jervis Bay* (a ship destined to make history in November 1940 when she took on a German battle cruiser, enabling 33 ships in the convoy of 38 to reach safety. Commander E. S. Fogary Fegen, RN, who went down with the *Jervis Bay*, was awarded a posthumous Victoria Cross). On 20th December aircraft 'M' found a raft with six men aboard and guided a launch to it, the Air Officer Commanding sending his congratulations to the 608 crew for their vigilance. Christmas saw the traditional ceremony of officers waiting upon their airmen at lunch and the usual exchanges of visits between messes – many undoubtedly wondering whether Christmas 1940 would see them still in uniform – or still in England!

January was a quiet month of training and convoy escorts but on February 3rd aircraft 'E' met three He.111 bombers and attacking the nearest without hesitation had the great satisfaction (and relief) of seeing all three turn tail and disappear for their base. Three days later the C.O. was promoted and as Wing Commander Shaw left to the regret of all, Squadron Leader Stead took command. In March, Pilot Officers J. C. T. Downey and T. C. Stansbury, serving in the RAF on regular commissions, joined the squadron. With the collapse in Belgium, Holland, and France, 608 Squadron was called upon to undertake more and more escorts, to release Coastal Command units based further south to attack ports and airfields as our forces made for Dunkirk and Calais. The squadron crews would have liked the chance to join this struggle but Coastal Command had received its first Blackburn Botha aircraft ('a machine built to an extremely exacting specification issued by Air Ministry in September, 1935, for a three-seat, land-based, twin-engined reconnaissance bomber with internal stowage for a torpedo' to quote aviation writer A. J. Jackson from his classic book *Blackburn Aircraft Since 1909*).

The eventful history of this machine is worth reading but we are only concerned here with 608 Squadron and after the first issues to the Royal Air Force on 3rd June, 1940, the trainees selected to fly the Botha in squadron service were from 608, to which, as A. J. Jackson reveals, a first allocation of serials L6164/5/6 was delivered to Thornaby on 28th June to begin replacing the Avro Anson. Seven other Bothas arrived on 5th July. A. J. Jackson points out that these were the first Blackburn aircraft to equip a land-based RAF squadron since the Kangaroo supplied to 246 Squadron in 1918! In the event it was Wing Commander Shaw, and Pilot Officers Washington and Tucker, who flew the first operational patrols on 10th August in L6173, L6170 and L6190 respectively. During the next three months, says A. J. Jackson, there were only twelve days on which the squadron's Bothas were grounded by bad weather. Airborne times were often 4–5 hours but, although there were recorded instances of the remaining Ansons engaging in combat with the enemy (Pilot Officers Reeve and Creed, with Sergeant Anson and A.C. Birtwistle in 'V' took on a Ju.88 on 1st August) the Bothas were given no opportunities of gaining battle honours.

89. Blackburn Botha.

Thirty Bothas were sent to Thornaby and were flown by the squadron from 10th August to 6th November mainly on convoy escorts, only one Botha being lost – L6165 – missing from a patrol on 31st August. Amazingly it was one of the few remaining Ansons – 'R' crewed by Pilot Officer Gibbs, Flight Lieutenant Johnson and Sergeants Gowing and Norton – which met with the enemy when two He.115 floatplanes attacked with cannons. Avoiding damage by skilful evasive action the Anson opened fire and hit both Heinkels which thereupon made off. After the patrols flown in Bothas L6198 (Pilot Officer Keates) and L6209 (Sergeant Burton) on 6th November, these machines were withdrawn from front-line use and sent to Silloth, then to other training units, for the various commitments as fully-described in A. J. Jackson's splendid book.

On 14th November, Anson 'P' damaged another He.115 and then followed a period of comparative quiet until, on 2nd February, 1941, the Bristol Blenheim began to reach the squadron, the aircraft being a mixture of the Mark I and IV. Conversion training was the priority broken only for a party on 14th March at the news of a Distinguished Flying Cross for Wing Commander Shaw. On 18th March three sub-lieutenants arrived from the Fleet Air Arm, Bramcote, to strengthen the squadron, and Pilot Officer Sir Iain MacRobert arrived to captain one of the squadron aircraft. Three Heinkels were encountered by one of 608's Anson aircraft out on escort and, despite her slower speed and poorer armament, the aggressive attack made caused the Luftwaffe trio to turn and disappear.

On 1st July, flying 'U', Pilot Officer MacRobert took off with his crew to search for a dinghy reported in the North Sea but it was fated not to come back. Thus Lady MacRobert lost a second son (the third was also to die in the RAF). This courageous lady not only paid for bombers and fighters but later gave her home to be a convalescent centre for members of the Royal Air Force. No. 608 Squadron was very proud to have had a member of this family in its ranks.

With the provision of more Lockheed Hudson aircraft for Coastal Command, No. 608 was next to be equipped with this military version of the Lockheed 14 Super Electra airliner, flown across the Atlantic after Captain (later Air Vice-Marshal) D. C. T. Bennett of BOAC, had proved that the Hudson could make the crossing by air rather than as deck-cargo on a ship. With endurance of six hours, maximum speed of 284 m.p.h., range of 2,160 miles and with five, six, or seven guns for defence, according to other loads, the squadron now had a machine which was to be a real thorn in the enemy side. The first sorties were flown in Hudsons on 8th July, 1941, when fishing smacks bringing patriots to serve with the Allies were protected into port. On 30th August aircraft 'F' bombed enemy naval vessels with three 250-pounders, taking cloud-cover against anti-aircraft fire but not before observing that one of the ships attacked had slowed-down and was probably seriously damaged. On 8th September an enemy merchant convoy was bombed and two days after this 'P', during patrol, spotted the guns firing at Redcar. Giving chase, a Ju.88 was hit and last seen with its port engine smoking as it made for base.

Leaflets were dropped over Denmark, exhorting the Danes to maintain their resistance. On 3rd October, using the experience of the 'Nickelling' sorties – the code-name for leaflet-drops – the squadron bombed the enemy airfield at Aalborg despite considerable ground-fire. Forty bombs plastered the runways and hangars and machine-guns were used on all the parked aircraft. On 20th October the Danish seaplane base was visited and on 5th November Wing Commander R. S. Darbyshire and Squadron Leader Disney joined the strength just before news came of an impending move to another squadron base. After Christmas leave for the lucky ones, January 1942 saw 608 settling-in at Wick in the far north of Scotland to join the hunt for U-boats. On 26th February three direct hits were scored on an icebound motor vessel, notwithstanding return fire, and at Egersund, the Norwegian port, a 4,000-ton ship was successfully attacked.

On 1st March, Wing Commander P. D. R. Hutchings arrived to command and on 17th May eight Hudsons flew a total of 49½ hours 'Ops' on a Shipping Strike, 'H' being slightly damaged when two Messerschmitt Bf.109 fighters pursued it; only to be out-flown by the Hudson pilot. Aircraft 'O' fired 250 rounds in support of his fellow-pilot's evasion and 'K' photographed the complete sortie. At this time there were Australian, Canadian, Polish, and American aircrew as well as from all parts of the British Isles, with the few Auxiliaries still flying, supported by the majority of the pre-war Yorkshire part-timers. Many hated the thought of promotion if it involved leaving 608, so strong was the team-spirit.

90. Wg Cdr Peter Hutchings, DFC, AFC.

On 3rd June a tanker was hit in the heavily-defended Skaggerak and on the 10th aircraft 'L' sent off on a special mission, refuelled at Sumburgh in the Shetlands, and then attacked a U-boat with three 250 lb Torpex depth-charges which fell short. The air-gunners thereupon fired all their ammunition at the surfaced submarine, scoring hits. When the Hudson had to leave the area the U-boat was still on the surface and other squadrons were alerted to try and finish off the enemy craft. On the 16th an attack was made on the German cruiser *Prince Eugen* and the Air Officer Commanding-in-Chief of Coastal Command and the AOC No. 18 Group signalled congratulations; these messages being followed by an Air Council letter thanking 608 Squadron for splendid work.

On 5th August, the squadron moved up to Sumburgh, at the foot of the Shetland Islands, to attack targets off the Norwegian coast and to help protect convoys moving to North Russia. On 25th

August, though, orders came for an immediate move south to Gosport in Hampshire and for all aircraft to be brought to a high state of readiness with the machine-guns tested for action. Aircraft 'V' took off to fly an air-test near Selsey Bill and was unlucky in running into three FW.190 fighters, the Luftwaffe's latest and fastest machine. Although the FW.190s had shot down both Hurricanes and Spitfires, the reliable and manœuvrable Hudson outwitted this trio, despite hits being scored by one of the enemy fighters. The Hudson landed safely at RAF Tangmere, Sussex, but the rear-gunner, Pilot Officer J. H. V. Nelson, was discovered to be dead, killed at his guns as he warded off this attack, a superb performance by the pilot and his gallant crew.

91. Sumburgh airfield from a 608 Hudson.

On 29th October, after leave, the ground personnel embarked at Gourock, Scotland, in His Majesty's Transport *Strathmore* (the P. & O. liner commandeered as a troopship) and the Hudsons, moving first to Exeter, flew out to Gibraltar, cleverly avoiding waiting Luftwaffe standing patrols over the Bay of Biscay. On 10th November the troopship bringing in the groundcrews was escorted into Gibraltar by two squadron Hudsons now painted white for their new role ahead in the Mediterranean sunshine. The next day began a fantastic run of successes when aircraft 'B' attacked a U-boat, seeing a mile-long oil-streak on the sea. With 'Operation Torch' – the first of the great Anglo-American landings – taking place in French North Africa, there was an immense task for 608 (and 500 [County of Kent]) Squadrons: to photograph ports, escort our ships and, most of all, destroy every U-boat and Italian submarine in the waters of the Mediterranean. Aircraft 'U' did not return from patrol on 11th November and on this day 'L' brought the first despatches from General Eisenhower in Oran after another squadron Hudson had flown to Taffaraari with personnel to operate a wireless station, after which the Hudson reconnoitred the Oran area before the allied landings occupied the port. Another Hudson flew General Haden from Gibraltar to Maison Blanche, Algiers.

92. 608 protect the Royal Navy, Gibraltar.

During 19th November, three separate attacks were made on enemy submarines and by 10th December the squadron was moved up to Blida, an airfield twenty-five miles from Algiers, to intensify the U-boat campaign. On 16th January, 1943, 'G' depth-charged a U-boat as it submerged, the pilot's report saying 'I am sure we gave it a good shaking!' Two days later aircraft 'K' attacked a U-boat on the surface and on the 20th the new 'U', after sighting a ship on fire in one of our convoys, attacked as a U-boat crash-dived. Three of the 250 lb depth-charges straddled the spot and the navigator of the Hudson saw whitish-blue flashes on the spot. The U-boat had fired in desperation from its conning-tower but no hits were made on the Hudson. On the 28th 'K' attacked another U-boat. After a lull, on 25th February, as 'E' was attacking a surfaced U-boat, the Hudson came under fire from a Ju.88 and a Messerschmitt Me.210 but managed to drive off both enemy machines which showed damage from the accurate firing of the Hudson's gunners. The following day Wing Commander C. M. M. Greece relieved Wing Commander Peter Hutchings who was awarded a well-earned DFC (he later got the AFC for instructing).

During March the squadron received the Hudson Mk.VI and Flying Officer A. Scholefield was awarded the DFC for his excellent work. On 5th April Aircraft 'B' crashed on take-off, with Sergeant E. P. O. Watson and his crew killed instantly, and, sad to say, on 20th April came the announcement of a Distinguished Flying Medal for Watson, and of his promotion, both recommended before his death. Aircrew members from Newfoundland and New Zealand joined the other nationalities already making up a happy unit and a DFC award for Squadron Leader J. T. Freeman rewarded several good attacks.

93. Hudsons of 608 on patrol.

During August the squadron moved to Protville, Tunisia, for anti-submarine warfare and to cover convoys in the Sicilian waters. In September there were further moves: to Augusta, Borizzo and, Palermo, as the war moved into Italy; and there were visits from Air Vice-Marshal Sir Hugh Pugh Lloyd and Air Commodore K. B. B. Cross. In October the squadron was thrilled to be given a Hurricane from No. 145 Maintenance Unit, to use as a communications machine, and this may have been connected with a visit made by Air Vice-Marshal Sir Keith Park, the new Air Officer Commanding, Malta, who had used a personal Hurricane since his command of

11(F) Group in the Battle of Britain. In November came a move to Montecorvino, Grottagli, then to Gando, and during the landings at Anzio three squadron machines were lost as the Luftwaffe fought a rearguard action. The months of January and February 1944 were extremely busy and on 18th March Vesuvius began to erupt. Twenty-two heavy falls of volcanic ash brought several inches of the stuff to Montecorvino airfield, the weight of the ash accumulating on aircraft wings, endangering the control surfaces and penetrating the gills and turrets, involving a most thorough check to ensure the clearance of this unexpected menace. Then between the 23rd and 25th a fine dust filled the whole of the air-space up to 10,000 feet, the volcanic dust polluting the water and blocking the road to Naples.

On 1st April came the award of a DFM to Flight Sergeant Wallace; and Wing Commander Don Finlay, OBE, the Olympic hurdler and one-time fighter pilot, assumed temporary command. Despite the lava dust everywhere, air-sea rescue sorties were flown and news came that Group Captain Finlay was being promoted to become Senior Air Staff Officer at No. 210 Group, British North Africa Forces. The squadron disbanded at Pomigliano, crews being posted to Nos. 17, 22, 25, and 27 South African Air Force Squadrons to carry on the Middle East fight. On 1st August, at Downham Market, Norfolk, the number-plate of 608 Squadron was re-activated as a tribute, one feels, to the pre-war Auxiliary volunteers.

94. Canadian-built Mosquito XX (B.20).

The de Havilland Mosquito Mk.XX (B.20) built in Canada was the squadron's new machine and the role was for light-bomber work in No. 8 (Pathfinder) Group, with Wing Commander W. W. G. Scott as C.O. The Air Officer Commanding, Air Vice-Marshal Don Bennett (who had led the first Hudson formation across the Atlantic), called to meet the squadron and to brief them on their duties. Four nights later the first squadron machine attacked Wanne Eickel with four 500 lb bombs and, from the 10th August, Berlin was visited almost nightly with visits to Hanover, Frankfurt, and Hamburg, as alternatives. On 23rd August the Mosquitos left their 'cookies' at Cologne, Dusseldorf, Bremen, and Brunswick and on the 10th

November came the first DFC award to the re-formed unit; to Flying Officer N. D. Wilkinson. About this time a new commanding officer appeared in Wing Commander R. C. Alabaster and throughout the winter of 1944–5 the tempo quickened and every serviceable machine was hitting at targets mainly in Germany. On the night of 14th January, for example, crews returning after a visit to Berlin (when seventeen squadron aircraft went to the Nazi capital) reported that fires started on their previous visit were still burning. DFCs were promulgated for the previous C.O., Wing Commander W. W. G. Scott, and to Flight Lieutenants Stanbridge and Cummin, followed by a further five DFC awards to aircrew members on 22nd January.

Squadron Leader McArdle, one of the flight-commanders, using 'Gee' the navigational aid, bombed from 23/25,000 feet over Magdeburg, avoiding Luftwaffe night-fighters. Other crews went to Erfurt and Munich and on 2nd May the squadron's final offensive saw sixteen Mosquitos going to Kiel with 4,000 lb bombs; meeting with no opposition. Then, with VE Day parades and short-leaves over, the groundcrews were given Cook's Tours over Germany in Lancasters and, after a few ceremonial flypasts in various parts of Europe, the squadron aircraft were delivered to Upper Heyford, Oxfordshire, on 28th August, 1945, and a note in the diary ends with 'Good luck to the new 608 when it forms again.' A late award announced at this time was a Bar to the Distinguished Service Order for Wing Commander Alabaster, DSO, DFC and Bar, who had been in the pre-war RAF Volunteer Reserve and who had flown more than a hundred operational missions. Following this came yet another postscript to squadron history when the DSO was awarded to Flight Lieutenant R. J. Cook, DFC, DFM, another RAFVR airman.

In July 1946 – again at Thornaby – the new post-war 608 Auxiliary Squadron began to re-form, designated as a Mosquito light-bomber unit but, in the event, receiving the night-fighter NF.30 with Squadron Leader W. A. Brown, DFC (a 1938 squadron member), as Commanding Officer and with the Rt. Hon Viscount Swinton, PC, GBE, CH, MC, continuing his appointment as Honorary Air Commodore. In 1948 the squadron exchanged its Mosquitos for the Spitfires F.22, and parted company with most of the navigators, although a few retained a link in other capacities. During 1950 Squadron Leader F. A. Robinson, DFC, RAF, who had flown with 17 and 92 Squadrons post-war, assumed command and the de Havilland Vampire F.3 jet fighters were received, followed in 1952 by the Vampire FB.5 and with Squadron Leader G. A. Martin, DFC, AFC, RAF, as C.O., formerly the training officer with 614 (County of Glamorgan) Squadron and with a splendid war record as a fighter-pilot.

Summer camps were successfully held at Manston, Thorney Island, Ta Kali (Malta) Gibraltar and Tangmere. In 1955 Squadron Leader H. D. Costain, RAF, became the Commanding Officer, having been with the squadron earlier on training duties from 1953 and having served with 615 (County of Surrey) Squadron in SE. Asia in the latter stages of World War II. The arrival of a Vampire

95. Vampire FB.5 at Church Fenton, August 1956.

FB.9 seemed to cancel out the rumours of the Royal Auxiliary Air Force's impending disbandment but, regrettably, in March 1957, along with the other squadrons, No. 608 ceased to exist. The members came together again, briefly, at Middleton St George in November 1959 when The Standard, approved by The Queen, was presented by Air Vice-Marshal G. H. Ambler, one of the founder-members, in the presence of Group Captain G. Shaw, DFC, President of the Squadron Association, and other former officers and airmen. The Standard was later laid-up in York Minster.

As access to post-war files is not yet permitted, it is difficult to list what has happened to many of the men who made the North Riding Squadron one of Coastal Command's great units and then a powerful member of the Pathfinder Force. We do know that Wing Commander Peter Hutchings, DFC, AFC, remained in the post-war Royal Air Force until 1958, farmed for a time, and then returned to flying as a civilian instructor in Shropshire. Wing Commander R. C. Alabaster, DSO and Bar, DFC and Bar, joined BOAC, and rose to become Captain (Senior 1st Class) and later Flight Manager of the Comets, proudly wearing his Pathfinder Badge on his BOAC uniform.

96. Captain R. C. Alabaster, DSO, DFC.

As this is written, at least two ex-members have reached air rank in the RAF: Air Vice-Marshal G. H. Ambler, CB, CBE, AFC, now retired, and Air Vice-Marshal John Downey, DFC, AFC, who has held many high appointments since the war and who captained the Avro Lincoln 'Aries III' on a global flight of 29,000 miles in 1949, during which records were broken.

As this chapter is being written news comes that on the old Thornaby airfield a pub has been built and named *The Spitfire*, honouring, one feels, the post-war North Riding Squadron.

So far no evidence has come to light of a wartime 608 machine being in existence, although there have been rumours that one of two Mosquitos Mk.B.20 at present in North America flew with 608 from Downham Market. To date no example of the Lockheed Hudson is displayed in England and if and when one is secured, many will feel it should wear the colours of the North Riding Squadron. The author would be most grateful for news of any squadron aircraft still in existence – anywhere in the world, flying or non-flying.

REPRESENTATIVE SQUADRON AIRCRAFT

Avro 504N		
Westland Wapiti		J9868 J9871 K1324
Hawker Demon	I	K4508 K4533 K8193 K8210
Anson	I	N5204
Blackburn Botha	I	L6164 L6165 L6166 L6170 L6173 L6209
Bristol Blenheim	I	K7120 L6693 V5572 (M.IV)
Lockheed Hudson	V	AE642 AM629
de Havilland		
Mosquito	B.20	KB212 KB242 KB265 KB358
	B.25	KB400 KB413 KB438 KB441
	B.XVI	PF483 PF505 RV360
	NF.30	NT373 RAO–A NT471 D NT548 B NT609 C
	T.3	VA866 K VA888 L VP351 P LR555 R
Airspeed Oxford	I	X6737 M HM604 N PH393 O PH514 M
Vickers-Supermarine		PK 337 A PK651 B PK665 G
Spitfire	F.22	PK671 K
Harvard	IIb	FT457 N KF772 R FX207 T
de Havilland Vampire	F.3	VF316 6T–A VF319 6T–E VF322 6T–G VF346 6T–R
	FB.5	VZ178 A WA203 C WA365 D VZ321 F
Gloster Meteor (1950–57)	T.7	WA671 6T–O, then O.WF820 U WH223 P

It is believed that the squadron's Demons carried the code letters PG and that these were briefly used on the first Ansons which, on outbreak of war, changed to OY, the squadron code for the remainder of the war, though the Bothas may have used UL.

Post-war in Reserve Command the code letters were RAO, changed later to 6T. When the Vampires arrived squadron insignia was introduced and it is said that 608 may have tried more variations than other RAuxAF units. A rectangle either side of the tail-boom's roundels was divided diagonally by a pale blue-green line, the upper segment being red and the lower segment blue. The badge was also carried on the Vampire nose. Combinations of blue, silver, blue and black are thought also to have been used in the Vampire era.

Badge: A falcon's leg, erased, belled and fessed. This indicated the squadron's readiness to fight in the air, attacking tooth and nail.

Motto (translated): 'With all talons'.

609
(West Riding of Yorkshire)
Squadron

IT WAS AT Yeadon, half-way between Leeds and Ilkley, where No. 609 Squadron came into being on 10th February, 1936, as part of the expanding Auxiliary Air Force, with Squadron Leader Harald Peake, MA, of the Yorkshire Dragoons Yeomanry, as the first commanding officer. Flight Lieutenant N. C. Odbert was appointed adjutant and flying instructor and early volunteers included Flight Lieutenant the Earl of Lincoln, Dr T. McM. Boyle and Messrs S. G. Beaumont, W. Hamble, P. R. Nickols, D. Persse-Joynt, and P. Drummond-Hay. Three Avro Tutors arrived for initial training, followed by Hawker Harts, and on the first anniversary of the squadron's formation, a celebration dinner was held at the Hotel Metropole, Leeds, with many distinguished guests in attendance.

On 31st July, 1937, the squadron left for its first annual camp at Manston, Kent, the twelve Auxiliary officers and ninety-three Auxiliary airmen including Messrs A. R. Edge, B. W. Little, J. C. Gilbert, P. H. Barran, J. Rylands, and G. Robinson – the latest of the part-time entrants. The Rt. Hon the Earl of Harewood accepted the invitation to become Honorary Air Commodore, and in time for the 1938 summer camp, at Thorney Island, Hampshire, newcomers J. C. Dundas and G. E. Moberley strengthened the unit. In November, Squadron Leader G. H. Ambler became C.O., and Pilot Officer D. M. Crook was commissioned as a trainee-pilot. On 8th December the squadron role was changed from bomber to fighter and during the 1939 camp, held at RAF Church Fenton, south of Tadcaster, the members were embodied into the Royal Air Force and on 27th August left for Catterick. Spitfires Mk.I serials L1081 to L1088 arrived from the Vickers-Supermarine factory at Eastleigh, followed by eight others from RAF Shawbury, Shropshire.

Co-operation with the Whitley bombers based at Dishforth helped aircrews to understand the problems of combat and evasive action. Then came a move to Drem, south of Edinburgh, from where vital convoy escort patrols were flown, before a move even further north to Kinloss, Morayshire, to protect the shipping lanes into Scottish ports. On Christmas Eve, 1939, Squadron Leader Ambler was promoted and became Wing Commander, Operations Controller at Wick, Squadron Leader M. T. Avent taking command of the squadron. On 7th January, 1940, came excitement when Flying Officer Russell had to bale out from Spitfire L1064 over Crook of Alves, following engine failure. A North American Harvard trainer was flown in so that new pilots could be brought to operational standard and then – on 29th January – a page of history was written as Red Section of three aircraft, during practice flying – were ordered to intercept an enemy aircraft which was bombing a trawler at the mouth of the River Tay.

97. The Earl of Harewood, Sqdn Ldr Peake and others inspect Yeadon, 1936.

98. Tutors and Harts, inspection by Air Commodore Quinnell, 1938.

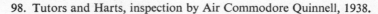

The bomber, an He.111, was sighted at a range of 400 yards and the squadron pilots opened fire almost immediately with the Heinkel's rear-gunner replying as the enemy made for clouds and disappeared. No claim was made but a few hours later Wick reported that a Heinkel had tried to land there and was, in fact, forced to put down, riddled with machine-gun bullets. The crew admitted it was the Spitfires which had damaged it so badly that it was compelled to turn back after making out to sea. First blood to 609, and it was a tonic indeed. On 27th February Red Section again scored a success after relieving Yellow Section over 'Alice', a convoy near St Abbs Head. Again a lone Heinkel was trapped in the cross-fire of Flight Lieutenant Persse-Joynt, Flying Officer G. D. Ayre, and Pilot Officer J. R. Buchanan – the enemy crew taking to their rubber boat as the Heinkel fell into the sea.

99. Sqdn Ldr Ambler scrambled, Kinloss, 1939.

In March the squadron moved to Grangemouth to defend the Royal Navy base at Rosyth and the Forth Bridge – already a target for the Luftwaffe. Then on 19th May – as the Nazis poured into France towards Paris – the squadron was instructed to fly down to Northolt in Middlesex, to help cover the British Army's retreat to Calais and Dunkirk, the Spitfires often penetrating far inland, too high for our desperate soldiers to see the RAF's valiant contribution to their evacuation. Squadron reports for this period are very confused and many enemy aircraft brought down are not credited to 609 although we do now know that, over Dunkirk on 30th May, Flying Officer Ayre was badly shot-up and that in making a forced-landing, near Harwich, Essex, he lost his life. The next day, with the Defiants of 264 Squadron and Hurricanes of 111 Squadron, the West Riding pilots had a field day with six enemy claimed destroyed and three others seriously damaged. Unfortunately Flight Lieutenant Persse-Joynt and Flying Officer J. C. Gilbert did not return; Sergeant Bennett, also reported missing, was later learned to be in Leavesden Hospital, Hertfordshire, having been picked up from the sea.

1st June saw the award of the DFC to Flying Officer I. B. N. Russell but delight soon turned to dismay when this officer – and

Flying Officer Dawson – failed to return from a later patrol. During this sortie a Messerschmitt Bf.110 was claimed shot-down and two Heinkels damaged. Mr Churchill and Mr Anthony Eden were escorted to and from France as they tried to persuade the French to fight on. Then, after 609 with the remnants of three other squadrons had made up the Gravesend Wing, to cover the final evacuations from the beaches which saved so many men to fight again, 609 was ordered to sweep the French airfields formerly in use by the RAF, destroying any enemy machines they found at Abbeville and Rouen-Boos. Incredibly they found none; for the Luftwaffe, it seemed, had returned to Germany to prepare for the invasion of England.

As Squadron Leader Avent moved away to become Senior Controller at St Eval, Cornwall, Squadron Leader H. S. Darley, an RAF officer of great experience, came in as C.O. On 6th July the squadron was moved to Middle Wallop, Hampshire, and then on to Warmwell, Dorset, in the newly-created No. 10 (Fighter) Group, responsible for the defence of SW England. Raids against Royal Naval bases began on 9th July and as Green Section intercepted Ju.87 dive-bombers escorted by Bf.109/110 fighters over Portland, Flying Officer D. M. Crook destroyed a Ju.87 Stuka and a Messerschmitt Bf.110 was shot down by others of 609 Squadron. Unfortunately Flying Officer Peter Drummond-Hay did not come back from this patrol. Next day, 10th July, the Battle of Britain officially began, but 609 Squadron had to wait until the early morning of 11th July when the 'Readiness' Flight of six Spitfires was ordered off to combat an attack on a South Coast convoy.

Three Spitfires took on the Junkers 87 force, the other trio endeavouring to hold off the Messerschmitt escorts. Flight Lieutenant P. H. Barran and Pilot Officer G. T. M. Mitchell did not return from this engagement and although it is believed they were in combat, it is not known if they scored successes before being brought down. On Saturday 13th July the convoy 'Bread' was sailing west near Lyme Bay when Flying Officer J. C. Dundas and Pilot Officer R. F. G. Miller sighted a Messerschmitt 110 fighter-bomber which Dundas attacked and damaged. A Do.17 was also attacked by Miller and by Hurricanes of 238 Squadron and was claimed as damaged. On the 18th a Ju.88 was shot down near Swanage by Flight Lieutenant F. J. Howell, Flying Officer A. R. Edge and Sergeant A. N. Feary but both Howell and Edge suffered from accurate return fire and Howell had to bale out from his Spitfire to be picked up from the sea by the Navy. Edge force-landed his machine near Studland and was unhurt when taken off by the Navy, the Spitfire being repaired later. During this engagement a second Ju.88 was attacked by Flying Officer J. D. Bisdee and Pilot Officer C. N. Overton and, from intercepted Luftwaffe sources, it was learned that it crashed on landing in France.

On 19th July both Dundas and Miller were in combat but no enemy aircraft were confirmed and the squadron diary reveals that pilots were experiencing considerable difficulty in obtaining their meals at the odd hours occasioned by 'Readiness' and other states of preparedness for action. A complaint was entered in the Officers' Mess suggestions book and the Station Commander replied 'I commanded a fighter squadron and *we* always had our meals at regular times'! It does not say if he was ever in action or if his command was limited to peacetime and, as though the chaps had not enough to complain about, they were flying in an area where the Royal Navy's trigger-happy gunners fired first and admitted their mistakes later! Happily a fairly quiet few days now followed and this enabled the squadron to train a small band of Polish and American pilots; the three from U.S.A. including Pilot Officer V. C. 'Shorty' Keogh, former professional parachutist, only 4 feet 10 inches, reckoned possibly the smallest of all Battle of Britain pilots. His companions were Pilot Officers A. Mamedoff and E. Q. Tobin; all the newcomers, Polish and American, were keen to get into the fight against the enemy.

100. The first American volunteers: P/Os Mamedoff, Keogh, and Tobin.

8th August saw the allied convoy 'Peewit', twenty merchantmen with escort ships, endeavouring to pass through the English Channel without engagement but the Luftwaffe sent every available dive-bomber and fighter to bomb the ships. Between the Needles and Weymouth 609 Squadron found the enemy and although the convoy lost most of its vessels sunk or damaged, Squadron Leader Darley, Flight Lieutenant J. H. G. McArthur and Pilot Officer M. J. Appleby all returned victorious, with McArthur destroying a Ju.87b and damaging a second, Appleby shooting down a Bf.110 and the C.O. damaging another Bf.110. No damage was inflicted on squadron machines and on the 11th, when the Luftwaffe approached Portland, morale was extremely high as the Spitfires left Warmwell. At a height of 23,000 feet Squadron Leader Darley headed for the enemy's fighter-bombers and within minutes Pilot Officer N. le C. Agazarian had shot down Major Ott who was leading the Bf.110 formation from ZG 2 (Zerstörergeschwader 2) part of Luftflotte 3. Flying Officers Bisdee and Dundas and Pilot Officer Crook of A Flight, following Flight Lieutenant McArthur, added four more Bf.110s to Noel Agazarian's success and the squadron landed without loss although Dundas had slight damage to his Spitfire from an escorting Bf.109 which failed to bring down our machine. Having taken on up to eighty Messerschmitts which they helped to rout, the squadron earned high praise from the Air Officer Commanding.

The next day, near Portsmouth, A Flight again flew straight into a force of fighters and fighter-bombers and Pilot Officer D. M. Crook scored a double-kill when he shot down two Bf.109s near the Needles, one pilot being killed, the other rescued from the sea. Several other Bf.109s and 110s were claimed destroyed or damaged but the true figure cannot be determined, though Luftwaffe records show that at least five of their aircraft were written-off during attempts to land damaged machines. Tuesday 13th August, unbeknown at the time to the Royal Air Force, was Hitler's 'Eagle Day' (Adler Tag) when the Luftwaffe began the final onslaught on RAF airfields and radar stations as a preliminary to the landings planned for the invasion of England. The morning weather was poor but in the afternoon a large force of Ju.87s was detailed to wipe out Middle Wallop airfield. The Spitfires of 609 were ordered off from Warmwell at tea-time and, over Lyme Bay, caught about forty of the dive-bombers, some of which had missed finding Middle Wallop and had been searching in vain for Warmwell. The Messerschmitt 109 escort, low on petrol, had begun to turn for home and 609 swept down on the luckless Stukas, destroying four, credited to Flying Officers Dundas and H. McD. Goodwin, Pilot Officers Miller and M. E. Staples and Sergeant Feary. Pilot Officer Crook got another Bf.109 and Flying Officer T. Nowierski, one of the newly-arrived Poles, destroyed one Bf.109 and damaged another. It was 'a fabulous performance', to quote contemporary reports, for not an aircraft or pilot was hit in the squadron's triumph.

Next day, the Commanding General of Luftflotte 3, Generalfeldmarschall Hugo Sperrle, probably at the direct order of Goering, sent a series of smaller bombing missions to try again and, unluckily for the RAF, some bombers did get through the defensive screen: three He.111s scoring direct hits on 609's hangar and squadron headquarters. Three of the squadron's airmen tried to shut the hangar doors as protection but were killed by bombs which brought the doors down upon the brave men. Flying Officer Dundas and Pilot Officer Crook managed to take off during the attack, and, attacking the leading Heinkel, the navigating aircraft, shot it down. In the wreckage were the bodies of the Geschwaderkommodore of KG 55 (Kampfgeschwader), with KG 55's navigation specialist and a passenger, later known to be the Chief of Staff of Luftgau VIII. It was a real blow to the enemy, especially as a second Heinkel of KG.55 crashed at its base with considerable loss of morale in the unit.

Next day the air fighting was mainly in the North East of England but a mixed force attempted a further attack on Middle Wallop and five of the raiders were either shot into the sea or limped back very badly damaged. Meantime all the vital equipment was moved from the bombed hangar and although unexploded bombs lay beside Spitfires and spares there were so many volunteers from the West Riding groundcrews that lots had to be drawn for the privilege of risking their lives to get the squadron at full strength for the next patrol. On 16th August, with the squadron's old chums from No. 249 Squadron, Church Fenton, coming into Boscombe Down, 609 were rested and on this day Fighter Command's only VC was gained by Flight Lieutenant J. B. Nicolson, who had transferred at Church Fenton from 72 to 249 and who lost his life after gaining the DFC in Burma leading 27 Squadron's Beaufighters as a Wing Commander.

On Saturday 24th August one of the Americans, Pilot Officer Mamedoff, tangled with Messerschmitt 109s over the Isle of Wight and was brought down, happily uninjured, though his Spitfire was destroyed. The next day almost three hundred enemy raiders were reported by radar and Observer Corps watchers as they approached Weymouth, the huge force splitting up with the intention of hitting naval bases and the airfield at Warmwell. Squadron Leader Darley's men pursued the force heading for Warmwell and only a few bombers got through to hit hangars and the medical officer's building. Five of the fighter-bombers and three of the escorting fighters fell to 609's guns and although two Spitfires received hits, both pilots landed safely. The month of August ended with a note in the diary: 'Under Squadron Leader Darley's quietly firm and competent leadership the squadron is gaining steadily in skill and confidence, remaining a veritable "Band of Brothers" not confined to pilots but reciprocally shared by the ground staff.'

For a few days the Luftwaffe concentrated on the Essex, Kent, and Surrey approaches to London, giving 609 pilots a respite until, on 7th September, came a call to reinforce No. 11(F) Group area. Flight Lieutenant James McArthur, acting C.O., led the squadron as the enemy bombers left London by the south-west route to the Cherbourg area. The squadron claimed a dozen machines destroyed or damaged but post-war analysis reduces this to six confirmed, five bombers and a fighter, for no loss except damage to one Spitfire. Again there was a few days of inactivity for the squadron pilots until, on Sunday 15th September, the squadron fought over South London. Four Dorniers were attacked with success, one falling near where Queen Wilhelmina of the Netherlands was staying, her personal congratulations being sent to Pilot Officer A. K. Ogilvie, the victorious pilot. Another piece of Dornier landed close to a Pimlico pub, the onlookers standing outside with glasses raised to the 609 aircraft. Pilot Officer G. N. Gaunt, alas, fell to the return fire from one Dornier as he attacked but in the afternoon two more Dorniers were caught near Rye, Sussex. Scrutiny of 609's combat-films revealing that one Luftwaffe airman baled out before our pilot opened fire, the squadron line-book noted 'He must have spotted the squadron code-letters'. The Chief of the Air Staff sent a 'Well Done' signal.

101. Squadron Spitfire in the Imperial War Museum.

On 24th September the squadron claimed victories above Swanage, including what was described as a 'Morane' though it could have been a Henschel Hs.126b which the Luftwaffe admit as being 'damaged in landing'. Enemy attempts to wipe out the aircraft factories near Southampton and Bristol involved 609 in a succession of engagements in company with No. 238 Squadron and several bombers and fighters were shared with the Hurricanes. The three American pilots left to help form the first 'Eagle' Squadron, No. 71 (RAF) coming into being at Church Fenton. On 27th September, Pilot Officer R. F. G. Miller, who had brought down a Ju.87 and was showing great promise, lost his life when he collided with a Bf.110 near Weymouth. Five other Messerschmitts were claimed and Sir Stanley White of the Bristol Aeroplane Company sent his thanks for the squadron's timely defence of the Filton factories. The Secretary of State for Air and the AOC-in-C. Fighter Command also sent signals of congratulation; and sympathy at the loss of Pilot Officer Miller.

On 30th September the squadron was scrambled to defend London but almost immediately diverted to the coast and over the Needles caught up with sixty enemy aircraft making for their bases. Three were shot down and two damaged. At tea-time, over Swanage, about a hundred enemy were sighted but only a few gave battle, three combats being recorded, with one enemy destroyed and two claimed as damaged. Pilot Officer Agazarian detached himself to chase a lone Heinkel of KG 55, the crew being picked up from the sea by a Luftwaffe Air Rescue Heinkel seaplane. On 4th October Squadron Leader Darley was promoted to command RAF Exeter, and when the award of the Distinguished Service Order was announced for his leadership he modestly said that it was really an award for all the pilots, and for the ground personnel too. Every member of the squadron, though, felt that the decoration was more than deserved. In, to command, came Squadron Leader Michael Lister-Robinson, formerly with 601 (County of London) Auxiliary Squadron and 238 Squadron, both Hurricane units. The new C.O. quickly acquainted himself with the Spitfire, a type he had not flown before and, to replace tour-expired pilots, in came two Poles from 234 Squadron, Pilot Officers Zurakowski and Olenski.

On 7th October about fifty enemy planes approached Portland Naval Base and the squadron caught them between the coast and Yeovil, claiming four destroyed or damaged, the new C.O. getting two Bf.110s. On the 9th came awards of the Distinguished Flying Cross to Flight Lieutenant McArthur, Flight Lieutenant F. J. Howell and Flying Officer J. C. Dundas. On the 15th a new-style hit-and-run foray by Messerschmitt 109s carrying bombs, stepped-up from 16,000 to 30,000 feet, attacked Southampton, 609 getting three of several machines brought down. On the 18th, Pilot Officers David M. Crook and J. Curchin, who had helped swell the squadron tally since July, were awarded DFCs. On 21st October there was an historic encounter when a Ju.88 on a mission against the Gloster Aircraft Works at Brockworth and Old Sarum airfield, Wiltshire, fell to the guns of Flight Lieutenant Howell and Pilot Officer S. J. Hill who happened to be airborne on a training exercise. From the wreckage of the bomber a piece of swastika-emblazoned rudder was retained by 609 Squadron to mark this, their hundredth claim.

On 27th October Pilot Officer P. A. Baillon engaged an unidentified machine in poor visibility, seeing his fire going home but as the stricken aircraft made for cloud-cover the rear-gunner hit the Spitfire, causing Baillon to parachute to safety. 29th October saw a gathering of 'The Century Club' at Middle Wallop with many V.I.P. guests including Air Chief Marshal Sir Arthur Barrett who had commanded the RAF in France 1939/40 and Air Vice-Marshal Sir Quintin Brand, AOC No. 10(F) Group, a famous South African aviator. Members of Nos. 238 and 604 (County of Middlesex) Auxiliary Squadron joined in applauding 609's fine achievement. In November Pilot Officer D. M. Crook, DFC, left for the Central Flying School to instruct (and to write his famous *Spitfire Squadron*, a classic story of 609's Battle of Britain combats). Marshal of the RAF Viscount Trenchard came to talk to personnel and the announcement was made of a DFC for the C.O., for his claims with 601, 238 and 609 Squadrons. Squadron Leader Lister-Robinson was the owner of several light aircraft and Pilot Officer Crook delighted the squadron with his flight in the C.O.'s 45 m.p.h. Drone which was followed by a Puss Moth and a 'Robinsonian' – a glider with an engine, two of these machines being coded 'PR-?' and 'PR-!' The artist Cuthbert Orde came to paint the decorated pilots and the press turned up to publicise the West Riding airmen's activities for Yorkshire and London newspapers.

102. Dundas versus Wieck – an artist's impression.

27th November saw a typical 609 action when, due to poor visibility, the squadron was refused permission to take off after a Ju.88 which the radar plotters picked up going along the coast. Newly-promoted Flight Lieutenant Dundas then sought approval to do some local practice-flying. He took off immediately consent was given and overhauled the enemy bomber over Cherbourg, shooting it down near a field full of Bf.109s. He turned for base; to face the Sector Controller's wrath and to submit his claim. Next day, though, Dundas, the last pre-war Auxiliary pilot of the squadron, radioed that he had shot down a Bf.109; after which there was a silence. Pilot Officer Baillon, out with Dundas, also failed to land. It was later admitted by the Luftwaffe that their Ace Messerschmitt pilot Major Wieck, had fallen to the guns of Dundas who, was, in turn, brought down, with Baillon, by other 109s. So was lost this brilliant member of the 'Yorkshire Post' team; a specialist in European affairs and product of Stowe and Oxford. (On 24th December a Bar to his DFC, for which he had been recommended before his death, was promulgated in the *London Gazette*).

On 2nd December, Agazarian and Nowierski brought down a Bf.110 and a Do.17 near Thorney Island, the DFC was awarded to Flying Officer Nowierski for this and his earlier combats. Flight Lieutenant F. J. Howell, DFC, was promoted to command No. 118 Squadron which was re-forming at Filton, and after a quiet January, a practice formation during February spotted a Ju.88 and chased and damaged it as it disappeared into cloud, making for France. The diary records at this time that the quality of the food improved; coinciding with the visit of the RAF's Inspector-General! On 24th February came the long-awaited move back into No. 11(F) Group and, at Biggin Hill, Kent, the Spitfires Mk.II of No. 66 Squadron were taken over from pilots who then left for No. 10(F) Group, taking 609's aeroplanes. At this time Flight Lieutenant Paul Richey, DFC, a top-scoring pilot in France who had spent most of the summer of 1940 in hospital, joined the squadron as flight-commander to replace Squadron Leader Howell.

On 26th February there began for the squadron the first of many successful offensive sorties into Occupied Europe in fulfilment of Churchill's orders that the Nazis were to be harried wherever they could be found. From now on very few days elapsed when at least a couple of the West Riding pilots were not hitting Luftwaffe aircraft on their airfields or shooting-up other targets. In April the squadron was strengthened by Belgian pilots who had joined the RAF after escaping from the enemy via Spain and other hazardous routes; some had suffered tortures at the hands of Spanish police which had given them additional reasons for wanting to get into the fight against tyranny.

Noël Coward and Beatrice Lillie provided a welcome entertainment for the men and this was followed by the Prime Minister's visit from his home at nearby Westerham. Losses were now inevitable, as most pilots brought down were almost certain to be taken prisoner, though a few did manage to evade capture, thanks to the brave patriots who hid and later returned them via Gibraltar. On 8th May, 1941, a remarkable incident was noted in the records, for the RAF

Air-Sea Rescue launch was approaching a Luftwaffe dinghy in the Channel when a flight of 109s dived down and drove the launch off. It seemed obvious that the enemy did not wish the occupant to fall into British hands. Luckily 609 was airborne at this time and when vectored to the spot, destroyed the Bf.109 flight and damaged three of another formation, for the loss of one Spitfire (the pilot was saved from the sea). What happened to the German in the dinghy is not revealed, but in the mêlée it is possible an enemy craft took the dinghy and occupant under its wing.

103. Airmen at Biggin Hill, 1941.

Wing Commander 'Sailor' Malan was leading the Biggin Hill Wing comprising his old squadron, No. 74 'Tiger', with 92 and 609, and the tally of victories mounted slowly during escorts flown to our daylight bombing missions. On 21st May Pilot Officer Count de Grunne did not return from accompanying Blenheims of No. 2(B) Group against Bethune Oil Refinery. He had flown 109s in the Spanish Civil War, then Hurricanes with No. 32 Squadron, after getting to England in 1940, and after destroying one Messerschmitt, had been shot down and burned, going later to Lisbon on a top-secret mission to get details of French and German bases in North Africa. Thus was lost the first 609 Belgian and his countrymen were determined to take their revenge particularly when, on 27th May, the Spitfire Mk.Vb arrived – then the most powerful aircraft in Fighter Command. During June, on 'Roadstead' sorties against enemy shipping targets, the squadron had a total of 14 destroyed, 5 probably-destroyed and 7 damaged Luftwaffe machines for the loss of three pilots including Flight Lieutenant J. Curchin, DFC (who had been credited with eight enemy in 1940) and Pilot Officer S. J. Hill, DFC.

One of the Belgians, Pilot Officer V. M. M. Ortmans, introduced to the squadron a mascot in the shape of William the goat, fed by Ortmans with a child's feeding-bottle in the early stages. Who then could have realised the heights to which Acting Pilot Officer William Goat would rise! The July total of enemy aircraft was 13, with 19 either damaged or probably destroyed. It is of interest to remember that 609's claims were regarded as most modest in official eyes, probably due to Squadron Intelligence Officer Flight Lieutenant Frank Ziegler being a stickler for confirmatory evidence: as one pilot remarked at this period 'If you brought back lava from Vesuvius on your flying boots Frank would want to see the outline of the Pope's autograph in the dust!'

A spate of well-earned decorations was now announced with the DSO and the Belgian Croix-de-Guerre for Squadron Leader Lister-Robinson; DFCs to Flight Lieutenant Bisdee and Flying Officer Ogilvie, a Bar to Paul Richey's DFC, and two DFMs and five Belgian Croix-de-Guerre awards to other successful pilots. On 4th July, Lord Haw-Haw radioed that Flying Officer Ogilvie, missing, was safe and a prisoner of war. As the C.O. left to become the Wing Leader, in came Squadron Leader 'Sheep' Gilroy, DFC, pre-war 603 (City of Edinburgh) Auxiliary and, of course, a farmer. Three of the squadron's pilots shot down over the Channel were rescued in one month and one fortunate pilot, picked up by the Navy, returned with a bottle, stowed safely in his borrowed clothing – a little 'consolation' for earlier attacks on our aircraft by Naval gunners.

The August tally was sixteen enemy aircraft destroyed or damaged again for loss of three pilots, all being replaced by more Belgians. Squadron Leader Richey left to command No. 74 Squadron and in September, with the score down to five destroyed or damaged, a DFC came for Flying Officer V. Ortmans (twice rescued from the 'drink') and a DFM for Sergeant Rigler. The introduction of the Focke-Wulf 190 by the Luftwaffe hit some squadrons hard but 609 pilots were not dismayed and in October seven enemy machines fell to their guns, though Flying Officer Ortmans, DFC, went missing and Sergeant Palmer, DFM, failing to return, was believed killed. When Air Commodore HRH the Duke of Kent paid a call his Aide was the former C.O., now Wing Commander M. Lister-Robinson, but he soon wangled a move from his 'mahogany fighter' desk-job and returned to flying to lead the Tangmere Wing. The month ended with Squadron Leader Gilroy getting two Bf.109s in the same sortie and November's score was six destroyed and damaged, with the loss of Sergeant Laing, a Canadian, later known to be a prisoner. Air Commodore Harald Peake, the first squadron commander, came to present the badge approved by the King; its motto 'Tally Ho' being most appropriate.

19th November saw the squadron moving out to Digby, Lincolnshire, William Goat making the trip by Harrow transport aircraft. Convoy patrols were now the drill and the monotony of these was enlivened by the good news that Flying Officer Vicky Ortmans was safe and a prisoner; also that Pilot Officer Nitelet, another Belgian, missing since 9th August, had evaded capture and was back in London, having journeyed via Brussels (where he visited his mother), Paris, Spain, and Gibraltar.

The year 1942 opened with 'Rhubarbs' over Holland. The Belgian Croix-de-Guerre came to Squadron Leader Gilroy but the genuine delight of the Belgian pilots was short-lived, for Flight Lieutenant 'Pykker' Offenburg lost his life. The diary read: 'So departed one of the kindest, nicest, best and bravest pilots.' On 12th February the squadron was alerted to move first to Biggin Hill, then to rendezvous over Southend where, in atrocious visibility, they shot down two Dorniers near the battleships *Scharnhorst* and *Gneisenau* which, with their escorts, were making their way to Germany from Brest.

In March the two flight-commanders, Flight Lieutenants D. V. C. Cotes-Preedy and 'The Duke' Monceau, DFC, led sorties in support of our light-bombers of No. 2(B) Group, on one occasion shooting down an FW.190, with four others left damaged. At the end of the month there was a move to Duxford, Cambridgeshire, with A Flight detached to Coltishall, Norfolk. Then on 18th April came the news that the squadron was to get the Hawker Typhoon, with the other Duxford unit, No. 56 Squadron, the first to be so-equipped and a tremendous honour for an Auxiliary Squadron. In May, as Squadron Leader Gilroy left, with Bar to his DFC, Paul Richey returned to command, and a well-deserved British Empire Medal was given to Flight Sergeant Abraham, one of the founder-members of the squadron. On 29th June, another milestone as Flight Lieutenant Roland Beamont, DFC, reported as flight-commander, a member of 87 Squadron in France in 1940 and later a test-pilot for the Hawker Aircraft Company. The diary note read 'By many he is regarded as an anachronism – he ought either to be dead or a wing commander'.

As this is written, in April 1972, Wing Commander Beamont is, happily, very much alive, and so one can only assume that it was his own interpretation of regulations which delayed his promotion in the 1940s. It was on 19th July, 1942, that the squadron's Typhoons made their first sweep, uneventful according to the diary, and although the Dieppe landings in mid-August engaged many other fighters, Matlaske was too far away to be concerned and it was 18th September before orders came for a return to Biggin Hill. Wing Commander Paul Richey, on promotion, left, taking with him, to fly as his No. 2, Belgian Flying Officer Christian Ortmans. Both flew in Burma, Richey being invalided home and Ortmans, flying with

615 (County of Surrey), was forced down but made his way to allied lines. It was Squadron Leader 'Roly' Beamont, more often called 'Bea', at last promoted, who took command and a more popular choice could not have been made. But soon after this appointment, Pilot Officer Dopere, a Belgian who had been tortured in Spain en route to freedom, was killed in an accident, tragically never ever achieving his ambition to have a combat with the enemy.

In November the squadron was moved to Manston, Kent, for operations and was joined by young Pilot Officer J. R. Baldwin, RAFVR, who had served as a groundcrew airman in France and on bomb-disposal during the rest of 1940 before going to the U.S.A. for aircrew training. The 'shooting season' opened with Beamont destroying a locomotive and, in December, an impressive list of successes including four FW.190s, with six others left damaged, plus a Ju.88 shot down. Ground targets included eighteen locomotives destroyed or disabled, much rolling stock left ablaze and a tug reduced to firewood. So low did squadron pilots fly to avoid detection by enemy radar that one aircraft returned with a fish in the radiator – in the beak of a seagull!

January of 1943 was a turning-point in the story of the Typhoon; rushed into RAF service ahead of time and before some of the teething troubles had been ironed-out. Hated by many Spitfire pilots, consistently attacked by our own fighters in mistake for the FW.190 (because in flight the 'Tiffie' radiator scoop gave the impression of a radial engine) and constantly fired-on by our own Ack Ack. It was largely due to Bea Beamont and some pilots of 609 that Fighter Command retained this tough, fast, and inelegant fighter when (in the words of Flight Lieutenant Ziegler) 'most pilots except the C.O. would have exchanged their Typhoons for Spitfires with a whoop of joy!' Bea Beamont had helped with production tests of the Typhoon during a rest from operations and he it was who had to convince his superiors that it should not be withdrawn from squadron service. Underwings were painted black and white like a zebra crossing, screaming 'Friendly' at the ground gunners and Spitfires; yet pilots were still brought down, and one gunnery officer following some sharp words over the telephone by Frank Ziegler actually replied 'Could you ask your pilots, tactfully, did we get anywhere near them?' One pilot, brought down by friendly fire really 'blew his top' when the coastguards addressed him in German as he waded ashore from his submerged Typhoon. The great radiator scoop soon plunged the heavy machine to the bottom and what with having to watch for Spitfires as well as the Luftwaffe, then avoid our Army and Navy guns, plus balloons, and at the same time watch engine temperatures of the 2,200 h.p. Napiers, it took all of Beamont's powers of leadership to maintain morale.

He had his own ways, for, provided the job of defending the

coast from Ramsgate to Dungeness against hit-and-run low-level raiders was accomplished, the Air Officer Commanding No. 11 Group promised him a free hand to attack enemy communications and Bea caused downright astonishment by demonstrating that the Typhoon could be used in Occupied Europe *by night* – particularly for 'train-busting' missions. 20th January will always be remembered by those servicemen and civilians who witnessed the events, as a pointer to eventual victory, for on that day Flight Lieutenant Baron de Selys Longchamps, a former cavalry officer, known as Jean, who got to England via Dunkirk and learned to fly at the ripe age of 29, took off on an unauthorised sortie – one which Fighter Command Headquarters had considered and rejected as impracticable. After blowing up a train near Bruges he told his No. 2 to return to base whilst he set off alone for Brussels. He had never seen his native city from the air and, after flying over his old barracks, he dived down on Gestapo Headquarters, raking the building's windows with cannon-fire and then, pushing open his cockpit-hood, he threw out a large Union Jack and the Belgian flag, following with hundreds of minia-ture flags as he tore across the countryside on his way back. Eye-witnesses later told of the cheering crowds and the stopped trams – and of the thirty casualties suffered by the Gestapo.

Jean was ordered to appear before the Air Officer Commanding and was 'carpeted' and reduced to the rank of flying officer. Shortly afterwards, though, a DFC was announced for the brave Belgian. As he was staging his one-man war over Brussels, the Luftwaffe also decided to put on a daylight hit-and-run against London. Ordered to intercept, the seven serviceable Typhoons roared off in pursuit and, over Margate, Flying Officer Baldwin shot down three Bf.109Gs, the latest Messerschmitt fighter in production. Three more enemy, FW.190s, fell to the guns of other pilots and a seventh enemy machine was claimed as damaged. Beamont got a Bar to his DFC, 'Johnny' Baldwin the first DFC to the squadron since 1941. It transpired, during 'Ziegly's' interrogations, that Flying Officer Lallemand, another Belgian with fellow-countryman Pilot Officer Van Lierde, and Pilot Officer Joe Atkinson (British) should all be credited with the three aircraft not shot down by Baldwin. One Luftwaffe pilot who fell to Baldwin's accurate fire presented him with his Mae West and another, also taken prisoner, gave Baldwin a clasp-knife. Neither pilot had heard of the Typhoon and one had called it a 'Vultee Vanguard'; the other thought he had met a Mustang!

On 14th February the squadron gave the Luftwaffe a Valentine by destroying seven FW.190s and damaging locos, barges, and a motor torpedo boat in addition. Baldwin was rescued from the Channel during March, and a Red Letter Day was the destruction of a Ju.52 transport at Chievres as it was taking off loaded, the squadron hoped, with high-ranking Nazis. A DFC was awarded to

Flying Officer Lallemand and on 17th April the hundredth train destroyed or damaged was logged. In May, Beamont came to the end of his second operational tour and to take over from the man who had put the once-despised Typhoon on the map, in came Squadron Leader Alec Ingle, AFC, a Battle of Britain pilot in 605 (County of Warwick) Squadron after a long spell of instructing. Things seemed against the new C.O., for the AOC, Air Vice-Marshal 'Dingbat' Saunders, a South African-born soldier who won the Military Medal in the ranks before getting the DFC and Bar in the Royal Flying Corps, came to tell Ingle that 609 had flown more hours per engine-change than any other 11 Group squadron and that because of engine shortages the squadron would be rationed to 300 flying hours a month. Alec Ingle then asked for – and got – bombs; supervising the provision of an improvised bomb-sight for the Typhoons. The first bomb to be dropped was covered in savings-stamps donated by RAF Manston and squadron personnel, and was dropped on a Luftwaffe hangar by Flying Officer Van Lierde during a dusk sortie. His excellent night vision spotted an He.111 in the circuit of this airfield and he smartly turned and shot it down. Squadron Leader Ingle then began to plan missions against enemy shipping, soon nicknamed 'Ingle's Tours of the Dutch Islands'. Four Typhoons carrying bombs followed four firing their cannons, the C.O. and Norwegian Flight Lieutenant Erik Haabjoern leading, the Norwegian no stranger to shipping in European waters.

104. Typhoon takes off from Manston with 'stamped' bombs, 1943.

These low-level operations were not without great risk and on one occasion Ingle landed at Manston with his Typhoon on fire; surprised at surviving the last minutes of his flight. On another, Haabjoern returned from Holland riddled by flak, belly-landing with not a drop of oil left but able to report five German vessels damaged near Flushing. Then on 19th May as the squadron machines

were coming in to land after a night intruder project, one of the aircraft being assisted down by searchlights looked somehow different.
Flight Lieutenant 'Johnny' Wells and Van Lierde suddenly realised
that it was not a Typhoon but a Focke-Wulf 190, and jumping in
to the C.O.'s car they reached the enemy machine as it stopped, with
its engine still running. Squadron Leader Ingle pointed his finger at
the Luftwaffe pilot (no officer having his revolver with him at the
time) and yelled 'hands up'. The pilot obediently switched off and
climbed out. He was bundled into the car and taken to the Intelligence
Officer, the German saying he thought he was at St Omer, having
mistaken the Thames Estuary for the English Channel! It was a
splendid present for the Air Ministry.

   On 1st June came another enemy hit-and-run, this time against
the Kent coast with Margate and Broadstairs coming under Luftwaffe fire as twelve or more FW.190s attacked. Flight Lieutenant
Wells, despite having his aircraft hit by our own Ack Ack, found
himself in the middle of an enemy formation heading back to sea,
the FW.190s seeming not to notice the stranger in their midst. Dropping back, Wells shot down one of the leaders and then, as the others
realised what was happening, he destroyed another 190 before doing
a steep climbing turn, watching the formation pass beneath him as
he made for base. At the same time, Flying Officer Davies, seeing
the enemy gunning the streets of Broadstairs after setting fire to
Margate's gasometer, chased five 190s between the house-tops, seeing
one pilot bale out from his crippled aircraft. Flying out to sea,
behind the formation now heading for Belgium, Davies shot down a

105. The squadron at Manston, 1943.
Bea Beamont second from left in doorway.

second aircraft into the waters, saving his remaining ammunition for defensive action – but with Ostend looming up – finished his combat with a burst into a third aircraft which promptly caught fire and hit the sea. Only then did some of the enemy turn on him, but it was too late and Davies outstripped them and soon landed back at Manston.

Squadron records say that this devastating success – five destroyed by two pilots for no loss – ended the Luftwaffe's mass daylight hit-and-run sorties and that afterwards they only came in small numbers. Thus the main purpose of the Typhoon fighter was vindicated and in late July the squadron was moved to rest at Matlaske having lost three pilots during that month of continuing offensives. Immediately on landing in Norfolk, though, permission was sought for more attacks against Luftwaffe airfields and two Bf.109s were destroyed, one hitting the ground without the Typhoon pilot opening fire. On 1st August Alec Ingle was awarded the DFC for his magnificent leadership and left on promotion as Wing Commander Flying, No. 124 Airfield, later becoming a prisoner of war. It seemed impossible that the squadron should again get a leader of top calibre (to quote Frank Ziegler's fascinating 609 records) but it happened when Squadron Leader Pat Thornton-Brown straightaway showed that he possessed all the qualities necessary (he had flown Hurricanes in 263 Squadron in the Battle of Britain).

Moving back to Lympne, Kent, in August, the squadron was quickly in action when the C.O., with Flight Lieutenant Baldwin, paid a visit to St Leger, France, there destroying two FW.190s to the obvious dismay of watching Luftwaffe personnel. On the last day of August, Pilot Officer Detal (Belgian) and Flying Officer Readhill (Canadian) proved that the Typhoon could go even further and at Laon, near the Swiss border, destroyed a Ju.52 and a Bf.110

106. Flt Lt Baldwin, Sqdn Ldr Wells, and P/O Evans (Canada), 1943.

on the aerodrome, seriously damaging two other machines as well as shooting-up a lorry and a nearby locomotive. Only two pairs of long-range tanks had been issued to the squadron and they were certainly being well-used. Air Marshal Sir Roderic Hill, incoming Commander-in-Chief of Fighter Command (re-named Air Defence of Great Britain from November 1943 to October 1944), came to hear the views of pilots on the operation of long-range sorties to catch the Luftwaffe napping at bases far beyond Paris. September, though, became the month of air-sea rescue sorties as the allies staged a fake invasion which, regrettably, did not draw the Luftwaffe from their airfields.

In October the squadron returned to attacks on Occupied Europe and on the 4th a remarkable performance by four of the pilots led by Flight Lieutenant Baldwin (the others were de Moulin, Geertz and Henrion). Far into Europe the quartet attacked and destroyed or damaged no less than four locos, three supply barges, a tug, two radio towers, a gasometer and three enemy aircraft in the air after the Luftwaffe had despatched no fewer than 24 Bf.109s to bring down the Typhoon pilots. It was a dramatic moment for it brought the squadron's score of aircraft claimed to 199 and a sweepstake was at once started for the pilot who got the 200th victory. In the event it was a man who was to make history in more ways than this. Accompanied by Pilot Officer Artie Ross, an American who refused to transfer to the United States Air Force despite higher pay, Pilot Officer 'Pinky' Stark, an Englishman, led the way to Soissons where a nearby Luftwaffe base had eight Messerschmitt 110 fighter-bombers neatly parked in tidy rows. One burst into flames on Stark's first burst and another broke into pieces as Ross also fired. German air-men rushed for shelter as their flak opened up, far too late, for the Typhoons were after other targets. A Ju.88 had been sighted, flying probably into or from this airfield, and Stark's first burst set the starboard engine ablaze as the second followed and hit the port motor. As the Junkers crashed into a wood an airman was seen to bale out and Stark's Typhoon caught the tops of the same trees, landing back at base with a quantity of illegally-imported timber aboard.

Van Lierde, who had taken off on another mission, also landed with a Ju.88 claimed destroyed in the air and another one shot up on its airfield. The times were carefully checked and Pinky Stark was credited with the 200th success by some twenty minutes. It was almost three years since the 100th victory and, of course, the occasion for an enormous party – the AOC wisely putting the squadron at 'released' – his message adding 'until such time as the C.O. decides it is capable of taking off again!' The aircraft, meantime, were being fitted with projectile-rails for rockets with 60 lb warheads and on 16th October, acting on a tip radioed in from the French underground, the Typhoons combed France in search of Von Runstedt's mobile headquarters – a private train. It was not at any of the places quoted by the patriots and the pilots had to be content with three enemy aircraft, a gasholder, two tugs and a dock-crane. In November attacks were directed against 'Noball' sites, the launching-platforms for what we later knew as the V.1 flying-bomb, hidden away in forests facing the coastline of England. As the aircraft returned they shot up enemy troops on parade-grounds and any other targets of opportunity they sighted.

Then came the posting-out of Flight Lieutenant Baldwin, to be promoted as C.O. of No. 198 'sister' squadron of Typhoons, the regrets being softened by the thought that he would be leading his new team alongside 609. On 4th December, just before dusk, the squadron sent five Typhoons to Holland and encountered a complete Geschwader of Do.217 bombers about to take off for a night raid on England. Seven of them fell to the guns of 609, and 198 (flying from Manston) caught another four, which left Eindhoven airfield littered with smouldering wreckage – a very severe blow to the morale of that Luftwaffe establishment. On 14th December the squadron moved from Lympne to join 198 at Manston and on the 21st the war's most senseless act robbed the squadron of a beloved C.O. The Typhoons were escorting a contingent of USAAF Marauder light-bombers, in company with Spitfires, a well-organised operation proceeding very smoothly until, for no acceptable reason, a squadron of USAAF Thunderbolts dived down, destroying Squadron Leader Pat Thornton-Brown's Typhoon and that of Flying Officer Miller, along with three of the Spitfires. Thus died a defenceless man who had led the squadron for all too short a time, but who had made his unforgettable mark. It was typical that Pat's last words over the radio-telephone were concern for Miller and not for himself. A few days later came the announcement of a DFC, for which Pat had, of course, been recommended before his untimely death, for this is not one of the very few decorations which can be awarded posthumously.

Flight Lieutenant Johnny Wells, DFC, with the squadron since May 1942 was promoted to take command, and all were delighted to learn of a Bar to the DFC for Squadron Leader Baldwin of 198, partly for his combats with 609 before promotion. The pilots were determined to make up for the tragic losses of the C.O. and Flying Officer Miller (a Canadian) and put all they could into an attack on the blockade-runner *Munsterland* off Boulogne, the five Typhoons coming back riddled with flak-holes. 'Every man,' said Squadron Leader Wells, 'deserved a VC for pressing-home such an attack in face of such blistering fire.' On 4th January, 1944, the squadron paid a call on Gilze-Rijen airfield between Breda and Tilburg in Holland, just as the Luftwaffe bombers were engaged in their NFT (night flying training). Before the base knew what had hit it, four Dorniers had fallen out of the skies, three more were ablaze on the ground and a Ju.88 was also destroyed where it stood. One Typhoon did not return but the pilot managed to get away from the area before crashing and later returned to the U.K., through the bravery of Dutch, Belgian and French patriots.

107. 'United Nations' *Left to right:* Ken Laing (Canada), Maurice Choron (France), 'Cheval' Lallemand (Belgium), Joe Atkinson (Great Britain).

During that month the pilots were 'shaken' when a civilian called to collect a Typhoon for return to the Hawker factory. Wearing an old overcoat and without a parachute the pilot took off quite unconcernedly: it was Jim Mollison, famous airman, flying with the Air Transport Auxiliary and not always wearing their uniform. A week later Pilot Officer Stark, with Pilot Officer Detal, flew to Brussels and there intercepted an all-silver Bf.110 (obviously a special aircraft, perhaps flown by a V.I.P.). Following its destruction they shot down a Bf.109 and then got a Caudron Goeland transport on the ground. Squadron aircraft were now equipped with both the 16 mm and 35 mm cameras and some interesting and funny films were obtained. In one, a peasant, complete with his horse, could be seen throwing his hat in the air with joy as he danced jubilantly; the smoke of five enemy aircraft destroyed on the ground at Roye-Creil in the background. A DFC came for newly-promoted Flying Officer Detal and Air Chief Marshal Sir Trafford Leigh-Mallory, Air Commander-in-Chief of the Allied Expeditionary Air Force now hardening-up under canvas in SE. England, called to thank the squadron for 'putting the Typhoon squarely on the RAF map'.

In March the squadron was moved into No. 84 Group of the 2nd Tactical Air Force, as part of No. 123 Airfield, spending some time at Acklington, Northumberland, and Fairwood Common near Swansea, for dive-bombing training and to demonstrate their abilities to General Eisenhower. By May, from Thorney Island, Hampshire, they were hitting enemy installations in preparation for allied landings, under the control of Group Captain D. E. Gillam (former C.O. 615 'Churchill's Own' County of Surrey Squadron). Pounding Rommel's headquarters the squadron suffered the loss of five aircraft in one sortie, so low did they go in to try and wipe out the key figures on the other side. As Squadron Leader Baldwin left 198 on promotion to a Wing Commander Flying post, Flight Lieutenant Davies of 609 moved over to command 198, with a DFC for his 609 work. On 5th June the squadron swept the Normandy coast hitting every gun to be found and the next morning – D-Day – they patrolled far into France keeping Nazi reinforcements away from the beaches, hitting tanks and troop-trains moving up to the front. On 14th June another page was turned as 609 landed in France to refuel, returning with souvenirs for those back at base (Funtington, a temporary airstrip near Chichester) including flowers picked from beside the Continental airstrip, for the Belgian and French members who did not fly on this mission.

Then came support operations to American forces attacking Cherbourg during which – on 22nd June – the C.O. 198, Squadron Leader Davies, DFC, one of 609's great warriors, lost his life. Two days later, on departure of Squadron Leader Wells, Squadron Leader Manu Geerts a Belgian, took command of 609. On 1st July the squadron moved into B.10 airfield, Plumetot, with 129 Airfield, and began intensive operations in face of fanatical enemy resistance. 'Group Captain' Goat, rapidly-promoted, was flown over and spent some time in slit trenches, to the disgust of those who had to throw themselves into the trenches when flak opened up on the British airstrip. The squadron then moved on to B.5 at Cammily, then to B.7 at Martragny, receiving a signal of thanks from HQs Army Group for the Typhoons' devastating rocket attack when about a hundred tanks of the Panzer Regiment were strafed at Vimoutiers, extricating the Polish Armoured Brigade from a rather ticklish situation. During the Falaise Gap battles the squadron flew 461 individual sorties claiming 42 tanks and 88 other transports disabled or destroyed – five more pilots were lost in achieving these successes. A DFC came for Pilot Officer Merrett and then, after eleven weeks' absence, in walked Warrant Officer G. Martin who, on D-Day, had broken his leg on the tail of his aircraft during a bale-out from near ground level after being hit by flak. He had landed successfully, though in great pain, and he swam five hundred yards down a canal but could not raise the strength to climb out. He was saved by a child who fetched the village priest. He was taken by horse and cart to the shelter of a patriot's house and when the Gestapo raided the premises he was passed off as a deaf and dumb bombed-out relative!

Squadron Leader R. A. Lallemand, long-serving Belgian, now assumed command but on 14th September, the squadron having moved into B.23 airfield at Morainville, for the liberation of Belgium; the new C.O. had to belly-land his Typhoon after flak-damage and was badly burned, after which he was evacuated to the U.K. for emergency treatment. Squadron Leader T. Y. Wallace, DFM, a South African, took over, leading the missions in support of the Arnhem drops from B.53 at Merville, an old Luftwaffe base with concrete runways and a few unblitzed billets. At this period a mongrel pup, acquired in Kent, faced a Selection Board and was 'commissioned' as Pilot Officer Blitz, being given permission to sleep on the adjutant's bed – to the adjutant's annoyance! Visits into Brussels were organised and the members of 609 rather puzzled the city's Mayor by suggesting that the famous statue of the little boy should be clothed in a pilot officer's best-blue uniform – the worthy dignitary failing utterly to see the point.

By November the squadron was at B.67, Ursel, Belgium and the Walcheren landings were covered. Over Dunkirk, where a hard-core of Nazis were holding-out defiantly, Squadron Leader Wallace's aircraft was hit by flak. Squadron Leader Chas de Moulin, DFC, became C.O., a pilot who, escaping to England in 1940, joined 609 as an Aircraftman 2nd Class, sweeping the squadron offices under an NCO who was still with the squadron, in the very same rank. This airman was diplomatically moved elsewhere as 609 moved into Holland and flew from B.77 Gilze-Rijen (a former target for the Typhoons) now cleared of Dornier and Junkers' wreckage. General Eisenhower called in person to express his thanks to the squadron members for their wonderful help to the American forces and as he left the squadron took off and hit oil storage tanks in Northern Holland, Squadron Leader de Moulin being hit and having to bale out. Squadron Leader E. R. A. Roberts, DFC, then took command and low-level strikes were made with considerable success against midget submarines off the Dutch coast. Christmas Day was properly commemorated by the traditional waiting-upon of airmen by officers and ended with a 609 favourite, the implanting of footprints on the mess ceiling by pilots supported by an unsteady pyramid of comrades.

With the unexpected thrust by the Nazis into the Ardennes the squadron was moved to an American airfield, A.84, at Chievres, then on to Y.32, but bad weather held up operations. Wing Commander Dring, the Wing's leader, took off to see for himself but, on landing, swung off the runway and was killed; a sad loss for he had led the Typhoon Wing since before D-Day. Flight Lieutenant Mason left on promotion to command 183 Squadron and in February, as the weather slowly improved, long-range sorties ranging across Germany saw a trail of disabled enemy vehicles left littering the roads and fields. From B.91 at Kluis Nigmegen it was only possible to fly on 18 days of March but 269 sorties were made and, once again, the C.O., Squadron Leader Roberts, was lost and two others with him, but news came later that they had been seen standing beside their crashed machines near Berlin and were probably prisoners of war. Squadron Leader Pinky Stark, DFC, destroyer of the 200th enemy aircraft, became C.O., and led the squadron as it helped the British Army over the Rhine, knocking out flak-posts and, according to official records, ensuring that very many soldiers' lives were saved. Allied gliders in particular had a very easy passage, thanks to 609's vigilance.

In April the squadron base was at B.103, Plantlunne, Germany, from where trains evacuating Nazi troops were well and truly plastered. At the beginning of May there was a feeling of anti-climax, the final operations being flown against Heliogland barges on 4th May and after a quiet meditative VE Day, the officers and NCOs produced a magnificent party on 9th May at Groningen, for their ground personnel, moving back into Holland for this one evening due to the 'No Frat' rule in Germany. The Dutch girls could not have been more grateful for the invitations to the dance and the arrival of the all-WAAF Gang Show set the seal on a month in which victory was at last achieved in Europe. To the joy of all, Squadron Leader Lallemand, DFC and Bar, recovered from his burns and now commanding No. 349 (Belgian) Squadron, came to visit, as did former C.O. Squadron Leader Manu Geerts and an old-timer, Flight Lieutenant Ogilvie, DFC, a prisoner of war since January 1941 and now en route from Germany to England. A Bar to his DFC was promulgated for Squadron Leader Stark; and DFCs for flight commanders Flight Lieutenants King and Inches. To mark the happy ending of hostilities, Group Captain Goat was promoted to Air Commodore!

After a short sojourn at B.116, Wunstorf, for the impressive Victory fly-past over Germany and Denmark, the squadron moved to Fairwood Common, South Wales, via Lasham, to demonstrate to the Army's 'top brass' the possibilities of using rockets – and Typhoons – against the Japanese. A DFC came for Flying Officer Harkness and then the squadron moved back to Wunstorf where, on 15th September, 1945, appropriately Battle of Britain Day, news came that the squadron was to disband so as to be able to re-form as part of the post-war Auxiliary Air Force in Yorkshire. The diary showed that 3 DSOs, 22 DFCs and Bars, 4 DFMs and many other decorations had been awarded to squadron members – some promulgated after pilots had been promoted to other units. That the squadron was first to claim 100 victories with Spitfires and first to get 50 with the Typhoon, and to end up as the highest-scoring 'Tiffie' outfit with 247 victories, were some of 609's boasts. The final war entry in the diary reads: 'We hand on to those who begin anew a West Riding Squadron of Auxiliary airmen. Peace has taken the place of war; the squadron has ended its travels in search of Nazis and now returns to Yeadon. "TALLY HO." '

108. Squadron and Mosquito, Tangmere camp, 1947.

In May 1946 the volunteers began to gather again at Yeadon and in July the de Havilland Mosquito NF.30 was received for 609 to serve as a night-fighter unit under Squadron Leader P. A. Womersley, DFC and Bar, formerly pre-war 609, then 59, 200, and 18 Squadrons. The Rt. Hon the Earl of Harewood, KG, GCVO, DSO, TD, resumed as Honorary Air Commodore and on his death, one-time C.O., Air Vice-Marshal G. H. Ambler, CB, CBE, AFC, assumed the office. In April 1948 the squadron changed to the Spitfire LF.XVIe and Squadron Leader A. Hudson, DFC, ex-295 and 570 Squadrons, took command. Summer camps were held at Tangmere, Manston, and Thorney Island, then at Chivenor, Devon, Malta, Celle and Sylt in Germany. In 1951/1952 the Gloster Meteor jet fighter was received and in 1953 Squadron Leader E. Evans, wartime Hurricane pilot with 32 Squadron, later with 691, 82, and 541 Squadrons, became C.O. In 1954 the coveted Esher Trophy was gained for all-round efficiency.

In June 1955 Wing Commander Bea Beamont, DSO and Bar, OBE, DFC and Bar, DFC (USA), ARAeS (better-known post-war as 'Roly') came to open the Royal Auxiliary Air Force Town Headquarters in Leeds, and in February of 1956 Squadron Leader David Shaw, formerly of the Leeds University Air Squadron, who had instructed in South Africa and had joined the RAuxAF in 1951, assumed command of the squadron until 609 Squadron had to disband in March of 1957, at RAF Church Fenton. Thanks to the efforts of Squadron Leader Shaw of Bramhope, and Flight Lieutenant S. H. 'Darky' Hanson, MBE, of Leeds, former members have gathered together again since 1964, especially for the unveiling of a commemorative plaque at Yeadon Airport in 1968. Squadron souvenirs are held mainly at RAF Church Fenton and maybe some will go on show at the Royal Air Force Museum at Hendon.

Of those who served – in the air and on the ground – between 1936–45 and 1946–57, a full-length book could (and ought to) be written. To select just a few, who can deny that Bea Beamont merits a high place – his faith in the Typhoon, his post-war triumphs in the Canberra and Lightning; he was the first English pilot and aircraft to fly at Mach 2 (twice the speed of sound) and his great work with the ill-fated but magnificent TSR.2 ensure that his name will ever live in British aviation annals. Did any squadron produce more 'scrambled egg' types (officers of group captain and above)? We think of Air Vice-Marshal G. H. Ambler, and of Air Commodore A. M. Ruston, CBE, DFC, who joined 609 as an airman while still at Leeds Grammar School in 1936 and who entered the RAF College in 1938, later flying Sunderland and Catalina flying-boats over Norway, the Mediterranean and SE. Asia; of Group Captains H. S. Darley, Sheep Gilroy, J. C. Wells, Johnny Baldwin (killed in Korea while on exchange posting with USAF) and Alex Ingle (who was one of 'The Few' to walk in Churchill's funeral procession); of Wing Commanders Paul Richey and Michael Lister-Robinson (killed in 1942 leading a Spitfire Wing); of Colonel R. A. Lallemand a leading Belgian Air Force jet pilot of post-war; and of Squadron Leader Tom Rigler, DFC, DFM, who rose from the ranks in 609 to command No. 603 (City of Edinburgh) Auxiliary Squadron in early 1945. Let us not forget the loyal groundcrews, including the already-mentioned Darky Hanson who was one of the originals and who rejoined in 1946; of Sergeants Geoffrey Walker and Eric Ingle, also originals, and Sergeants Olaf Priestley, John Payne, Robert Walling, Douglas Andrews and Harry Simpson. Or Corporal

109. Mosquito 'prang', Yeadon, 1947.

Bernard Walker, said to be the last Auxiliary, and Corporal Roland Walker of the Orderly Room. No squadron was ever better-served by its airmen, said Bea Beamont, and every C.O. before and after him surely says 'Amen' to that.

Fortunately for posterity there are a few aircraft preserved which have a 609 association, although the Spitfire Mk.V at Church Fenton painted in 609's code-letters was never with the squadron, and one hopes that in time a genuine 609 machine may stand there or at Yeadon as a tribute to the West Riding airmen. The authentic surviving machines are as listed below, for enthusiasts to see: Imperial War Museum SE.1 – Spitfire Mk.I R6915 of Battle of Britain. RAF Bicester (for static exhibitions) Spitfire Mk.1 PR–F X4590 of 1940. RAF Henlow (ex-Leconfield) Spitfire XVI RW382, ex 609 Church Fenton. RAF Henlow (maybe for RAF Museum, Hendon) Meteor 8 WH301 (but in 85 Squadron markings). Let us hope that other 609 aircraft will be displayed throughout the country when the Royal Air Force Museum has decided upon a display. The Typhoon (the world's only example) recovered from the U.S.A. may perhaps be painted as a Bea Beamont machine? Let us hope so.

In the limited space in a book of this type only a fraction of the many aircraft flown by 609 can be mentioned and to pilots and fitters, riggers, armourers, searching for the aircraft they flew or serviced I express sincere regrets that all cannot be included. The squadron songs, though, can be shared by all and these, I'm told, are the words:

SQUADRON SONG (Tune 'Eton Boating Song' approx!)

1. We're the 609th West Riding Squadron, occasional Air Force are we;
We only fly Saturdays and Sundays, when the hard-working regulars are free.
And if ever you've landed a Meteor, then you know just how fast they can roll;
When you roll 'em and land 'em and roll 'em,
Tally Ho 609, Tally Ho.

REFRAIN: Oh we'll roll 'em and land 'em and roll 'em,
Mach descents when the weather is fine;
Oh we'll roll 'em and land 'em and roll 'em
Tally Ho, Tally Ho, Six-o-nine.

2. On occasions we do some night flying, dusk landings can be rather fun:
But we really prefer to be flying, in 8/10ths blue sky and a sun.
As you'll know if you've landed a Meteor, that you're far better off when it's light;

For if Meteors are dicey by daylight they're a bl . . . sight dicier at night.

3. We're the beer-drinking working man's squadron, some say we just joined for the brass;
   But you'll never get rich on this squadron, whilst ever you've a hole in your ass.
   If you're thinking of flying a Meteor, and quietly making your pile;
   A rate A and day's pay are peanuts (Oh, and 3d 3 farthings a mile).

4. We've worn down a few Regular officers, long and lean, short and fat, big and small;
   They arrive knowing far less than nothing, and leave knowing less than . . . us all!
   But at least they have had the right training, they're sure they will reach the top shelf;
   For the biggest Brasshat in the business, was once an Auxiliary himself.

5. They've converted the Regulars to Hunters, those things that go faster than sound;
   They do forty minutes at fast speeds – and the next seven weeks on the ground.
   They get frightfully cross if one breaks one, you're too old when past twenty-nine;
   But to get some more b . . . . . s to fly some, they'll soon have to call six-o-nine.

6. Now one day you'll retire from the squadron, which has had the best years of your life;
   You'll have spent far more time in a Meteor, than at home in the arms of your wife;
   When you get your last notice of rating, and you're feeling like shooting a line;
   Just report where the bullsh lies the thickest, and you're bound to find old six-o-nine.

7. They've disbanded the 609th squadron; civilians now full-time are we;
   We'll try a Civvy Street weekend – with crumpet and butter for tea.
   When the Regulars are throwing a party, and bar-profits show a decline;
   If they're needing a hard-core of boozers – we'll be glad to send round six-o-nine.

LAST REFRAIN: Ohhhhhhhhhhhhhhhhhhhhhhhhhhh we'll roll 'em and
land 'em and roll 'em,
Mach descents when the weather is fine;
Ohhhhhhhhhhhhhhhhhhhhhhhhhhh we'll roll 'em and
land 'em and roll 'em
Tally Ho, Tally Ho, Six o-nine.

FLYING WING LAMENT (Tune 'Clementine')

1. There's a village, called Church Fenton, with two-five it's dead
in line;
Every Sunday in St Mary's, Vicar 'blesses' Six-o-nine.

REFRAIN: Oh my darlin, oh my darlin, oh my darlin Six-o-nine,
Th'art lost and gone forever, dreadful sorry, Six-o-nine.

2. Came on Saturday, stayed till Sunday, drank their bottles to
the dregs,
Playing dice and utt'ring cries of 'Never mind her skinny legs!'

3. It was oft heard up i't Tower, 'Dinger' Bell there in a haze;
Q.G.H.s with white faces, G.C.A.s that did amaze.

4. In the bar that Friday morning, it was closed, so cold and still;
Back came 'Darkie' with his toolkit – now we haven't got a
grille.

5. 'Horns' are blowing 'Gongs' are sounding, we remember all
the time,
Happy days with our third squadron, 'Tallyho' for Six-o-nine.

6. They've disbanded – left Church Fenton, but the bar will not
decline,
For the mess will still be haunted, by the ghosts of *Six-o-nine*.

REPRESENTATIVE SQUADRON AIRCRAFT

Avro Tutor		K3323 K3433 K6095
Hawker Hart		K3011 K3839 K3870
Hawker Hind		K5421 K5496 K6847 K6850
North American		
Harvard	I	P5865
Vickers-Suparmarine		
Spitfire	I	L1082 L1088 R6769 PR–D X4642
	IIa	P7305 P7734 P8235
	Vb	AB859 BL335 BL486
Hawker Typhoon	Ia	R7577 PR–A R7708 R7855
	Ib	JP851 PR–Q MN282 PD449 SW566

DH.98 Mosquito	NF.30	NT422 RAP–D NT568 RAP–B
		NT615
	T.3	VA883 VA926
Airspeed Oxford	I	MP449 RAP–Y
Vickers-Supermarine		
Spitfire	LF.16e	SL609 RAP–C (PR–C) TB294 TE477
Gloster Meteor	F.8	VZ501 K WA969 A WE969 WF645
		WF743

Throughout World War II the squadron carried the code letters PR on its Spitfires and Typhoons. Post-war, in Reserve Command the code was RAP but it reverted to PR on return to Fighter Command. With arrival of the Gloster Meteor the squadron wore its own insignia which comprised a blue rectangle each side of fuselage roundels with two yellow X's superimposed.

Badge: In front of two hunting horns in Saltire, a rose. The white rose was to show the connection with Yorkshire, the horns to indicate the squadron role.

Motto: 'Tally ho'.

610
(County of Chester)
Squadron

IT WAS AT Hooton Park, the old home of the Stanley family, between Birkenhead and Chester, that No. 610, one of three new Auxiliary Air Force squadrons, was formed on 10th February, 1936. As part of the expansion programme of the Royal Air Force at that time it was designated a light-bomber unit. Squadron Leader I. R. Parker was appointed to command with Flight Lieutenant J. A. C. Stratton as adjutant. A visit from Brigadier General Sir W. Bromley-Davenport, KCB, CMG, DSO, TD, Lord Lieutenant and President of the Cheshire Territorial and Air Force Association, was followed by the arrival of the first aircraft, an Avro Tutor and a few Hart bombers, On 29th October H.M. King Edward VIII approved a badge in the Chester colours of red and blue.

During the summer of 1937 the first annual camp was held at Hawkinge, Kent, after which it was unanimously decided to invite Sir William Bromley-Davenport to become the squadron's first Honorary Air Commodore. In May 1938 Hawker Hinds were received and during that summer the camp was at Abbotsinch, the home of No. 602 (City of Glasgow) Auxiliary Squadron. Then came the Munich crisis and at this time the nominal roll included Squadron Leader Parker, Flight Lieutenant T. F. U. Lang (adjutant and flying instructor), Flight Lieutenant B. J. Paul (assistant adjutant), Flying Officers G. M. T. Kerr, A. T. Smith, J. K. Wilson, E. B. B. Smith, A. R. J. Medcalf, D. S. Wilson; Pilot Officers M. C. Topham, G. L. Chambers, W. H. C. Warner, J. H. C. Albrecht, P. G. Lamb, C. R. Pritchard, P. J. Davies-Cooke, A. D. Graham, A. H. Graham, M. G. Pascallis, T. A. Mason and A. L. B. Raven.

On 19th January, 1939, the squadron was transferred into Fighter Command but it was not until the summer of 1939 that the Hind bombers were gradually replaced by the Hawker Hurricanes. During summer camp, again at Abbotsinch, Scotland, Squadron Leader Lang moved away on promotion, together with Squadron Leader B. J. Paul, the former to Headquarters No. 11 (Fighter) Group, Hillingdon, Uxbridge, Squadron Leader Paul to RAF Andover.

110. Hawker Hart of 610 Squadron.

111. Squadron's Fairey Battle at Abbotsinch, with Alfred Briston, 1938.

By 5th September, with the squadron embodied into the RAF, the squadron's Hurricanes were at war readiness but before they could see any action they were transferred to No. 605 (County of Warwick) Squadron and on 28th September the first Spitfires were flown in, to the joy of all. On 10th October the squadron was at Wittering, near Stamford, and it carried out its first operational patrol on the 21st, only to intercept a friendly machine. Moving over to Sutton Bridge, Lincolnshire, air-gunnery courses involved a useful liaison with No. 101 (Bomber) Squadron. In December Wing Commander I. R. Parker was promoted to command Royal Air Force, Digby, Lincolnshire; Squadron Leader A. L. Franks, AFC, a Royal Air Force officer, came in to command and patrols were flown from West Raynham and Bircham Newton, Norfolk, mainly to escort our convoys against occasional Luftwaffe raids.

112. AOC's Inspection. Sqdn Ldr Parker on AOC's right,
behind the C.O., Flt Lt Lang.

In April 1940 a move was made to Prestwick, Scotland, for intensive training and then, when the Nazis invaded the Low Countries, the squadron was ordered into Biggin Hill, Kent, nicknamed 'The Bump'. Then as the British Army withdrew from France and Biggin Hill's new runway became busy with incoming transports, the squadron was moved into Gravesend, taking off to patrol the Dunkirk area and beyond. On 27th May came the first recorded victories in the air when an He.111 bomber and six Messerschmitt Bf.110 fighter-bombers were engaged and either destroyed or seriously damaged. On the 29th four Bf.109 fighters were shot down but Squadron Leader Franks and Sergeant Jenkins had to bale out from their crippled Spitfires. The following day only six Spitfires were serviceable and they joined other Biggin Hill squadrons, with Flying Officer Medcalf and Sergeant Medway still missing from the encounter of 27th May.

On 31st May two Do.215 bombers were shot down but Flying Officer Chambers and Pilot Officer Keighley were hit by return fire; Keighley baled out into the Channel and was picked up by a trawler and taken to Ramsgate by the Royal Navy. Flight Lieutenant Ellis and Pilot Officer Litchfield, the successful combatants, were soon airborne again only to see a wing break off from Sergeant Wilson's Spitfire; luckily the pilot took to his parachute in time. As Flight Lieutenant John Ellis tried to attract the attention of a destroyer to the spot where Wilson was struggling in the sea, the Navy's guns almost blew Ellis out of the sky. On 4th June the squadron flew its last sortie over Dunkirk and then came welcome respites at Digby and Acklington, Northumberland.

Between 26th and 29th June Mr S. C. Bentley of de Havilland's came to Gravesend with an NCO and two fitters and they converted the Spitfires to constant-speed propellers to enable the squadron to match the opposing Bf.109s in performance. Sergeant-Pilots R. F. Hamlyn, P. Else and N. H. D. Ramsay had arrived and Squadron Leader A. T. Smith took over command. There were a few quiet days and then Flight Lieutenant Ellis and Sergeant Arnfield were scrambled and, flying at full-throttle, overtook and shot a lone raider into the sea off Margate.

It may not be generally known that even during the Dunkirk evacuation the RAF was carrying out offensive sorties far into Occupied Europe to hit Luftwaffe bases and 610 Squadron was escorting our Blenheim bombers during June with little or no enemy aircraft to be seen in the air. Not until 3rd July was a solitary Do.17 found over France – and shot down. Then, on 8th July, the airfighting increased. Over a convoy near Dover, Pilot Officer A. L. B. Raven was shot down into the sea and believed drowned, a Bf.109 being damaged in the fight. Next day a Do.17 was engaged and probably destroyed by the C.O. and Sergeant Parsons. On the 12th Sergeant Ireland lost his life during training when his Spitfire plunged into the ground but Pilot Officer Litchfield levelled the score on the 14th when he shot down a Bf.109 over a convoy. Tragically, Litchfield did not long survive his victory, for on 18th July he was brought down and killed by a formation of Bf.109s between Dover and Calais.

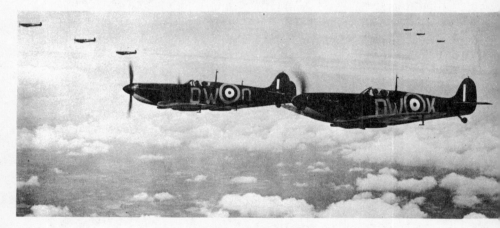

113. Battle of Britain, summer 1940.

On 20th July Pilot Officer G. Keighley baled out after a dog-fight near Canterbury and on the 24th a mixture of delight and dismay when Squadron Leader Smith, Flight Lieutenant Ellis and Sergeant Gardener destroyed three Bf.109s between Dover and Margate. Coming in to land his damaged aircraft at Hawkinge, Squadron Leader Smith stalled and was killed. Flight Lieutenant John Ellis was promoted to command, and next day between 6.45 p.m. and 7.0 p.m. with only seven Spitfires serviceable, two more Bf.109s were brought down; one by Sergeant Else, one shared by Squadron Leader Ellis and Flying Officer D. S. Wilson. John Ellis said of this engagement:

I was leading 610 Squadron, consisting of 7 aircraft, ordered to take off from Hawkinge at 1827 hours. While patrolling Dover we saw a destroyer being bombed 2 miles out to sea. I personally did not see the bombers but saw about 20 Bf.109s at 7,000 feet so I gave orders for the squadron to attack them. I attacked the last e/a [enemy aircraft] of one section and fired about half my ammunition at him at between 100 and 10 yards' range. I must have taken the section by surprise as they did not break up or adopt any evasive action except gentle turns. My target rolled over and plunged down towards the sea out of control. As I climbed into the clouds after the attack I saw a 109 hit the sea and believe that this was the one I attacked. After this I cruised around just in the cloud where it was possible to see clearly downwards. While doing this I sighted another section of 4 Bf.109s in line astern. I dived down below this section and carried out a climbing attack on the last e/a. I emptied the remainder of my ammunition into him at point-blank range and he fell out of the sky burning furiously as he hit the sea.

The squadron, in fact, claimed 5 destroyed and 3 damaged including what was thought then to be a captured Chance-Vought of the French Air Force, in use by the Luftwaffe. This would seem – from post-war research – to be an error of identification by a new pilot and as the enemy only show two 109s missing from this engagement, it is thought that one or two of the others limped back to French bases in varying stages of damage.

On 29th July a lone Dornier jettisoned its bombs into the Channel as 610 Squadron approached and although no shots were fired, some merchantman was probably spared disaster. Then came a break until Sunday 11th August when, on the Prime Minister's personal orders, He.59 ambulance seaplanes were attacked as it was known they were carrying out far more than their missions of mercy. Off Calais Flight Lieutenant Edward Smith shot one down, but unfortunately, escorting Messerschmitts, unseen until too late, shot down Sergeants J. H. Tanner and W. J. Neville, both of whom were killed. Early next morning two Bf.109s were shot down near New Romney, Kent, but Flight Lieutenant Edward Smith had to bale from his blazing machine, with serious burns; Sergeant B. G. D. Gardner was also wounded, one Spitfire being lost and four damaged, the other two pilots unhurt. Next day was a respite, but on the 14th Sergeant Gardner was again wounded and force-landed, his Spitfire being a write-off. Two Ju.87 dive-bombers were destroyed and a Bf.110

badly damaged (an He.113 was claimed in error on this sortie).

On 15th August the squadron was detailed to protect Biggin Hill from attack during the afternoon and the pilots were 'released' from operations in the morning. The Dorniers which set out for Biggin Hill bombed West Malling airfield in error and five bombers and fighters were claimed as destroyed by 610 Squadron, though some may also have been claimed by other units in the air. The following day, refuelling first at Hawkinge, a Ju.88 was claimed as damaged, one Bf.109 as destroyed and another damaged. Post-war examination of Luftwaffe archives shows that the Ju.88 may not have got back and that both 109s were, in fact, destroyed near Dungeness and their pilots taken prisoner: Flight Lieutenant W. H. C. Warner was lost in this action. On the 18th, the squadron earned the praise of the Air Officer Commanding by putting *fifteen* Spitfires into the air in formation and, between 1.00 p.m. and 2.00 p.m. between Sevenoaks and the Kent coast, waded into a mass of bombers and fighters approaching London. Two Do.17 bombers were shot down, with aid from Hurricanes, and other bombers and fighters damaged with no loss of aircraft or pilots to the squadron.

The Luftwaffe licked its wounds for a few days and then on 22nd August, in proceeding to drive the enemy away from our convoy code-named 'Totem', Sergeant D. F. Corfe was bounced by Bf.109s and crashed near Hawkinge unhurt, though the Spitfire was burned out. The convoy attack was, happily, frustrated. On the 24th three precious Spitfires were lost in the fierce battles over Kent and Essex, Pilot Officers D. McI. Gray and C. Merrick and Sergeant S. J. Arnfield suffering various wounds. Squadron claims of four destroyed and others damaged are not confirmed by post-war figures but 610's attacks doubtless enabled others to finish off damaged machines trying to get away. On Sunday 25th one Bf.109 was claimed destroyed and Pilot Officer F. T. Gardiner, wounded in this combat, was forced to crash-land at Sandwich, Kent, his Spitfire a write-off. So anxious were pilots to try and save their aircraft, even when crippled, that lives were sometimes lost, and on 26th Pilot Officer F. K. Webster died after vainly bringing his damaged Spitfire down at Hawkinge; the aircraft was totally destroyed. Sergeant Else also baled out seriously hurt and his Spitfire, too, was a complete loss after combats over Folkestone when five Messerschmitts were claimed – but one was later credited to No. 54 Squadron.

On Wednesday, 28th August, Pilot Officer C. O. J. Pegge and Sergeant R. F. Hamlyn scored victories off the Kent coast during enemy attacks on our radar stations but Pilot Officer H. F. Cox was killed by return fire and his aircraft lost. On the 29th, in a fierce engagement near Mayfield in Sussex, Sergeant E. Manton was killed, Flying Officer P. G. Lamb inflicting damage on a Bf.110. Sergeant A. C. Baker, who was also shot down, managed to land at what is now

Gatwick Airport, though his Spitfire was a useless wreck. A later sortie by the squadron added two more Bf.109s to the tally and the squadron was in excellent heart for the big battles of the 30th when over a hundred enemy machines were sighted heading for London. Sergeant Hamlyn was attacked by five Bf.109s but he managed to outwit them and claimed one as probably destroyed. He later dived down on a lone He.111 when out of ammunition and thought he saw the bomber hit the sea as it tried to take avoiding action. Sergeant H. H. Chandler destroyed a 109 over Biggin Hill at tea-time and Sergeant R. A. Beardsley also got in a good attack on another Bf.109. A Luftwaffe rear-gunner, captured after being shot down, was the guest of 610 Squadron and asked for his hosts' names and addresses so that he could keep in touch with them when they came to Germany as prisoners, so sure was he that Hitler's forces would be landing quite soon! Biggin Hill suffered badly this day from Ju.88 bombing when 610 Squadron was absent. Night came with orders for the squadron to prepare to move out but before the groundcrews could get packed to leave there was a further raid and four of 610's loyal airmen lost their lives. On the 31st the Spitfires flew up to Acklington, Northumberland, for the defence of Newcastle and NE. England. The one compensation was news that airmen were to get sixpence extra per day war pay!

114. Servicing at Biggin Hill, August 1940.

Patrols over the coastal convoys brought no action and it was welcome news that in mid-December the squadron would be returning to No. 11(F) Group area, this time to be based at Westhampnett (now Goodwood racing circuit) a satellite airfield to RAF Tangmere. The squadron began the escorting of our first daylight bombing raids of 1941 to targets in Occupied Belgium and France, joining Nos. 65 and 302 (Polish) Squadrons. Casualties rose; and pilots, if and when they baled out or managed to put their Spitfires down for emergency landings, were fortunate to evade early capture, though a few were lucky enough to get into the hands of patriots before the

Germans could reach the spot (some of these later made their way back to England via the Pyrenees and Spain, to return from Gibraltar to fly and fight again). 5th March, 1941, for example, cost the squadron three pilots missing and one killed during relentless offensives against Luftwaffe airfields and ground installations. The score of enemy aircraft shot down mounted very slowly although an He.111 was brought down during a rare night patrol by the C.O. A Ju.88 'milk-train' was damaged in an early morning encounter and after this Squadron Leader John Ellis, DFC, was posted away to instruct at No. 55 Operational Training Unit, as was Flight Lieutenant S. C. Norris, DFC. Into the squadron to command came Squadron Leader H. de C. A. Woodhouse, AFC, with Flight Lieutenant J. N. W. Farmer, DFC, the latter having flown during the Battle of Britain with No. 302 (Polish) Squadron.

Now flying 'Rhubarb' sorties against ground targets, transportation of all types, flak-posts, parked aircraft, etc., the squadron was part of the Tangmere Wing of Nos. 145, 610 and 616 (South Yorkshire) Squadrons, led by Wing Commander Douglas Bader, DSO, DFC. A fine record of claims was built-up on the squadron board though a sad moment came when, after Flight Lieutenant Farmer and his section brought down a Ju.88 off Portsmouth, Pilot Officer A. R. Ross was shot down by the despairing return fire of the Junker's air-gunner. Squadron Leader Woodhouse and Flight Lieutenant Gaze hit barges off Dieppe and Le Treport and, accompanied by Pilot Officer Stoop, the C.O. intercepted and shot down a Ju.88 off Brighton, two men baling-out before it hit the sea. Escorts to our own air-sea rescue Lysander aircraft and launches made breaks from the offensive patrols and half a dozen enemy aircraft were shot down during a spate of dusk attacks from the Luftwaffe fighter-bombers when 610 Squadron was detailed for 'Fighter Nights'.

When Squadron Leader Woodhouse left to take command of No. 71 (Eagle) Squadron (mainly American volunteers in the RAF) Squadron Leader Ken Holden, pre-war Auxiliary Air Force pilot, moved from 616 (South Yorkshire) Squadron at Westhampnett to become C.O., the squadron now being based at Tangmere. Flight Lieutenant Hamlyn, promoted and with a DFM for his 1940 successes, left to command a flight in No. 242 (Canadian) Squadron and into 610 as flight-commander came Flight Lieutenant Denis Crowley-Milling, DFC, a pre-war RAF Volunteer Reserve Sergeant-Pilot and Rolls-Royce engineering apprentice who had flown in France with 615 (County of Surrey) Squadron and in 242 Squadron with Bader during the Battle of Britain. At this time the squadron was re-equipped with the Spitfire IIb armed with two cannons and four machine-guns instead of the eight machine-guns of the Spitfire Ia and the Station Commander, Group Captain Woodall, paid 610 the compliment of flying with the Tangmere Wing using one of the squadron machines. On 9th August Wing Commander Bader was brought down over France, and in his place to lead the three squadrons came Wing Commander H. de C. A. Woodhouse, the former squadron commander.

During a great two-stage operation on 21st August, with thick cloud from 19,000 to 28,000 feet, enemy fighters jumped our Spitfires and Flight Lieutenant Crowley-Milling and three NCO-pilots did not return. Happily, news came through later that Denis Crowley-Milling had successfully evaded capture and, with the aid of the French Underground Movement, had reached Gibraltar after a terrible period in a Spanish prison during which he contracted typhoid. Awarded a well-earned Bar to his DFC for his 610 sorties and his escape from Occupied Territory, he was later posted to command No. 181, one of the first Typhoon fighter-bomber squadrons. With a move to Leconfield, Yorkshire, for a rest-period, Flight Lieutenants P. P. C. Barthropp, who had flown in 602 (City of Glasgow), and H. S. L. 'Cocky' Dundas, an Auxiliary of 616 (South Yorkshire) Squadron, both Battle of Britain veterans, joined the squadron. Squadron Leader B. J. Wicks, DFC, who had flown in 56 Squadron and had returned to England in 1940 after being shot down over enemy-held territory near Dunkirk, came in as C.O., when Ken Holden, awarded the DFC for his 616 and 610 combats, left for a staff appointment at No. 12(F) Group Headquarters (Ken Holden later commanded No. 64 Squadron and, after the war, his old unit, 616 [South Yorkshire] Squadron).

115. Squadron at Ludham, September 1942. F/O Brown, Lt Huinden, Lt P. A. Biat, P/O Watson, P/O Malton, P/O Jones, P/O Pearson, P/O Musgrove, P/O Sanderson, F/O Cameron, Sqdn Ldr Poggs, Sqdn Ldr Johnson, Flt Lt Collinge, P/O Smith, Flt Lt Watson, P/O Wright, Eng/O, Doc.

In November, after a busy period of escorts to our four-engined Stirling and Halifax bombers and the first Boeing B–17 Flying Fortresses (of No. 90 Squadron, RAF), a new C.O. arrived: Squadron Leader J. Pegge, DFC, and when he left for overseas in February 1942 he was replaced by Squadron Leader G. S. K. Haywood, with Flight Lieutenant R. N. H. 'Buck' Courtney as a flight-commander. The squadron moved to Hutton Cranswick, near Driffield, Yorkshire, and then into Ludham, north-east of Norwich, to fly anti-shipping operations against German vessels in Dutch waters, sometimes hitting the sea with their props as they tried to fly under the Nazi radar screen. The waving of Dutch fishermen was a tonic to both sides, as were the occasional victories when enemy aircraft put in an appearance. In June the squadron was ordered to West Malling, Kent, to act as close-escort to Hurribombers, and with 951 operational hours logged in this month the 'Spy' (Intelligence Officer) announced that a check on records showed that 610 Squadron had claimed 120 enemy aircraft destroyed, 40½ probably destroyed, and 37 damaged (these totals, of course, do not allow for the post-war research into Luftwaffe figures).

The next officer selected to command the squadron was Squadron Leader J. E. 'Johnnie' Johnson, DFC, who had flown briefly with 616 (South Yorkshire) Squadron in 1940 but due to an injured shoulder had no Battle of Britain combats, his first victory coming in early 1941 on his return from hospital. Group Captain HRH the Duke of Kent paid a welfare visit, and for 'Operation Jubilee', the Dieppe landings of 19th August, the squadron flew four sorties, squadron records noting that breakfast at 6.0 a.m. comprised egg and chips, unusual though much-appreciated fare. For some months the Spitfire Vb had given good service but in this month came the Vc version with the universal wing capable of carrying a 500 lb bomb in addition to normal cannon-machine-gun armament. During September the first Messerschmitt Me.210 fast-bomber was intercepted and destroyed as the squadron flew close escort to Flying Fortresses of the USAAF, on their way far into Germany, taking them to or meeting them at the limits of a Spitfire's fuel endurance.

15th October brought chilling news, a move to Castletown, an airfield on the northernmost shores of Scotland, facing the Orkney Islands and close to John O'Groats. There were some compensations in the form of warm billets, a modern camp cinema, good local hospitality and excellent squadron all-ranks' parties. There was also a Bar to Squadron Leader Johnson's DFC, for his part in the destruction of a Focke-Wulf 190 on 19th August and for helping to destroy two others. Hind carcases from the estate of Sir Archibald Sinclair, Secretary of State for Air, and other kind hosts helped with the rationing, and as the C.O. flew off to Norwich to marry (with ex-610 pilot, now Wing Commander, H. S. L. Dundas as best man) the Air Officer Commanding No. 14(F) Group, Air Vice-Marshal Raymond Collishaw, CB, DSO, OBE, DSC, DFC, Ace of the RNAS, flew up to present Squadron Leader Johnson with a cigarette-case, the gift of squadron personnel. The diary says 'The C.O. dispensed our portions of hind with the air of a proud father ministering to the needs of an outsize family.'

By 20th January, 1943, the squadron was back at Westhampnett, Tangmere, now commanded by Group Captain H. D. McGregor, DSO, and here they were joined by that other legless pilot, then Flying Officer, Colin Hodgkinson, ex-Fleet Air Arm, straightaway nicknamed 'Hoppy' to his own delight. Several pilots were lost over Europe but some returned, one being Flying Officer Skibinski, a Polish officer in the squadron, who was awarded the MBE for his adventurous evasion and return to England. Flying Officer L. A. Smith was awarded the DFC for his victories against the Focke-Wulf 190 fighters, and Flight Lieutenant P. I. Howard-Williams, who had saved many lives when he destroyed another FW.190 attempting to attack one of our air-sea rescue launches containing picked-up aircrews, was also given the DFC for his fine work with 610 and for his Battle of Britain flying in 19 Squadron.

On 16th March, 1943, Johnnie Johnson was promoted to lead the Kenley Wing and in his place came Squadron Leader W. A. Laurie, DFC, the squadron now turned to all-out blitzing of trains and other vital enemy communications. A feature of squadron life was the close link between pilots and ground personnel, the pilots being shown how to service their machines against the day when this could be necessary after a landing in Europe took place. Free French, Belgian and Norwegians joined the squadron, one of the Belgians being airborne on a cine-gun photographic exercise when a lone FW.190 tried to bomb Brighton, only to fall to the guns of the Belgian's Spitfire. On 21st April Flight Lieutenant Collinge, DFC, longest-serving pilot with 610, was reported missing. Then came a move down to Perranporth, Cornwall, to escort 'Whirlibombers' (Whirlwind twin-engined fighters carrying bombs) against the Cherbourg Peninsula and Bay of Biscay targets. Squadron Leader J. M. Littler joined the squadron for experience before taking command of No. 276 Air-Sea Rescue Squadron replacing ex-610 Squadron's Squadron Leader R. F. Hamlyn, AFC, DFM.

On 29th May the squadron's timely arrival saved the crew of a USAAF Fortress in their dinghy well out to sea and this was followed by a move into Bolt Head for 'Rhubarb' sorties against trains in the Cherbourg area. Flying Officer Crew, missing, was later known to be a prisoner of war. A Mustang pilot, Flight Lieutenant Holloway of 16 Squadron, showed his appreciation after being picked up from the sea due to 610's vigilance, by presenting a silver ashtray to the squadron. At this stage there were only fourteen pre-war Auxiliary airmen left with the squadron, the others having been promoted and posted to strengthen new squadrons and, with the formation of the Allied Expeditionary Air Force, most squadrons, including 610, parted with their own groundcrews, with some regret, though the idea of servicing echelons already based on the airfields to which squadrons flew proved very successful and exceptionally efficient in action.

The crew of the Flying Fortress 'Ole Battleaxe', rescued when the squadron beat off attackers near their dinghy, flew in to present a load of gifts to mark their gratitude. This was a happy moment, for two USAAF pilots had joined the squadron to fly Spitfires. Four Bf.110 fighter-bombers fell to squadron guns, the first enemy seen for many months, and a light relief was the joint squadron and echelon production 'Fighter Follies' which delighted its audience. Flight Lieutenant A. R. Costello left to be trained as a controller. Re-equipping with the Spitfire XIV, the Griffon-engined version with top speed of 446 m.p.h. and capable of carrying 1,000 lb of under-slung bombs, the squadron flew sorties across the Bay of Biscay hitting every possible target and interspersing this with escorts to bombers and to V.I.P. aircraft coming in from North Africa.

Squadron Leader R. A. Newbury, DFC and Bar, became C.O. in January 1944 as, from Culmhead, the squadron attacked a Gestapo Headquarters in Normandy, then led 'Bomphoons' (Ty-phoons with bombs) against targets in Dinard. Just before D-Day, alas, both flight-commanders lost their lives during the build-up period when 610 hit everything within range. From Bolt Head and then from Harrowbeer, Devonshire, the squadron hammered the pre-invasion targets and on D-Day, 6th June, escorted Typhoons carrying rocket-projectiles on their mission against enemy targets in the Channel Islands to prevent forces there from reinforcing the Nazis in Normandy. Then, led by Wing Commander H. A. C. Bird-Wilson, and in company with No. 41 Squadron's Spitfire XII, formation and No. 263 Squadron's Typhoons, 610 hit shipping along the coast of France to prevent supplies and troops reaching Rommel.

On 19th June, though, came a very different commitment, for the squadron was moved back to West Malling, Kent, to help combat the arrival of the V.1 flying bombs then hitting Southern England. On the first day of operations the Spitfires shot down four of these doodlebugs and by the end of July had destroyed forty-three, Flight Lieutenant Gaze, holder of the DFC and Bar, showing a rare aptitude for these pilotless aircraft. Spells at both Westhampnett and Friston, Sussex, helped the pilots to increase their victories against the flying bombs and a move back to Kent, to Lympne (now Ashford Airport), saw the attachment of long-range petrol tanks for close-escort to the Arnhem airborne forces during 'Operation Market' in mid-September. Then came inoculations all round which indicated to most that the squadron was earmarked for some overseas destination. Rumours abounded but, in the event, the first landings by squadron aircraft were made on airfields near Antwerp and as the enemy was shelling and sending both the V.1 and the V.2 rocket which fell without warning and could not be intercepted, pilots returned to England after their sorties with some relief.

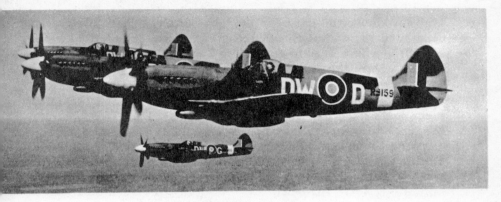

116. Spitfires Mk.XIV in 1944.

During October, the Prime Minister and King George VI were escorted (separately) to the Continent and Royal Air Force bombers, lifting the new 12,000-pounders, were shepherded far into the Third Reich territory. December was a bad month as the squadron settled-in at B.56 (British airfield 56) at Brussels, Evere, under Wing Commander Johnnie Johnson's leadership of an offensive Spitfire Wing for armed reconnaissance into Germany. The terrible weather contributed to the loss of four pilots and newcomers as replacements included Flight Lieutenant Finucane, brother of the much-lamented Paddy who had served in 602 (City of Glasgow) Auxiliary Squadron.

On 1st January, 1945, Goering staged his last great gamble, 'Operation Hermann' or 'Big Blow', against allied airfields in Holland, Belgium and Northern France. The Brussels bases were strafed but Flight Lieutenant Gaze managed to take off and shoot down a Focke-Wulf 190. Many Luftwaffe machines – which had certainly destroyed many of our aircraft on the ground – were caught on their way back to Germany, out of ammunition in most instances, by RAF fighters returning from escorting our bombers. The enemy thrust into the Ardennes, helped by the continuing bad weather, caused a squadron move to airfield Y.32 (Zeelst) and then to B.78 at Eindhoven with a full-scale attack being waged against all enemy transportation to be seen. Air Chief Marshal Tedder called in person to thank the squadron for a splendid effort and was pleased to hear that living conditions in a requisitioned school were an improvement, if not ideal.

History was made on 14th February when Flight Lieutenant Gaze's Valentine for the Luftwaffe was the destruction of an Me.262 jet, the first of the Messerschmitt rocket-carriers to fall to No. 125 Wing and a brilliant performance against a 500 m.p.h. enemy. Then came a move back to Warmwell in Dorset, with Flight Lieutenant J. B. Shepherd, DFC, acting as commanding officer at the armament practice camp where, in generous tribute, the official log read '610 Squadron did twice the flying of any other visiting unit'. It showed the enthusiasm of the pilots of the County of Chester Squadron who wanted to get back to Europe and action. 3rd March, therefore, brought a shock to every member when a signal arrived announcing the impending disbandment of the squadron. The scoreboard at that time read: Enemy Aircraft destroyed 132, probables 46½, damaged 53, Flying Bombs destroyed 50, Trains, Barges, Wagons: no complete tally kept but over 200 disabled.

Wing Commander Keefer, the Canadian C.O. of No. 125 Wing, British Liberation Armies, added the last word to the war diary when he wrote: 'Led by keen and courageous pilots, and ably supported by a loyal and efficient ground staff, this squadron is one of which not only the County of Chester, but indeed the whole of Britain should be proud. It never let its Country down during its distinguished history. All who leave this squadron will forever hold a memory of many happy friendships.' Seven of 610's pilots died fighting the Battle for Britain and nineteen of those who survived the 1940 combats gave their lives before VE Day came on 8th May, 1945. A few decided to remain in the post-war Royal Air Force but, in June 1946 at Hooton Park, Cheshire, a new County of Chester Auxiliary Squadron began to form under Squadron Leader P. G. Lamb, AFC, one of the squadron's Battle of Britain veterans.

117. Pilots at annual camp, Tangmere 1948. *Left to right:* Duffey, Baxendale, Watt, Spencer, Twomey, Mercer, Law, Bamberger, Lee, Rigby (C.O.), Ainsworth, Tilston, and Leete (seated).

In July 1946 the old-timers, with many new volunteers, joined the squadron and soon the first post-war machines, Spitfires Mk.XIV, arrived. Sir William Bromley-Davenport, TD, again accepted the appointment of Honorary Air Commodore and in 1948 came the Spitfire F.22. In 1950 came a change of command when Squadron Leader C. S. Bamberger, DFC and Bar, relieved Squadron Leader Lamb. This was a most interesting appointment as Squadron Leader Bamberger had joined as an Auxiliary airman in 1936 for ground duties and, there being no NCO-pilots in the pre-war AAF, had transferred to the RAF Volunteer Reserve for pilot-training, re-joining 610 as a Sergeant-Pilot on 27th July, 1940. He moved to No. 41(F) Squadron in September of 1940, destroying one Messerschmitt Bf.109 before the Battle of Britain ended, receiving first the DFC and later a Bar to the decoration after being commissioned, flying in Nos. 64, 93, 243 Squadrons.

118. Meteor F.8 low-flying at Hooton Park.

During 1951, the Gloster Meteor F.4 was received, followed by the Meteor F.8 a few months later, and in the year 1953 Air Commodore I. R. Parker, OBE, the squadron's first C.O., became Honorary Air Commodore. The Esher Trophy, gained in 1952, was presented during 1953 by Major the Viscount Leverhulme, TD, at an impressive and very proud gathering of members and former members. During 1954, the year in which Squadron Leader J. E. Storrar, DFC, AFC, assumed command, the squadron forged a link with No. 3 Squadron, Royal New Zealand Air Force, Canterbury, New Zealand, a unit which had seen distinguished war service in the South Pacific. Squadron Leader Storrar, a Chester Veterinary Surgeon, had flown with Nos. 145 and 73 Squadrons, also with No. 421 Flight, during the Battle of Britain, being credited with several enemy aircraft and had afterwards served his country well as an instructor on fighters.

Summer camps were held at Tangmere, Thorney Island, Horsham St Faith, and Sylt in Germany, and when the squadron had to disband it was noted that of the 610 Squadron RAuxAF pilots, *fourteen* held degrees and – to a man – offered to carry on their flying without pay or allowances, a gesture of which the pre-war Auxiliaries would have been very proud had they been there to share the genuine dismay at the decision to cease this part-time flying. There was, alas, no reprieve and squadron property was dispersed, the history, in two volumes known as *Hevucnit*, presented to Squadron Leader Williams, Medical Officer and Hon Historian (H. O. Williams, FRCS, of Little Sutton, Wirral).

119. Squadron personnel and Spitfire F.22s at Hooton Park, February 1949.

The record of the squadron, in peace and in war, ranks with the best and, happily, a Spitfire coded DW–A serial TD248 (later 7246M as a maintenance instructional airframe) stands at Royal Air Force, Sealand, Cheshire, as a tribute to all who flew and serviced the squadron's machines. In Canada, Spitfire Vc AR614, which once operated with 610 Squadron, may be made airworthy and perhaps will fly in its old markings. At Shoreham, Sussex, is Spitfire XIV NH904, formerly of 610 Squadron, acquired for the Battle of Britain film and re-sold afterwards to a wealthy farmer as part of his 'stable' of World War II aircraft. At Ternhill, Shropshire, Meteor F.8 WK988 was saved from the scrapheap to be used for firefighting drill but, as this is written, may no longer exist, after doing a vital job after ending its flying at Sylt.

Of former members one thinks immediately of Air Vice-Marshal J. E. Johnnie Johnson, CB, CBE, DSO, DFC, now retired and a Deputy Lieutenant for the County of Leicester; also of Air Vice-Marshal Denis Crowley-Milling, CBE, DSO, DFC, Air Officer Commanding No. 38 Group, Royal Air Force, one of few RAF officers to fly the F–111 and who played a key part, during his tour of duty as Air Attaché, Washington, in helping to sell the Hawker Siddeley Harrier to the U.S. Marine Corps. It is of passing interest to note that the Spitfire F.24 serial VN485, flown by No. 80 Squadron RAF and then by the Hong Kong Auxiliary Air Force, has been painted DW–X in honour of Air Vice-Marshal Crowley-Milling, who was Air Officer Commanding, Hong Kong, before going to the U.S.A. On Battle of Britain Day every year this Spitfire is taken across the harbour from Kai Tak to stand before the Cenotaph in Hong Kong and one hopes that for as long as airmen are asked to explain the code letters they will be briefed to tell the world that they stand for 610 (County of Chester) Squadron. One who joined when a student at Liverpool University and who left the AAF to take a permanent commission in the RAF, retired as Air Commodore James Leathart, CB, DSO, C.O. No. 54(F)Sqdn, 1940. One of his great regrets was being a staff officer in Reserve Command when the RAuxAF was disbanded – perhaps his happiest recollection that he met his wife through his 610 Squadron flying.

REPRESENTATIVE SQUADRON AIRCRAFT

Avro Tutor		K3311			
Hawker Hart		K3881 K4441			
Hawker Hind		K5400 K6615 K6625			
Fairey Battle		N2107			
Hawker Hurricane		L2117 L2121 L2123			
Vickers-Supermarine	I	P9503	DW–D	R6694	DW–F
Spitfire		R6976 DW–A			
	Vb	AD512	DW–A	BL564	DW–E
		BM378 DW–H EE745			
	XIV	RB150	DW–A	RB159	DW–D
		RB170 DW–G RB174			
	(post war) XIV	NH646 RAQ–K SM876 TZ144			
	F.22	PK511	RAQ–N/DW–N		PK544
		RAQ–U			
Gloster Meteor	F.4	RA368 VT187 VT235			
	F.8	WA776 WH273 A WH447 H			
		WL110			

The squadron was allotted the code JE just before outbreak of war and it may have appeared on the Hurricanes although DW was carried on the various Spitfires flown until disbandment in 1945. From 1946–8 the code RAQ was allotted by Reserve Command and this changed back to DW on return to Fighter Command. Finally, on the Meteors, the squadron's own markings of black/white rectangle and serrated dividing line was painted either side of fuselage roundels and also either side of the badge on the engine nacelles.

Badge: A garb. A wheatsheaf was chosen as such charges appear in the City of Chester's armorial bearings.

Motto (translated): 'Ceres rising in a winged car.'

611
(West Lancashire)
Squadron

THE OFFICIAL RECORDS state that No. 611 Squadron of the Auxiliary Air Force formed at Hendon, Middlesex, on 10th February, 1936, but Lancastrians will feel that the squadron really began to shape at the St George Building in Lime Street, Liverpool, on 1st April, 1936, when Squadron Leader Geoffrey Langton Pilkington was commissioned and appointed the first commanding officer of the squadron, which was destined to be known locally as The City of Liverpool Squadron. On 6th May, at Speke, the city's airport, the first equipment arrived, a Hucks Starter (an example of which can be seen today at the Shuttleworth Collection, Old Warden, Bedfordshire). On 11th May the first volunteers for pilot-training were attested, Messrs W. J. Leather and W. L. Lang, commissioned as pilot officers to begin flying the Avro Tutor. The records show that a total of one hour's flying was achieved in May.

By the end of July, with the arrival of a Hawker Hart Trainer and Hawker Hart day bombers, the flying hours rose to fifty-seven. Two more potential pilots, A. W. Richards and D. W. S. Howroyd, enrolled and Dr W. D. Peock, MB, ChB, became the squadron medical officer. The Air Ministry provided a hard-core of RAF officers and airmen for continuity and administration, together with flying instructors, and an early tragedy, which could so easily have affected morale and progress, involved the Regular RAF assistant adjutant, Flying Officer P. S. Salter, who was taxying out in Hart K3044 when it came into collision with Percival Mew Gull G–AEKL whose pilot, Tom Campbell, was killed. It was not merely a local disaster but an international calamity as Tom, a well-loved pilot, had been co-pilot of the de Havilland DH.88 Comet which had won the Mildenhall to Melbourne Air Race of 1934.

This temporary cloud was soon dispersed, however, by a flow of recruits for training and with the arrival, from London, of Flying Officer J. E. McComb who had been a member of No. 600 (City of London) Squadron, with Flying Officer J. H. Little from No. 601 (County of London) Squadron. On 11th October the Chief of the Air Staff, Air Chief Marshal Sir Edward Ellington, paid a visit and said that he was well pleased with what he saw. Pilot Officer Robin Birley joined as adjutant, AAF, and the year ended with Kenneth Maxwell Stoddart becoming an officer-pilot. On 16th January, 1937, four more Hawker Harts arrived from Sealand, Cheshire, and the first weekend camp was attended by eleven officers and fifty-seven airmen volunteers. Newcomers E. C. Fieldsend, S. H. Bazley, J. W. Carmichael, J. N. O'Reilly Blackwood and R. K. Crompton joined for flying training and Pilot Officer Leather had the distinction of being first to qualify for the pilot's badge, soon followed by Messrs Stoddart and Bazley.

120. Squadron officers, 1937.

A popular tradition was established with a squadron outing to Blackpool for all ranks, following a most successful summer camp at Manston, Kent. A combined force of ninety-six Auxiliaries and fifty-three Regulars produced a record total of 271 flying hours for the West Lancashire Squadron whose official badge had been approved and signed by the King. The year ended with a visit from Manchester Corporation officials to investigate the possibilities of forming their own squadron, which later came into existence at Ringway as No. 613 (City of Manchester) in March 1939.

During 1938 – with the threat of trouble in Europe – the RAF adjutant, Flight Lieutenant C. H. Parker, who had taught many of the pilots to fly, left to command No. 40(B) Squadron on promotion. Flight Lieutenant Lea-Cox replaced him as the Hawker Hind arrived as the new squadron aircraft. On 28th May, as Empire Day was staged at Speke, another change brought in Flight Lieutenant H. S. Darley from No. 602 (City of Glasgow) Squadron, AAF, as adjutant and instructor. Darley was a brilliant RAF fighter pilot and his arrival was soon followed by the great news that the squadron role was to be changed from light-bombers to fighters. On 1st January, 1939, the squadron was transferred into No. 12 (Fighter) Group and Messrs C. H. McFie, W. P. Barrell, J. R. G. Sutton and T. D. Williams enlisted for pilot-training. On 19th May came the first Spitfires, a high compliment to a part-time unit when many RAF squadrons were anxious to acquire one of the world's finest fighter types.

121. Squadron inspection 1938, Hawker Hinds on parade.

On 12th June, 1939, Barrie Heath was commissioned and by 13th August the squadron was at Duxford, Cambridgeshire, for annual summer camp where it was learnt, on 24th August, that 611 was now embodied into the Royal Air Force for the duration of hostilities. With Squadron Leader Pilkington as C.O. and Flight Lieutenants McComb and Stoddart as flight-commanders a total complement of 196 officers and airmen were called-up for full-time service, only one man being found less than a hundred per cent fit, a wonderful start to a glorious page in squadron history. A sad moment came, though, on 2nd September, when Pilot Officer H. Fiddes was killed in Spitfire K9985 near Wattisham, Suffolk, as he was flying to Watton, Norfolk, for the daily stand-by in case war broke out. Then, as the Nazis entered Poland, Squadron Leader Pilkington was moved and Squadron Leader J. E. McComb assumed command.

On 10th October the squadron flew into RAF Digby, Lincolnshire, seventeen Spitfires taking off and forming into a swastika pattern, only to break quickly into two units of nine and eight machines in traditional RAF fighter formations, indicating to any one watching their determination to break the forces of Hitler if and when the chance came. They joined, at Digby, Nos. 46 and 229 Squadrons of the Royal Air Force, flying Hurricanes and Blenheims respectively, and this gave the West Lancashire pilots useful hours of flying on affiliation exercises, also with the Hampden light-bombers of Nos. 44 and 144 Squadrons. The bomber crews congratulated 611's pilots on their attacks and both sides derived advantages – not least in aircraft recognition – which some squadrons neglected, to their cost.

122. Spitfires taking off from Digby.

On 21st October a call 'Bandits at 15,000 feet coming from the north-east' sent A Flight climbing through cloud between Mablethorpe and North Coates. No. 72 Squadron was also scrambled from Church Fenton, near Leeds, to meet this Luftwaffe attack. In the clouds Sergeant Mather of 611 joined up with two of 72 Squadron's Spitfires and, on sighting ten-plus enemy aircraft, this trio attacked at once with Sergeant Mather opening fire on the flank enemy aircraft which turned away, diving steeply towards the sea. No. 72 Squadron later claimed two enemy destroyed but 611 made no claim, though they felt their pilot had made some small contribution. On 2nd November, King George VI paid a visit to Digby to meet squadron personnel whose duties were now mainly as escorts to North Sea convoys. On 30th November the Spitfires were taken out of the front-line to be armour-plated!

Command of RAF Digby passed, on 8th January, 1940, to Wing Commander I. R. Parker, formerly C.O. No. 610 (County of Chester) Squadron AAF, one of the first 'weekend warriors' to be given com- of a Royal Air Force station. A commendation came from the Admiral, Humber Fleet, for the squadron's fine work over the convoys but a sobering note was the news that Pilot Officer J. N. O'Reilly Blackwood, a one-time 611 pilot who had taken a short service RAF commission, had lost his life over Germany with No. 57(B) Squadron. During February 1940 the squadron gained first place in No. 12 Group's re-arming trials; twelve Spitfires in fourteen minutes! Probably as a result of this, the squadron's Mk.I Spitfires were transferred to a newly-formed squadron (No. 152) and 611 Squadron received a new batch of Spitfires.

123. King George visits the squadron at Digby, 2nd November, 1939. Station Commander on the King's right; AV-M Leigh-Mallory behind S.C.; ACM Sir Cyril Newall behind the King; Sqdn Ldr McComb, the C.O., far right in black flying suit.

On 28th February, Green Section, comprising Flying Officer Hamilton, Pilot Officer McFie and Sergeant Bruce, stuck to their task of escorting merchant shipping despite terrible visibility, often flying below mast-height to check on their charges. Sergeant Bruce, alas, did not return to base, and the Air Officer Commanding, Air Vice-Marshal Trafford Leigh-Mallory, signalled: 'Very much regret to hear Sergeant Bruce missing on what was gallant effort to carry out difficult duty. At same time wish to congratulate Green 1 and 2 on continuing convoy patrol in face of great difficulties.' Sergeant Bruce would have been commissioned a few days later had he lived and his loss was a real blow to all in the squadron.

A detachment was now based at RAF North Coates, where conditions were so primitive that pilots slept on the floor of the

Watch Hut between patrols. A typically-AAF note in the squadron records says 'Sent airman to buy enough aspirin and Alka Seltzer for three pilots with six headaches.' Flight Lieutenant Geoffrey Clapham, formerly Chief Flying Instructor at Liverpool Aero Club, Speke, and an Honorary Member of 611 Squadron, came to Digby as Operations Room controller, to the delight of all. When Marshal of the RAF Viscount Trenchard called he found the personnel in magnificent heart, despite lack of action so far. Then came the Nazi invasion of Norway and Denmark and orders for 611 Squadron to come to an advanced state of readiness and to ensure that night-flying training was maintained. Sergeant Levinson was caught and held in our Army's searchlights over Grantham until, completely blinded, he was forced to bale out when in a spin.

The entry of the Nazis into the Low Countries on 10th May brought orders for all airmen to take turns on guarding the Spitfires against surprise paratroop drops and then, on 23rd May, came instructions from Fighter Command for the squadron to go to Dunkirk. In company with Nos. 32, 66, 92, and 266 Squadrons (the last led by Flight Lieutenant Bazley a former 611 pilot) the squadron was detailed to engage enemy fighters as 92 Squadron took on the Luftwaffe's bombers trying to reach the stranded British Expeditionary Force. In the fighting, often far into France, No. 611 Squadron opened its tally of victories with claims of eight enemy destroyed (Ju.88s, Bf.110s and Bf.109s). Flying Officers Crompton and Little were reported missing and Flight Lieutenant Stoddart force-landed at Martlesham, Suffolk, his Spitfire 'like a sieve'.

About this time came a letter written aboard HMS *Glorious* by 46 Squadron, the chaps who'd shared Digby with the West Lancashire lads and with whom a friendly rivalry had been established. It read:

> We're sending all our pink pills home to you,
> Our glim-lamps, and our goosenecks too;
> We have no use for them out here,
> The sun never sets for half the year.
> This is the land of the Midnight Sun –
> Oh what a place for Six-One-One.

Good Luck to you deadbeats, we're flying off tonight. From the Bing Boys.

(Squadron Leader Cross was their C.O., hence nickname, 'Bing' Cross.) The references to pink pills, goose-neck flares, glim-lamps, were to the night-flying aids at Digby. No. 46 Squadron battled bravely over Norway after flying off their Hurricanes and then, to save their precious Hurricanes, decided to try and land them back on the deck of *Glorious*, which they did, but *Scharnhorst* and *Gneisenau* sank their ship. Only Squadron Leader K. B. Cross and Flight

Lieutenant P. G. Jameson survived, after seeing twenty-five of their comrades die on a Carley Float before they were picked up by a fishing boat. Bing Cross retired as Air Chief Marshal Sir Kenneth Cross, and Jameson as an Air Commodore, both receiving high decorations for their World War II and post-war service.

No. 611 Squadron now helped to re-form 46 Squadron at Digby, some of that squadron having returned by other means from Norway; one of them Flight Lieutenant Peock had once been the 611 Squadron doctor. News was received that a former squadron pilot, later Squadron Leader Cooke, awarded the DFC for his fine work leading 264 Squadron over Dunkirk, was believed killed. Pilot Officer C. A. T. Jones went to Farnborough to fly trials against a captured Bf.109 and later joined No. 312 (Czech) Squadron and 166 (South Yorkshire) Squadron, getting the DFC. His place in the West Lancashire squadron was taken by a young RAF Volunteer Reserve pilot, Pilot Officer David Scott-Malden, of whom much was to be heard.

On 2nd July there was excitement when a Do.215 was intercepted off Withernsea by a Section of the squadron led by Flight Lieutenant W. J. Leather who had Pilot Officers J. R. G. Sutton and J. W. Lund as his No. 2 and 3. The enemy machine, probably on early morning reconnaissance, was shot down into the North Sea. A Flight was now detached to Ternhill in Shropshire for defence of this vital training area which, on 23rd July, was attacked by the enemy, happily without casualties. Pilot Officer D. A. Adams had to make an emergency landing on the Colwyn Bay beach following technical failure and Sergeant Burt damaged his Spitfire landing at Ternhill; neither pilot was injured. The other flight, on 5th July, had fought an inconclusive combat near Spurn Head with a Ju.88; the pilots made no claim since they did not see the end of the fight. Post-war research, though, indicates that this Ju.88 was written-off completely when it tried to make a landing at its base in France, so the squadron tally should be increased accordingly.

On 28th July Pilot Officer Lund had to make a belly landing (wheels retracted) at Digby but was unhurt. Then came a frustrating period as squadrons to the south and to the north saw action but 611 was kept at readiness to meet any penetration to the Midlands. Not until Wednesday 21st August did opportunities arise when three Dorniers were reported seen off Mablethorpe. Spitfires led by Squadron Leader McComb (Sergeants A. D. Burt and A. S. Darling were his No. 2 and 3) destroyed two Do.17Zs off the Lincolnshire coast and Flying Officer D. H. Watkins with Pilot Officers M. P. Brown and J. W. Lund shot down another Do.17Z near Burnham Market, Norfolk, after a short chase. Four of the Spitfires were damaged by enemy return-fire and after he had landed without combat damage to his Spitfire, Sergeant Darling's aircraft hit an obstruction on the runway and so a fifth machine suffered minor damage. Fortunately no pilot was hurt, in this, the best day's work so far in the Battle of Britain.

On 30th August, with the air fighting concentrated on the London area, the squadron moved temporarily into Duxford, the records noting that in the year since becoming embodied, 3,916 hours had been flown on operations. On 5th September, back at Digby, a Luftwaffe reconnaissance plane crossed the Midlands, and ordered by the Sector Controller to 'Buster' (achieve top speed) the squadron Spitfire registered a true air speed of 390 m.p.h. via the emergency boost, using 71 gallons of fuel in 80 minutes. The enemy machine, sighting the climbing Spitfire over Nottingham, turned and made for the coast. A short time later another Spitfire was ordered off but the fighter was recalled, Sector telling our machine that it was a friendly aircraft after all. A few seconds later bombs fell in Lincoln!

On 8th and 9th September, to their great disappointment, the squadron pilots were held on patrol over North Weald but it was vital work, even if without sighting the enemy. On the 11th, though, came the long-awaited tussle and during the afternoon's fighting six claims were made of Bf.109s destroyed or damaged. Two Spitfires were lost, Sergeant F. E. R. Sheppherd losing his life and Sergeant S. A. Levenson making an emergency landing in Surrey without harm to himself. On 15th September, as part of Bader's Duxford Wing, the squadron claimed several enemy aircraft shot down or damaged but we now know that many aircraft were claimed by more than one pilot in the hectic fighting.

The 15th September was a turning-point, for our fighter reserves were almost negligible and only the reluctance of the Luftwaffe to attack again in force enabled us to build our squadrons up to strength with pilots and aircraft. It was 18th September when the five squadrons of the Duxford Wing met a mixed enemy bomber and fighter force and whilst 611 kept the fighters at bay, a number of bombers fell to the guns of the other squadrons and although, flying at 30,000 feet, 611 did not fire a single shot, they made a valuable contribution to this success. Then on 21st September, Pilot Officer D. A. Adams was sent up from Ternhill to investigate a Bogey (an unidentified aircraft) over Liverpool and, emerging from thick cloud, found that it was indeed an enemy, a Do.215 on photographic-reconnaissance of the area. Chasing it for fourteen minutes he shot it down at Dolgellau, Merioneth, seeing two men climb out. Thus the citizens of Liverpool were probably spared at least one raid which would certainly have followed the successful return of the machine with its vital pictures of potential targets.

Two days after this incident came the first decoration and, appropriately, it was a DFC for Flight Lieutenant Leather, the first of the volunteers to gain his wings at Speke.

A terse note in the records referring to the constant shuttling of pilots and ground personnel from Digby to Ternhill says 'What Group wants is not airmen but gypsies, with Carter Patterson as C.O.!' In one month, twelve of the experienced pilots were transferred to newly-forming squadrons, a tribute to 611 but disappointing for the loyal groundcrews who, it was noted, had attached affectionate nicknames to their pilots, including 'Kidney Bean' Bazley, 'Fanny' Adams, 'Farquar' Leather, 'Hack-Mack' McFie, 'Senator' Dewey, and 'Kenny' Stoddart. Flight Lieutenant McFie left to command a flight in 616 (South Yorkshire) Squadron and Flight Lieutenant Scott-Malden to command a 603 (City of Edinburgh) flight, thus maintaining their Auxiliary links. With a constant flow of trainee pilots a wag re-named the squadron No. 611 Flying Training Squadron but on 11th October came a welcome change when the Ternhill Flight intercepted a force of Dorniers attacking Liverpool in the early evening. Three Do.17Z's were attacked, two of them falling in flames, one, shot down by Sergeant Pattinson, managed to hit the Spitfire and Pattinson crashed near Kidderminster and died from his wounds. The third Dornier, set alight, and from which two of the crew parachuted to safety, managed to fly back to France and crash-land; so Luftwaffe records confirmed.

On 16th October, during a night raid on Birmingham, one of the Dorniers dropped a mine on Ternhill, hitting a hangar and destroying twenty training aircraft, though no Spitfire was touched. What was at that time thought to be a reprisal for the squadron's victory on 11th October was later believed an error of navigation by a crew which, having missed their Birmingham target, unloaded the mine on the first airfield seen in the early-morning light. Three days later Squadron Leader J. E. McComb, awarded the squadron's second DFC, left for a rest from operations and Squadron Leader E. R. Bitmead, RAF, a most experienced day and night pilot, took command. On 13th November a lone raider was intercepted between Newark and Nottingham and eventually shot down over Newbury, Berkshire; a fortnight later, 29th October, a Ju.88 was diverted from bombing Cromer and jettisoned its bombs into the sea as it scorched for home. On 7th December another bomber, caught and damaged over Mablethorpe, turned for home but changing its mind, landed in Lincolnshire, disgorging four prisoners.

Then on 12th December came orders to move into Rochford with the task of helping to implement Churchill's directives and to escort RAF daylight bombers over Occupied Europe. Pilot Officer W. G. G. Duncan Smith arrived and news came that Squadron Leader P. S. Salter, the squadron's first instructor, had been awarded the Air Force Cross for teaching very many pilots to fly. Now part of the Hornchurch Wing under Wing Commander (now Air Chief Marshal Sir) Harry Broadhurst, the squadron participated in 'Circus' and 'Rhubarb' operations – the former escorting bombers, the latter our offensives of fighters and fighter-bombers intended to hit airfields and other targets to try and force the Luftwaffe into the air over France, Belgium, and Holland.

The Spitfire IIa was received as 611's old machines went to form No. 485 (NZ) Squadron and one of the squadron's new machines was donated by Mr George Heath of Birmingham and named Grahame Heath in memory of a son killed in the RNAS as he shot down a German Ace over Sylt in World War I. Now flown by his younger son, Barrie Heath, a 611 pilot, it did magnificent work and when Barrie left to command No. 64 Squadron on promotion, he took the Spitfire with him and was later awarded the DFC for his sorties with 611 and 64 Squadrons. In March came the sad news of the death of Flight Lieutenant Bazley in an accident and the better news that another former member, now Squadron Leader J. H. Little, had been awarded the DFC for his command of 219 night-fighter squadron.

In April the squadron received three Dutch pilots who had escaped to England and who wanted operational experience before going out to the Dutch East Indies. On their first mission – by fate it was over Holland – one did not return and was thought to have been shot down near Flushing. Flight Lieutenant D. H. Watkins was awarded the DFC, and during April of 1941 a record total of 800 hours was flown on sorties over Europe. A light-hearted diary entry, though one which might have had serious consequences, relates that when Pilot Officer Askew was sent to collect a Miles Magister communications aircraft from Cranwell, he had to force-land in a field near Epping, Essex, due to weather. Airmen removed the mainplanes to tow the machine into RAF North Weald and they then re-assembled the 'Maggie' and telephoned Askew that it was ready to be flown into Rochford. He went over to collect the aircraft but rang 611's engineering officer to tell him that the aileron controls had been wrongly-rigged and sought advice. 'Fly it back upside down or sit facing the tail' was the retort from the busy engineer. A few minutes later the Magister landed at Rochford and the engineer was visibly shaken to find that the ailerons had not been re-rigged! Two officers were now promoted; Squadron Leader Leather, DFC, to command No. 145 Squadron and Squadron Leader F. C. Hopcroft to lead No. 91 Squadron. Jeffrey Quill the Vickers-Supermarine test-pilot came to liaise with the squadron and to fly on operations, drawing the admiring quip 'He flies – we only drive' from 'Chips' Carpenter who spoke for all 611 members. Jeffrey was later made an OBE and awarded the AFC for his superb airmanship.

Squadron Leader F. S. Stapleton, who had joined the RAF Volunteer Reserve as a Sergeant-Pilot, later accepting a permanent RAF commission, came in as C.O. and on 7th May the squadron shot down four Bf.109s over a convoy near Deal, Kent, and in the afternoon destroyed another and damaged one during an escort to Blenheim bombers. The squadron records amusingly note 'This was no mean effort when it took another (Regular) squadron all day to get just one.' Prince Bernhard of the Netherlands, a brilliant pilot, flew in to meet the squadron Dutchmen and when the Luftwaffe turned to a series of night raids on London and SE. England, 611 reinforced the night-fighters, Pilot Officer Duncan Smith damaging one raider over Canterbury. Flight Lieutenant S. T. Meares, an American, nicknamed 'Lord Charles', took over a flight as the squadron received the Spitfire Vb, naming one 'City of Liverpool', another 'Fleetwood', one 'City of Hull' and another 'Saddleworth' in acknowledgement of the funds raised to purchase these machines for the RAF.

Twelve Spitfires flew over Essex dropping 'Lend to defend the right' pamphlets and, after refuelling, attacked targets in France during which Flight Lieutenant Buys, one of the Dutchmen, got a Bf.109 over the Channel. By June there were only two of the Auxiliary Air Force pilots left and one, Flight Lieutenant T. D. Williams, was awarded the DFC for his excellent work. Two days later the squadron had its best bag since Dunkirk when, over Hazebrouck, they shot down seven Messerschmitt 109s, probably destroying or damaging three others. Next day, as congratulations poured in, Flight Lieutenant Buys was lost, his replacement, Flight Lieutenant E. S. 'Sawn-off' Lock, DSO, DFC and Bar, of Shrewsbury, coming in as flight-commander, a high-scoring member of No. 41 Squadron in 1940, rated by many as the finest of all fighter pilots.

Squadron Leader Stapleton, awarded the DFC for his great leadership, moved out on promotion to lead the Hornchurch Wing and in came Squadron Leader E. H. Thomas, DFC, another Battle of Britain veteran ex-229, 19, 266 Squadrons. Sir Archibald Sinclair, Secretary of State for Air, signalled 'Many congratulations on magnificent results' and the newspapers headlined the squadron's successes. Escorting Short Stirling four-engined bombers in July, the Hornchurch Wing included Group Captain Broadhurst, now the Station Commander and he paid 611 the honour of flying with them, using one of their machines. Flight Lieutenant Lock, Flying Officers Duncan Smith, Dexter and Gilmour got enemy aircraft and Group Captain Broadhurst got two. Dexter landed to learn that a DFC had been promulgated and the last of the Dutchmen, Flight Lieutenant J. B. H. Brunier, crash-landing after enemy fire had wrecked his seat, apologised for damage to his machine, saying 'I was not taught to fly sitting on the floor'. He later left for Java and, happily, survived the war to return to Holland.

Flight Lieutenant Meares, writing to his parents in the U.S.A. about this time, gave them some graphic facts about one of his own sorties with 611 when, after attacking a Bf.109, he found himself alone over St Omer aerodrome where two more 109s, on defensive patrol, gave chase. This is what he went on to add:

> I waited until the first was in firing range and then pulled the stick back and turned as tightly as I could. 'To me 'orror and amazement' I found the Hun was turning inside my turn which meant he could fire and hit me, and I started to perspire a bit. I could not climb away because he could outclimb me, and I could not dive as I was already flat on the 'deck', and it struck me that I was fighting for my life, which is the strangest of sensations. I knew with terrific clearness that unless I did something within the next split second I would be one of those who did not get home. I was flying about five feet above the ground, and pulled the stick back until it would not go any further. I blacked out for what seemed to be minutes and when I came to again I was flying about twenty feet behind the Hun, and he was obviously wondering where I had got to.
>
> I gave him a little squirt to let him know I was behind him. He then started to do the most amazing display of aerobatics I have ever seen but I found it quite easy to follow him and every time he made a mistake I squirted him. He bolted straight back to the aerodrome and I chased him down his hangars, in between them, over the flying field, and back. He was trying to get his ground defences to shoot me down, then in desperation he turned on his back at about fifty feet and I gave him a long burst and in he went, but it took all the rounds I had and now I had empty guns.
>
> I headed for home but the other Hun arrived on the scene. So I had to turn and fight him without guns. This lasted for about ten minutes and every time I turned for home he came at me again and I was still fifty miles from the French coast. This went on until I was almost exhausted and in a last frantic effort, I got on his tail and when he turned to shake me off, I went the other way, and dived over the top of a hill I had spotted and, turning as quickly as possible, flew under the level of the trees about a foot off the ground, and he never saw me again. I flew at ground level to Le Touquet and home via Dungeness. *I never learned how well I loved England until I saw her shores again. I had learned more about tactics and flying in twenty minutes than in all my flying years.*

Shortly after writing this letter home Flight Lieutenant Meares, to the regret of all in 611, was sent to No. 71 'Eagle' Squadron, and in the absence of the C.O., he was leading this squadron, later in 1941, when he was killed.

On 14th July a squadron record of three victories in one sortie was established by Sawn-off Lock, bringing his total confirmed victories to twenty-six. He was invited to speak at an aircraft factory but sent along Flight Lieutenant Duncan Smith as his substitute. Duncan was lavishly entertained by the Rootes workers and came back to the squadron with a cheque for £80,000, with which to buy Spitfires! On 23rd July Flight Lieutenant Williams, DFC, moved to command a flight in 602 (City of Glasgow) Squadron and the only other Auxiliary pilot then remaining – Flying Officer J. G. R. Sutton – was killed over France, Sergeants Fair and 'Mushroom' Smith (a farmer) being taken prisoner. On 3rd August a tremendous blow to all in the Royal Air Forces was the news that Flight Lieutenant Eric Lock, DSO, DFC and Bar, had failed to return from operations over France. He was last seen diving down on a column of the enemy near Calais; posted missing, his body was not reported found and the manner of his death remains a mystery. Because of our peculiar system, no award was made for his victories with 611, as posthumous decorations are limited to the VC, GC, and (at that time) a Mention in Despatches, for members of the RAF. He would have had a second Bar to his DFC, but the recommendation had not gone through the channels when he was reported missing.

Sawn-off Lock's replacement, Flight Lieutenant R. G. A. Barclay, DFC, from 249 Squadron, was also reported missing soon after he joined the squadron but returned to the United Kingdom five months later after exciting adventures with the French Underground Movement who helped him to get back to England to fly again. As the squadron's second war anniversary came round the adjutant worked out that it had accomplished over 10,000 flying hours, had flown over two million miles – equal to Liverpool–New York every day since war started – and had used 410,000 gallons of petrol, 10,000 gallons of oil and, in scoring 68 victories, with another 60 probables or damaged; had lost 25 pilots killed or missing, 20 during 1941, indicating the offensive press-on into Europe spirit called for by the Prime Minister.

At Hornchurch they were joined by No. 54 Squadron, with Squadron Leader David Scott-Malden, DFC, promoted from 611 to command that RAF squadron whose history dated back to 1916. The West Lancashire team now included Australian, Canadian, more Dutch, New Zealand, Polish, South African and American pilots including Pilot Officer Antonio Glowacki, holder of the Polish VC, Polish 'Pour le Merite', and our own Distinguished Flying Medal and DFC, gained with No. 501 (County of Gloucester) Squadron. Then came orders for a rest period and the squadron flew up to Drem, near Edinburgh, and as Squadron Leader E. H. Thomas departed, with a Bar to his DFC, he was replaced by an 'old boy' Squadron Leader D. H. Watkins, DFC, AAF. The British Empire

Medal went to Sergeant R. Markey who was then moved to Air
Ministry as a specialist on Spitfire maintenance. Although there was
a night-fighter squadron based at Drem, equipped with Boulton
Paul Defiant two-seaters, it was 611's Spitfires which logged most
night-flying hours, a feat obviously noted at Fighter Command and
Air Ministry for, in a short time, fourteen pilots including both flight-
commanders, were sent to Malta and Middle East, the flight-
commanders to command new squadrons on promotion.

Fortunately, at a time of some depression at so many departures,
Flight Lieutenant Gilmour, DFM, a one-time NCO-pilot of 611,
rejoined to become a flight-commander. He was accompanied by
Prince Emanuel Galitzine who had flown with the Finnish Air
Force against his 'Red' countrymen. In June came a return to the
11(F) Group area to be based at Kenley, Surrey, joining the Wing
led by Wing Commander Paddy Finucane, with Nos. 402 (Cana-
dian) and 602 (City of Glasgow) Squadrons. Belated but well-
deserved awards to some of the squadron's pre-war Auxiliary Air
Force groundcrew members included British Empire Medals for
Flight Sergeant Belgrove and Corporal Butler, with Mentions in
Despatches for Pilot Officer Griffiths and Flight Sergeant Findlay.
Then in July came the Spitfire Mk.IX, developed to counter the
Luftwaffe's Focke–Wulf 190 fighter. During the Dieppe Raid of
19th August the squadron escorted our day bombers and Flight
Lieutenant W. V. C. 'Bill' Compton, DFC, a young New Zealand
pilot, flew his first patrols as flight-commander.

124. Sqdn Ldr Armstrong and pilots, Bill Compton holding dog.

On 1st September, 1942, commemorating the third anniversary of call-up, a reunion was held in London with the Honorary Air Commodore, Air Commodore G. L. Pilkington, AAF, the first C.O., Air Marshal Trafford Leigh-Mallory, Group Captain Broadhurst, Wing Commander Peock, the first medical officer, and many old members and friends. The King and the Duke of Lancaster were toasted and Squadron Leader D. W. S. Howroyd, in his speech, mentioned that when he volunteered at Speke he was told that he was too young! The squadron was now commanded by Squadron Leader H. T. Armstrong, DFC, an Australian, with one flight under Flight Lieutenant Bill Compton, the other a Czech, Flight Lieutenant Vancl, DFC. The Wing was led by former C.O., now Wing Commander, E. H. Thomas, DFC and Bar, and, on moving over to Biggin Hill, Kent, the squadron joined Nos. 609 (West Riding), which flew Typhoons, and 340 (Free French), another Spitfire squadron. The Station Commander was Group Captain 'Sailor' Malan, DSO, DFC, former Merchant Navy officer and Battle of Britain pilot, and operations included refuelling in Cornwall for patrols out over the Bay of Biscay.

Mrs Eleanor Roosevelt came to see a typical Biggin Hill briefing, take-off and de-briefing after landing, but missed the big moment a few days later when as the squadrons were lunching an FW.190 thirty-plus hit and run attack sought the airfield but missed it and bombed a school in Bromley, Kent, in error. In only eight minutes from leaving the dining-tables, 611 were airborne and, over Beachy Head, caught some of the enemy, shooting down three and probably destroying or damaging four more. Then Squadron Leader Armstrong was lost in the Channel, his replacement being Squadron Leader Charlton Haw, DFM, Order of Lenin, one-time Sergeant-pilot in 504 (County of Nottingham) Squadron in 1940 and member of the RAF Hurricane Wing sent to Russia. In early 1943, Squadron Leader E. F. J. Charles, DFC, who had flown with 54 and 64 Squadrons, came to relieve Squadron Leader Haw and all the squadron trophies and every available man who could be spared left for Liverpool to boost the Wings for Victory campaign.

Down at Biggin Hill history was about to be made as the moment approached when the Thousandth Enemy Aircraft claimed by this base was to be chalked-up. A great sweepstake was organised, the successful pilots getting the 998th, 999th and 1,000th victories, to collect the prizes. It was on 15th May, 1943, when Nos. 611 and 341 (F.F.) (which had replaced 340) Squadrons, led by Wing Commander 'Al' Deere, DFC and Bar, with Group Captain Malan also flying a 611 machine, set off to escort bombers to Caen. Some ten miles SE. of the target a dog-fight ensued below the main force as Blue Section of 611, led by the C.O., dived down and destroyed two Focke-Wulf 190s. At about the same time the C.O. of 341 also claimed another FW.190 and as it was quite impossible to separate the times of the kills the two C.O.s, Squadron Leader Charles and Commandante Mouchotte, sportingly agreed to share the prize-money – which they immediately gave to their groundcrews – as the pilots were right-royally entertained in London.

125. 611 Spitfires from Biggin Hill, 1943.

On 30th May Flight Lieutenant Johnny Checketts, another popular 'Kiwi', scored the squadron's hundredth victory and although Norwegian Lieutenant Tradin was reported missing it was known that he, too, had shot down a Focke-Wulf 190: all hoped he would return from enemy territory if, in fact, he had baled out. Sergeant Lancaster also claimed an FW.190 and in celebrating the century-not-out, tributes were paid to the groundcrews who had helped keep up the magnificent serviceability and morale. Flight Lieutenant Count Franz Colloredo-Mansfeld, an Austrian, became a flight-commander and just before his DFC was announced, trapped an FW.190 into a high-speed stall seeing the enemy aircraft dive to destruction without a shot being fired by either pilot. On 30th June, 1943, after thirteen months in No. 11(F) Group, having flown, 6,898 hours and with a score of 27 destroyed and 45 either probably destroyed or damaged, the time came for another rest period, this time at Matlaske in Norfolk. With regret the Spitfire IX was left and at their new base the squadron took over the old Spitfire Vb aircraft of No. 315 (Polish) Squadron. The squadron was soon in action, though, in what they had thought would be a quiet backwater and, off Ijmuiden, Holland, shot down two of four FW.190s encountered, proving that even with obsolete machines they could out-wit the enemy.

Squadron Leader Charles and Squadron Leader Bill Compton (who got a Bar to his DFC for his 611 sorties and who now commanded 64 Squadron) were awarded the U.S.A. Silver Star for leading escorts to the USAAF Liberators and Fortresses but, alas, Squadron Leader Charles lost his aircraft on 25th July when, after destroying a Focke-Wulf 190 at close range, he was hit by the flying debris and forced into the sea twenty-five miles from the Dutch coast. After a fierce battle over his dinghy, Squadron Leader Charles was picked up and promoted to become a Wing Leader and received the DSO for his 611 leadership. Moving for brief attachments to Ludham then to Coltishall, Norwich, the squadron earned high praise from Wing Commander 'Laddie' Lucas, DSO, DFC, for splendid escorts to the 'Bomphoons' – the Hawker Typhoons now carrying up to two 1,000 lb bombs under their stout wings. Squadron Leader P. B. G. Davies, DFC, came in as C.O., and Flight Lieutenant Colloredo-Mansfeld, DFC, left to command 132 Squadron, later losing his life in action. Then came another blow for 611 when Squadron Leader Davies disappeared in his dinghy after successfully baling-out on 23rd August, 1943. In to command came Squadron Leader W. A. Douglas, DFC, an Auxiliary of 610 (County of Chester) Squadron, and with a move to Rochford, Essex, came the 'Ramrod' operations – penetration further into Occupied Europe to pave the way for eventual invasion. Unfortunately for the fighters 'Starkey', a fake invasion staged on 9th September, 1943, with empty landing-craft in the Channel, failed completely to draw up the expected hordes of Luftwaffe aircraft. A move back to Coltishall saw Flying Officer Colin 'Hoppy' Hodgkinson becoming a popular member of the squadron before he moved on to join No. 501 (County of Gloucester) Squadron.

126. Squadron personnel, Biggin Hill, 1943.

Some unusual tasks included the shooting down of some USAAF bombers which sometimes flew in over East Anglia crewless after their airmen had baled out over the sea or coastline. Extreme care had to be taken to bring them down away from populated areas. On occasions the squadron directed air-sea rescue craft to dinghies for the picking-up of these crews. Lieutenant R. G. 'Bob' Gouby, DFC, a Free French pilot, became a flight-commander, his decoration awarded for service with 164 Squadron and for sorties with 611. When the squadron was selected to be part of the Allied Expeditionary Air Force a move was made to a tented site at Deanland, Sussex, in April of 1944 to harden-up before the hoped-for advance into Europe. On D-Day – 6th June – the squadron was airborne at 0300 hours to protect U.S. forces landing on 'Gold' and 'Omaha' beaches in Normandy. Few enemy aircraft came up to oppose the allies until 10th June when Squadron Leader Douglas shot down a Ju.88 bomber at night and on the 14th three more enemy aircraft were claimed.

With the advent of the pilotless bombs flying over the camp by day and night, loss of sleep was a problem with the local Ack-Ack batteries firing all the time, and it was something of a relief for the pilots when they were at last able to land on the Normandy airstrips to refuel and re-arm for a second sortie before returning to Sussex. On 24th June, though, a move was made to Predannack in Cornwall, via Harrowbeer in Devonshire, and the escorting of RAF Lancasters on daylight bombing of U-boat pens and repair bases in Western France. One Free French pilot actually caught a glimpse of his father as the squadron flew low over St Brieuc but, on 14th August, Flight Lieutenant Bob Gouby, who had flown with the RAF since escaping from France in 1940, did not return from a mission. In September came a return to Essex, this time at Bradwell Bay, flying the Spitfire IX again under Squadron Leader McGregor. But in October it was a real blow when orders came for a move up to Orkney and Shetland, one flight based at Skeabrae and the other at Sumburgh at the foot of the Shetland Islands.

127. Squadron with Mustang, 1945.

Notwithstanding the distance from major activity the squadron managed to play its part and shot down a Junkers 188 attempting to photograph the Fleet at Scapa Flow, and, a few days later, during an escort to Coastal Command's torpedo-bombers, shot down a Ju.52 transport off the coast of Norway. On 1st January, 1945, as Goering ordered a big onslaught against our airfields in Belgium and Holland, the squadron was rushed down to Hawkinge, Kent, then across to Ursel in Belgium, to escort the streams of RAF and USAAF daylight bombers flying relentlessly into the heart of the Nazi war industries. The jet aircraft of the Luftwaffe were sometimes sighted and it was clear to all that the war in Europe must be ended soon if we were to avoid enormous casualties from these and the V.2 rockets then being launched.

In March the squadron re-equipped with the North American Mustang long-range fighter, powered now with the Rolls-Packard engine, but the pilots were dismayed to learn that they were not to indulge in ground-strafing but to stick closely to bombers until any enemy fighters showed inclination to fight. On 6th April came the first welcome break in routine as Focke-Wulf 190s tried to get at the fifty Lancasters in 611's charge. Three of the enemy fell to the Mustangs for loss of one aircraft, the pilot had engine trouble and, after baling-out near Minden, escaped capture and reached the allied lines. The day before the war came to an end in Europe the squadron was ordered to Peterhead, near Aberdeen, where Auxiliary, Group Captain Archibald Hope, DFC, was in command. A few escorts to high-ranking missions going to Norway were interspersed with the first real relaxation since the war started, when No. 234 Squadron was opposed on the cricket field and, dismissing 611 for only 42 runs, it looked easy for 'the Regulars'. However, the Lancastrians skittled their opponents out for only 28 – upholding the friendly rivalry of this station. Squadron Leader D. H. Seaton was replaced as C.O. by Squadron Leader P. C. P. Farnes, DFC, DFM, an appropriate appointment as he had flown as Sergeant-Pilot in 501 (County of Gloucester) in the Battle of Britain.

On 15th August, VJ Day, as war ended in the Far East, Air Marshal Sir James Robb, Air Officer Commanding-in-Chief of Fighter Command, signalled that 611 Squadron was to be disbanded so as to be able to re-form as soon as possible in the post-war Auxiliary Air Force. Corporal Bert Selwood wrote a poem recording the squadron's thoughts at this bitter-sweet moment as the men went their separate ways from Peterhead. It was not long, though, before many were volunteering again for part-time duties and in May 1946 under Squadron Leader W. J. Leather, DFC – first of the original Auxiliaries to qualify as a pilot – the squadron re-formed at Speke. This was, however, a 'paper' location as the expanding Liverpool Airport was not suitable and the squadron, in fact, began to re-form at Hooton Park on 16th June, 1946, moving over to Woodvale on 22nd July, 1946, and back to Hooton Park on 9th July, 1951. The Vickers-Supermarine Spitfire XIV and the North American Harvard trainer were allotted to get the squadron into the air. Squadron Leader Leather (who had ended the war as a Group Captain in the Far East) was typical of men who cheerfully dropped rank to re-enter the squadron. The pre-war adjutant, ex-Squadron Leader Robin Birley of Milnthorpe, Westmorland, came back, dropping a 'ring' to act again as adjutant. After a spell with the Spitfire F.22, the squadron re-equipped with the jet Gloster Meteor as Squadron Leader R. P. Beamont, DSO and Bar, DFC and Bar, wartime leader of 609 (West Riding) Squadron, test pilot with English Electric (now B.A.C.), took command. Summer Camps were held at Leuchars, Scotland, Sylt and Celle, Germany, and at Takali, Malta, and as the aircraft again changed to the Meteor F.8, Squadron Leader S. G. Nunn, DFC, became C.O., handing over in 1955 to Squadron Leader S. Kirtley, DFC, RAF, who had flown with 118 Squadron in war and with 257 post-war.

128. Squadron at Woodvale, 1947. Sqdn Ldr W. J. Leather centre.

In March 1957 came the news that all the twenty RAuxAF Squadrons were to disband and after a ceremonial parade the silver and trophies were handed on to No. 3611 Fighter Control Unit from the Town Headquarters, Everton Road, Liverpool. Some members kept up their flying – one of them Flight Lieutenant Bob Gaskell, a post-war flight commander, flying at the Royal Aircraft Establishment, Llanbedr, North Wales. Others have retained a link with aviation – notably 'Roly' Beamont, awarded the coveted Britannia

Trophy in 1953 and holder of many post-war records. The squadron's post-war medical officer, David A. P. Cooke, Fellow of the Royal Photographic Society, has contributed magnificent air-to-air pictures of 611's Meteors to the Royal Auxiliary Air Force collection. An interesting fact which has just come to light is that the surviving Dutch pilot of the trio who flew with 611 – ex-Flight Lieutenant Bruinier – a pre-war member of the Air Force of the Netherlands Indies Army, who left for the Far East on 18th October, 1941, rejoined his old squadron (3rd Aircraft Group) and was taken prisoner by the Japanese on 8th March, 1942. After his return to the Netherlands he rose to become Chief of the Air Defence Staff with many honours and awards.

Several of the one-time squadron pilots have reached high rank, including Air Vice-Marshals J. A. C. Aikens, CB; F. S. Stapleton, CB, DSO, DFC; F. D. S. Scott-Malden, DSO, DFC; W. Crawford Compton, CB, CBE, DSO, DFC; Group Captain W. G. G. Duncan Smith, DSO and Bar, DFC and 2 Bars; Group Captain S. G. Nunn, OBE, DFC; and Wing Commander K. M. Stoddart, OBE. Colin 'Hoppy' Hodgkinson, keen member of 'The Guinea Pig Club' for those badly burned, has made his mark in Public Relations and there are others who have maintained the great traditions of the squadron wherever they have gone. Ask them what they remember most and some will say 6th June when the squadron's Spitfires were – they believe – first across the Normandy Beaches in advance of the landing craft. Others recall that 611's Mustangs were probably the first RAF machines to meet Russian aircraft over Berlin. Older members will remember that the squadron badge is one of very few signed by King Edward VIII before he abdicated. A rarity for a very rare squadron to which a DSO, 14 DFCs, 4 Bars to DFCs, two DFMs, 3 BEMs and a U.S.A. Silver Star were awarded.

129. Squadron with Meteors, Celle, Germany, 1955.

REPRESENTATIVE SQUADRON AIRCRAFT

Avro Tutor		K3383 K3429 K3434
Hawker Hart		K3044 K3878 K6474 (T)
Hawker Hind		L7214 K5390 L7187
Fairey Battle		N2101 (T)
Vickers-Supermarine		
Spitfire	I	N3262 FY–O P9429 R6887 X4547
	IIa	P7314 P7553 P8035 P8567 P8593
	Vb	R7274 R7293 W3328 BL636 BM303 AR336 (LF.Vb)
	IX	EN133 FY–B BS475 FY–F BS387 FY–Y
North American Mustang	IV	KH638 KM132 FY–S KM368 FY–H
North American Harvard	IIb	KF223 KF255 RAR–Z KF640 RAR–X
Vickers-Supermarine Spitfire	XIV	NH784 RAR–D RM792 RAR–J TZ141 RAR–F
	F.22	PK632 RAR–A PK652 FY–G PK625 FY–H PK669 FY–H
Gloster Meteor	F.4	VT294 VT289 VW276 VW278 G
	T.7	WA718 X WF770 W
	F.8	VZ551 B WE899 J WH359 K WH365 D WK852 C WL110

It is thought that the Spitfire Vb formerly at the entrance to RAF Credenhill, Hereford, painted as AB871/M4353, is actually BL614 which served with 611 Squadron. This machine will be in the Royal Air Force Museum and it would indeed be a splendid thought to display it in the markings of the West Lancashire Squadron. Spitfire F.22 serial PK481, once with the squadron, is now in Perth, Western Australia, in care of the local Air Force Association (hence the code). It was formerly with the RAF Association in Sussex.

Prior to 3rd September, 1939, the squadron code letters were GZ from the arrival of the first Spitfires. On outbreak of hostilities the code changed to FY but on re-forming in Reserve Command this changed to RAR and reverted to FY on transfer back into Fighter Command in 1949. When, with advent of the Meteors, the squadron acquired its own markings, a black rectangle with red/yellow segmented diamonds was used, either side of the fuselage roundels.

Badge: In front of a trident, a rose, Drawn from the armorial bearings of Liverpool and the red rose of Lancashire.

Motto: 'Beware! Beware!'

503
(County of Lincoln)
Squadron

In January 1927 a recruiting office opened in Saltergate, Lincoln, for the Royal Air Force Special Reserve, to obtain volunteer part-timer aircrew and groundcrew personnel for No. 503 (County of Lincoln) Squadron, formed at Waddington in November 1926 with a nucleus of regular officers and airmen under the command of Squadron Leader R. D. Oxland. Flight Lieutenant W. R. Cox, MC, AFC, was adjutant and instructor, and Flight Lieutenant H. E. Walker, MC, DFC, with Flying Officers E. F. Haylock, C. P. Wingfield, C. E. Aston in charge of accounts and stores. Douglas Allison, a 22-year-old bank clerk, called to get details of the General Duties (flying) commissions and, approaching a chap who was wearing a tweed sports jacket and smoking a pipe, decided that he must be the C.O. and so called him 'Sir'. Given a pamphlet, Douglas was told to take it away and read it and that on the next Monday a squadron leader would be there to conduct interviews.

After a chat on this Monday, Douglas was invited to meet the 503 Squadron C.O. for lunch on the Wednesday at Boot's Cafe and there he was introduced to Wing Commander the Hon L. J. E. Twistleton-Wykeham-Fiennes 'whose steely-blue eyes looked right through one, weighing one up to an ounce, but nevertheless making one feel at home'. Douglas admits he was a little taken aback when asked if sandwiches and coffee would do, as he was very hungry. No matter; he was introduced then to Flight Lieutenant Cox (he of the sports jacket and pipe) who, in uniform with MC, AFC, and World War I campaign ribbons, filled Douglas with confidence. On 23rd April, 1927, Pilot Officer Allison was gazetted in the RAF Special Reserve, the first for 503 Squadron, and two days later Squadron Leader Oxland took him for his first flight – in a Fairey Fawn, the two-seat day bomber with a 470 h.p. Napier Lion II engine. A few days later Messrs R. H. Maw, T. North and R. Wardrop joined as volunteers and on 26th April Flight Lieutenant Cox commenced giving dual instruction in an Avro 504K, a type replaced at the end of that month by the Avro 504N, powered by the Armstrong Siddeley Lynx engine.

130. Squadron officers and airmen, Waddington, 1927.

131. Fairey Fawn III J7981, Waddington.

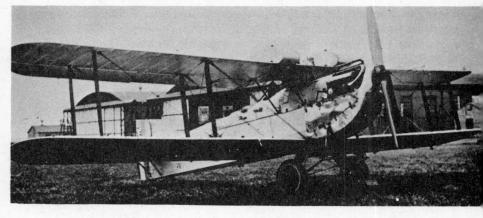

The brothers T. H. and G. A. Worth, Lincolnshire farmers, joined for pilot-training and by April 1929 the squadron had been named 'County of Lincoln' and was using the county's coat of arms although, for some unknown reason, the badge was never made official and given the Royal approval via the Chester Herald's office – the only Special Reserve badge to remain unofficial, unfortunately. During 1929, though, the strength had increased to thirteen Special Reservists officers – the highest number the squadron ever had – with nine RAF officers making up the establishment. During 1928 a summer camp was held at RAF Tangmere and officers who were to do extremely well in World War II, then Squadron Leaders Hugh Walmsley and C. B. Cooke, were the flight-commanders. In March

1929 the Fairey Fawns were replaced by the Handley Page Hyderabad and on 15th February, 1930, Wing Commander H. P. Lale, DSO, DFC, a most experienced pilot, became C.O., with Squadron Leader H. E. P. Wigglesworth, DSC, a former Royal Naval Air Service pilot, commanding A Flight, the operational flight, with B Flight the training flight.

Flight Lieutenant O. E. Worsley – who had helped gain the Schneider Trophy for Britain at Venice in 1927 – left 503 Squadron at this time and a note in the squadron diary recalls that the squadron occupied the old RFC hangars at the SE. corner of what was then an all-grass aerodrome at Waddington and adds that the walk across the aerodrome from the officers' mess was an excellent 'prairie oyster', especially in winter! The diarist later became Squadron Leader Arthur Young, MBE, who took a short service commission, as did many Special Reservists, and who now lives in Bamford near Sheffield in retirement. I am greatly indebted to him and to Douglas Allison for their contributions to expand the meagre official data of the 'Cinderella' unit of the SR/AAF.

On 11th May, 1931, Wing Commander H. I. Hanmer, DFC, took command, with Squadron Leader P. J. Barnett commanding A Flight. In July a new Reservist, Jack Peel, joined and became a most enthusiastic member. Flight Lieutenant Douglas Allison, the first part-timer to gain his wings, left to take up a civilian post in Malaya with many memories of his years with 503, especially of the 1930 Hendon Air Pageant when 503 were only narrowly beaten by a team

132. Special Reserve Officers, 503 Squadron, 1928. *Back row:* Groves, G. R. Worth, de Moleyns, Thompson, Brooke, Lindley, Canning. *Front row:* Maw, Barrow, Wardrop, Allison, T. H. Worth, Morris, Horsfall.

from 601 (County of London) in the race for Special Reserve and Auxiliary units; also of his last summer camp, held at North Coates, Lincolnshire. Tragically, Jack Peel lost his life, the first fatality in the squadron; and, because of business commitments, there were only six Special Reservists flying by April 1932. More Regular RAF officers had to be posted-in, including Flying Officers H. J. Piper and H. E. Power (the former remembered for his prowess at snooker, seldom, it is recorded, pocketing a ball without it vibrating between the cushions, gaining it fame as 'The Piper Shot' in the RAF).

Flying Officer Henry Power, grandson of a well-known ophthalmic surgeon, had been shot down over Holland on 1st September, 1918, when serving as an observer, subsequently training as a pilot at No. 4 FTS, Abu Sueir. He came to 503 Squadron from No. 2 FTS, Digby, where he had been crashed by a pupil-pilot and severely burned in the face. He was a strong character with a mischievous sense of humour, a modest man who shunned publicity and an exceptional pilot and instructor who, more than any other single officer, was to have a strong influence in the training and spirit of the squadron over the next five years. Although he could have strict discipline when essential he took full advantage of the minimum of red tape (which he detested) which prevailed in Special Reserve squadrons.

Wing Commander A. P. V. Daly, AFC, assumed command on 9th August, 1933, a former Morane Bullet pilot of 60 Squadron RFC. Squadron Leader Arthur Young, who joined the squadron in December, found (after he transferred later to the Royal Air Force) that the difference in atmosphere and enthusiasm between 503 and some Regular units was almost startling. In retrospect, he says, it seems that under the influence of Daly and Power the spirit in 503 must have been closely akin to that of the Royal Flying Corps. A notable recruit in 1933 was J. H. Smith, quickly followed by Michael Smith and Paul Ruston in January 1934, with C. W. Rees joining in February. Squadron Leader J. L. M. de C. Hughes-Chamberlain took over A Flight in April and the squadron, part of No. 1 Air Defence Group, became part of Western Area which commanded all bomber squadrons, under Air Vice-Marshal P. H. L. Playfair, CB, MC.

The squadron was being re-equipped with another obsolete aircraft, this time the Handley Page Hinaidi and of the machines delivered from RAF Cardington it was noted that one at least had only thirty hours to fly before its 'life' of 700 flying hours was up. An amusing (?) entry in the diary was that the appropriate serial number of one Hinaidi was K1066 (ex-No. 99 Squadron, RAF). Height tests were made and Pilot Officer Ruston won with 18,500 feet, with Pilot Officer Rees climbing to 18,400 feet, there being a 500-foot difference in reading between the cockpits despite that they were both zero on the ground! On 7th and 8th December full war-load tests were made with the reputed best and worst Hinaidi on strength, K1070 climbing to 500 feet in 1 minute 3 seconds whereas K1063 took an additional 16 seconds. To 10,000 feet K1070 took 44 minutes 47 seconds, but K1063 failed to rise above 7,400 feet, in just over 39 minutes. The maximum speed achieved by K1070 was 97 m.p.h. and K1063 85 m.p.h. Some pilots considered their old Hyderabads slightly superior to the incoming Hinaidi but when, after a flight, an NCO struck a penknife through the longeron of a Hyderabad and discovered 'fungae lachrymosis' it was deemed best to settle for the all-metal newcomer with the two 440 h.p. Bristol Jupiter VIII engines (against the Hyderabad's two 454 h.p. Napier Lion engines).

133. Handley Page Hyderabad, 503 Squadron.

134. Handley Page Hinaidi, on altitude test, October 1934.

Training on the Hinaidi commenced only a few hours after going solo on the Avro 504N and pupils flew, at the instructor's discretion, in all but the very worst weather conditions. Generally speaking (says Arthur Young) if one could see the trees on the Sleaford road, half a mile to the east from the hangars, flying took place. The technique of carrying out forced-landings in fog was academically learned by all and practised in thin fog by some on occasions. Part of the printed instruction read: 'Assuming the fog to be 100 or 200 feet thick, fly round the supposed location of the aerodrome and if no lights are fired within a minute or two you will know that the Duty Pilot is a mug and you will get no intimation of the whereabouts of his wretched hovel. It is hoped you will not decide to land unless there is a hole through which you can see some definite mark, such as a corner mark or a circle. Take the first, the better of the two; it gives more room to land if used well.'

Thursday 24th May, 1924 was Empire Air Day and Waddington was opened to the public with 503's Hinaidi and Avro 504N formations the attractions; one Reservist pilot even gave an aerobatic display. On 22nd July the squadron flew down to Manston for the Special Reserve and Auxiliary exercises, taking six Hinaidi and three Avro 504N aircraft. Manston was shared with 500, 501 and 502 Squadrons and the Fighter Stations of Biggin Hill, Hornchurch, and North Weald provided the 'opposition'. Arthur Young flew as second pilot bomb-aimer and navigator to Henry Power, their first night target a Dagenham factory which they 'bombed' with sachalite bulb flashes – in thick haze the sight of another aircraft's lights coming head-on produced a violent turn to starboard – to miss a Lufthansa Junkers mail aircraft heading for Croydon! In pea-soup conditions Henry Power handled the Hinaidi like a fighter, putting her down at the unfit-for-night-flying Hawkinge in sweeping side-slipping turns.

The next night F. D. Bradbrooke, editor of *The Aeropilot*, flew with Power and Young, he wrote of his flight:

Off Southwold the Hinaidi took to waltzing over the North Sea in broad moonlight – killing time before crossing the coast. I lounged on my promenade deck, gazing aft over the restless tail as it heaved and swung across the moon, till I knew its sixteen bracing wires by heart. Flight Lieutenant Power has a happy hand on the wheel of his great kite, and its antics were most graceful. I was leaning idly over the gunwale, braced casually against the knife-like hurricane when the light materialised. The airscrew discs and wire glowed like molten metal. I have never really considered a situation in which I might be falling from two miles high over sleeping London and wanting to fall faster. However, for a second or two I quite wished I could drop rapidly enough to keep up with the bomber, to which I was attached officially but insecurely, as Power dived to escape the searchlight. I had heard of power-dives! In a few seconds we were droning peacefully towards Dagenham while bereaved beams combed the night sky far to our rear.

Next time I was ready. Our pilot had a dislike of the limelight, rather unusual in distinguished aviators. One inquisitive beam caught us and was joined by a second – so I braced myself in the gun ring. The Jupiters bellowed in wrath and the Hinaidi reared, shook herself, stood on her head and dived like a giddy comet until she howled in all her wires, and the wind nearly planed me off neatly at the waist. We, with a thousand thunderous horse power, cut planetary capers in the thin, sharp, midnight air, and a few million candle-power groped for us in vain. If the fighters had come my hands were full; I could only have spat at them, but I was ready for a squadron or two. All in a night's work and a dull technical exercise – for some. Not for me, by Jove!

During September a new Air Ministry Order came out stating that all ab-initio training aircraft were to be painted yellow; the entire fuselage, mainplanes and tail unit. Prior to this all aircraft were silver dope finish. On 2nd October the squadron's first Avro 504 so painted was rolled out of workshops. It was a hideous sight, promptly dubbed 'The Flying Banana'. Then, at the end of the year rumour became rife; Royal Engineer personnel arrived and surveyed the airfield, it being said it was intended to extend it eastwards over to the Sleaford road; the squadron was to be moved and two day-bomber squadrons moved in! In mid-March 1935, work started on building the present hangars in the NW. corner.

135. Rehearsal for the Royal Review of the RAF, Mildenhall, 21st March, 1935. *Clockwise:* M. A. Smith, J. H. Smith, P. Ruston, R. Bradford, I. A. Critchley.

On 21st March, 1935, three Hinaidi aircraft flew down to Mildenhall, then the biggest and most modern RAF base, to rehearse for King George V's Jubilee Inspection of the Royal Air Force. On the actual day the King so disliked the turn-up uniform trousers that they were dispensed with soon afterwards for the straight-cut bottoms. During this year four new Reservists joined – Pilot Officers J. S. Bell, J. S. F. Hood, M. P. Forte, and R. H. Smith – Arthur Young left on being granted a six-year short service commission. In January 1936 Squadron Leader A. F. James arrived to command the squadron on the departure of Wing Commander Daly, AFC, and Squadron Leader Hughes-Chamberlain. On 1st May the squadron was transferred to the Auxiliary Air Force as a member of No. 6 (Auxiliary) Group, then Bomber Command, No. 502 (Ulster) being the only remaining S.R. squadron.

Following the arrival of at least one Westland Wapiti trainer the squadron began to re-equip with the Westland Wallace, the Mk.I with open cockpit and the Mk.II with closed cockpit. Harold Willers, of Rufford Green, Lincoln, was one who joined as an airman, became an armourer and, in 1936, qualified as a Corporal air-gunner. Pilot Officer G. Hellyer joined, and Flight Lieutenant E. J. Palmer was posted-in. With the departure of Squadron Leader James, Henry Power was promoted and became acting C.O., adjutant and instructor for a time. The Hawker Hart and Hawker Hind (many from No. 57 Squadron) had replaced the short-lived Wallace, and Avro Tutor trainers also arrived for pilots to convert to the new types.

On 6th February, Pilot Officer Forte, a young company director from Cleethorpes, was giving Leading Aircraftman East a flight in Hart K3025, when the machine crashed near Waddington, killing both instantly. For those interested in these matters it was stated that the day before the crash Michael Forte, in winding his office clock, accidentally knocked down a photo of himself which hung on the wall below a photo of his aeroplane. The clock was later found to have stopped at *exactly* the time of his death!

By April of 1937 a new station, Royal Air Force, Waddington, had been created and Wing Commander P. H. Cummings, DFC, arrived as the first Station Commander, his unit coming within No. 3 (Bomber) Group, though 503 was the only flying squadron there for some time, still part of No. 6 (Auxiliary) Group. Flight Lieutenant R. G. Harman came in from No. 7 Flying Training School, Peterborough, to instruct, leaving Henry Power as acting C.O. On Empire Air Day, 30th May, 1937, the Royal Air Force at home and overseas was shaken to hear that Squadron Leader Power had been killed. He was flying a Hawker Fury fighter in what was described as the finest and most daring aerobatic display ever seen at Waddington when, attempting a slow roll at high speed across wind and very low, he found himself drifting towards the hangars. He checked his roll, did an inverted turn away from the hangars – but then had insufficient speed to recover. To perform aerobatics so low down was quite unlike him, and so an exceptional instructor and first-class leader of men was lost to the Service.

By January of 1938, with the great expansion of the Royal Air Force taking place, many opted for full-time service and 503 Squadron was left with only six Reservist/Auxiliary pilots and one Regular – Flight Lieutenant Harman. RAF Waddington was moved into No. 5 (Bomber) Group (Headquarters Grantham) and Nos. 44, 50, and 110 Squadrons – destined to make history in World War II – were forming on the station. The 1938 Auxiliary Air Force camp was held at RAF Hawkinge, Folkestone, but the writing was on the wall; there was a pressing need to build up Bomber Command's Lincolnshire-based squadrons and no longer was there accommodation or provision of Regular 'hard-core' for the County of Lincoln Squadron. In truth the response for volunteers had not come up to expectations, as from areas of greater population like Nottingham or Birmingham. It was decided to disband No. 503 Squadron and to form a new unit, No. 616 (South Yorkshire) Auxiliary Squadron, at Doncaster, in the hope that the remaining part-timers of 503 would find it possible to make the journey to Doncaster to carry on, under Squadron Leader the Earl of Lincoln, who was appointed to command 616 Squadron.

136. Summer camp, RAF Hawkinge, 1938.

It was a pity that some of the airmen – chaps like Corporal Harold Willers – could not be absorbed at Waddington as part-timers, for many could not find time to get to Doncaster for evening sessions. Some became part of the RAF's Reserves but Pilot Officers J. S. Bell (killed in the Battle of Britain), Pilot Officer Hellyer and Pilot Officer

E. St Aubyn (killed in 1943) joined No. 616 Squadron and helped defend Lincolnshire against the Luftwaffe when war came. Other ex-503 members re-joined in August and September of 1939, Sergeant Harold Willers surviving No. 46 Squadron's fighting in Norway to go out to Middle East where he met other 503 members. Squadron Leader Young returned from his tour of duty with No. 60 Squadron and as a test-pilot in Karachi, to earn the MBE before retiring. Wing Commander J. R. T. Bradford, OBE, who joined 503 in 1932, also had a distinguished career. After leaving 503 on moving house in 1936 he joined No. 501 (County of Gloucester) Auxiliary Squadron and still flies himself around as an executive of British Oxygen.

One of the most interesting stories is of 503's very first Special Reservist pilot – Douglas Allison – who left to take up a position in Malaya. Returning later to the U.K., he realised that flying was his metier and, after obtaining the necessary qualifications, he became Chief Flying Instructor at the Herts and Essex Flying Club, Broxbourne, Hertfordshire, moving later to be C.F.I., at other aerodromes in England and Scotland. Two of the men he taught to fly are today Squadron Leader Jack Jones, AFC, Founder and Chairman of Channel Airways, and Squadron Leader Bernard Collins, MBE, the Airport Director, Luton. When war came, Douglas Allison returned to the Royal Air Force and whilst serving as Deputy C.O. at No. 4 Elementary Flying Training School, Brough, Yorkshire, saw two Blackburn B.2 trainers crash after their wingtips had touched. Douglas was flying at the time, but landing quickly, ran to the bank of the river into which one B.2 had dived, and swam out to a barge making for the spot. Feeling the B.2 with a barge-pole he again dived in, locating the cockpit he was amazed that there was no body there. When the aeroplane was raised to the surface it was seen that the safety-straps were broken. The body was found two days later, twenty miles away, carried down by a 15-knot current. For his gallant attempt Douglas Allison received the Royal Humane Society's bronze medal. Later he was appointed to command No. 17 Elementary Flying Training School, first at North Luffenham, Rutland, then at Peterborough where, to his delight, Pilot Officer Jack Jones arrived to be one of his instructors. Wing Commander Allison was awarded the Air Force Cross for his magnificent instructing and leadership (more than 600 pilots went solo at just one of his commands). He later commanded No. 5 Pilots' Advanced Flying Unit and ended the war as No. 21 Group's Accident Investigation Officer, based at Cranwell, not far from where his interest in flying began in January, 1927.

Douglas now lives in Nottingham and takes an interest in the Newark (Lincolnshire and Nottinghamshire) Air Museum where a Westland Wallace (the world's only example) is being restored and repainted one side as a 503 machine, the other as a 504 (County of

Nottingham) aircraft. Ask him his favourite memory of the County of Lincoln Squadron and you may be surprised that it is of the occasion when he was ordered to fly a bomber to pick up the C.O.'s field boots. This reminded Douglas of a squadron poem written when Air Ministry Order A.93 of 1936 appeared, abolishing these boots as part of Royal Air Force uniform – here it is:

The Squadron Leaders' Farewell to their Field Boots

Our lovely boots! Our lovely boots! You stand so sleekly there;
With proudly arched and glossy feet, all polished everywhere.
We may not put you on again, from now you are taboo,
We have to show a trousered leg, above a sordid shoe. . . .
No more upon smart Church Parades you'll be our splendid wear,
No more we'll seem Cloud Cavalry – bold riders of the air.
Below our breeches' manly curve how soldierly you shone,
But now we all are quite undone – our breeches too, are gone.
Farewell to both! At times maybe for you we yet shall yearn,
And even hope that some Command may cause you to return. . . .
Return? But, if by chance you're sold, what will your masters do?
They'll have to save for months to buy such other pairs as you.
Yet you must go. For Freedom's sake. 'Tis vain all this delay,
The Air Force has to dress for work and not for mere display.
Farewell! Our free unfettered limbs hence cheerfully will roam,
On lengthy tours with AOCs, about the aerodrome.
No longer shall our airmen see that highly-pleasing sight –
Those limping officers of rank in boots and breeches tight.
Nor when the Marshal's plane arrives and he climbs out of it,
And bends too much – shall juniors hear the august breeches split.
Yes; you must go. With ankles free and unconstricted knees,
Henceforth we'll climb into our planes with nimble careless ease;
Where once our legs were stiff or numb and knew not how to bend,
We gladly say 'Goodbye' to you, Old Boots, it is the end.

137. Squadron Hart K3007.

Others who made important contributions to the Royal Air Force in war and peace include Air Marshal Sir Hugh Walmsley, KCB, KCIE, CBE, MC, DFC, Air Marshal Sir Horace Wigglesworth, KBE, CB, DSC, Group Captain R. H. Maw, CBE, and others from groundcrew personnel who were commissioned in World War II, retiring with many decorations, reflecting much credit on their 503 Squadron training. You may search the official histories in vain for news of the squadron but its existence must never be forgotten; certainly by those who served at RAF Waddington. They took over where 503 Squadron left off.

REPRESENTATIVE SQUADRON AIRCRAFT

Fairey Fawn	II	J7211
	III	J7980 J7981 J6991 (5th prototype)
Avro 504N		J8592 J9271 K1965 K2368 K2416
Handley Page Hyderabad		J7742 J7782 J8321 J9035 J9294
Handley Page Hinaidi		K1063 K1066 K1909 K1925
Westland Wapiti Trainer		K2244
Westland Wallace	I	K3227 K5072 K5078 K5080
	II	K6013 K6042 K6057 K6058
Hawker Hart	I	K3006 K3023 K3046 K3816 K3900
		(T) K6486
Hawker Hind		K5473 K5481 K6747 L7193 (T) 7226
Avro Tutor		K3340 K3466

No badge was officially authorised but the unofficial badge combined the County of Lincoln arms with the eagle.

504

(County of Nottingham)
Squadron

ON 14TH OCTOBER, 1928, at Hucknall aerodrome NNW. of Nottingham, No. 504 Squadron came into existence as a Special Reserve unit in the light-bomber role, with Hawker Horsley aircraft. The first commanding officer was Squadron Leader Charles M. Elliot-Smith, AFC.

By the summer of 1931 it was possible to put ten aircraft into the air for summer camp at Hawkinge, Kent, a special train taking the remaining 20 officers and 111 airmen from Nottingham. The following year came the first casualties when an Avro Tutor trainer crashed on Bulwell Hall golf links. In July of that year Wing Commander Orlebar, famous Schneider Trophy pilot, came to examine volunteers for flying training and the Lord Mayor entertained the squadron to dinner, after which the City Council accepted hospitality at the squadron's mess. On 26th November, 1933, a Unit Chapel was dedicated by the Lord Bishop of Southwell in the presence of Sir Albert Ball, father of one of the greatest airmen of all time, the late Captain Albert Ball, VC, DSO and two bars, MC.

Eric Sharman, who was a Corporal Air-Gunner from 1932 to 1938, describes typical training sessions of the pre-war Special Reserves-Auxiliary members thus:

> We would be collected by bus in Trinity Square, Nottingham, on Saturday afternoons, early Sunday morning, and a few evenings each week, to be taken to Hucknall aerodrome where, after parading outside the guardroom, we would march off to our respective sections. The pilots, all officers, arrived separately in their cars, except for Pilot Officer J. C. Reynolds, who flew in from London in his Hornet Moth. The airmen were from all

138. 504 aircraft, 22nd July, 1932. *Right to left:* Avro 504K, Avro 504N, Avro 504K, then Horsleys.

walks of life, and speaking for the air-gunners, we would find that the regular RAF staff always arranged an interesting programme. Flight Sergeant (later Wing Commander) 'Chick' Edge and Corporal 'Jobbo' Jobbins would lecture us on such subjects as the Lewis Gun, theory of bombing, sighting, tactics, navigation, air pilotage, or perhaps the practical use of various synthetic training devices. We were never more happy, though, than when airborne and putting into practice what we had been taught.

Our formation flights over Nottingham were a very familiar sight to local citizens. We carried out cross-country exercises and camera practices during which it was necessary to perform violent aerobatics whilst engaging other aircraft in mock-combat. We gunners, standing upright in our open cockpits, would feel the terrific force of air resistance on the upper part of our bodies, unprotected from the waist up. We were fastened to the aircraft by a length of wire, one end attached to the cockpit floor, the other to the D ring on the lower part of our parachute harness (the parachute pack was not worn but tucked away in a stowage). When flying upside-down for a spell we dangled by our bottoms on the end of the safety wire. Whilst changing film in our camera-gun we would be in a crouching position out of wind, engrossed in threading film into the slot in the take-up spool. On standing upright to put the magazine into the camera mounted on the scarf ring we would glance upward to look for our attacker but would probably see green fields at an acute angle above us and blue sky below. We would just be coming out of a loop, or roll, or 'Immelman' turn; such were the thrills of air-gunnery which we all enjoyed immensely in those far-off carefree days.

On other occasions we would be lying in the prone position, feet towards the tail, head and shoulders suspended over a large opening. We had pushed forward the sliding floor of our cockpit and were carefully watching objects on the ground thousands of feet below appearing to move slowly up the drift wires on the course setting bombsight. We were engaged in the process of finding the wind-speed and direction with the aid of the bombsight by the 'three course', '90 degree', or 'timing the bead' methods. During these exercises it was always necessary to yell with all force down the Gosport tube to give orders to the pilot. Our voices would be almost indistinguishable above the deafening roar of the engine and also the rush of air.

There were two main bombing practices; the Camera Obscura method where, when the 'tit' was pressed, instead of releasing a bomb a magnesium flare occurred in a bulb attached to the bomb-rack. A 'plotter' sitting in the Camera Obscura room on the aerodrome (which was our bombing target) watched the track of our aeroplane moving on a chart as it was being projected through a large lens in the roof, following our path with a pencil and marking the chart where he saw the flash, he could then calculate the accuracy of bombing. Live bombing usually involved a flight to Upper Heyford, Oxon, on Saturday afternoons to bomb-up early Sunday mornings. Armourers would attach eight $8\frac{1}{2}$–$11\frac{1}{2}$ lb bombs on the racks and we would head for Otmoor Ranges, each making eight individual runs over target, releasing one bomb per run. As bombs burst the chloride filling gave off a white vapour, easily seen from the air, and we were able to plot on Form 3073 the position and time of each strike. Competition was tremendous, bomb-bursts also being plotted on the ground by two observers, to decide which crew had the best results.

There were two annual events to which the whole squadron

139. Pilots and air-gunners, 1935.

looked forward, the chief being the compulsory continuous 14 days' training camp at Hawkinge, Kent, when we lived under canvas, carrying out an intensive programme including about 25 hours' flying for every air-gunner, with bombing and air-to-ground firing with live ammunition at Lydd, and the Leysdown Range on the Isle of Sheppey, bombing-up at Eastchurch aerodrome. Another part of our training was affiliation with the fighter squadrons when our manœuvrable Westland Wallaces (which replaced the Horsleys in 1934) would dog-fight with Bristol Bulldogs or Hawker Furies. For our photographic missions we would guide our pilot towards the centre of each run line by gripping his right or left shoulder and he would continue turning to port or to starboard until the grip was released. The Gosport tubes from the earpieces on our helmet would not reach the speaking-tube plug-in point in the cockpit whilst we were leaning over the side looking vertically down at the targets.

The other annual event was Empire Air Day held at Hucknall when our squadron would put on a display for the crowds. Imagine our pride when 504 was chosen to take part in the Review of the Royal Air Force at Mildenhall to commemorate the Silver Jubilee of King George V in 1935. We sent four Wallace aircraft with aircrews, fitters and riggers. We spent hours metal-polishing the cowlings and how magnificent was the array of 500 aircraft representing every type in current service all silver and white except the night bombers which looked very formidable in their matt black finish. In front of the aeroplanes each side of the upright blades of the propellers stood pilots (and gunners where applicable) with groundcrews at wing-tips. This was a sight that had never before been seen in England, the largest congregation of aeroplanes ever assembled.

140. Westland Wallaces over the River Trent, 1935.

After exchanging the Wallace for the Hawker Hind in 1937 (the squadron had become part of the Auxiliary Air Force in May 1936 under Squadron Leader Sir Hugh Seely, Bart, MP, the first part-time C.O.) further changes came when 504 was designated a fighter unit. After a short spell with the Gloster Gauntlet, which, unfortunately, saw the departure of the loyal air-gunners, some being persuaded by Squadron Leader Seely to train as NCO-pilots, the Hawker Hurricane was received just before outbreak of war as the Rt. Hon Lord Mottistone, PC, CB, CMG, DSO, agreed to be the first Honorary Air Commodore. The 1939 summer camp was held at RAF Duxford, Cambridgeshire, and as the squadron was embodied into the Royal Air Force for active service, Squadron Leader Seely took a post in the Duxford operations room, Pilot Officer Lord Allerton rejoined the Coldstream Guards, and Squadron Leader Victor Beamish, AFC, a regular RAF pilot, assumed command as 504 Squadron moved into RAF Digby for intensive war training.

141. Hawker Hind trainers of 504, 1937.

Convoys along the Lincolnshire–Yorkshire coast were protected and then the squadron moved into Debden, Essex, keeping detachments at Wattisham and Martlesham Heath for the escorts to shipping. In January 1940, Victor Beamish handed over command to Squadron Leader Hartley Watson, with Pilot Officers Renison, Wendel, Count Czernin, and Prince Obolensky (the great rugby player) becoming operational on the Hurricane. On 2nd April, 1940, history was made as Blue Section of three fighters sighted two Heinkel 59 floatplanes approaching a convoy. Opening fire at extreme range our fighters first silenced the enemy's rear-gunners and the two Heinkels turned and made off for their German bases. A few days later Pilot Officer A. G. Lewis left to join No. 87 Squadron in France, there to make a name for himself and to earn the DFC and Bar.

May was a disastrous month as on the 1st, the C.O., Squadron Leader Watson, took off just before midnight to try and intercept a night raider, only to lose his life when trying to land near Bungay. Squadron Leader J. Parnall took over and between 12th–22nd May the squadron fought in France from Lille-Marcq and from Norrent Fontes. On 14th May a Ju.88 became the squadron's first confirmed victory. Squadron Leader Parnall, Squadron Leader Hill and Flight Lieutenant W. B. Royce all commanded the squadron during this hectic month and Royce became the first of the Auxiliary members to be awarded the DFC for his leadership and combats. When the squadron was down to only four serviceable Hurricanes, instructions came for evacuation and unfortunately all the records and a great deal of equipment and personal kit were destroyed. The squadron was ordered to Wick in the far north of Scotland to re-form under Squadron Leader J. Sample, DFC, a veteran of air-fighting over France with 607 (County of Durham) Squadron.

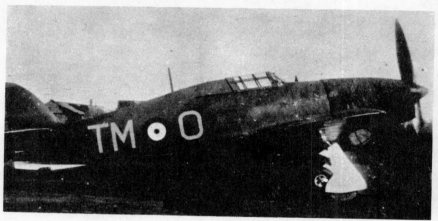

142. Hurricane I, serial L1931.

Charged with the defence of the important Royal Navy base at Scapa Flow in the Orkneys and with protection of our Scottish convoys, the squadron 'champed at the bit' as the Battle of Britain grew into a major conflict. They did, however, score two successes: He.111s on 24th and 28th July (the second not claimed but known from post-war Luftwaffe evidence to have been lost to a 504 interception near the Orkneys). At last their pleas were answered and on 5th September they flew into Hendon, rested on the 6th and next day destroyed two enemy bombers and damaged others over the Thames Estuary. Pilot Officer K. V. Wendel was killed and Sergeant B. M.

Bush had to make a forced-landing at Eastchurch but was uninjured, Hurricane P3021 being slightly damaged. As the squadron maintained defensive patrols over London and SE. England a grateful Hendon firm presented a bulldog, 'Suzy', as a mascot. On the 11th September Pilot Officer A. W. Clarke was shot down and killed and on this day Pilot Officers J. V. Gurteen and Michael Rook experienced technical troubles, their Hurricanes having to be taken out of service. Count Czernin, who had left 504 to join No. 17 Squadron, added to his growing tally of victories, a tribute to the training of Victor Beamish who was now commanding the RAF base at North Weald, flying whenever he could and claiming several successes in the air combats.

After comparatively quiet days on 12th–14th September, the 15th saw the squadron battling high over London, claiming five Dorniers shot down and five more damaged. Post-war figures show that in fact three Do.17s were destroyed by the squadron and two more damaged, a splendid achievement. One Dornier, shot down by Sergeant R. T. Holmes near Victoria Station, had attacked Buckingham Palace. Sergeant Holmes had to bale out, Pilot Officer J. V. Gurteen was killed and Flying Officer M. Jebb baled out with severe wounds and died the same evening. Flight Lieutenant Royce dropped Gurteen's ashes over his comrade's home, keeping a pact requested by the dead pilot.

On 17th September a new pilot, Sergeant D. A. Helcke, baled out during training and was killed over Kent. The next few days saw

143. Dispersal scene 1940. Sqdn Ldr Sample, centre, Sgt Haw far right, Flt Lt Rook reading on table, Flt Lt Royce with gramophone.

the squadron patrolling against the decreasing Luftwaffe attacks and then, as the enemy switched to night bombing of the capital and to day raids into the West of England, with a successful bombing of the Bristol Aeroplane Company's works, No. 504 Squadron was ordered into Filton to protect the approaches to Bristol. The Luftwaffe, whose forces had wreaked havoc unopposed on the 25th, returned on the 27th and were routed by 504 Squadron whose pilots claimed six enemy destroyed, though post-war checking indicates that three Messerschmitt Bf.110s fell and one more landed back at its French base badly damaged. Nevertheless, the factories were saved from further harm and the grateful Bristolians sent a barrel of beer and a parcel of cigarettes, the Lord Mayor calling to thank the Nottinghamshire squadron for their timely work. Lord Beaverbrook, then Minister of Aircraft Production, wired 'Your fine courage saved the aircraft factories'. Who can say what effect this defensive action had on the war, with the night-fighter Beaufighters just coming into full production at the Filton works? It ranked as one of 504's great days.

September ended with another Luftwaffe raid, this time intended to wipe out the Westland Aircraft works at Yeovil. The Heinkels and Messerschmitts which evaded two squadrons of our fighters over Dorset were met by 504's Hurricanes and, again, the factories were saved as the enemy bombs were jettisoned wildly into the countryside or on civilian targets such as Sherborne. One He.111 was chased as far as Portland and then shot down and a second Heinkel was shot into the sea. The squadron losses this day were two Hurricanes (P3021 which Sergeant Bush had force-landed on 7th September was this time again landed after an enemy attack and was written-off, the pilot uninjured). The other Hurricane crashed into the sea from enemy fire and Flying Officer Hardacre's body was later washed ashore. Two other Hurricanes were hit by enemy return-fire and damaged, their pilots unwounded.

144. The squadron at Exeter, 1940.

During October the enemy made a further attempt on Yeovil's factories without much success, though some workmen were killed when a shelter was hit. One squadron aircraft had to make an emergency landing on 16th October but Pilot Officer R. E. Tongue was unhurt. Two enemy aircraft were claimed during this month and the squadron's known score during 1940 was about twenty enemy destroyed with others damaged for the loss of four pilots (three on operations). The Bristol workers had a whip-round and the sum of £39.0.0 donated to the squadron was passed to the RAF Benevolent Fund, though the 2,000 cigarettes which accompanied the gift found good homes in the pilots' and groundcrews' huts. Night-fighting was attempted and although a Ju.88 was chased as far as Banbury and left smoking, no firm claim could be established. Squadron Leader Royce, DFC, promoted to command No. 260 Squadron, departed, leaving only four Auxiliary pilots as the year ended, though 114 of the NCOs and airmen were Nottinghamshire volunteers.

A move was made to Exeter and, in March 1941, Squadron Leader Michael Rook assumed command. On 8th April came the first casualties to groundcrews when Leading Aircraftman Parr and Aircraftmen Armstrong and Bickford died as a result of a hit-and-run Luftwaffe attack. The main tasks now were to escort our daylight offensives to the Cherbourg Peninsula and to strafe ground targets such as enemy airfields or transports. In July, Flight Lieutenant A. H. Rook was promoted to command No. 81 Squadron and left, along with the 504 Squadron adjutant, for an unknown destination,

145. Re-arming between patrols.

later revealed as Russia where he gained the DFC and was awarded The Order of Lenin. Sergeant C. Haw, who shot down one of the Messerschmitt 110s near Bristol and who got the DFM later, also went to Russia and was commissioned, gaining the DFC.

After spending part of July and August at Fairwood Common near Swansea, flying shipping sorties over South Wales, the squadron moved to Chilbolton, Hampshire, for a few days before being sent to Ballyhalbert in Northern Ireland, there to re-equip with the Spitfire IIa and to train a band of newcomers including Pilot Officer Prince Galitzine, a Russian naturalised British, who had fought with the Finns against the Communists. Free French, Royal Australian, and Royal New Zealand Air Force pilots swelled the ranks and Squadron Leader P. T. Parsons, who had joined 504 as a junior officer, assumed command, handing over in February 1942 to Squadron Leader R. Lewis, DFC, a flight-commander before being promoted to C.O. The occasional enemy reconnaissance machines visiting Northern Ireland were pursued to the limit of the Spitfire's fuel, some being shot down into the sea with a few making emergency landings in neutral Eire. Flight Lieutenant Gowers was awarded the DFC, and detachments were sent to Eglinton and Kirkstown.

In October of 1942 the squadron returned to England and, from Middle Wallop and Ibsley, Hampshire, became top cover squadron for daylight sorties by Boeing B–17 Flying Fortresses, using the recently-acquired Spitfire Mk.Vb for these and 'Rhubarb' operations – the penetration of Occupied Europe's defences to force the Luftwaffe to refrain from strengthening their squadrons on the Russian Front. Squadron Leader J. I. Kilmartin, DFC, took command from January to March of 1943, handing over to Squadron Leader R. C. Kilian as 'Exercise Spartan' took place, to prepare the British Army for possible invasion. The squadron then participated in deck-landing practices, giving rise to all sorts of rumours but the next move was

146. Squadron personnel in 1943 with mascot 'Suzy'.

from Church Stanton on the Somerset–Devonshire borders into Redhill, Surrey, where a few Spitfire VI high-flying interceptors were added. Then came a move to Castletown, near John O'Groats, for the defence of the Fleet, followed by a spell at Peterhead near Aberdeen where new pilots were brought to operational efficiency to replace the many experienced pilots sent out to Middle East squadrons.

Squadron Leader P. J. Simpson, DFC, had been replaced on his promotion by the experienced Squadron Leader H. J. L. Hallowes, DFC, DFM and Bar. In January 1944 the squadron flew down to Hornchurch, Essex, to join a Wing of Spitfire IX's carrying out offensives into Europe, particularly against the enemy's top-secret weapon, later known to be the flying bomb, but at this time known as a 'Noball' target. During February a rare sneak raid by the Luftwaffe on Hornchurch destroyed or damaged fifteen of the squadron's Spitfires but the Vickers-Supermarine factories were turning out replacements faster than our losses and only a few hours' activity was lost. In March, Squadron Leader Banning-Lover, AFC, assumed command and 504 was given the task of flying 'Jim Crow' sorties – early-morning reconnaissance flights in advance of the big daylight operations mounted by both the RAF and United States Air Force bombers.

When Bomber Command Lancasters successfully hit the V.1 sites and later blocked the railway tunnels in which Hitler's terror-weapons were being stored, it was 504's Spitfires which flew above to shield the bombers from Luftwaffe intervention. For D-Day the squadron again provided cover and when the Prime Minister visited our troops in Normandy it was 504 which had the honour of acting as protective escort. For the ill-fated Arnhem landings the squadron covered the armada of transports and gliders, being based at these times at Lympne and Detling, Kent, after a brief rest period back at Castletown with detachments at Digby, Lincolnshire (the squadron's 1939 war station), and Acklington, Northumberland.

From Manston in Kent with the Spitfires now carrying bombs and quickly nicknamed 'Bomfires' a series of 'Channel Stop' missions was flown to prevent German vessels from attacking our reinforcements moving over to Europe. Refuelling in France, the Spitfires flew on to hit targets ahead of our forces and as airfields became available in Holland the squadron detached some pilots to operate as bomber-escorts far into Germany. Several pilots, though, had moved to the Gloster Aircraft airfield for training on the RAF's first jet, the Meteor, and, after a short spell at Hawkinge and at Maldeghem in Belgium, the Spitfires were handed over and at Colerne, near Chippenham, Wiltshire, No. 504 Squadron became the second (after 616 [South Yorkshire] Squadron) to be given the Gloster Meteor III fighter. Squadron Leader M. Kellett, DFC, a Battle of Britain pilot, was now in command, and Flight Lieutenant Anthony Snell, DSO, who had escaped from the Germans in Italy though badly wounded, became a flight-commander.

To the disappointment of all members, 504 Squadron's jet training could not be turned into action before the war in Europe ended, but a detachment was sent to Lübeck in Germany and it flew some impressive formation displays during July 1945. In August, though, came orders to disband and the Meteors were handed to No. 245 Squadron. In May 1946 the squadron began to re-form, firstly as a light-bomber squadron at Syerston, but this was soon changed to the night-fighter role with the de Havilland Mosquito NF.30 under Squadron Leader A. H. Rook, DFC, AFC, who had served with distinction at No. 57 Operational Training Unit after his return from Russia. On becoming a night-fighter unit the squadron moved to Hucknall and there transferred to the day-fighter role, using the Spitfire F.22. Squadron Leader J. M. Birkin, a pre-war RAF Volunteer Reservist with a magnificent war record, took over command in 1948 and Lord Sherwood, who as Sir Hugh Seely had been C.O. 1937–39, became Honorary Air Commodore.

147. Squadron Meteor F.4 in 1950.

In March 1950 the squadron received the Meteor F.4 following a move to Wymeswold, and Squadron Leader G. J. Beardsall, a Nottingham-born pilot who had served in Nos. 214 and 102 (Bomber) Squadrons, joining the Auxiliary Air Force at Hucknall in 1947, assumed command. The Meteors were flown to Celle, Germany, for summer camp as a break from those held in the U.K. and in March 1952 the squadron received the Meteor F.8. In 1954, Squadron Leader P. I. Briggs, DFC, a Shirebrook, Nottingham, airman, another ex-bomber pilot of Nos. 199, 171, and 157 Squadrons, became C.O. The Honorary Air Commodore from 1956 was Air Commodore J. M. Birkin, CB, DSO, OBE, DFC, AFC, the Chilwell officer who had commanded the squadron before becoming Inspector of the Royal Auxiliary Air Force. The 1956 camp was held in Malta, and early in 1957 came the presentation and consecration of The Standard, awarded by Her Majesty for the squadron's twenty-five years of meritorious service. Air Chief Marshal Sir Francis Fogarty, GBE, KCB, DFC, AFC, a pre-war adjutant and flying instructor with 604 (County of Middlesex) Squadron, made the presentation, and The Standard, at first laid-up in St Mary's Parish Church, Nottingham, was later to go into the RAF Chapel in Southwell Minster and finally to the RAF Church, St Clement Danes, in London. Battle Honours shown were France and Low Countries 1940; Battle of Britain 1940; Home Defence 1940–42; Atlantic 1941–42; Fortress Europe 1942–44; Normandy 1944; Arnhem 1944; France and Germany 1944–45.

Many at The Standard ceremony re-lived their personal experiences: over London during the Battle of Britain; fighting off the attacks on Bristol and Yeovil aircraft factories; trying to draw the flak away from our airborne forces at Arnhem by flying at only 2,000 feet over the dropping zones. It was a gathering of men who had helped to make history. Of the nineteen pre-war pilots eight had been killed in action and two seriously wounded and a further eight others who joined during war also gave their lives. In addition to the combat decorations (some of which were promulgated after pilots left 504 and cannot in all cases be traced) there were Air Force Cross awards to Group Captain K. Gough, Wing Commanders G. Greaves, J. C. Reynolds and M. M. Hutchinson (the last-named was later killed in action). Many had gone to the top in the post-war Royal Air Force, including Air Commodore A. G. P. Brightmore (first commissioned in 504 in 1938) and Air Commodore L. H. Snelling, CBE, AFC, who also served with the squadron.

The decision to disband the Royal Auxiliary Air Force was a severe blow to the volunteers of Nottinghamshire. Some of the squadron's possessions were transferred to the County Territorial Association Hall on Derby Road, Nottingham, and as this is written plans are afoot to open a Newark (Nottinghamshire and Lincolnshire) Air Museum, in which will be displayed the world's only known Westland Wallace, bearing the colours of 504 on one side and 503 (County of Lincoln) on the other. There will be a Meteor to honour the post-war 504 squadron pilots and groundcrews and efforts are currently being made to try and acquire other types flown by the squadron and to exhibit, at the old airfield at Winthorpe (now the County Agricultural Showground), other souvenirs of No. 504 (County of Nottingham) Squadron, RAuxAF, where they can be seen by former members, their families and their friends. The squadron may have been disbanded but the glorious pages of history it helped to write will never die.

REPRESENTATIVE SQUADRON AIRCRAFT

Hawker Horsley		J7993 J8018 J8019 J8614 (Mk.II)
Avro 504K		H2995
Avro 504N		J9256 J9703
Westland Wallace		K3907 (1813M) K4015 (Wapiti airframe K1344) K5082 (Wapiti K1413)
Hawker Hind Trainers		K6715 K6716 K6785
Hawker Hurricane	I	L1615 L1931 TM–O N2481 N2705 P2987 P2414 R4178 (became Sea Hurricane)
	IIb	Z5082 Z5539 Z5704
Vickers-Supermarine Spitfire	IIa/b	P7690 P7734 P8576 P8666
	Vb	BL966 EN773 EP651 EN907
	VI	BR473 BS437
	IX	NH587 PL256 PL396 TM–E
Gloster Meteor	III	EE286 EE293 TM–V EE302
de Havilland Mosquito NF30		NT561 NT562 RAD–M NT566
North American Harvard	IIb	KF577 RAD–X
Vickers-Supermarine Spitfire	F.22	PK495 RAD–A PK595 RAD–H PK621 RAD–T
Gloster Meteor	F.4	VZ403 RAD–A/TM–A VZ404 VZ406 RAD–E/TM–E
	T.7	WA610 WA615 WF823 WL475
	F.8	WF682 C WH307 WH310 J WH344 B WH464 F WH504 U

Just before World War II the squadron aircraft were coded AW but this was changed on outbreak of war to TM. The letters HX may have been used during the Spitfire Vb period. Upon re-forming after the war RAD was the code in Reserve Command and this was changed to TM when the squadron moved into Fighter Command again. From 1951 the squadron had its own markings comprising green rectangle outlined in red either side of fuselage roundels.

It may be of interest to some that Spitfire Vb AR501, kept at the Royal Aircraft Establishment, Thurleigh, Bedfordshire, but owned by the Shuttleworth Collection, Old Warden, and awaiting hangarage there, was once with 504 Squadron. In the Battle of Britain film it flew as N3314, N3316 and N3320 and was coded at various stages AI–E, AI–G and DO–A. It also has a civil registration of G–AWII and it is good to know that it may one day be seen again in the air – perhaps wearing the TM code?

Badge: An oak tree fronted and eradicated – the 'Major Oak' of Sherwood Forest from the armorial bearings of the county, thought very apt for a Hurricane squadron.

Motto (translated): 'It avenges the wind'.

501
(County of Gloucester)
Squadron

ON 14TH JUNE, 1929, No. 501 (County of Gloucester) Squadron formed at Filton aerodrome, Bristol, as a Special Reserve bomber squadron. Flight Lieutenant the Hon L. P. Winters came from No. 7(B) Squadron as temporary C.O., and Flying Officer B. E. Moody from No. 2 (Army Co-operation) Squadron to be the first instructor. On 23rd August came an Avro 504N from No. 605 (County of Warwick) Auxiliary Squadron, known as the Lynx-Avro powered by the Armstrong Siddeley Lynx IV or IVc engine. With the arrival of Squadron Leader R. S. Sugden, AFC, to take command Flight Lieutenant Winters became adjutant and with an enthusiastic response to the appeal for part-time volunteers to supplement the nucleus of Regular personnel, Messrs D. C. Beauchamp, R. A. Hall, A. T. Laws, W. F. Pharazyn and the Honourable H. C. H. Bathurst were enrolled as pilot officers for flying training. On 6th December, 1929, the first recruits for ground trades were attested on production of satisfactory certificates of efficiency from employers and the usual intelligence and medical tests.

Flying Officer V. S. Bowling arrived from No. 503 (County of Lincoln) Squadron, Flight Lieutenant R. A. A. Cole from No. 14(B) Squadron and Flight Lieutenant E. A. Hodgson and Flying Officer J. B. Neal from the Central Flying School. Dr F. G. Mogg, a local practitioner, was commissioned to be the squadron M.O., and on 13th March, 1930, the de Havilland D.H.9A became the first operational machine. Pilot Officer Pharazyn made local history on the 30th April when he received the RAF flying badge: the first of the squadron volunteers to qualify as a pilot. On 1st May the squadron was designated 'City of Bristol' and on 31st May when HRH Prince Albert, Duke of York (later King George VI), flew into Filton prior to the opening of Whitchurch aerodrome, the squadron was on duty, strengthened by Pilot Officers N. Alexander, G. Bearne, with G. N. Warrington from No. 2 Flying Training School, Digby. At that summer's annual Special Reserve and Auxiliary camp, twelve officers and eighty-eight airmen attended for training and Pilot Officer Pharazyn was so attracted to Royal Air Force life that he accepted a short service commission for full-time duties. Pilot Officer A. N. Luxmore and Flying Officer M. C. Collins were posted-in and, soon afterwards, the Westland Wapitis, built at nearby Yeovil, became squadron aircraft.

The 1931 summer camp, held at Manston, Kent, saw newcomers Messrs H. Clarke, P. Holman, H. S. Laws, D. G. Lewis, A. D. Pickup and C. N. Shaw swelling the ranks of potential pilots. Nine aircraft were flown over Cardiff for Civic Week and during the 1932 Air Defence of Great Britain exercises the Air Officer Commanding-in-Chief congratulated 501 on a fine performance. Tragically, though, the first man to gain his wings, Flying Officer Pharazyn, RAF, lost his life in an air accident at Bekesbourne, Kent, on 27th July, 1932. On 17th December came a new commanding officer, destined to rise to the very top, though he, then Squadron Leader William Elliot, DFC, would have been the last to make such a prediction. In January 1933 the Westland Wallace superseded the Wapiti and it was a signal honour when the squadron was selected to participate in the famous Hendon Air Pageant though, alas, bad weather prevented the flying that year.

The squadron, however, excelled at the Bristol Air Display, staged at Whitchurch, and demonstrating that keenness typical of the Special Reserve units, clubbed together to buy a glider for additional experience. September of 1933 saw the squadron co-operating with the Gloucestershire Hussars and there were also long-distance flights to Abbotsinch, Scotland, to liaise with 602 (City of Glasgow) Squadron. Bombing practice took place at Boscombe Down, Wiltshire, and front-gun firing at Lydd Ranges, Kent. During 1934, Pilot Officer D. O. Young came from No. 503 (County of Lincoln)

148. Squadron pilots 1934. Sqdn Ldr Elliot fifth from left.

and Flying Officer M. K. Le May from 500 (County of Kent), with Flying Officer L. F. Sinclair as instructor. March of 1934 was marred by the death of Aircraftman Griffiths, Special Reservist, when a Wapiti crashed; Flying Officer Le May baled out successfully. Empire Air Day attracted over 2,000 visitors and after the flying the Bishop of Bristol dedicated the RAF Chapel. Flight Lieutenant W. E. Staton, MC, DFC, came in as adjutant and in May 1935 C. E. Malfroy and M. H. Taylor joined as pilots-under-training.

The squadron was represented at the Royal Review, Mildenhall, and when Flying Officer Holman decided to take a short service commission he was posted to No. 99(B) Squadron. 1st May, 1936, was another squadron landmark on the change from Special Reserve to the Auxiliary Air Force, being designated 'County of Gloucester' with Flight Lieutenant H. M. 'Toby' Pearson coming in as adjutant and, on being promoted, to command. Camp was at Donibristle, near Edinburgh (No. 500 [County of Kent] coming to Filton). Following a short period as adjutant, flying instructor, and then acting C.O., Flight Lieutenant F. W. Stannard departed and Squadron Leader M. V. M. Clube, AAF, became the first Auxiliary Air Force C.O. The coronation of King George VI brought the commemorative medal to Pilot Officer E. S. Williams, the squadron's nominee, and an assistant adjutant was appointed, Flight Lieutenant G. N. Amison filling this post.

For Empire Air Day in May 1938 the country's growing awareness brought 11,000 spectators to Filton with special recruiting

149. Sergeant-Pilots of 501 at Filton, September 1939.
Douglas Crabtree on ground.

flights laid on to attract more volunteers; the custom of a five-year stint in the Auxiliary Air Force, necessitating new blood to replace the original members, many of whom had been World War I veterans. On 14th July HRH the Duke of Gloucester, KG, KT, GCMG, GCVO, accepted appointment as Honorary Air Commodore and on 26th September the squadron was mobilised for the Munich crisis. Flying Officer E. R. Bitmead arrived at this time and after the 'panic' the great news was released that 501 was to become a fighter squadron, competent to fly by night in defence of this country. His Majesty King George VI approved a squadron badge; and a Fairey Battle fitted with the Rolls-Royce Merlin engine arrived for advanced dual-training. The first Hawker Hurricane followed, with others arriving in time for summer camp at Manston during which the squadron was embodied into the Royal Air Force 'for the emergency'.

Returning to Filton to become part of Bristol's defences it was not until 11th November that the first war patrol was ordered when six aircraft took off but made no contact with the enemy. On 27th November the squadron was moved to Tangmere, Sussex, and a newly-trained batch of NCO-pilots joined, including Sergeant J. H. 'Ginger' Lacey. The time was occupied in affiliation exercises with the locally-based Blenheim night-fighters and in searchlight co-operation. With the Nazi blitzkrieg came instructions to move to France with all speed and on 9th May, 1940, the advance party left, with sixteen Hurricanes flying off on 10th May to Bethieneville. Soon after landing came the squadron's first combat when Flying Officer A. D. Pickup destroyed a Do.17 some fifteen miles NW. of Vouziers when, after a burst of 140 rounds from the Hurricane's eight guns, the Dornier pilot baled out of his crippled bomber – what happened to his crew is not recorded.

The next day, 11th May, was disastrous, as the last of the transport machines bringing in the remaining pilots and some ground personnel crashed on touching-down. Flying Officer A. C. J. Percy, Sergeant Whitfield and Sergeant Barnwell were killed and the crew of the aircraft and six other 501 members were taken to hospital. There was little time for mourning, though all who could be spared attended the service for their comrades. A devastating toll was exacted that day from the Luftwaffe as six of 501's pilots – Flight Lieutenant Williams, Flying Officer Malfroy, Pilot Officer Hulse, Flight Sergeant Payne, and Sergeants Dafforn and Morfill, ploughed into a formation of some twenty Dorniers, Heinkels, and Messerschmitt Bf.110s, between Bethieneville and Rheims, and shot down six without loss. Next day, with visibility up to thirty miles and a large force of Luftwaffe bombers overhead before dawn, fighting continued all through the hours of daylight. When the reckoning came that evening 501 claimed twelve Luftwaffe machines but

Flying Officers P. H. Rayner and M. F. C. Smith were believed killed. Sergeant J. E. Proctor claimed a Do.17 and a Bf.110; the squadron's first double.

13th May was again fine and Sergeant Lacey opened his personal account with an He.111 and the squadron's first Bf.109 near Sedan, claiming a Bf.110 near La Chesne on a later patrol. Other pilots claimed four more enemy aircraft in all and next day Sergeant Proctor claimed a pair as Flying Officer Cridland, Flight Sergeant Payne and Sergeant Dafforn also registered two Heinkels and a Dornier between them. 15th May was cloudy but not enough to prevent Flight Sergeant Griffiths shooting down a Dornier near the airfield, a member of the Luftwaffe crew, who baled out, was picked up by two of 501's airmen who happened to be driving in Bethiene-ville. Flight Sergeant Payne shot down another Dornier and Sergeant Proctor a Bf.110 near Mourmelon. During that evening Flying Officer Cridland and Pilot Officer Hairs came upon seven Dorniers; Cridland's first burst killing the nearest enemy air-gunner, after which the Hurricane's fire totally destroyed the bomber, the other Dorniers making off at top speed.

On 16th May the squadron moved to Anglure but the Luftwaffe kept out of sight for three days, the smoke from burning towns being the only evidence of enemy activity. On the 24th, a lone Henschel 126, probably on reconnaissance, was damaged during a squadron escort to an RAF Blenheim's photographic sortie. On the 25th, after refuelling at Rouen, the squadron patrolled over Hesdin as our bombers hit back at Nazi ground forces. Over Abbeville intense flak brought down Pilot Officer Sylvester, last seen using up his ammunition on a gun-post, before gliding out towards the sea. Next day the squadron moved on to Boos, near Rouen, delighted to hear that Sylvester had managed to land his crippled Hurricane and that he claimed to have damaged a Dornier.

150. Hurricane L1659.

27th May was a record day for 501: as twenty-four He.111s were intercepted and as soon as the Hurricanes (thirteen, led by Flight Lieutenant E. Holden) dived into the formation the Messerschmitt 110s, supposed to be escorting the bombers, flew off leaving the Heinkels, eleven of which were promptly shot down, with others damaged. One Messerschmitt 110 was pursued and destroyed, all for no loss to the Hurricanes. Next day there was no action for 501 and although an escort was flown to a French Air Force Potez on recce over Soissons on the 29th the enemy did not come up to fight, nor were any squadron combats recorded for 30th/31st. It is known that there were combats on 1st June, though squadron records are incomplete as most were burned on orders from Air Force Headquarters. On 2nd June ground personnel moved to Le Mans, leaving aircraft and pilots at Boos and on this day Pilot Officer A. J. Claydon was killed, and buried at Rouen. Wing Commander Clube left on promotion and other experienced pilots went to the U.K. to strengthen newly-forming fighter squadrons. The ground personnel then left for Dinard by air and by road with the pilots – thought to be the last based in France – staying over the British Expeditionary Force until 18th June, returning via the Channel Islands after covering the evacuations from Cherbourg.

On 21st June the squadron re-assembled at Croydon under Squadron Leader H. A. V. Hogan and began intensive training of new pilots. On 2nd July Air Marshal Sir Arthur Barratt, Air Officer Commanding-in-Chief, RAF in France, came specially to thank the surviving pilots for their magnificent achievements. The Distinguished Flying Medal was awarded to Sergeant Lacey and there were probably awards to others, though squadron records of this period are not clear. On 4th July the squadron moved to Middle Wallop, Hants, joined there by Midshipman Lennard, one of many Fleet Air Arm volunteers to fill gaps in the RAF squadrons after the fighting over France. Convoys were escorted and Sergeant Dixon was jumped and shot down by Bf.109s, he baled out but was drowned.

Moving to Warmwell, Dorset, a new airfield satellite for Middle Wallop, Pilot Officer D. A. Hewitt was lost attacking a Dornier over a convoy near Portland Bill, followed a week later by the loss of Pilot Officer Sylvester, veteran of France, killed in combat over Lyme Bay. On 25th July the squadron was moved to Gravesend, Kent. Next day Flight Lieutenant P. A. N. Cox, who had two successful combats to his credit, lost his life near Dover, thought, alas, to have been the victim of our own guns firing at the enemy.

Over Dover on 29th July a major engagement with a large force of Ju.87 Stuka dive-bombers resulted in 501 making claims for six destroyed and others damaged but post-war figures credit the squadron with two confirmed and another damaged, giving the others to Spitfires who also claimed, presumably, the same machines shot down. Pilot Officer R. S. Don had to bale out and was injured on the 31st and Pilot Officer E. G. Parkin was seriously injured when trying to land his damaged Hurricane at Gravesend, the aircraft was written-off.

In early August four Polish pilots, having escaped across Europe, arrived on the squadron strength after refresher training, and 501 flew to Hawkinge, near Folkestone, each morning, Squadron Leader A. L. Holland being attached for combat experience before he took command of No. 65 Squadron. On 7th August, when landing after an early-morning patrol in terrible weather, two Hurricanes collided at Gravesend and were totally destroyed, but Sergeants E. F. Howarth and W. A. Wilkinson were happily unhurt. There was coastal skirmishing by the Luftwaffe for a few days as they built up their reconnaissance prior to 'Eagle Day', the preliminary to invasion, but it was not until 12th August 'Adler Tag' minus-one, that 501 got into the action by claiming two Bf.109s with two others damaged, for the loss of Pilot Officer K. Lukaszewicz. Squadron Leader Holland's Hurricane was damaged in combat and he made an emergency landing in fields near Dover without personal injury.

On 15th August the squadron engaged about twenty Ju.87s over the Thames Estuary and others attempting to dive-bomb Hawkinge airfield. Claims that fourteen Stukas had been destroyed or damaged have been reduced by post-war analysis to three definitely shot down with damage to others later finished-off by other squadrons. Two Hurricanes were brought down but Flight Lieutenants J. A. A. Gibson and A. R. Putt were uninjured. Next day three Dorniers were engaged but as their destruction was not confirmed, claims of damaging them were submitted. Post-war evidence, however, shows that at least one Do.17 was destroyed by a 501 attack and another had to be written-off after the crew had been picked up from the Channel by German rescue services. Then came a setback on 18th August when, in a series of dog-fights over Kent, seven of the squadron Hurricanes were shot down by the crack Luftwaffe Jagdeschwader 26s II Gruppe (III/JG26) under the redoubtable Major Adolf Galland. Flight Lieutenant G. B. Stoney and Pilot Officer J. W. Bland were killed, Pilot Officers K. N. T. Lee and F. Kozlowski seriously wounded, and Sergeant D. N. E. McKay baled out with burns. Veterans of France Pilot Officer R. C. Dafforn and Flight Sergeant P. F. Morfill were unhurt.

As an indication of the confused claims of this period, no Luftwaffe aircraft were credited to 501 for the morning battle though during an afternoon attack by the enemy on Biggin Hill, two Bf.110s were claimed and post-war figures show that these were, in fact, shot down by 501 and that a third Bf.110 was so damaged by their Hurricanes that it had to crash-land in France. Then came a welcome respite for re-equipping with new Hurricanes and not until 24th August did the squadron have to take on the Luftwaffe again when thirty Dorniers with fighter escort attacked Hawkinge and Manston airfields. In the first raid one Bf.109 was claimed but the squadron lost Pilot Officer Zenker, killed. At lunch-time two Ju.88s were destroyed, one by Ginger Lacey, the Bf.109 escorts shooting down Pilot Officer K. R. Aldridge who suffered a broken arm when he baled out. Marshal of the RAF Viscount Trenchard braved the bombing to visit the squadron; a real tonic for all ranks.

On 27th August Squadron Leader Hogan's aircraft was hit but he managed to land with the glycol tank punctured. Meanwhile a Do.17 was chased into France: two of its crew baled out and post-war evidence indicates that the machine crashed. Next day three Bf.109s were destroyed and on the 29th the squadron was bounced in the evening and Flight Lieutenant Gibson and Sergeant W. J. Green baled out and lost their Hurricanes, two 109s being shot down, one by Ginger Lacey. On 30th August Ginger claimed a share of four Heinkels believed shot down near Southend, his Hurricane was hit in the radiator, forcing him out of the fight. He was back in the air that afternoon, claiming an He.111 destroyed (and a Bf.109 the next day). The same day Sergeant Glowacki baled out unhurt. The following day over Tunbridge Wells three Hurricanes damaged a Bf.110, forcing it back to its base and on 2nd September Gravesend airfield was bombed. The squadron claimed a mixed bag of enemy destroyed or damaged but lost Pilot Officer A. T. Rose-Price killed, Pilot Officer S. Skalski and Sergeant W. B. Henn wounded, and a fourth Hurricane when Sergeant H. C. Adams was shot down, though he was unhurt.

Signs that the Luftwaffe crews were losing heart for the fight showed on 4th September when a formation of fifteen turned back rather than face 501's Hurricanes. On the 5th the unlucky Skalski was shot down over Herne Bay, baling-out wounded, his Hurricane falling to destruction. Ginger destroyed a Bf.109 near Folkestone in the afternoon patrol and Sergeant Gent claimed one as probably destroyed. During the first patrol of the 6th, though, three pilots were brought down, Sergeants Adams and O. V. Houghton being killed, with Sergeant G. W. Pearson unhurt; although only one Bf.109 was claimed, the Luftwaffe admitted to a couple, so one of the dead pilots must have got one. Next morning Flight Lieutenant Gibson, back in harness, claimed a Messerschmitt 110 as damaged but later evidence showed that it did not, in fact, get back to its base. The Luftwaffe now turned to night bombing of London and although this was followed up on Sunday 8th September by a small daylight offensive enemy losses were great in comparison with those of the RAF, 501 Squadron destroying one of the Bf.109s.

On 10th September the squadron was moved into RAF Kenley,

to man the Maidstone Line with 253 Squadron, to prevent the Luft-waffe reaching London. Three Heinkels were either destroyed or damaged on the 11th and Sergeant T. G. Pickering had to bale out when an escort Bf.109 shot up his Hurricane. On the 'unlucky for some' Friday 13th, Ginger destroyed an He.111 but his Hurricane was badly damaged by the Heinkel's fire and Lacey baled out. Next day Sergeant Farnes damaged a Do.17 (which crash-landed at Cherbourg according to Luftwaffe files) and on Sunday 15th Septem-ber the squadron flew several sorties from early morning to dusk. Claims were inextricably confused with those of other squadrons who attacked the same machines either before or after 501's pilots had fired. Post-war investigations show that at least three Dorniers were destroyed by the squadron and that Ginger Lacey claimed a Heinkel which had bombed Buckingham Palace. Squadron Leader Hogan had to bale out after being attacked, and Pilot Officer Van den Hove was killed on his first patrol. Next day was quiet but on the 17th, with Squadron Leader A. D. Murray flying with the squadron for experience, Squadron Leader Hogan claimed a Messer-schmitt 109 as damaged but Sergeants Egan and Lacey failed to return, Egan was later found dead in his Hurricane near Ashford but Ginger, having baled out to safety, returned to Kenley in the evening.

On 18th September, Squadron Leader Hogan was again forced to bale out after combat with 109s and Sergeant C. J. Saward also jumped from his shattered Hurricane after 109 cannon-fire. Pilot Officer Hairs claimed one enemy aircraft as damaged and Squa-dron Leader Hogan thought he had probably destroyed one before leaving his Hurricane. The weather next day was poor but Ginger took off after a lone He.111 (which in the rain he identified as a Dornier) firing at 300 yards and making no claim though post-war records show that the Heinkel was hit but that it got back to its base. The Secretary of State for Air, Sir Archibald Sinclair, called to meet the squadron and Squadron Leader Murray left to command 73 Squadron (and to get the DFC). Fighter Command signalled awards of DFCs to Flight Lieutenants J. A. A. Gibson and E. Holden. On the 27th claims were made of four enemy aircraft shot down but two Hurricanes were lost, Pilot Officer E. M. Gunter losing his life when his parachute failed to open and Sergeant V. H. Ekins jumping successfully, though wounded.

Next day two more Hurricanes were lost near Deal to Bf.109s, Pilot Officer F. C. Harrold losing his life; Pilot Officer E. B. Rogers baling-out unharmed. On the 30th Sergeant Farnes got his third confirmed kill when he destroyed a Junkers 88 near Gatwick and the month ended with twenty-one pilots still in action and nine more non-effective, either in hospital or on sick leave. On 4th October, the Luftwaffe, obviously affected by their heavy losses, started hit and run raids, a solitary Ju.88 claimed as damaged near Kenley later known to have crashed in France. On the 5th a force of Bf.109s carrying bombs attacked the railway workshops at Ashford, Kent, three being hit by 501's fire, one definitely destroyed, the other two probably getting back to France. On the 7th the enemy tried again and this time the squadron destroyed three and a fourth fell into the Channel after Pilot Officer MacKenzie had rammed the Bf.109, MacKenzie making a forced-landing near Folkestone with his damaged Hurricane. Flying Officer N. J. M. Barry lost his life in this encounter.

On 12th October, Flight Lieutenant Holden and Sergeant Lacey claimed to have damaged Luftwaffe machines in inconclusive combats with the hit and run attackers and on the 15th came news of a DFC award for Pilot Officer MacKenzie. During another sneak raid by the enemy, Sergeant S. A. Fenemore was killed and Sergeant R. W. E. Jarratt was forced to land at Rochford and his Hurricane was written-off. Flying Officer R. C. Dafforn's Hurricane was damaged in combat and he landed it at Rochester where it was found to be repairable. The night of 17th/18th October was marked by a bombing attack on Kenley and four Hurricanes were damaged but luckily our aircraft production was now overtaking losses. On the 25th, combats at 25,000 feet with the high-flying Bf.109s brought down two of the raiders but the operation was marred by a mid-air collision between Pilot Officers V. Göth and K. W. MacKenzie, the former losing his life as MacKenzie baled out to safety. Sergeant S. A. H. Whitehouse and Pilot Officer V. R. Snell were also lost, with their Hurricanes, in this engagement.

During sporadic incursions by the enemy on 27th, 29th and 30th October, the squadron claimed six Bf.109s hit, possibly accounting for some of the post-war evidence that some of these machines did not get back, though definite combats could not be checked. DFCs were announced for the C.O., Squadron Leader Hogan, and for Pilot Officer K. N. T. Lee and with the promotion of Wing Commander Hogan to No. 58 Operational Training Unit, Squadron Leader E. Holden, DFC, assumed command. On 8th November during a visit by Group Captain HRH the Duke of Kent, the squadron was scrambled and, over Maidstone, Sergeant Farnes shot down a lone Messerschmitt 109, chasing and firing at a second soon afterwards. Flight Lieutenant D. A. E. Jones, posted-in from No. 3 Squadron, got another Bf.109 on his first sortie with 501 and Sergeant Whitehouse also claimed one, with Blue Section having shared one between the three pilots. Sergeant Groves did not return from this minor battle; a rare event at this time.

On 12th November Red Section shared a Ju.88 and although Pilot Officer MacKenzie was jumped on the 15th by a Bf.109 he managed to get on to its tail and shoot it down. By December, though, the occasional visiting Messerschmitt fighter-bombers were flying above 30,000 feet and although Flying Officer Dafforn got his Hurricane to 32,000 feet to damage a Bf.109, his aircraft was also hit and as he made an emergency landing at Detling, he learned that 74 Squadron's Spitfires had brought down his attackers. The DFM was promulgated for Sergeant Farnes who was granted a commission shortly afterwards, as was Sergeant Whitehouse. Flying Officer K. N. T. Lee, DFC, left for a special-duty post with Rolls-Royce and although Kenley was again singled-out for a Luftwaffe night bombing, no squadron machines were affected. Pilot Officer Skalski was awarded the Polish Flying Cross as orders came for a move to Filton near Bristol, the squadron's birthplace. A quiet period, with occasional hit and run raiders and a share of the convoy patrolling, was interrupted by a tragedy when Sergeant R. J. K. Gent, a promising pilot who had a Bf.109 to his credit, died when ferrying the squadron's Miles Magister from Kemble, Gloucestershire, to Filton.

The January Honours List brought the DFC to Flying Officer R. C. Dafforn, DFM, and a Bar to the DFM for Pilot Officer Ginger Lacey who had just been commissioned. Many of the battle-worn pilots left to instruct others, including Flight Lieutenant Jones and Pilot Officer Farnes, but in their stead returned Flight Lieutenants Cridland and Malfoy who had completed a tour of instructing at 70 OTU. Many of the squadron's Polish pilots now left to join the new all-Polish units, Nos. 306 and 316. Sergeant Grimmatt, a comparative newcomer, hit the balloons near the airfield in poor visibility and was killed, HRH the Duchess of Gloucester conveying her husband's sympathy during a personal visit to the squadron. Then, after a brief sojourn at Colerne, near Chippenham, the squadron moved to Westhampnett, and contributed to the Prime Minister's directive to 'set Europe ablaze' escorting bombers to targets in Occupied Europe. HM The Queen Mother paid an informal call which coincided with the arrival of the first Spitfires, in April 1941, and four Czech pilots arrived to swell the flying strength and Fighter Command allocated night interceptions to the squadron, although Spitfires were hardly the most suitable aircraft. However, as if to uphold the 'chairborne' ruling, the new commanding officer, Squadron Leader A. H. Boyd, DFC and Bar, taking off from the squadron's new base at Chilbolton, Hampshire, scored the squadron's first night victory over Portsmouth. The flight-commanders were now the ex-NCO pair Flight Lieutenants Dafforn and Lacey, and it was regarded as a real honour for the squadron when 501 was chosen to do the flying sequences for the film *The First of the Few*.

It was not until 10th June that another combat was logged when Squadron Leader Boyd and Flight Lieutenant Lacey claimed one enemy aircraft destroyed and another one damaged during an escort to Blenheims bombing ships at Cherbourg. The High Commissioner

151. Spitfire IIs of 501 on patrol.

for Australia came down to present to Ginger a personal parachute and scarf donated by Australians to mark his many combats. A short detachment was made to Predannack, Cornwall, for Bay of Biscay patrols during which two Bf.109s coming in to attack Lacey fell to destruction after Lacey had used up his ammunition and was avoiding combat – the Messerschmitts colliding! As Wing Commander Boyd moved to Middle Wallop on promotion, Squadron Leader C. F. Currant, DFC, ex-605 (County of Warwick) Squadron, came to command and a move was made to a newly constructed airfield at Ibsley, on the edge of the New Forest, the ponies having to be shepherded off the runways before operations. Ginger moved away to instruct, having added an He.59 seaplane to his tally and 'The Fighting Five-O-One', as the proud groundcrews referred to the squadron, led a new three-squadron wing, including Nos. 118 and 234 Squadrons.

Pilot Officer John Dennehey joined at this time and with the Mk.Vb replacing the earlier Spitfires the squadron now carried out anti-shipping strikes and, for a break, practised escorting the Army's gliders during exercises. A lone Ju.88 was shot down as it tried to reconnoitre the area and permission was sought – and obtained – for 'Rhubarb' sorties. Casualties were high and any pilot brought down was usually taken prisoner, but some managed to escape. Flight Lieutenant (now Air Marshal Sir) Harry Burton, the first man to escape from Germany in World War II, came to talk to the pilots but most, if their aircraft were disabled, tried hard to get back as far as the sea rather than be taken prisoner. If they then had to 'ditch' and take to a dinghy, our air-sea rescue system did a magnificent job and many were saved to fight again.

Pilot Officer R. Wheldon, who had to left join an overseas squadron, came back after the Wellington in which he was a passenger crashed between Gibraltar and Malta, he being one of two survivors from the sea. Now that the RAF's four-engined bombers, the Short Stirling and Handley Page Halifax were operating by day, the squadron was given the task of close-escort on raids against Brest. Unhappily for the allies, permission was refused early on 12th February, 1942, for the squadron to carry out a B Flight shipping reconnaissance. At noon, though, the squadron was ordered to fly to West Malling, Kent, there to refuel and take off immediately afterwards in search of *Scharnhorst* and *Gneisenau*, now creeping up the North Sea, a convoy which 501 might have spotted hours earlier if the authorities had allowed their early-morning reconnaissance. Readers will know the outcome of this day's blow to our pride, but it was no fault of the squadron. Wing Commander Ian Gleed now flew with 501 as he led the wing, though the Luftwaffe rarely took the bait and it was 25th April before the squadron met opposition, and trouble, as six Bf.109s dived out of sun and Flying Officers Palmer-Tomkinson and Wheldon were reported missing with two of the Czech pilots also shot down.

There were awards of the DFC for Flight Lieutenants Ekins and Newbery and a Distinguished Service Order for the C.O., Squadron Leader Currant, DFC, who had often led the wing and who was promoted to command RAF Ibsley. The incoming C.O. was Squadron Leader J. W. Villa, DFC and Bar, of Battle of Britain combats in 72 and 92 Squadrons. In mid-July the body of Flight Sergeant Thomas, missing since April, was washed ashore and news came that Sergeant Potelle, a Belgian pilot, was a prisoner of war. The DFC was announced for Flight Lieutenant Stanbury and the glossy magazine *The Tatler* featured the County of Gloucester pilots as a much-decorated team. Flying now from Harrowbeer as escort to the Douglas Bostons bombing St Malo involved almost 300 miles of sea and an He.59 floatplane was one of very few enemy aircraft seen, and shot down. For the ill-fated Dieppe landing of August 1942 the squadron moved into Tangmere, flying four sorties that day, sharing several victories with other squadrons. Pilot Officer Lightbourne had to bale out and, with his parachute caught on the tail, fractured his right leg and was paralysed in the arm. He nevertheless managed to extricate himself just in time to hit the sea and later climb into his dinghy, no mean feat in his condition.

The Czech Government in exile awarded decorations to their 501 squadron pilots and the Croix-de-Guerre was awarded to Frenchman Lieutenant B. Fuchs. Then came a real rest from action when, in October, the squadron moved to Ballyhalbert in Northern Ireland, with a detachment at Eglinton. Squadron Leader A. J. Robinson took command with Flight Lieutenants C. J. Cox, DFC, and A. J. B.

Friendship, DFM, as flight-commanders. New Zealand Ace of the Malta air battles, Flying Officer Ray Hesselyn, DFM and Bar, joined the squadron in time for a return to No. 11(F) Group's area in April 1943 with Westhampnett again the base. Squadron Leader B. Barthold took command and a one-time Fleet Air Arm pilot, the legless Colin Hodgkinson, also joined the squadron. Escorting Air-Sea Rescue aircraft and launches and covering escapes of gallant Frenchmen rowing the Channel enlivened the daily 'Jim Crow' early-morning weather flights which the squadron now flew from Hawkinge, after brief sojourns at Martlesham, Suffolk, and Woodvale, Lancashire.

It was rare for combat opportunities to offer themselves as all the No. 11 Group squadrons depended upon 501's reports before the day's big operations but the squadron pilots pressed on into France to photograph the Luftwaffe airfields and to watch for signs of the secret-weapon sites which it was known the Nazis were constructing. A mixed bag of nationalities included Australian, Belgian, Canadian, Czech, French, New Zealand, Polish and American pilots with, of course, members from all parts of the British Isles, a happy band now commanded by Squadron Leader M. G. Barnett, a Kiwi, awarded the MBE, for his adventurous return after being brought down in enemy territory.

Equipped now with the Spitfire IX, the squadron's patrols ranged from Western France to the Dutch–German borders, flying the dawn sorties and then following the mass daylight raids to photograph the damage. In February (1944) 501 notched 341 missions of all types and then, in April, came a move into Friston, Sussex, and under canvas in preparation for what all knew was to come – the invasion of Occupied Europe. The airfield was shared with No. 350 (Belgian) Squadron and the wing leader was Wing Commander Don Kingaby, DSO, DFM and 2 Bars, a famous Sergeant-Pilot of the Battle of Britain. An all-out blitz on enemy targets: off-shore shipping, transportation, airfields, continued until D-Day when, at 0300 hours, the squadron took off to cover the eastern end of the beaches. Few enemy aircraft challenged the allied landings and it was not until 8th June that 501 scored a victory in the air when Flight Lieutenant D. C. Fairbanks, a Canadian, shot down a Bf.109 and damaged a second, and Flight Lieutenant L. P. Griffith, DFC, from New Zealand, also claimed a possible victory. On 11th June the squadron landed in Normandy, refuelled at the first airstrip in the American Sector (A.1) and then escorted 36 Mitchell light-bombers attacking the 'Noball' sites, the Vergeltungswaffe or V.1 retaliation weapon.

The following day the first V.1 flying bomb was launched against Southern England and the squadron had an early success when Squadron Leader Barnett, testing his Spitfire, overtook and shot one down. Back to Westhampnett came pilots who had been detached to France, bringing news that Warrant Officer Vid, lost in March, was buried beyond the beaches. On 18th July news came that the squadron was to re-equip with the Hawker Tempest which was 30 m.p.h. faster than the Spitfire IX, at 434 m.p.h. (only the Spitfire XIV was faster, at 448 m.p.h.). From Manston, Kent, the squadron staged a daily battle against the flying bombs with Squadron Leader J. Berry, DFC, from the Fighter Interception Unit as C.O., with Squadron Leader Barnett and twenty of the pilots leaving to form No. 274 Squadron as another Tempest unit, also at Manston. The County of Gloucester Squadron was chosen to be the night-operational squadron and soon achieved a high score of doodlebugs shot down with thirty-three destroyed by the end of August; Flight Lieutenant Bonham, DFC, got four in one patrol, including a V.1 tipped-over out of control by the Tempest's wing.

In September, with the flying bombs now being launched from Holland and from Heinkels in mid-air, the squadron was ordered to Bradwell Bay in Essex to catch them before they crossed the East Coast. For a busman's holiday Squadron Leader Berry led his pilots across the sea to strafe Luftwaffe airfields and the V.1 launching sites. In October, unhappily, he was hit by fire from a single flak-post and killed, a Bar to his DFC having earlier been announced. Post-war information reveals that he was the top-scoring pilot against the flying bombs with 61 shot down and another which he shared with two other pilots. What is owed to him is beyond words. Squadron Leader A. Parker-Rees, DFC, took command, and sad to relate, the other high-scoring pilot, Flight Lieutenant Bonham, was ordered off in bad visibility to try and intercept an incoming V.1. Trying to get back to base he crashed and lost his life.

As the enemy was pushed back into Germany the V.1 was replaced by the V.2 rocket which could not be intercepted in the air, though 501 helped to attack many of the sites from which Hitler's second terror-weapon was being launched. In March 1945 the squadron moved to Hunsdon, Hertfordshire, and disbanded there on 30th April; members who had time to serve moved over to other squadrons. Flight Lieutenant A. J. Grottick joined No. 611 (West Lancashire) Squadron and had to bale out into enemy-held territory on his very first sortie. True to type he evaded capture near Bremen and later rejoined his squadron. Other pilots joined the Mustang squadrons at Bentwaters and some flew aircraft out to the Far East or, like the C.O., moved into chairborne jobs until they were released from the Royal Air Force.

In May 1946 the squadron was re-formed at Filton and was allocated the Spitfire XIV under Squadron Leader T. James, an Australian who had flown with Nos. 84 and 88 Squadrons in World War II. The adjutant was Flight Lieutenant R. F. W. Cleaver, DSO,

DFC, who had happy memories of Bristol, for it was at Whitchurch that he had landed on 17th June, 1944, having flown in from Gibraltar after successfully evading capture, with the assistance of patriots. (As captain of a Halifax of No. 644 Squadron on a special operation over France in April 1944 his aircraft had been hit by flak and, after seeing all his crew bale out, he found himself too low to jump and, in the darkness, made a magnificent landing in a field with the bomber ablaze.)

152. Spitfire LF XVIe SL669 at Filton, 1948.

During February 1949 the squadron received the jet de Havilland Vampire F.1 and Squadron Leader A. C. Henderson, DFC, another pilot who had successfully evaded capture, took over. Summer camps were held as far away as Malta and in 1950 Squadron Leader P. J. Simpson, DSO, DFC and Bar, a Battle of Britain pilot who had held high rank during wartime, became C.O. of 501 Squadron. During 1952 the Vampire F.5 was received and Squadron Leader G. B. Mercer took command. In 1953 the squadron re-equipped with the Gloster Meteor F.8 and Squadron Leader C. D. Griffiths handed over command in 1955 to Squadron Leader M. C. Collings, one of the pre-war volunteer pilots. In company with the other squadrons of the Royal Auxiliary Air Force, 501 disbanded in March of 1957 but was re-born for a glorious day in 1964 when, on 9th May, HRH The Duchess of Gloucester, Air Chief Commandant of the Women's Royal Air Force, presented The Standard, awarded by The Queen, at a ceremony on College Green, opposite the Council House, Bristol. The Standard was consecrated by the Chaplain-in-Chief, RAF, the Venerable F. W. Cocks and was afterwards laid up in Bristol Cathedral.

The Battle Honours on the Standard are: France and Low Countries 1940; Battle of Britain 1940; Home Defence 1940–45; Fortress Europe 1940–44; Channel and North Sea 1940–44; France and Germany 1944; Normandy 1944. The last adjutant, Flight

Lieutenant Frank Skuse (who transferred to the Territorial Army when the RAuxAF squadrons disbanded) was so encouraged by the attendance of old members at The Standard ceremonies that he immediately started to form an Old Comrades' Association to include all ranks – many of them having made their mark in military and civil aviation since their 501 days. One thinks of the late Air Chief Marshal Sir William Elliot, GCVO, KCB, KBE, DFC, who

153. Squadron scramble during Exercise Foil, 1949.

154. Squadron Vampires airborne, 1949.

became Air Officer Commanding-in-Chief, Fighter Command; of Air Vice-Marshal Sir Laurence Sinclair, GC, KCB, CBE, DSO (the George Cross was won in 1940 when he entered a blazing bomb-laden Blenheim to rescue the crew), who became Controller of the National Air Traffic Control Services; of Air Vice-Marshal H. A. V. Hogan, CB, DFC, who commanded No. 83 Group of the 2nd Tactical Air Force before retiring to take up a post with a helicopter firm. Air Commodore H. M. Toby Pearson, CBE, pre-war adjutant, after commanding No. 54(F) Squadron 1939–40, served at No. 11(F) Group in the Battle of Britain as a controller and, post-war, joined Bristol Siddeley Engines Ltd. Air Vice-Marshal W. E. Staton, CB, DSO, MC, DFC, taken prisoner in Java, became AOC. No. 46 Group post-war.

The epic film *Battle of Britain* must have revived very many memories for ex-members of 501 Squadron and how right it was that Squadron Leader Ginger Lacey, DFM and Bar, should be one of the film's advisers, a tribute to the squadron and to the pilot credited with the top score during the actual air-fighting over the British Isles in that fateful summer of 1940. The squadron may no longer exist but the spirit of the County of Gloucester airmen has inspired, in Bristol and district, a fine contingent of the Air Training Corps with Godfrey Auty, FRAeS, of Filton as Chairman.

155. The Battle of Britain film background boys – Sqdn Ldr Ginger Lacey far left with arms folded, Derek Wood third from left, Wg Cdr Stanford-Tuck far right.

REPRESENTATIVE SQUADRON AIRCRAFT

Avro 504N		J8689
de Havilland D.H.9A		No serials recorded
Westland Wapiti	IIa	J9869 K1367 K1373 (C.O.) K1374
Westland Wallace	I	K3566 K3567 K3568 K3569 K3570 K3572 K3573

(rebuilt Wapiti airframes K1347, 1331, 1345 1348, 1349, 1352)

Hawker Hart		K2439 K3018
Hawker Hind		K5410 K5550
Fairey Battle		K7571
Hawker Hurricane	I	L1578 L1866 N2329 N2549 P3803 P3808 V6644 V7234
Vickers-Supermarine		
Spitfire	I	X4645 X4989 X4990
	IIa	P7990 P8196
	Vb	BL632 SD–S EN956 EP118 EP570 BR168 (Vc)
	IX	MH855 MJ129 MJ311 TB532 SD–A
Hawker Tempest	V	EJ585 SD–A EJ608 EJ763 SN328
Vickers-Supermarine		
Spitfire	LF.XVI	SL541 RAB–F SL699 SL571 TE474
de Havilland Vampire	F.1	TG304 RAB–J TG437 TG441 VF272 VF282 (later SD–R)
	FB.5	VX984 WA261 WA303 D
Gloster Meteor	F.8	unknown. T.7 VZ638

As this is written the following ex-501 machines are known to be exhibited and the writer would be pleased to hear of others which may exist:

Spitfire Vb EP120/5377M (restored with Mk.XVI components) now at RAF Wattisham, Suffolk.
Spitfire LFXVIe SL674 Battle of Britain Chapel, RAF Biggin Hill.
Spitfire LFXVI TE288 Canterbury Brevet Club, Christchurch, N.Z.
Spitfire LFXVI TE384 RAF Henlow (formerly RAF Syerston).
Spitfire LFXVI TE456 Auckland War Museum, New Zealand.
Meteor T.7 VZ638 Historic Aircraft Museum, Southend.

The pre-war squadron code letters were ZH which, on outbreak of war, became SD, changed in 1946 to RAG when the squadron was part of Reserve Command. Returning to Fighter Command in 1949, the code reverted to SD until 1951 when individual squadron colours were carried by RAuxAF units, the County of Gloucester's insignia becomir.g a rectangle of interlocking triangles of black and stone, each side of the Vampire's tailboom roundels and on the fuselages of the Meteors.

Badge: A boar's head couped. The animal noted for courage taken from the arms of Gloucester.

Motto: 'Nil time.'

500
(County of Kent)
Squadron

THE PRIVILEGE OF bearing the first number ever allocated to a Special Reserve squadron was given to No. 500 (County of Kent) Squadron although in the event it was actually the thirteenth of the twenty SR and AAF part-time units to form – on 16th March, 1931, at Manston – commanded by Squadron Leader S. R. Watkins, AFC, RAF, with Flight Lieutenant T. B. Prickman, RAF, as adjutant. On 4th June that year the Mayors of Margate and Ramsgate named the squadron's first Vickers Virginia 'Isle of Thanet'. This was one of the three bombers and two Avro 504N trainers then on the strength.

On 28th July, 1931, Wing Commander L. F. Forbes, MC, RAF, assumed command and an intensive recruiting campaign began to persuade the Men of Kent and Kentish Men to balance the nucleus of regular officers and airmen. There was a warm response from the county and by May 1933 it was possible to send a strong representation to Tangmere, Sussex, for annual camp; sixty Special Reservists accompanied the hard-core of RAF personnel under Squadron Leader T. F. W. Thompson, DFC, RAF, the flight-commander. In July, Wing Commander R. Halley, DFC, AFC, RAF, took command and the squadron, now equipped with the Hawker Demon light-bomber, gave a demonstration for the Observer Corps, en route to Porton Ranges for bombing exercises. Boys of King's School, Canterbury, were given flights, many later serving in the Royal Air Force as a result of this indoctrination.

On 6th May, 1935, came the first award when Corporal Charles Edward Marsh, Special Reservist carpenter-rigger, received the King George V Silver Jubilee Medal as squadron representative. Wing Commander Halley was posted to HMS *Glorious* as senior

RAF officer and Wing Commander G. M. Lawson, MC, RAF, took over. In that year's Royal Review at Mildenhall, Suffolk, the squadron was chosen to appear before King George V and the Prince of Wales (later Duke of Windsor) who were accompanied by RAF pilot, HRH the Duke of York (later King George VI).

156. Virginia X serial K2330.

On 5th December, 1935, the squadron converted to Hawker Harts and in May 1936 was transferred into the Auxiliary Air Force as a single-engined day bomber squadron. The County of Kent Territorial Army and Air Force Association assumed responsibilities and worked closely with the then-adjutant, Flight Lieutenant A. McKee. When the squadron again re-equipped, this time with the Hawker Hind, McKee left on promotion to command No. 99 Squadron and in came Flight Lieutenant P. H. Dunn as adjutant until March 1938 when he left to join the Long Range Development Flight. Following the visit of Air Officer Commanding No. 6 (Auxiliary) Group to present the Lowe-Holmes Miniature Rifle Shooting Trophy, No. 87(F) Squadron arrived for fighter affiliation exercises and on 5th August, 1938, HRH the Duke of Kent, KG, KT, GCMG, GCVO, agreed to be the squadron's first Honorary Air Commodore. With a move to Detling, Squadron Leader the Reverend H. R. Carmichael became Chaplain as an Auxiliary officer.

No. 500 Squadron was now transferred to the control of No. 16 (General Reconnaissance) Group of Coastal Command, and with the arrival of the Avro Anson Mk.1, it became known as a G.R. unit. On 6th May, 1939, a march through Maidstone marked affiliation of the squadron to the county town and Mayor Councillor Percy Brown took the salute. Local residents showed their interest by turning up 15,000-strong for Empire Air Display a fortnight later; and on 24/25th August came embodiment into the Royal Air Force and active service. On 9th September Anson N5052 had to be abandoned owing to engine trouble, the crew, Flying Officer R. B. Jay, Leading Aircraftman Baldry, and Aircraftmen Cunningham and Ridley, all making parachute descents with only minor injuries. That same day another Anson landed on the sea, the crew being picked up and brought into Whitstable with only superficial injuries. In terrible weather the squadron continued to contribute patrols to cover our convoys and again engine failure forced an aircraft down near Benenden. Leading Aircraftman Messent baled out to safety from N5233 but Flying Officer D. G. Mabey, Pilot Officer A. M. Patterson and Corporal J. F. Drew lost their lives – the first casualties of 500 Squadron.

Photography of shipping and warning by radio of loose mines off our coasts, with the occasional driving-off of approaching enemy aircraft, kept the crews busy, and on 10th December another Anson crashed near Detling, one crew-member later dying from his injuries. In January 1940 the leave-boats from France were escorted and Squadron Leader Le May was promoted to command. The squadron gunnery officer, Flying Officer Harold Jones, concerned about the Anson's vulnerability in combat, obtained his C.O.'s permission to fix extra guns, two additional .303 machine-guns being fitted to fire from positions along the fuselage sides. On 15th May, 1940, came a rare occurrence, reminiscent of World War I air-fighting. An He.111 flying above Anson MK–B dropped bombs aimed at our machine, the Anson retaliating by putting several bursts of fire into the Heinkel which made off into cloud.

157. The squadron, with Group Captain HRH the Duke of Kent, Detling, 1940.

Three aircraft from No. 48 Squadron arrived to help 500 Squadron with patrols over France as our soldiers tried to escape. The Ansons hit enemy surface vessels trying to attack the armada of small boats picking up servicemen. Anson 'U' crashed into the sea after being hit, the crew were picked up by a destroyer. Anson

MK–N failed to return from bombing enemy-held harbours on 29th May and on the night of the 31st 'W' returned to Detling with bombs aboard, crashing on touch-down. This incident gained for the County of Kent Women's Auxiliary Air Force Company a very high honour when Corporal Daphne Pearson, medical orderly, ran to the scene of the crash, and despite warnings that the bombs and ammunition would explode, rescued the pilot throwing herself on the wounded officer as the explosions hurled him to the ground. For her heroism Daphne received the Medal of the British Empire for Gallantry (EGM) which, in September 1940, became the George Cross. The Anson's observer, alas, lost his life.

158. F/O Daphne Pearson, GC.

During May 1940 the squadron flew 1,386 hours, and 1st June started in dramatic fashion when 'V' piloted by Pilot Officer Philip Peters was jumped by nine Messerschmitt Bf.109s. Co-pilot Sergeant D. Spencer ran to man one of the side guns, the other being operated by Leading Aircraftman Pepper. The enemy over-estimated the Anson's speed and shot straight past. Peters hauled the nose up and as the Messerschmitts turned he fired, causing one to go down into the sea. Leading Aircraftman Smith, in the turret, scored another direct hit and a second Bf.109 dived into the 'drink'. On landing back at Detling only one bullet hole from return fire could be seen but no bullet was traced, it was found some months later when Peters had his parachute re-packed! For this sortie and for one other Messerschmitt damaged Pilot Officer Philip Peters was awarded the DFC, and DFM awards came to Sergeant Spencer, newly-promoted Corporal L. G. Smith and to Leading Aircraftmen L. S. Dillnutt and Cunningham (aircrew were not yet automatically of NCO rank).

On 14th June 'MK–M' failed to return from a sortie; on the 24th Sergeant Prentice rear-gunner of 'N' shot down a Bf.109; and on the 28th 'MK–E' did not come back. July was a very distressing month as 'MK–F' crashed in flames on take-off, all the crew losing their lives. On the next night 'D' failed to return to base from a fight in which nine Heinkels attacked our machines protecting a convoy. Anson 'L' claimed one and Spitfires coming to the rescue destroyed another. On 18th July 'G' shot down a Messerschmitt Bf.110 menacing our ships, the Anson observer and rear-gunner taking turns to pour 500 rounds into the enemy. As the first mountings for the unofficial guns tended to work loose when guns were fired, Tilling-Stevens Ltd of Maidstone manufactured a more suitable mounting as a gift to the squadron.

On 19th July came change in command as Wing Commander C. H. Turner took over and although the squadron maintained vigil over our coastal convoys losses increased, particularly on the ground as the Luftwaffe mistakenly thought Detling to be a fighter base. On Tuesday 13th August at tea-time, forty Ju.87 dive-bombers hit Detling just as personnel were going to the messes, three of which were demolished along with all the hangars. The station commander, Group Captain Davis, and sixty-six other servicemen and civilians were killed. The operations block was destroyed along with twenty-two aircraft in hangars or dispersals along the cratered runways. Devastating as it was, it in no way weakened Fighter Command and thus it was a very hollow victory for the enemy. Squadron ground-crews, helped by their aircrews, toiled to repair runways, refuel and re-arm aircraft and Pilot Officer Peters and his crew narrowly escaped death when 'Y' crashed on take-off. The squadron was entrusted now with the unusual task of flying over London after dusk to check on the blackouts and to report to the Air Ministry their suggestions on where things could be improved.

September was exceptionally busy as the Ansons continued to protect convoys despite the overwhelming superiority of the enemy's forces and the Anson's lamentable lack of speed when pursued. As a break from escorting our own ships, attacks were made on German vessels; and barges, thought to be ready for invading troops, were destroyed in harbours. One Anson, after driving off two Henschel 126s, damaging one, was further attacked by three Messerschmitt 110s and although the Anson pilot was wounded, he brought the aircraft back, claiming a second enemy machine probably destroyed. For this and earlier sorties Pilot Officer Armstrong Brown received a well-earned DFC.

For the squadron's shipping strikes a cannon was mounted to fire downwards, the special mounting made and presented to 500 Squadron by the British Cannon Manufacturing Company; No. 500's Ansons were said to be the first aircraft in the world to fly with a free-mounted cannon. When the cannon was fired rearwards the recoil added an extra five knots to the Anson's speed!

On 8th November, relaxing after the arduous spell, Pilot Officers

Chaffey and Mallalieu were flying the squadron's Miles Magister communications machine when it crashed near Ightham; both men being killed. On 27th November Wing Commander G. I. Pawson became C.O., and after a quiet December the New Year opened with *London Gazette* announcements of Mentions in Despatches for ten members, three of these, alas, killed before they could know of the award. Rumours abounded of moves and change of aircraft and at midnight on 7th April, 1941, the squadron temporarily ceased operations with the versatile 'Annie' and exchanged their Avro Ansons for the Bristol Blenheim Mk.IV, on 15th May leaving Detling for Bircham Newton, Norfolk, to take over responsibility for North Sea convoys from Yorkshire down to the Thames. Interspersed with this rather monotonous though important work came the occasional search and rescue sorties which saved many valuable lives and, during one rescue, brought combat with three yellow-nosed Bf.109s, one of which was left smoking by Blenheim 'T' Tommy, the other 109s retreating in some haste.

159. Aircrew and NCOs at Bircham Newton, late 1941.
C.O. Wg Cdr Gilbert.

In September of 1941 permission was at last given for the squadron to begin 'Intruder' missions over enemy airfields in Occupied Europe, alternating with some day sorties escorted by a squadron of Spitfires, to attack the enemy's ships. On 31st October a 10,000-ton merchantman was set on fire for the losses of Squadron Leader Phipps and Sergeant Mowan and their crews. Wilf Butler, who flew Blenheim Z6161 on this attack, later understood from the Air Officer Commanding No. 16 Group, that the enemy vessel had been completely destroyed and that he (Butler) would receive an immediate DFC, but no such decoration ever came his way. Awards sometimes misfired if channels between recommendation and approval broke down, as apparently occurred on this occasion.

As a reward, it seemed, for the squadron's consistent efforts, the Lockheed Hudson replaced the Blenheim and this marked perhaps the finest phase in the County of Kent Squadron's history. Wing

Commander Denis Spotswood (who had joined the Royal Air Force in 1936 and who had flown flying-boats before ferrying Hudsons across the Atlantic) came to command, his arrival almost coinciding with that of Pilot Officer M. A. Ensor, a new captain of a squadron Hudson. On 30th January, 1942, Ensor hit an enemy ship off Sylt, Germany, and, illuminated by the shore batteries, dived for the darkness of the lower altitudes but, with his altimeter registering 200 feet, the Hudson hit a submerged rock and the starboard engine failed, as did the electrical systems including the wireless. He set course for base and despite a further burst of flak, flew on. After a total flying time of 5½ hours his fuel tanks were virtually dry and, hoping he was over friendly land, he fired the recognition cartridges at a height of 300 feet, seeing a largish field into which he belly-landed without injury to the crew.

In March the squadron was based at Stornoway in the Hebrides, with a detachment at Limavady, Northern Ireland, helping to combat the U-boats in the Atlantic shipping lanes. Despite the heavily-armed enemy craft, when met on the surface the Hudsons pressed home their relentless attacks, though they were often unable to witness the end of the mission. Both 'A' and 'Q' claimed some success in April when U-boats were left with bows in the air. In May ten Icelandic sailors were picked up from rafts: their ship had shot down the Luftwaffe aircraft which had sunk them and a trawler collected the sailors after the Hudson had radioed for assistance.

In July Mike Ensor received a well-earned DFC after attacking a surfaced U-boat in a dive from 3,000 feet. Two of his four Torpex charges straddled the enemy craft, blowing off the bow. On a later patrol Ensor dropped his depth-charges only to see a very dead whale rise to the surface, an all-too-common happening for Coastal

160.
Air Chief Marshal Sir Denis Spotswood,
KCB, CBE, DSO, DFC, ADC,
now Chief of Air Staff.

Command crews. Aircraft were sent to fly from Iceland and Flight Lieutenant C. J. Mackenzie got the DFC and Flight Sergeants McCourt and Andrew Mentions in Despatches for these patrols. One Hudson had to ditch during August but a nearby trawler soon picked up the crew.

At the end of that month orders came for the aircrews to move to Gosport, Hampshire, and for the ground personnel to go to Wilmslow in Cheshire, prior to moving overseas. As they waited, news came of a Bar to the DFC for Flying Officer Ensor and on 5th November, following a further move down to Portreath in Cornwall, the first nine white-painted Hudsons flew from there to Gibraltar. The very next day five aircraft were out on patrol and soon in action over the Mediterranean. Two U-boats were attacked but no firm claims were submitted as the departure of diving U-boats leaving large oil patches was often a ruse to persuade our aircraft to break off attacks when, in fact, the enemy craft was pushing out the oil deliberately. But on 14th November survivors landed at Oran stated that they were from a U-boat attacked and sunk by a white Hudson lettered 'U'. In the interim period three more U-boats had been attacked and one, hit on 7th November, was later confirmed as sunk by the Royal Navy.

On 12th November, a dozen squadron aircraft covered the allied landings at Oran and although 'A' was attacked by a Ju.88 and an He.111 it returned with only minor damage. Aircraft 'J', painted in French colours, flew General Giraud, his son, his Aide, and his Secretary to Oran and then on to Blida which was still in French hands. As a gesture the Air Ministry handed this Hudson to the gallant French General who had escaped from Germany but, after a few days, General Giraud returned it saying it was of more use in 500 Squadron

161. Airmen bombing-up a Hudson.

hands to wipe out the remaining enemy submarines. A Ju.52 transport was shot down by 'G' and the squadron now made base at Tafaroui. Success followed success and on 15th November Squadron Leader Ian Patterson forced a U-boat to beach and another surrendered with the crew waving white towels as they stood on the deck waiting for a ship to make them prisoner.

Flying Officer Ensor, piloting 'S', dived from 7,000 feet to only 50 feet as a U-boat submerged and got a direct hit on the magazine or torpedoes, the U-boat's gun pointing straight upwards as the conning tower ripped open. The Hudson was severely battered by flying debris and flew as far as Algiers Bay where the port engine cut. With the aircraft then spinning Ensor ordered his crew to bale out, two of them, alas, losing their lives, Ensor and Sergeant H. J. Roe the rear-gunner escaped and were picked up by a sloop. This was Ensor's last sortie on this tour of operations with the squadron and he left for England, promotion and a staff post at Coastal Command Headquarters, Northwood, Middlesex. A Distinguished Service Order was promulgated for his magnificent work with the County of Kent Squadron.

Wing Commander Spotswood had not been idle and, in company with Flying Officer H. M. S. Green, dived down on a U-boat just as it was submerging. Heavy explosions from the depth-charges opened up the seams in the enemy craft and it surfaced with the crew firing sub-machine-guns at the two Hudsons. For almost an hour there was a duel, with other aircraft standing by to lend a hand. Eventually, though, the U-boat sank close to the shore and survivors from the crew waded inland to be taken prisoner by waiting French troops. Wing Commander Spotswood was awarded the DFC for this and other sorties and for leadership. Hudson 'Z' successfully straddled another U-boat which immediately surfaced in surrender and the Hudson flew in circles above it, directing it into an allied port. Unfortunately a Fleet Air Arm Albacore aircraft, not appreciating that the U-boat had surrendered, unleashed its torpedo and sank the enemy submarine.

As the squadron moved into Blida personnel found the French barracks alive with vermin, the bedsteads being burned as the medical officer and his orderlies struggled to wipe out the bugs. By the last day of November, 201 sorties had been made in the 24 days of operations in 34 attacks recorded and confirmation by the Royal Navy that five U-boats had been sunk, with the possibility of others probably also at the bottom of the Mediterranean. Admiralty added their congratulations to those of the Air Officer Commanding and in December the fine work proceeded as 'W' got both the Italian submarine and the Cant 1007 bomber-reconnaissance aircraft which was escorting it. Unfortunately Hudson 'W' was later lost in an accident and 'M', after destroying another Italian submarine, was brought down, the crew being picked up by a Walrus amphibian of our air-sea rescue detachment.

Flight Lieutenant Holmes arrived from the U.K., flying out a Hudson Mk.III, carrying mail for all ranks in time for Christmas. The assassination of Admiral Darlan on Christmas Eve stopped visits into Blida and Algiers but a traditional Christmas Day, in the competent hands of Flight Lieutenant Paine, DFM, was an outstanding success. The DFC was announced for Squadron Leader Ian Patterson also for Flight Lieutenants A. W. Barwood, J. B. Ensor, A. Holmes and Pilot Officer Criswell, with the Distinguished Flying Medal for Sergeant H. J. Roe. Throughout January and February intensive training took place as the Hudsons Mk.V and VI arrived and newly-trained crews were brought to operational standard to fill losses and end-of-tour departures, the patrols were maintained against some aggressive U-boat retaliation. When the troopship *Windsor Castle* was torpedoed it was 'D' of 500 which first destroyed the U-boat and then escorted the stricken liner until help came. Flying Officer S. A. Gilman's DFC was for his 'courage and devotion to duty on air operations'.

The appearance of the sirocco, a hot and blighting wind which blew unceasingly, failed to halt the squadron's sorties and General Spaatz, commanding North West African Air Forces, sent thanks to the C.O. for ensuring the safe landing of American troops. On 23rd April, 1943, came a magnificent entry in the records noting that 'N' had descended to 200 feet above the sea after picking up a radar contact some twelve miles away and shadowing a surfaced submarine. As the bomb-doors opened the U-boat's cannon scored a direct hit on the Hudson, killing the pilot. Flight Sergeant Kempster took over the controls and kept the Hudson from hitting the sea as the body of the captain was removed from the pilot's seat. Meanwhile Sergeant Blackwell closed the bomb-doors, an act of quick-thinking which saved the machine. As they passed over the U-boat Flight Sergeant Carruthers fired 600 rounds into it, seeing strikes and, as the Hudson neared base, Sergeant Blackwell took over the controls and, realising a landing was impossible, climbed the aircraft to 5,000 feet, from which height all the survivors baled out to safety. An immediate award of the Conspicuous Gallantry Medal came to Sergeant Blackwell and the DFM to Flight Sergeant Kempster.

As Wing Commander Spotswood left to join the Directorate of Air Tactics he was succeeded by Wing Commander D. G. Keddie and when No. 614 (County of Glamorgan) Squadron came out with their Blenheims V (Bisleys) it was 500 Squadron's responsibility to 'parent' them; these two squadrons, and No. 608 (North Riding) Squadron, adding more kills to their tallies, bringing a DFC for Flying Officer D. A. G. Blakeley of the County of Kent unit. Flights were at this time stationed at Blida, Bone, and Tafaroui, and Air

Vice-Marshal Sir Hugh P. Lloyd flew in to thank the squadron for enabling the Sicilian Campaign to open as scheduled. Although five U-boats were known to be threatening the landing areas none got through to the small craft heading for the beaches. One Hudson damaged a U-boat, which was finished-off by a No. 13 Squadron aircraft, and in the meantime the crew of a 36 Squadron Wellington were protected after taking to their dinghy. A DFC for Flight Lieutenant J. R. Pugh and a Mention in Despatches for Warrant Officer Hipwell marked another busy phase of operations.

On 9th December the squadron took over the Lockheed Venturas of No. 13 Squadron and co-operated with the Royal Navy in the sinking of a submarine outside Oran harbour. Then came a move into Corsica, with Wing Commander C. K. Bonner, formerly 614 Squadron, as C.O., and with Flight Sergeant (later Pilot Officer) Jackimov receiving the DFM. The Air Ministry signalled that for the second successive year No. 500 Squadron had topped the G.R. Squadrons' accident tables with only five accidents in 5,000 hours of flying. Then from Borizzo, Sicily, and La Senia, the squadron aircraft claimed two more enemy submarines. Wing Commander C. E. Garton (who had been associated with the squadron in the early Manston days) was appointed to command, just as news came of disbanding and of the return to England of the pre-war Auxiliary Air Force airmen.

162. The Martin Baltimore.

As with many other rumours, this proved false and within days this was changed and although by this time some crews had left to join No. 27 (South African) Squadron, taking their Venturas, orders now came to re-form with the Martin Baltimore light-bomber and to join the Desert Air Force. Wing Commander H. N. Garbert arrived to command, and the men sailed in the liner *Ville d'Oran* from Algiers for Taranto and, after many unforgettable incidents, finally reached Pescara, only to find that the Baltimores became bogged down in the mud. A move was then made to Perugia for intensive training and by 10th December the first operational sorties were possible from Cesenatico, against German troops in Italy and on their supply dumps, all forms of transport, and on marshalling yards. The squadron was selected to bomb Kesselring's Headquarters and every machine was hit by the concentrated anti-aircraft fire, though all returned safely to base.

The anti-radar device, code-named 'Window', the metallised strips, often picked up in England in 1944, was used with success by 500 Squadron and bundles of leaflets were also dropped to encourage the Germans to give up the fight. Sorties were made over Yugoslavia to help the partisans, firstly attacking the enemy and then dropping containers of food and arms to the patriots. The Archbishop of York, Dr Garbett, called to talk to squadron-members and on 1st May, 1945, Air Vice-Marshal A. E. Borton, CB, CMG, DSO, AFC, the County of Kent Regional Liaison Officer, visited the squadron with a message from the Rt. Hon Anthony Eden who was the Honorary Air Commodore, following the death on active service of HRH the Duke of Kent in a Sunderland flying-boat crash.

With the ending of the war in Europe the squadron, now based at Villa Orba near Udine, led No. 253 Wing in the Desert Air Force Victory Flypast. The only other excitement was when Flight Lieutenant Mason and crew on one of the squadron's communications flights was posted missing, only to turn up three days later, having been forced down near Graz by Russian fighters, a foretaste of things to come. Notwithstanding this lack of co-operation from our new ally the squadron carried on its vital link with bases throughout Europe until Transport Command aircraft took over the duties. In October 1945 the squadron was disbanded in Kenya and immediately re-numbered No. 249 (Gold Coast) Squadron, Royal Air Force, to keep in use the number-plate of the fighter squadron in which the late Wing Commander J. B. Nicolson, the Tonbridge schoolboy, had gained Fighter Command's only Victoria Cross on 16th August, 1940.

In June 1946 No. 500 (County of Kent) Auxiliary Squadron began to re-form at West Malling as a night-fighter unit equipped with de Havilland Mosquito NF.30 aircraft under Squadron Leader Patrick Green, OBE, AFC, who had served in 500 Squadron as a young officer 1936–40 and had later flown with 221 and 621 Squadrons (commanding the latter) instructing also at 7 OTU. He took the squadron to summer camp at Tangmere in 1947; later handing over command to Squadron Leader H. C. Kennard, DFC, when the decision was reached at Ministry level that all Auxiliary squadrons be day fighters. Squadron Leader Kennard, who flew with 66 Squadron in the Battle of Britain and later with 610 (County of Chester) 306 (Polish) and 121 (Eagle) Squadron, which he commanded, saw 500 Squadron become the first part-timers to fly the Gloster Meteor when, in 1948, the Mk.F.3 was received, followed in 1950 by the Meteor F.4 and in 1952 by the Meteor F.8.

The squadron's Honorary Air Commodore, Sir Anthony Eden, made regular visits to West Malling and often flew in the two-seater Meteor T.7 trainer. Squadron Leader Desmond de Villiers, AFC, who had joined the squadron post-war as a junior officer after flying with Nos. 608, 68, 288 and 252 Squadrons in World War II, took

163. Anthony Eden visits the squadron at Thorney Island camp, 1949. Sqdn Ldr Kennard on Eden's left, then Gp Cpt Eeles.

command in 1952 as a break from his test-pilot flying for de Havilland's (and later for the British Aircraft Corporation). Summer camps were held at Horsham St Faith, Norfolk; Thorney Island, Sussex; Leuchars, Fife; Takali (Malta); and Celle (Germany). In 1954, Squadron Leader D. M. Clause, AFC, relieved Desmond de Villiers and Flight Lieutenaht Bonney, a former aircraft apprentice who flew Thunderbolts and Spitfires in the Far East, came in as the RAF adjutant. In October 1955 Squadron Leader D. H. M. Chandler, RAF, came from the Central Fighter Establishment, West Raynham, Norfolk, as C.O., and the squadron followed-up its 1954 Cooper Trophy success with the Esher Trophy in 1956. At this time it was decided to revive the custom of the 1930s and give appropriate names to squadron machines. Unfortunately the award of The Standard for 25 years' service (Battle Honours were Channel and North Sea, 1939–41; Dunkirk, Biscay Ports, 1941; Atlantic, 1941–42; North Africa, 1942–43; Mediterranean, 1942–44; Italy, 1944–45) and the Freedom of Maidstone, did not halt the squadron's disbandment when the Royal Auxiliary Air Force squadrons were ordered to stand-down in 1957.

On Saturday 21st September, 1963, a ceremony unique in Royal Air Forces' history took place at Maidstone Barracks when No. 500 (County of Kent) Squadron, was re-mustered for one day to receive The Standard from the Earl of Avon, KG, MC, DCL, JP (formerly Sir

164. Meteor F.8 formation, 9th February, 1954.

Anthony Eden). Flying Officer R. de V. Rudolph, a former squadron pilot, carried The Standard, after consecration by the Chaplain-in-Chief, Royal Air Force, and at All Saints Church it was received for safe-keeping by the vicar, an address being given by the Rt. Rev S. W. Betts, Bishop of Maidstone. Former members of the squadron (under Group Captain W. K. Le May, President of the Old Comrades Association) paraded in plain clothes with a marching contingent from the Queen's Colour Squadron of the RAF supported by the RAF Central Band. Distinguished guests included Lord Cornwallis, Lord Lieutenant of Kent, and Air Marshal Douglas Morris, Air Officer Commanding-in-Chief, Fighter Command. The Air Ministry's press release mentioned the squadron's unofficial Anson fire-power modification and added that it was later the leading maritime squadron in the West Mediterranean, and the most highly decorated; also that it was the first Auxiliary Air Force squadron to receive jet aircraft.

The squadron may have disappeared from the RAF Order of Battle but it will never be forgotten. Many who led it, or who served in 500 Squadron, have left their mark on military and civil aviation – Air Marshal Sir Andrew McKee, KCB, CBE, DSO, DFC, AFC, RAF (retd.), one-time squadron adjutant and later a great bomber pilot and Air Officer Commanding-in-Chief, Transport Command, before returning to his native New Zealand to become Chairman of New Zealand National Airways and Tasman Empire Airways Ltd. His successor in the squadron, Air Marshal Sir Patrick Hunter Dunn, KBE, CB, DFC, became Commander-in-Chief, RAF Flying Training Command. Of the post-war officers, to mention just two again, Squadron Leader Desmond de Villiers, AFC, has made a magnificent contribution to the development of the English Electric P.1 which became the RAF's Lightning supersonic fighter; and Wing Commander Bonney, ex-adjutant, later flew Javelins with No. 33 Squadron and commanded No. 83 Squadron, flying Vulcan V-bombers. As this is written, every former member rejoices that the Chief of the Air Staff is Air Chief Marshal Sir Denis Spotswood, KCB, CBE, DSO, DFC, who commanded the squadron 1943/1944 and who afterwards held such important posts as Commandant of the RAF College, Commander-in-Chief RAF Germany and Commander 2nd Allied Tactical Air Force and, from 1968, Air Officer Commanding-in-Chief RAF Strike Command.

REPRESENTATIVE SQUADRON AIRCRAFT

Avro 504N		K1811 K2407 K2412
Vickers Virginia	VII	J7566
	X	K2330 K2668 K K2669
Hawker Hart (T)		K3751 K3757
Hawker Hind		K4643 K6700 K6701
Avro Anson	I	N5052 N5233
Bristol Blenheim	IV	Z6161 T
Hudson	III	V9094 MK–W
Lockheed Hudson	VI	FK657 FK712
Lockheed Ventura	V	FP546 JT895
Martin Baltimore	IV	(A–30A) FA517 FA618
	V	(A–30A) FW699 FW791 FW866 FW880
de Havilland Mosquito	NF.30	NT245 NT279 NT288 NT351 NT430 NT606 RAA–H
North American Harvard	IIb	KF423
Gloster Meteor	F.3	EE352 RAA–A EE420 RAA–B EE403 RAA–E
	F.4	VT169 S7–F VT288 VT330
	T.7	WF788 L Isle of Thanet WH224 Z Isle of Sheppey
	F.8	VZ545 B Dartford WK725 P Dover WL169 V Maidstone

The code carried on the Ansons and Hudsons 1940–43 was MK but on re-forming in 1946 in RAF Reserve Command the letters RAA were allocated, changed to S7 from 1950 on the transfer into Fighter Command. When in 1951 this code was discontinued the squadron used its own marking, a blue rectangle with green zigzag horizontally across it, outlined in white.

Badge: A horse forscene—the white horse of Kent.

Motto (translated): 'Whither the fates may call.'

612
(County of Aberdeen)
Squadron

AT DYCE AERODROME, on 1st June, 1937, The County of Aberdeen's own Auxiliary Air Force squadron came into being under the command of Squadron Leader Finlay Crerar, with Flight Lieutenant R. B. Wardman as adjutant and with two Avro Tutor trainers. First to gain his flying badge was Mr R. B. Thomson who was commissioned as a pilot officer, as were Messrs A. M. Scott, S. A. Middleton, D. G. E. Benzie, N. S. F. Gilchrist, R. R. Russell and I. G. F. Stephen. Hawker Hart and Hawker Hector aircraft arrived for Army Co-operation duties and by April 1938 fifty-four local men had been attested for groundcrew duties including Flight Lieutenant D. Mackintosh, DCM, the equipment officer. In July the squadron was able to fly down to Hawkinge, Kent, for summer camp and, to the surprise of the old-established units, walked away with the Inter-Squadron Sports Cup; a feather in the Aberdeen caps.

Soon afterwards the squadron was transferred from No. 6 (Auxiliary) Group of Fighter Command into No. 18 (Reconnaissance) Group of Coastal Command to become No. 612 (G.R.) squadron flying the twin-engined Avro Anson. Alan Hendry, MC, MB, ChB, a local doctor and a pilot of the 'Kaiser' war, was commissioned as squadron medical officer. For Empire Air Day, 20th May, 1939, almost 5,000 locals flocked to Dyce to see the squadron and visiting aircraft in action. On 14th June the aircraft conveying Group Captain HRH the Duke of Kent on a visit, overturned on the aerodrome but happily without casualties. During the squadron dinner in August news came of call-up and embodiment into the Royal Air Force and next day patrolling began between Aberdeen and Dundee, Lieutenant-Commander Wisden, RN, briefing crews on likely enemy tactics and later flying in the Ansons to act as liaison officer.

On October 28th Anson N5274, piloted by Pilot Officer Frain, was attacked by a Spitfire, Aircraftman Cruickshank being seriously wounded. In happier vein, news came that Flying Officer J. P. Smythe's attack with 100 lb anti-submarine bombs on a U-boat seventeen miles east of Aberdeen, leaving large patches of oil, had brought congratulations from the Commander-in-Chief, Rosyth. Air Commodore C. D. Breese, Air Officer Commanding No. 18 Group flew up from Donibristle to add his personal thanks for the squadron's vigilance.

In November, Wing Commander Finlay Crerar was promoted to be Station Commander, RAF Dyce, and Squadron Leader A. M.

165. Squadron officers, July 1938, with Hawker Hector. Sqdn Ldr Finlay Crerar, C.O., second from left in front row.

166. 612 Squadron on outbreak of war. *Front row:* Thomson, Scott, Crerar, Hendry, Smyth, Stracey. *Second row:* Middleton, Russell, Raffan, Sadler, Brotherstone, Davie, Stephen, Nelson, Young. *Back row:* Officer of Gordon Highlanders, Frain, Gordon, Campbell, Macaldowie, Crockart, Watt, Berry, Benzie.

Scott became C.O. 612 Squadron. On 16th December Flight Lieutenant Davie attacked a submerged U-boat without visible results and the rest of that winter passed fairly uneventfully though many local seamen were glad to see the faithful 'Annie' overhead when warned of U-boats in the vicinity. It was in April 1940, with the Nazis invasion of Norway, that war came to Aberdeenshire in the shape of a Norwegian seaplane courageously flown into Peterhead from under the noses of the enemy by gallant airmen offering their services to the allied cause. During May the squadron Ansons flew down the coast as far south as Bircham Newton, Norfolk. King George VI, then staying at Sandringham, drove over to meet 612 crews; and Marshal of the RAF Viscount Trenchard, 'Father of the Royal Air Force', flew up to Dyce to chat informally with all ranks.

In July, Wing Commander J. B. Wallis, RAF, took command as information was received that the squadron would exchange the Anson for the Armstrong Whitworth Whitley, to cover the longer patrols now necessary for protecting our vital convoys. On 18th July, still operating the Anson, 'A' of 612 attacked and drove off a Do.17 menacing our merchant shipping. On the first anniversary of war the Secretary of State for Air, Sir Archibald Sinclair, arrived to thank the squadron for their convoy escorts and for escorting the fleets of de Havilland Tiger Moth trainers being ferried up to Montrose for the urgent training of pilots now that training bases in the south were under daily Luftwaffe attack.

167. A Flight with Avro Anson, May 1940.

5th November was a tragic day as news came that Squadron Leader A. M. Scott of Inchgarth, Pitfodels, one of the original volunteers, had lost his life at Kinloss with Flying Officer A. R. Nivison-Smith, RAF, during the conversion course to the Whitley, full military honours being paid to both men at Springbank and Newhills cemeteries. The conversion training, though, had to proceed at top speed until February 1941 when, for Aberdeen's War Weapons Week, Flight Lieutenant Ramsay Roger Russell of Kingswells flew Whitley T4325 on a leaflet-dropping sortie in support of the appeal and to display the squadron's new machine, other aircraft joining in the publicity flights. Later that week the C.O., Wing Commander Wallis, made a brilliant landing after one engine had failed, demonstrating that the Whitley could be handled in such an emergency. The two flight-commanders were now Squadron Leaders S. A. Middleton (awarded the DFC for his Anson sorties) and B. A. Sisson, RAF.

During March an FW.200 was driven off and bombs were dropped on a submerged U-boat. On 6th April, Flight Lieutenant R. B. Thomson, flying aircraft 'P', found himself south of Skye owing to faulty radio fixes. He had been airborne then for nine hours and, to quote his own report 'I then hopped over the mountains, jettisoned the bombs into a loch and landed at Kinloss at dawn with one engine stopped'. As he touched down, the other engine failed and the landing was a masterly display of airmanship which instilled confidence into other crews, particularly the new arrivals.

On 23rd April Wing Commander Wallis again experienced engine-failure in flight and made a forced-landing on North Rona, the RAF's air-sea rescue launch from Kirkwall, Orkney, picking up the crew after they had spent the night aboard. The next day aircraft 'L' crashed into Wick Fever Hospital as it was landing for a new assignment at the nearby RAF base, the aircrew and, alas, two members of the hospital staff were killed. The Luftwaffe, it seemed, knew of the squadron's move to Wick, for a hit and run He.111 bombed the airfield two days later, damaging four of the Whitleys which squadron ground personnel speedily repaired. With the *Bismarck* known to be out at sea the squadron patrolled wide areas within range to try and prevent attacks on our convoys. On 4th June another hit and run raider, this time a Ju.88, carried out a pinpoint bombing of the airfield and three Whitleys were pushed from the blazing hangar by courageous officers and airmen, thus being saved from total destruction. In record time the results of the bombing were cleared-up though when one unexploded bomb was discovered several new records were established for the hundred yards!

On 7th June, 1941, the first strike was staged by No. 612 Squadron (in company with six Lockheed Hudsons of No. 220 Squadron) and, unlike some post-war efforts, this was all-action. The target was Bergen, Norway, where the U-boat docks and workshops were completely obliterated: a conspicuous success for the men from Aberdeenshire. On 19th July Wing Commander Wallis was posted to command No. 3 Officer Training Unit, Cranwell, and Wing

Commander D. Ross Shore from No. 502 (Ulster) Squadron at Limavady, Northern Ireland, was flying over to take command of 612 when he sighted an FW.200 long-range reconnaissance machine actually attacking our shipping. Shore managed to drive it off with one of its engines smoking, but, hit by the enemy's return fire, he was forced to ditch, landing the Whitley skilfully on the sea. Picked up by a destroyer he reached 612 in time to learn of the awards of DFC to Flight Lieutenant Benzie and DFM to Sergeant Pirie 'For gallantry and devotion to duty in the execution of air operations'.

Two days later Pilot Officer Carter in 'H' intercepted a Do.18 which limped away damaged after the Whitley had poured a rain of bullets into it from front and rear turrets. A detachment of four Whitleys was then sent to Northern Ireland to fly out far into the Atlantic to protect food convoys and troopships. On 18th August 'E' had both engines cut out near the Shetlands and had to land on the sea, luckily attracting the attention of a Blenheim which reported their dinghy to Lerwick for the despatch of an RAF launch. A passing Sunderland flying-boat acted as top-cover but was shot-up by a Ju.88; the Sunderland making a safe landing back at its base.

Three of 612's Whitleys had now been ditched most successfully with no loss of crews, a record probably unequalled at that time. In mid-September aircraft were despatched to Iceland for patrols and although two U-boats were attacked no claims were submitted. Whales proved a time-waster as nothing that moved could safely be ignored. In October, during a return flight from Iceland and carrying out a 'sweep' en route, 'O' suffered engine-trouble, landing in the Faroe Islands without casualties although the machine was a write off. Rear-Admiral Tovey, a famous Naval commander, was flying with Squadron Leader Thomson in 'U', landing at Wick without incident. Congratulations and thanks were signalled by the Air Officer Commanding in Iceland and, without respite, 612 was asked to help cover the Bay of Biscay from St Eval in Cornwall, a tribute to the squadron's growing record of efficiency. Pilot Officer T. J. Raffan was posted to join No. 271 Transport Squadron at Doncaster, engaged in flying urgent supplies to RAF bases everywhere. He was soon seen at Dyce and Wick renewing old friendships. On Christmas Eve Pilot Officer Bow received a most unseasonable greeting from one of the ships he was escorting, a trigger-happy Naval gunner hitting one of the Whitley's engines. On one engine he managed to cover 150 miles towards the Faroes and as the other engine began to fail he got his wireless-operator to tap out 'Am landing in sea any minute now' (giving his position) and ending with 'A Merry Christmas to all in Iceland'.

The AOC instructed that the message be acknowledged and reciprocated but, happily, by splendid piloting, the Whitley safely got down at Kaldardarnes, a new airstrip carved out of the Faroes.

On Christmas Day two more Whitleys set out for Iceland but the weather deteriorated badly and they were ordered to return. Unfortunately 'A' had radio trouble, may not have heard the order, and was lost. The machine carried Flying Officer Fiddes, the new medical officer, Flying Officer Scholefield, intelligence officer, and Flight Lieutenant Spikins, squadron torpedo officer. Squadron Leader Thomson took over search duties and flew to the limits of his fuel but found nothing, a most grievous blow to all. During a sojourn in Iceland, Squadron Leader Thomson and Pilot Officer Bow flew Wellingtons which had made landings there, later piloting them back to Wick for No. 221 Squadron to operate again.

Early in 1942 gales of up to 110 m.p.h. lifted even aircraft moored to concrete blocks and, with forty airmen hanging on desperately to each Whitley, they were finally tethered to the refuelling bowsers and saved from the disasters which hit many other aircraft in Iceland, Faroes, Shetlands and Orkneys. On 18th February, after a successful attack on a U-boat, one 612 crew suffered engine failure and landed in a field some distance from Rekjavik, Iceland. After two days in a farmhouse they reached their airfield by various primitive transports, the last leg being in a small open boat.

Wing Commander Terence Corry, one of two brothers in pre-war 502 (Ulster) Squadron, came in now to command and when an Icelandic Airlines WACO crashed with two killed, two other passengers were saved by the prompt attention of 612's medical officer. On Terence Corry's promotion, Wing Commander R. M. Longmore (son of Air Chief Marshal Sir Arthur Longmore) arrived as the new C.O. and soon qualified for 'The Noble Order of Bluenoses' having

168. Whitley Q 'Queenie' down on Foula.

penetrated into the Arctic Circle. On 10th September came Squadron Leader A. H. Tollemache, GC, a pre-war Auxiliary Air Force pilot with 600 (City of London) Squadron. The squadron moved down to Thorney Island in Sussex, equipped now with the Whitley Mk. VIII, and then came another change, this time to Chivenor in North Devonshire to attack tankers in the docks at Cherbourg and to learn that Flying Officer Santell had hit a U-boat. The squadron diary at this time included 'Not since Dyce has the squadron been at any station near to civilisation until now. This is far more preferable than Iceland or Wick (that extremity which even Scots disown!)'.

In the autumn the squadron left Devonshire to return to Wick as the great convoys, including P.Q.14, left Scottish ports for Murmansk, with 612 helping to cover the ships as far as their fuel permitted. Good news was that the Vickers Wellington would replace the Whitley and, after training at Skitten, the Wick satellite airfield, crews were soon ready to return to operations, disposing of a Ju.88. and a Blohm & Voss Bv.138 in early missions with the new type. There were still a few Whitleys on strength and just as 'Q' was due to leave the squadron the aircraft had to crash-land on the Isle of Foula, the local schoolmistress and the minister billeting the crew until they could be taken to RAF Sumburgh to be flown back to Wick.

Then came another move, down to Davidstow Moor, Cornwall, on 15th April, 1943, and, a month later, a transfer to Chivenor, Devon. There, tragically, a new commanding officer for the squadron, Wing Commander Kendrick, was lost, when his machine dived into the river at Barnstaple on his early training flight. Wing Commander J. B. Russell, DSO, who had formed and led No. 172 Squadron at Chivenor, moved in as temporary C.O., only to have to return again when another officer from 172, Wing Commander Palmer, appointed

169. AV-M J. B. Russell, CBE, DSO.

to command 612 Squadron, also died in an accident. The squadron might well have been shaken to pieces by these two blows but, under Wing Commander Russell's splendid leadership, morale remained excellent. From both Chivenor, and St Eval, Cornwall, the squadron flew many successful sorties, Wing Commander Russell attacking a surfaced U-boat just before handing over the command to Wing Commander D. M. Brass before a move to Limavady in Northern Ireland.

Pilot Officer M. H. Paynter carried out a textbook kill in 'O' for Orange with a perfect straddle on a surfaced U-boat which brought debris and the familiar orange lights (attached to lifejackets of German sailors in the water). Flying Officer Staff-Brett, the squadron signals officer was acting as wireless-operator for this sortie and the award of an immediate DFC for Paynter's magnificent attack was coupled with an invitation for all ranks to visit Short and Harland's factories and local Royal Naval ships, pleasant breaks in routine.

As the U-boats in the Atlantic moved beyond the Wellington's range the squadron was sent back to Chivenor to operate the Leigh Light patrols in the Bay of Biscay (Wellingtons equipped with powerful searchlights in the nose to illuminate surfaced U-boats and other vessels for an attack). The fast German E-boats, which menaced our ships with quick attacks from French ports, were targets for the squadron. Although 'K' was hit by anti-aircraft fire, the petrol tanks and engines were just missed and, despite an enormous hole in the fuselage the aircraft made a safe landing. Flight Lieutenant Orloff hit a surfaced U-boat in the Bay of Biscay and several Mentions in Despatches were promulgated to hard-working airmen. Losses were rather high at this time as attacks were being delivered from as low as fifty feet and U-boats equipped with cannons were putting up a tremendous fight.

Selected as first to get the new Mk.VI radar, the squadron was sent back to Limavady to help train new crews for No. 36 Squadron and to release experienced 612 personnel for other units. Squadron Leader G. A. B. Cooper (a pre-war Auxiliary airman who had been seconded to BOAC 1941–43 but had insisted on returning to the RAF) was posted from 612 to take command of No. 282 Air-Sea Rescue Squadron which was to operate the life-boat carrying Warwick aircraft, to rescue the large crews from the heavy bombers. A captured U-boat gave the allies the opportunity to examine the secrets of 'Schnorkel', the device which enabled U-boats to 'breathe' when submerged for days. It was 612's task to work with Admiralty and Air Ministry on tests which had far-reaching results.

Flying Officer J. W. McKay, Paynter's navigator, received the DFC for his fine work, and as Squadron Leader Alan Blackwell left to become Chief Flying Instructor at No. 60 Operational Training

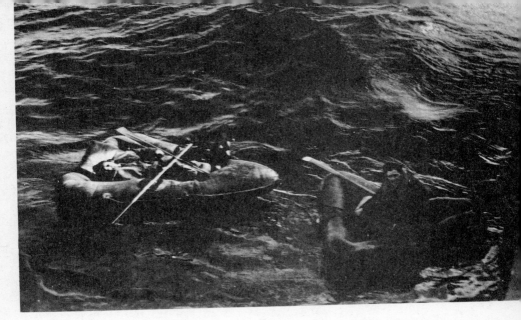

170. Exhausted crew-members about to be picked up by a flying-boat.

Unit, Silloth, Flight Lieutenant Orloff moved to RAF Leuchars, Fife, and Paynter was promoted to join Coastal Command's anti-U-boat staff, all complimentary to the squadron's war contribution. Then on 18th December came another move, this time to Langham, Norfolk, for a new role against the E-boat threat, with the Wellingtons carrying 250 lb bombs for low attacks. Much success was achieved in conjunction with Beaufighters and with the cover of Spitfires. The V.1 and V.2 launchings were often sighted leaving their Dutch sites and useful reports radioed to the Air Ministry so intercepting fighters could be directed to the V.1's likely coast-crossing point. Very many lives were saved through 612's co-operation. Our bombers, too, were enabled to hit the sites, often before the Nazis could move those which were now mobile.

In January 1945, thanks partly to 612's devastating attacks on the E-boats, it was said that not one enemy surface craft managed to interfere with allied shipping bound for Antwerp. Armed reconnaissance sorties ranged as far north as the Heligoland Bight and four Mentions in Despatches came for squadron personnel in the New Year Honours. Flight Lieutenant Rounce, attacking four ships in line astern, returned for a second bombing to find only two afloat, using up his remaining ammunition on a low-level strafing of the decks. Soon after this, with a DFC he left for No. 131 OTU, Killadeas, Northern Ireland, to instruct others in the tactics he had found so rewarding. Wing Commander Brass ('Brasso' to all) was awarded the Distinguished Service Order as he ended his fine tour of duty, leaving for No. 3 School of General Reconnaissance, to be Chief Flying Instructor.

Wing Commander A. M. Taylor was posted as C.O. but illness

caused him to hand over to Wing Commander Gordon Henderson. On 3rd March, as squadron aircraft were returning to Langham after pounding the E-boats off the Dutch coast, about a hundred Luftwaffe intruder aircraft came inland to attack Bomber Command bases. Incredibly they ignored the Wellingtons which prepared for an air-to-air tussle, with what ammunition remained, but, in the event, lived to fly again as the outcome would probably have gone against 612, short of fuel for a lengthy combat.

Air Vice-Marshal Hopps, the Group AOC, came in specially to congratulate the squadron on their successes since Wick (which he was commanding in 1942) and to tell Flying Officer K. Coulter that a DFC had been approved for his work. On 18th March a fully-loaded aircraft caught fire, exploding and damaging others, but thanks to the bravery and initiative of Sergeants Lynn and Marston, helped by Corporals Smith and Styles, other machines were quickly towed out of the danger zone. The records, regrettably, do not indicate what awards – if any – these gallant airmen received.

171. Vickers Wellington in Coastal Command camouflage.

As the German Navy began to evacuate Rotterdam the squadron piled on the offensives and Flight Lieutenant Johnson was forced to put his machine down on the sea after engine damage. A Flying Fortress spotted the dinghy and a Catalina picked up the crew, a broken arm for Flying Officer Strafford being the only casualty. For thirty-eight successive nights squadron aircraft had bombed the enemy's ships and harbours and as the midget submarines began to operate, this new threat was countered and Pilot Officer Shuttleworth got a DFC for his great work during this period. As May opened, with the end of the war in Europe in sight, the squadron aircraft pressed home attacks as far north as Denmark, the fanatical Nazis putting to sea hoping to get to South America or some place where they could continue their activities.

VE Day on 8th May came as an anti-climax and one's thoughts were of those who had given their lives in squadron service. Ground-crews got the chance to see Germany from the air in a series of Cook's Tours and some of the Wellingtons remained semi-operational to stop scuttling where possible, to photograph captured ships, and to fly V.I.P.s to accept surrender and take over ports and installations throughout Europe. A DFC was promulgated for Flying Officer H. Smith and with it came six more Mentions in Despatches awards for airmen who had kept the aircraft on the top line. Then on 9th July, 1945, orders to disband were received and personnel with time still to serve left for other units while others obtained their release and return to civilian life.

During 1946 arrangements were made to re-form the Auxiliary Air Force squadrons and on 1st November, No. 612 (County of Aberdeen) was re-activated under Squadron Leader R. R. Russell, a former Aberdeen Grammar School student who had first joined the squadron in 1937. After leaving 612 at the end of 1940 he had served as a flight-commander in No. 502 (Ulster) Squadron, then as Wing Commander, Controller at 19 Group Headquarters before commanding No. 179 Squadron of Leigh Light Wellingtons and ending the war as the Station Commander at Sullom Voe, Shetlands. Flight Lieutenant L. H. Cherry became first post-war adjutant and the Honorary Air Commodore was Sir Ian Forbes-Leith. Spitfire Mk.XIVs were issued with some Harvard trainers and in 1948 the Spitfire LF.XVIe. From the Manston summer camp seven Spitfires flew to Dinard to give an aerobatic display before 30,000 enthusiastic spectators and it is of passing interest that in addition to Squadron Leader Russell (who was in his father's building contractor business) pilots included a master plumber, an agricultural student, and an ex-Bomber Command DFC now happy to fly as an NCO. The squadron's Anson took along ground personnel.

Squadron Leader Child took over command from Squadron Leader Russell but on 3rd September, 1948, only two weeks after becoming C.O., he was leading six Spitfires to Linton-on-Ouse, Yorkshire, for 'Exercise Dagger' when after entering cloud south of Acklington, his machine crashed near Durham and he was killed. Squadron Leader Webb assumed command in October and shortly afterwards jet equipment was mooted for the squadron, but as Dyce was then unsuitable for this type of aircraft, conversion was postponed. The 1949 summer camp was held at Thorney Island, the 1950 camp at Sylt, Germany, and after the 1951 camp at Acklington, the squadron began to re-equip with the de Havilland Vampire FB.5, training on the type at RAF Edzell until the Dyce runway improvements could be completed. A big recruiting drive was mounted from city headquarters at Fairfield House with Squadron Leader Cory now commanding the squadron, which flew to Malta for the 1952 summer camp, a return to Dyce being made in November.

For the Royal Visit to Scotland in 1953 the squadron joined others of the Caledonian Wing to do a flypast over Hampden Park. In 1954 the summer camp was held at Bruggen, Germany, followed by a Battle of Britain Display at Dyce when the crowd had their legs pulled as Flying Officer Jim Healy dived a Vampire from 20,000 feet, coinciding with the double-firing of a Bofors gun behind a hangar as the commentator announced that the specially-stressed Vampire had flown through the sound barrier!

172. Vampire FB.5 at Tangmere camp, 1953.

The 1955 summer camp was at Coltishall, Norfolk, the C.O. now being Squadron Leader T. E. Johnston, DFC, and in the New Year's Honours of 1956 there was a well-merited award to Flight Lieutenant Robertson, one of the flight-commanders, who was made an MBE for his splendid services to 612 Squadron. The summer camp for 1956 was held at RAF Thornaby, home of No. 608 (West Riding) Squadron which proudly displayed a Spitfire as a tribute to former members. Before leaving, the members of 612, in traditional RAuxAF style, discreetly towed away the 608 Spitfire which when next seen bore the new 608 (Horse Riding) Squadron wording. In October Air Marshal T. Pike, Air Officer Commanding-in-Chief, Fighter Command, visited Dyce and spoke of 'a definite future for the Royal Auxiliary Air Force'. The squadron's autumn ball saw the debut of the kilt as the official mess kit of 612 Squadron, the ancient Hunting Gordon tartan being used, this bringing the squadron in line with others of the Caledonian Wing. A memorial salver presented to the squadron was handed over to Aberdeen Council for local retention in the event of any disbanding of the RAuxAF, of which rumours were increasing.

At this time Flight Lieutenant Robertson became C.O. but only a week or so later orders were given to ground the aircraft following a farewell parade and flypast. Pilots of RAF Transport Command arrived and flew the machines to St Athan, S. Wales, a home being found locally for 'Flight Sergeant Butch' a mongrel picked up and brought back from the Thornaby Camp. A poem in the squadron diary, probably written with tongue in cheek reads:

There's some that will and some that won't,
Some that do and some that don't;
Some that shall and some that shalln't,
    Come out to Dyce on Sundays.

There's some that work and some that slack,
Some come out once and don't come back;
There's some we see so very often,
They're known to one and all as 'Boffin',
    Out at Dyce on Sundays.

There's married men that get no life,
From greetin' bairns and nagging wife;
Whose only joy you'll hear them say,
Is when at last they get away,
    Out to Dyce on Sundays.

Some come for reasons mercenary,
Get their pay and only tarry,
Long enough for the cookhouse rush,
Then off they go without a blush,
    Away from Dyce on Sundays.

Yet be it snow or hail or rain,
We'll see their faces once again,
That's when they come from town and country,
To collect their annual £8 bounty,
    Out at Dyce on Sundays.

As my old grandmother used to say 'If the cap fits. . . .'

So another fine chapter in the Royal Auxiliary Air Force history was closed but the County of Aberdeen has left its imprint, not least in the service of Air Vice-Marshal R. B. Thomson, CB, DSO, DFC, who rose to become Air Officer Commanding No. 18 Group and AOC Scotland. The first C.O., rising to become Air Commodore Finlay Crerar, CBE, was Commandant of the Royal Observer Corps, Inspector of the RAuxAF and ADC to King George VI and HM Queen Elizabeth II. Another to reach high rank was Air Vice-Marshal J. B. Russell, CB, CBE, DSO, who commanded 612 at Chivenor. Sadly there is no wartime squadron aircraft preserved but outside the Chapel at RAF Biggin Hill, Kent, stands Spitfire LF.16e SL674 which was RAS–H and later 8W–H in 612's service. Perhaps one day it will be moved to Dyce Airport to remind all who see it, of the squadron's great history.

REPRESENTATIVE SQUADRON AIRCRAFT

Avro Tutor		K6106 K6107
Hawker Hart (T)		K3753
Hawker Hector		K8100 K8104 K8108 K9786
Avro Anson	I	K8838 M K8839 C N5274
Armstrong Whitworth Whitley	V	T4325 Z6633 WL–G P5062 P5071 P5080
Vickers Wellington		HX690 HX575 HX771
Vickers-Supermarine Spitfire	XIV	RM901 RAS F TZ182 RAS D TZ140 RAS H TZ183
	LF.XVIe	SL718 RAS D TD384 8W C TE400 8W M TE395
North American Harvard	IIb	FS881 KF475 KF996
Avro Anson C.XIX		TX213 VV246
de Havilland Vampire	FB.5	VZ131 WA397 8W I WA402 J WG828
Gloster Meteor	T.7	WA718 T WL378 U

173. Spitfire LFXVIe SL674 of 612 Squadron, now at Biggin Hill.

The code letters carried on the early Hectors and Ansons were DJ and on the Whitleys WL, changed to 8W on conversion to the Wellingtons. Post-war codes were RAS in the Reserve Command era but on transfer into Fighter Command in 1949 the code became 8W. Finally an official insignia was authorised, a tartan design in green, blue and white, carried on the Vampires' tails.

Badge: In front of a trident and a harpoon in saltire, a thistle dipped and leaved.

Motto (translated): 'We stand guard by vigilance.'

614
(County of Glamorgan)
Squadron

THE ONLY Auxiliary Air Force squadron formed in Wales, No. 614, came into being at Llandow (between Bridgend and Llantwit Major) on 1st June, 1937, as an Army Co-operation unit with a proportion of Reserve and Regular officers and airmen, part of No. 22 Group. Squadron Leader R. Cadman was the commanding officer and Flying Officer M. G. F. Pedley the adjutant. Before a full complement of aircrews could be fully trained, war came and on 1st September, 1939, the squadron moved into its war station at Cardiff Airport with seven pilots still undergoing the Army Co-operation training course at Old Sarum, Wiltshire. The squadron's machines at this time were a mixture of Hawker Hinds and Hawker Hectors with an Avro Tutor for initial flying training.

An early 'prang' happened when the engine of Hind L7238 cut at 2,000 feet and the aircraft nosed over on emergency landing in a field, but Pilot Officer D. F. H. Smith escaped serious injury. On 18th September there was a squadron inspection by the Rt. Hon the Earl of Plymouth, the Lord Lieutenant of the County, and by Lord Tredegar. Squadron Leader Cadman was posted to become Station Commander, Royal Air Force, Cardiff, and Flight Lieutenant L. J. Stickley, RAF, became squadron commander with Flying Officer R. E. C. Cadman as adjutant. On 2nd October the squadron moved to RAF Odiham, Hampshire, and on the 10th a new squadron, No. 225, RAF, started to form from B Flight of 614, known for a few days as 614A Squadron. At this time 614 was flying the Westland Lysander II and much confusion has arisen since the war because whereas the 614 code letters were 'LJ', those allocated to 225 Squadron were 'LX' and at least five of the Lysanders bore both codes at different times during October 1939.

On 8th November, Squadron Leader W. R. Wills-Sandford was appointed to command and some of the Hind and Lysander aircraft were transferred to the last-formed Auxiliary Air Force squadron, No. 613 (City of Manchester), which was also at Odiham for intensive training to bring crews to operational standard. Some pilots, when deemed ready, left the squadron to strengthen the Air Component in France, for liaison work with the British Expeditionary Force. Personnel from both the Army and Royal Navy arrived for training as air observers and on 21st January, 1940, Squadron Leader Wills-Sandford was moved to No. 52 Wing in France, his replacement as C.O., being Squadron Leader A. A. N. Malan, formerly a Major in the Royal Tank Regiment.

174. Hawker Hectors in formation near Cardiff.

175. Officers at pre-war Hawkinge summer camp.

With the Nazi push into the Low Countries in May 1940, the squadron came to readiness and six aircraft were ferried to Amiens-Glisy aerodrome, to act as airborne spotters for the British and French gunners trying desperately to stem the blitzkreig which ended at Dunkirk. The squadron was then ordered to Grangemouth near Edinburgh to assist in training the British Army for the day of retaliation, and also to carry out vital convoy escort patrols to release our Hurricanes and Spitfires for the defence of London and SE. England, and the Luftwaffe's targets from Plymouth and around the coast to Tynemouth. Crews of B Flight moved up to Evanton in North East Scotland to carry out tactical reconnaissance exercises and A Flight maintained shipping cover from Montrose down as far as Berwick-on-Tweed.

As the post of commanding officer was upgraded, Wing Commander D. J. Eyres assumed control, and B Flight moved down to Inverness for dive-bombing practice. Young pilots including Flying Officer B. R. Macnamara and Pilot Officer P. de L. Le Cheminant (both later rising to high rank) flew from dawn to dusk helping to train our soldiers before the Army moved to the Middle East, the Argyll and Sutherland Highlanders and Scottish Command paying tribute to the squadron's valuable help. Pilot Officer Le Cheminant made a successful forced-landing after a mid-air collision but, alas, the other machine crashed and Flying Officers Merrett and J. F. Harper lost their lives.

During August, Hurricanes of No. 263 Squadron, veterans of the Norwegian Campaign, became the 'enemy' to give 614 crews vital combat practice and with the appeal for pilots to replace Battle of Britain casualties, Flying Officer Macnamara moved to No. 7 Operational Training Unit for fighter-pilot training and fifteen of the squadron's groundcrew members volunteered for aircrew, a remarkable achievement for the unit. On 7th September for 'Operation Cromwell' the Lysanders were bombed-up awaiting the sound of church bells announcing the Nazi invasion but when Churchill's illustrious 'Few' successfully repelled the Luftwaffe, opportunity was again taken to form a new squadron on a nucleus of 614's personnel, No. 241 Squadron beginning to form at Inverness. Readers of *The Unseen Eye* by Air Commodore Millington, should remember that it was from the County of Glamorgan's Squadron that Nos. 225 and 241 were formed to become magnificent photo-reconnaissance units.

Advance Landing Grounds were sited for the future training of Army volunteers who were given initial training in de Havilland Moth Minors before going on to become Glider Regiment pilots. Then, with the Battle of Britain reaching its peak, the squadron detached Lysanders to help with air-sea rescue from RAF Tangmere in Sussex, helping to save many who later flew with distinction on offensives into Occupied Europe, thanks to 614's vigilance over the English Channel. On 9th October the squadron received the Lysander Mk.III and when volunteers were sought for Boulton Paul Defiant night-fighters, four pilots left to help form yet another new squadron. On 24th October the Air Officer Commanding, Air Vice-Marshal C. H. B. Blount, OBE, MC, was killed in a crash at Hendon en route for a squadron inspection; the grief of all was partially dispelled by the visit of Ivor Novello and his company who entertained, a show particularly enjoyed by the Welsh members.

176. Westland Lysander II.

Squadron Leader Malan left to take over 225 Squadron and an unusual top-secret project was a scientist's visit to examine the possibilities of fitting cannons to the Lysanders for strafing purposes. No. 309 (Polish) Squadron was considerably assisted in its formative weeks and 614, now commanded by Squadron Leader Tailyour, was divided between Tranent, East of Edinburgh, and Westhampnett, Sussex (from where sorties were flown to drop dinghies to pilots down in the Channel during the early attacks on the enemy in France). Then in April 1941 detachments at Macmerry, Inverness, and Elgin, learned with delight that Air Ministry felt the squadron had done its share of forming other units and was now entitled to a part in the growing offensive.

The Bristol Blenheim Mk.IV light-bomber was allotted to 614 and under Wing Commander Skelton, joined by an old friend, Squadron Leader B. R. Macnamara (who had scored victories with 603 [City of Edinburgh] Squadron in the Battle of Britain after leaving 614), conversion was so rapid that some crews flew down to West Raynham, Norfolk, during May to operate 'Intruder' missions against Luftwaffe airfields at Leeuwarden, Twente, and Vechta, in Holland. In support of the RAF's first 'Thousand Plan' attack on 30th/31st May against Cologne, 614's Blenheims attacked Bonn aerodrome to prevent the Luftwaffe night-fighters taking off to intercept our bombers. All our aircraft returned safely and reported that they could see Cologne's fires at tremendous distances.

By July, under Wing Commander Sutton, there were twenty-two trained crews on the strength – the highest ever – and for Operation 'Dryshod' the crews again worked smoothly with the Army. One genuine moment of regret was the departure of Squadron Leader Macnamara to 296 Squadron but, as had happened previously, there was consolation in the news that the Blenheim Mk.V was coming, but with a move overseas! From Odiham the squadron flew to Portreath, Cornwall, and in November set off for Gibraltar, one aircraft failing to arrive but whether due to technical troubles or enemy action was not known. By 18th November, the squadron was part of No. 326 Wing at Blida, Algeria, commanded by Group Captain Laurence Sinclair, GC, CBE, DSO and Bar, a most distinguished Blenheim pilot.

No. 18 Squadron's groundcrews hurriedly affixed bomb-racks to 614's Bisleys (the name for the Mk. V Blenheim) and, next day, led by Squadron Leader Le Cheminant, seven aircraft attacked Bizerta airfield, all returning after a successful sortie. Raids then continued by day and night against enemy targets in Tunisia; airfields and harbours receiving the squadron's pinpoint bombing. The unlucky ground personnel, arriving in the P. & O. liner *Strathaird*, discovered, too late, that the troopship had returned hurriedly to the U.K. carrying most of their kit back in the holds, what had been unloaded

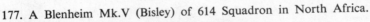

177. A Blenheim Mk.V (Bisley) of 614 Squadron in North Africa.

then suffered during an enemy air attack, nevertheless these airmen cheerfully accepted conditions and joined the squadron full of enthusiasm for the tasks ahead.

On 4th December, 1942, No. 18 Squadron was asked to relieve pressure on the British Army by bombing enemy fighter bases and Pilot Officer Georges and his crew volunteered to fly with 18 Squadron against the Cheuigui airfield, Tunisia. Ten Blenheim Vs set out – there was no time to try and get a fighter escort – and after a successful bombing from only 200 feet about sixty Messerschmitt 109s, called up from another airfield, dived on the Bisleys which were all shot down, with only a few survivors from the crashed machines taken prisoner and three from one crew who miraculously returned to our lines. After the war a member of the 2nd Lancashire Fusiliers, dug in thirteen miles from Bizerta, who watched the destruction of the Bisleys, sent to No. 18 Squadron a torn fragment of map, thrown from an aircraft to prevent it falling into enemy hands. Wing Commander Hugh Malcolm, who led that raid, received a posthumous Victoria Cross and the Malcolm Clubs were so named in his memory. All members of 614 honour Pilot Officer Georges and his gallant crew who flew in that epic raid.

After the squadron had moved on to fly from Canrobert, Flying Officer Irving's aircraft was forced down but he walked back across the desert to fight again. Group Captain Sinclair often flew with 614, whose morale was high despite frequent enemy dive-bombing

178. King George VI visits the squadron. Air Commodore L. F. Sinclair, GC, and Air Marshal Sir Arthur Coningham in background.

attacks on the airfield, now at Terbourba. The C.O. made a habit of taking all the aircrews into his confidence, inviting comments before and after attacks and several outstanding missions were credited to the squadron, Tunis Docks being just one target from which every aircraft returned unscathed. By Christmas Day, 1942, a Liberty Run was laid-on into Constantine for hot baths and relaxation, and a gift of £50 from the No. 614 Territorial Association, Cardiff, with splendid fresh pork for the traditional serving of the airmen by officers, helped brighten the Christmas away from home.

The squadron initiated the idea of single aircraft carrying out moonlight sorties to survey enemy airfields and wireless back coded instructions for follow-up raids, a most rewarding venture as results bore out. The next base, Oulmene, provided an underground operations room which enabled the squadron to plan mixed-force sorties, some aircraft taking food-containers to our front-line troops, with others wiping out Luftwaffe aircraft on the ground to prevent their interference. The Kasserine Pass break-through was assisted by 614's attacks on enemy transports and both 'Monty' and Air Marshal Tedder signalled commendations as the Bisleys left the roads littered with useless Nazi vehicles. General Alexander visited the squadron to give them his personal thanks, after which newly-promoted Air Commodore Sinclair flew him on to 'Paddington' (Souk el Kemis). Former C.O., Wing Commander Skelton, arrived to fly on operations and as many as fourteen aircraft were airborne on attacks between Soussee and Sfax; the results delighted the General Commanding 2 Corps, who expressed warm thanks.

Joining up with No. 13 Squadron, in one night *fifty-nine* sorties were flown, some crews flying as many as four missions to keep the enemy on the run. On 26th April, 1943, it was announced that the County of Glamorgan squadron had flown 155 operational missions totalling 433 hours, dropping 268,200 lbs of bombs on enemy positions and targets in the first 25 days of that month! Squadron Leader MacLaren received an immediate DFC, and as soon as organised enemy resistance ceased in Tunisia, the squadron aircraft ferried U.K. mail into the various bases. In late May came a different task: patrols against U-boats and Italian submarines in the Mediterranean, sharing the duties with No. 500 (County of Kent) Squadron from Tafaroui, with welcome breaks for rest and bathing at Les Andalouses.

In June a further 137 sorties were flown and DFCs were awarded to Flight Lieutenants D. Smyth and D. R. Wallace. So publicised was 614's record of achievements that some pilots flew with No. 39 Squadron's Beaufighters, and observers and air-gunners with No. 14 Squadron's Marauders, to infuse experience into these units, a loss to 614, but a tribute indeed. By August the squadron was at Borizzo in Sicily with Wing Commander C. K. Bonner in charge. Vital air-

sea rescue searches were flown and during one of these Flight
Lieutenant Holloway was himself forced down, to be picked up from
the sea by a Polish destroyer. Air Marshal Sir Keith Park, Commander-in-Chief, Middle East, flew over to thank 614 crews for saving
many valuable lives and authorised the attachment of a captured
Macchi C.200 fighter to give pilots a busman's holiday.

Squadron machines were now flown into Malta for major over-
hauls and when rations at Catania ran low the friendly Americans
lent a helping hand. International soccer was organised and a first-
rate concert party from talented 614 types entertained personnel of
other units. In February 1944 the squadron disbanded on paper at
Borizzo and, in early March, re-formed as a heavy bomber squadron
by taking over No. 462 (Royal Australian Air Force) Squadron's
Halifax II aircraft at Celone, under command of Wing Commander
W. T. Russell. On 11th March the squadron sent seven machines to
attack the marshalling yards at Genoa, leaving 24 thousand-pound
and 54 five-hundred-pound bombs on target. On the 14th/15th came
the long haul to Sofia in Bulgaria, again to attack marshalling yards.
Bad weather caused the loss of four aircraft and three crews, Flight
Sergeant Dingwall making his way back and Warrant Officer Atwell,
pilot of BB420, making an emergency landing on a satellite field near
Bari, receiving an official commendation for his fine airmanship.

Acting as target marking force for 205 Group, the squadron
bombed, with 4,000 pounders, such targets as the Ploesti Oilfields,

179. Squadron Halifaxes of 1st Pathfinder Force, 1944.

the Iron Gates Canal (Roumania's key waterway) and, from Stornara, as part of a joint RAF–USAAF Group, hit targets in Yugoslavia, Greece, Bulgaria, Italy and Hungary. Then came visits to Munich as day and night priority attacks were mounted ahead of the Army paths to victory in Europe.

On the night of 20th/21st April, Warrant Officer Atwell and crew were lost during a visit to Mestre, Northern Italy, when an abortive operation was blamed on poor meteorological forecasting. The bodies of three of Atwell's crew were recovered from the Adriatic later. Then came the allied invasion of Southern France which the squadron supported from Amendola. On 14th August Halifax JN912 was being flown back to base when it caught fire and was ditched. Leading Aircraftman Isaac, a groundcrew member, swam for nineteen hours (about twenty miles) accompanied most of the way by Pilot Officer J. E. Holmes who, alas, died from exhaustion. Warrant Officer F. W. Beare got a well-merited Distinguished Flying Medal for his fine work prior to his promotion, and the trusty Halifaxes were now exchanged for the Consolidated B–24J Liberator B.VIII. Aircrews as well as ground personnel worked hard to build a shanty-town from packing cases in preparation for a winter likely to be tough on tent-dwellers.

On the signing of the USSR–Roumania peace treaty, four crews, detained in Roumania as prisoners of war after squadron raids, were returned to 614, with interesting stories to tell of their captivity. The DFC was awarded to Flying Officer Prange for supply drops to Yugoslav partisans and a splendid occasion was the presentation to crews of the coveted Pathfinder badges by Brigadier J. D. Durant, DFC, the South African commanding the Group; and then four more DFCs came to pilots. Ammunition was flown into Greece as

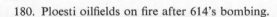

180. Ploesti oilfields on fire after 614's bombing.

a change from dropping bombs. Pooled finances at Christmas 1944 provided treats for local orphans, and carol-parties collected from their comrades to donate to the Red Cross P.O.W. fund. Once again a cheque came from the County of Glamorgan Territorial Association for Yuletide comforts.

On the promotion of Wing Commander J. S. Laird, who had led the squadron on a series of missions which had ranged from co-operation with the French patriots to minelaying in the Danube, Wing Commander E. B. R. Lockwood assumed command, the squadron continuing the offensive with bombing of an ammunition dump at Pola and in support of our 8th Army and the U.S. 5th Army push into Austria and Germany. Decorations came for Squadron Leader A. Dunning, Squadron Leader D. Q. Watson, Squadron Leader W. Simpson, Flight Lieutenants W. Irwin, C. H. Muggeridge, and H. Wheeldon, Flying Officer McFall, Pilot Officers Francis and Ross, and a DFM for Flight Sergeant G. B. Briggs, a flight engineer. Leaflets were dropped over a wide area warning the Germans that the end was near and as VE Day at last came, food was dropped. Then began the evacuation of our prisoners of war released from their camps, in parties of twenty-five in each Liberator: British personnel were flown into the U.K.; Frenchmen were picked up from Belgrade and flown into Istres, France; South Africans were taken to Cairo to await ships for their home ports. Almost a thousand men were flown to freedom during these missions.

Then came a series of Cook's Tours for ground airmen, to fly them over operational areas, followed by organised parties to Rome for a short break. The last formal parade was for the presentation of the Pathfinder badges to Major J. G. Maritz and Captain L. Pienaar, two South Africans who had served the squadron well. In July 1945 came the order to disband, No. 214 Squadron, RAF, taking over the Liberators which they later transferred to No. 37 Squadron, old rivals of 614, not least on the soccer pitch.

On 26th August, 1947, the squadron re-formed at Llandow in the Auxiliary Air Force (RAuxAF from 16th December, 1947) with the Spitfire LF.VXIe, exchanging these for the Spitfire F.22 a few months later. The first post-war C.O. was appropriately Squadron Leader W. H. Irving, DFC, who had flown with the squadron in 1942 and had made his way back to fly again after his Bisley had been forced down in the desert. He had served with distinction in Nos. 18, 100, 626, and 76 Squadrons, after leaving 614 in North Africa. The Honorary Air Commodore, likewise most appropriately, was Air Commodore R. Cadman, who had formed the squadron in 1937.

In July 1950 the squadron re-equipped with the jet de Havilland Vampire F.3, and Squadron Leader E. H. 'Sam' McHardy, DSO, DFC and Bar, Croix-de-Guerre, a regular RAF officer, took command; a New Zealand-born pilot who had led Nos. 248, 404, and 143 Blenheim and Beaufighter Squadrons of Coastal Command during World War II. The squadron's RAF adjutant and instructor was then Flight Lieutenant Peter Latham, who later made news when he led the 'Treble One' aerobatic team of No. 111(F) Squadron and received the famous Britannia Trophy from HRH Prince Philip, Duke of Edinburgh, being awarded the Air Force Cross for his inspired leadership. Squadron Leader H. J. E. Howe, who had been adjutant to RAuxAF squadrons, took over as C.O. in 1954 when the Vampire Fighter-Bomber Mk.5 was being flown (a few Mk.FB.9s arriving later). Then in March 1957 came the blow when all RAuxAF squadrons were told to disband.

181. Sqdn Ldr Sam McHardy, DSO, DFC.

182. Vampire F.3 VT799 in 1951.

A 614 Squadron Association was formed to organise reunions, and on Battle of Britain Sunday, 17th September, 1961, a unique page of history was written when in Llandaff Cathedral, the Bishop dedicated a chapel in memory of squadron members who had died in war and peace; the cost raised by ex-members. In the presence of Air Commodore M. K. D. Porter, CB, CBE, Air Officer Commanding in Wales, and other distinguished guests, the Dean of Llandaff, the Very Reverend Eryl S. Thomas, received for dedication and safe-keeping in the chapel the Squadron Colours presented by Air Ministry as an RAF Ensign, a very special award made at that time only to 617 (Dambusters) Squadron, for that unit, like 614, had not been in existence for the normal 25 years to earn The Standard given to the older RAuxAF squadrons. The Colours were borne by former Wing Commander H. C. Edwards, supported by the Squadron Association Hon Treasurer ex-Squadron Leader H. J. W. Coward, and the Hon Secretary S. Morgan. Funds were made available by the Association to provide fabric and hymn books, also for the welfare of ex-squadron members or their dependants in need. Holidays for deserving families were another project and few RAuxAF squadrons have a more public-spirited bandof ex-members.

As this is written (February 1971) there are two known 614 Squadron machines preserved; Spitfire F.22 PK624 at RAF Abingdon, Berkshire, and Vampire F.3 VT812 at RAF Colerne, Wiltshire, and one or both may go to the Royal Air Force Museum, Hendon. The remains of a Hector are said to be in Eire and could be of a 614 machine. Let us hope the authorities acquire the pieces for restoration as a tribute to the pre-war members of the squadron. Several members remained in the post-war Royal Air Force for some years, one of the early pilots retiring as Group Captain Richard Rhys, another as Air Vice-Marshal B. R. Macnamara, another as Air Marshal Sir Peter de Lacey Le Cheminant, DFC and Bar (the Bar awarded for leading 209 Squadron of Sunderland flying-boats during the Korean War). Former adjutant, now Group Captain Peter Latham, is serving at this time and, like all former members, whatever their rank, is proud to have been in Six One Four.

REPRESENTATIVE SQUADRON AIRCRAFT

Hawker Hind Trainer		L7238
Avro Tutor		K6104
Hawker Hector		K9727 K9729 K9762 K9766
Westland Lysander	II	L4756 L4761 L6855
	III	R9022 R9025 T1461 T1559
Bristol Blenheim	IV	Z6104
	V	BA734 BA800 BB180 EH334
Handley Page Halifax	II	BB420 H JN912 D JN943 X JP111 M JP183 C
Consolidated B–24J Liberator	VIII	KG945 KG949 KH227 KH375

Vickers-Supermarine Spitfire	LF.16e	TE120 RAU–A TE208 RAU–F TE385
	F.22	PK542 7A–O PK604 7A–E PK619 7A–G
de Havilland Vampire	F.3	VF348 G VT860 T VT667 V
	FB.5	WA291 N WG799 A WG829 R
	FB.9	WR157 WR253
Gloster Meteor	T.7	WL341 WG991 S VZ636 V

Squadron code letters appear to have been YX in the Hector period, then LJ and, on re-forming post-war in Reserve Command, RAU was allotted. This changed to 7A when the squadron moved into Fighter Command in 1949 and the code was finally dropped in favour of red and green interlocking triangles each side of the tail-boom roundels.

Badge: On a demi-terrestrial globe, a dragon passant.

Motto (translated): 'I rise to search.'

615
(County of Surrey 'Churchill's Own')
Squadron

ON 1ST JUNE, 1937, approval was given for a new squadron to be formed at RAF Kenley, to be known as No. 615 (County of Surrey) Squadron, Auxiliary Air Force, initially to co-operate with Territorial Army units in the area. Squadron Leader A. V. Harvey was appointed to command and Flight Lieutenant R. C. M. Collard arrived as adjutant and flying instructor. In November three Hawker Audax flew in from RAF Hawkinge, followed by a Hawker Hart trainer and one Hawker Hector – from RAF Waddington, Lincolnshire. Flight Lieutenant N. de W. Boult came as assistant adjutant and recruiting began for the other 35 officers and 164 airmen needed to keep the squadron airborne. First candidates for pilot-training included G. A. B. Cooper, E. C. Fieldsend, L. T. W. Thornley, J. R. H. Gayner, W. O. Stern, P. N. Murton-Neale, P. Collard, B. J. R. Brady, L. Fielding, P. F. Coyeneve, F. G. Bowling, A. Eyre and K. T. Lofts, with E. J. Smart and R. J. Kilby for ground duties as accountant and administrative officers.

By the time of the 1938 Munich crisis the squadron was able to move to its war station, Old Sarum, Wiltshire, as an Army Co-operation unit. Soon afterwards, though, on 7th November, it was transferred to Fighter Command and a mixture of Gloster Gauntlets and Gladiators was flown in by squadrons hastily re-equipping with Hawker Hurricanes. Mr Winston Churchill was approached and immediately accepted the appointment as Honorary Air Commodore. When the squadron moved to Ford in Sussex for the 1939 annual camp, Acting Pilot Officers Obolensky (the famous rugby player), Hanbury, Hancock, Jackson, McClintock, Rose and Truran joined the party for intensive flying practice. All 164 airmen turned up, indicative of the enthusiasm which was characteristic of the pre-war AAF.

183. Hawker Hector 1937.

After the excitement of intercepting French Air Force 'raiders' before they 'bombed' Brighton, news came of the squadron's embodiment into the Royal Air Force on 24th August, 1939, with a move into Croydon Airport as the first wartime base. Officers were billetted in the Aerodrome Hotel and airmen shared Imperial Airways' new hangar. The twelve Gladiators were dispersed over in the north-west corner of the airport with the four reserve machines sharing the airmen's bed-space. Pilot Officer W. O. Stern became adjutant to release another regular pilot for an RAF squadron, and a training flight was established at Kenley to bring to operational standard those who had recently joined. On 9th September Flying Officer Collard and Pilot Officer D. J. Looker left for a Hurricane conversion course and two nights later came tragedy when Pilot Officer A. St. C. Rose was killed a mile north of Bletchingley during training.

184. Squadron on presentation of squadron badge, 12th February, 1938. A/M Sir Hugh Dowding front row centre, with Sqdn Ldr Harvey on his right and Wg Cdr Mercer on his left.

185. Squadron officers with their autographs, 1st September, 1938.

Mr Churchill paid the first of his many visits and then, alas, another crash during night flying cost the life of Pilot Officer C. C. M. Hanbury. News then came that the squadron was earmarked for France, with 607 (County of Durham) to strengthen the regular units already there. A veritable stream of well-wishers called including Air Marshal Sir Hugh Dowding, AOC-in-C. Fighter Command, Air Vice-Marshal E. L. Gossage, AOC No. 11(F) Group, and, of course, Mr Churchill. No. 607 Squadron arrived from County Durham and on 15th November, 1939, the two squadrons were airborne from Croydon followed closely by four Ensigns, four DH.86s, two Scyllas, one Magister, one Avro 10, and one Fokker transport. There were forty-five machines in the air, one of the largest formations seen leaving for France at that time.

At Merville, they came under No. 61 Fighter Wing, commanded by Air Commodore Boret a World War I Ace. Three days later the first operational patrols were flown as far as Amiens and Le Touquet, enabling pilots to familiarise themselves with their 'parish'. Air Vice-Marshal C. H. B. Blount addressed officers and airmen on their reponsibilities and when King George VI came to see his troops and to present the first war decorations, a Gladiator of 615 was flown to Seclin for him to inspect and for the pilot to be presented.

As the 'Blighty' leave-boats commenced their Channel crossings 615 and 607 escorted them and, alas, returning to St Inglevert from one of these patrols in terrible visibility Pilot Officer S. M. Wickham stalled and was killed. His replacement was Pilot Officer P. H. Hugo, a South African, destined to make the headlines later. On 29th December the guns of 615 were fired in anger for the first time as Flight Lieutenant J. G. Sanders, on a weather-test, sighted an He.111

above him. Chasing it up to 23,000 feet, Sanders used up all his ammunition from 200 yards only to lose the enemy in cloud.

New Year's Day saw the visit of Captain Balfour, Under Secretary of State for Air, accompanied by Air Vice-Marshal Sholto Douglas, Assistant Chief of Air Staff. To their delight the members of 615 learned that they would be getting Hurricanes within weeks (it was more than three months in fact). The news was a great morale-booster during the depression of the 'Phoney War'. Mr Churchill then called, only to find his pilots dispersed between three airfields, Vitry, St Inglevert and Abbeville, affiliation sorties being flown with our Blenheim light-bombers to give their crews and 615 pilots experience of combat techniques. As the C.O. left on being promoted, in came Squadron Leader J. R. Kayll from 607 to take over and on 27th April the first Hurricane arrived and the squadron hastily started re-equipping at Abbeville, feeling that it was only a matter of time before Hitler made his move. It was, in the event, 9th May, when Abbeville was bombed, the squadron being at Le Touquet at this time. Pilot Officer Fredman took the only Gladiator from Abbeville and attacked an He.111 without being able to see the result. Two days later this same pilot failed to return and was last seen pursuing the enemy.

186. Gladiators of 615 at St Inglevert, France, April 1940.

Next day, during escort to our bombers, Flying Officer Murton-Neale went missing and on 15th May, Flight Lieutenant Hedley Fowler, an Australian in the RAF, flying with 615, failed to return from a mission against the German advance in the Ardennes. Who could then know that Hedley Fowler would be one of only thirty members of the Royal Air Forces to escape from German P.O.W. camps and make the journey back to the United Kingdom to fly and fight again. In one of the finest of all the Colditz breaks, he left Oflag IV.C in October 1942 reaching England via Spain and Gibraltar in March 1943; his adventures deserve a full-length book. He was awarded the Military Cross and, becoming tired of lecturing other aircrews on escape and evasion tactics, begged to be allowed to fly again. He was selected to act as a test pilot for the Hawker Typhoon fighter-bomber, during which he was killed in diving the machine, the notes found on the pad strapped to his knee helping to resolve some of the initial problems with this aircraft. Thus Hedley Fowler, in losing his life, probably saved many others and he will always be remembered with pride as one of 615's pilots.

187.
Sqdn Ldr Hedley Fowler, MC.

The day of Fowler's crash and eventual capture near Dinant, Belgium, was also the squadron's first confirmed victory when a Henschel 126 was shot down, though Pilot Officer Looker's aircraft was damaged by return-fire and he made a forced-landing near Brussels. Next day near Moorseele, Belgium, two pilots were lost but one was later reported through the Red Cross as a prisoner of war. On 17th May Flight Lieutenant Sanders destroyed a Ju.88 near Lille and 615 was forced to amalgamate with 245 Squadron to put twelve machines into the air.

On 19th May the squadron's Miles Master communications aircraft left to check on squadron machines left at Vitry and was intercepted by a Bf.109 en route. Brilliant evasive flying resulted in only one bullet hitting the Master and next day it accompanied thirteen Hurricanes to Norron Fontes. On the way an enemy convoy was spotted and seven lorries were left in flames; later two Heinkel He.111s were also sighted and shot down. As orders came for a return to Kenley, a DFC was announced for Flight Lieutenant J. G. Sanders – the first decoration to 615 Squadron.

A special G Flight, under Sanders, was positioned at Manston to protect that airfield against possible invasion and on 2nd June several pilots left to strengthen No. 242 (Canadian) Squadron including Pilot Officer Bush, Flying Officer Horne, and Pilot Officer

Denis Crowley-Milling. Squadron aircraft were still reaching Kenley, and Keith Belcher (a top engineer in civil aviation at Southend Airport after the war) says that when he was evacuated from Moorseele, Belgium, he was amazed to find Gladiator N2310, which he and L.A.C. Prosser had looked after and which had been flown by Flight Lieutenants Murton-Neale and Sanders, Flying Officer Gaunce and Pilot Officers Hugo and Lofts, safely back at Kenley; probably flown back by a pilot of another squadron.

On 8th, 9th, 10th, the squadron took off from Kenley, refuelled at Hawkinge and then, with No. 111 Squadron, flew to Le Treport-Aumale; refuelling again at Dreux, they found Rouen in flames but, surprisingly, saw no Luftwaffe aircraft in the air on any of these three days. On 11th June, however, between Le Treport and Fécamp they intercepted Ju.87 dive-bombers with Bf.109 escorts, probably bound for Dover: two Messerschmitts were damaged and a Stuka probably destroyed. On landing the squadron learned that Fowler was a prisoner of war and that Pilot Officers Looker and Pexton, logged as missing, were in U.K. hospitals, both with leg wounds.

Few people realised that the Royal Air Force was already on the offensive over Occupied Europe and it was 615 and 607 Squadrons which escorted a small Bomber Command force on attacks against Luftwaffe-held airfields in France and Belgium, destroying many machines on the ground, some of which would certainly have operated against England. On 22nd June during a sortie over Rouen, nine Hurricanes of 615 met a Ju.52 transport accompanied by nine He.111s and Messerschmitt 110s. One Bf.110 was destroyed, five others claimed as probably destroyed and one feels that the V.I.P., in the transport, must have felt slightly uneasy. Pilot Officer J. R. Lloyd, though, failed to return from this patrol.

On 27th June the squadron escorted a photographic machine over French airfields and, on landing at Kenley, found King George VI awaiting the pilots. He decorated Squadron Leader Kayll with both Distinguished Service Order and Distinguished Flying Cross for his fine work, and pinned the DFC on Flight Lieutenant Sanders' tunic. Remaining for tea, the King heard first-hand accounts of the County of Surrey's combats and experiences. Three days later whilst escorting Blenheims, an overwhelming force of Bf.109s jumped the bombers out of sun and shot down three, though the 615 Hurricanes accounted for several of the 109s without loss. On 3rd July, Kenley was bombed by a hit and run raider, damage was negligible, and the Luftwaffe aircraft was shot down over Maidstone by 32 Squadron.

Convoys were being escorted from Beachy Head round to the North Sea and on 12th July Mr Churchill – now Prime Minister – came in his Flamingo transport to chat to the squadron at Hawkinge, escorted by a lone Hurricane piloted by the AOC No. 11(F) Group, Air Vice-Marshal Keith Park. The Prime Minister stayed overnight and left just before a mixed force of Ju.87s and Bf.109s dive-bombed a convoy. The 615 pilots claimed two of the 109s and a Junkers 87 and B.B.C. commentator Charles Gardner recorded an on-the-spot interview which included congratulations to his squadron from Mr Churchill. Pilot Officer Mudie, forced to bale out during the mêlée, died later in Dover Hospital, the squadron's first home-battle loss.

On 17th July Pilot Officer Hugo damaged a Do.17Z off Folkestone, the enemy machine making a forced-landing at 615's old base, St Inglevert. After two days of convoy-escorting, action came again on 20th when Flight Lieutenants Gaunce and Hugo, with Flying Officer Tony Eyre (from Whitgift School, Croydon), destroyed three Messerschmitt 109s over Convoy 'Bosom' near Dover, claiming others which although damaged, apparently got back to France. On 25th July both Gaunce and Hugo had inconclusive combats and on 27th July, following direct orders from the Prime Minister that Luftwaffe machines carrying the Red Cross emblem but thought to be spotting for German long-range guns be engaged, an He.59 floatplane was sighted. The formation of 615 pilots shot the Heinkel to pieces ten miles NE. of Dover before they landed back at Hawkinge for supper.

The early days of August were uneventful for the squadron and it was good to learn that Pilot Officer Jackson, missing months earlier, was known to be a prisoner and was well. Pilot Officer J. A. P. McClintock overturned his Hurricane on landing at Hawkinge on the 11th but was happily unhurt. Next day Messerschmitts were intercepted near Beachy Head, claims being made of two destroyed and one damaged. On landing a signal awaited Flight Lieutenant Gaunce, Flying Officer Collard and Pilot Officer Hugo, announcing awards of the DFC – a cause for much celebration. On Wednesday 14th August, though, both Collard and Pilot Officer C. R. Montgomery were shot down and killed near Dover by a strong force of Messerschmitt 109s and 110s and although Flying Officer Gayner's Hurricane received hits, he brought it back. In this same engagement Pilot Officer Keith Lofts shot down a Ju.87 and Flying Officer Tony Eyre and Sergeant J. Porter shared another. That evening a high-flying Ju.86 was claimed as damaged.

On 15th August the Luftwaffe bombed Croydon instead of Kenley and West Malling instead of Biggin Hill (errors which were to cost the enemy dear). Pilot Officer A. J. J. Trurans' Hurricane was severely damaged in combat near Dungeness and he was wounded, nevertheless managing to land his aircraft so that it could be repaired and return to the fight. Sergeant D. W. Halton was shot down and killed but his death was partially avenged when Flying Officer Eyre and Pilot Officer Lofts destroyed a Messerschmitt.

On 16th August the squadron destroyed two Heinkel 111 bombers before they could hit SE. England, Pilot Officers Lofts and Young scoring the victories, with others claiming aircraft damaged as they approached Brighton. The next day was quiet but on the 18th Kenley was again bombed and Flight Lieutenant R. S. Cromie and Leading Aircraftman Holroyd lost their lives, and Leading Aircraftman Tanner, who was wounded, died later. The squadron fought bravely to defend its home ground but several Hurricanes were lost on the ground and those which got airborne met a second force of Messerschmitts which arrived to cover the withdrawal of the bombers. Surviving 615 pilots were ordered to land at Croydon but the Luftwaffe was there in force and two more Hurricanes were damaged. Ten squadron Hurricanes were destroyed this day but, luckily for the country, only one of the four pilots shot down died (Sergeant P. K. Walley on Morden Park golf course). Flight Lieutenant Gaunce and Pilot Officers Hugo and Looker escaped unhurt or with minor injuries. It is of passing interest to note that a classic Battle of Britain book states that Looker's Hurricane was destroyed but it was, in fact, repairable, and today exhibited in the Science Museum's aircraft gallery in Kensington.

188. Battle of Britain Hurricane, now in the Science Museum, London.

Claims of three destroyed and four damaged Luftwaffe aircraft were made at the time but there was much confusion with other squadrons and post-war research credits 615 with four Dornier 17Zs, one of them possibly shared with Spitfires. Next day Group Captain HRH the Duke of Kent called and the squadron rose to the occasion by getting two more Dorniers, one shared by Tony Eyre with 65 Squadron, the other shared by Squadron Leader Kayll and Pilot Officer Young; both Dorniers crashed near Eastchurch, Kent. In the evening the Prime Minister and Mrs Churchill joined in squadron rejoicing, particularly when Tony Eyre's DFC was announced.

On 22nd August Pilot Officer D. H. Hone got his Hurricane safely down after being shot-up by another Hurricane (whether it was one captured and flown by the enemy has never been confirmed).

The unfortunate Pilot Officer Hone was again forced down on 24th, this time over Essex during a battle in which Squadron Leader Kayll and Pilot Officer McClintock shot down an He.111 near the Thameshaven Oil Refineries, the Heinkel crashing near Hornchurch where McClintock landed and spoke to the German pilot and crew. That night history was made when Flight Lieutenant J. G. Sanders took off and shot down a Ju.88 near Hastings receiving the Air Officer Commanding's warm congratulations for a remarkable feat in the darkness.

Pilot Officers 'Buck' Casson and Brewster were attached from 616 (South Yorkshire) Squadron for combat experience (Buck later getting a DFC and commanding 616 after the war, he also gained the AFC). On 26th August the squadron lost four Hurricanes, Flight Lieutenant Gaunce was admitted to hospital suffering from shock, Flying Officer Gayner also went to hospital slightly wounded, and the luckless Pilot Officer Hone crash-landed at Rochford and was also admitted to hospital. Pilot Officer McClintock baled out unhurt. One enemy aircraft was credited to the squadron this day.

By 28th August, with only nine Hurricanes airworthy, the strain was telling and Pilot Officer S. J. Madle was forced down near Ashford, several enemy aircraft being damaged near Sandwich. The Air Ministry decided the time had come to give the squadron a wellearned rest and ordered them to move up to Prestwick in Scotland, leaving some new pilots with other 11 Group squadrons. In Scotland four Free French airmen joined, including Adjutante Mouchette, and as pilots were trained to operational requirements some were sent to reinforce squadrons still in the battle zone. Six Polish pilots came for combat training and on 10th October a move back to Northolt to replace No. 1 (Canadian) Squadron and then, three days later, over to Heathrow, at that time a newly-constructed airfield, now London Airport. Patrols were increased in strength and 615 led a three-squadron wing which included Nos. 229 (RAF) and 302 (Polish) though the beaten Luftwaffe was now licking its wounds and was rarely in evidence.

On 18th October a terrible happening distressed all members when news came that four of the squadron airmen, out for an evening in Harrow Wealdstone, had been killed by a bomb from a lone raider. Three days after this came news of a DFC for Flight Lieutenant Keith Lofts (posted to 249 Squadron). On 25th October Squadron Leader Kayll damaged a Bf.109 and on the 29th Sergeant E. T. Cosby destroyed a Bf.109 and claimed a Junkers 88 as damaged. Unhappily Pilot Officer N. D. Edmond was shot down, his Hurricane destroyed and the officer badly hurt. On this day came the promotion and departure of Flight Lieutenant L. M. Gaunce, DFC, to command No. 46 Squadron and on 1st November Mr Churchill came to see 'his boys'. On the 6th Sergeant Hammerton failed to return from patrol and was found dead in his crashed machine in Kent. Two days later the squadron flew three sorties, Sergeant Moore damaging a Heinkel and Pilot Officer Landells, after destroying a Bf.109, was brought down but luckily was unhurt.

On 19th November Flying Officer Christopher Foxley-Norris came in from No. 3 Squadron and a quiet spell followed, disturbed on 25th November when Pilot Officers McClintock and Truan, old warriors of the squadron, died in an accident in the Miles Magister. Their cremation at St John's, Woking, was a sad occasion for all. On 5th December Squadron Leader Orzechowski left to command No. 308 (Polish) Squadron and as 615 returned to Kenley, Squadron Leader Kayll departed on promotion and an Australian pilot Squadron Leader R. A. Holmwood took command with Flight Lieutenant Tony Eyre, DFC, elevated to flight-commander.

On 8th January, 1941, came the first act for 615 in the Prime Minister's 'Set Europe Ablaze' programme when the squadron began a series of close-escorts for daylight bombing of Occupied Europe by our small force of Blenheims and Hampdens which, in early February, were supplemented by the RAF's first four-engined bomber, the Short Stirling. These escorts brought inevitable losses. Sergeant Jenkins was reported missing and then when two aircraft collided, one of the Polish pilots died. As a break from escorting the bombers, 'Rhubarb' operations were flown and losses continued; Flying Officer Stewart and Sergeant Fotheringham failing to come back from Belgium on 15th February.

The more powerful Hurricane II was received but a sad start made as on climbing between Dover–Folkestone on 26th February the squadron was jumped by Messerschmitt 109s and the C.O. was killed when his parachute caught fire and failed to open. Flying Officer Foxley-Norris baled out successfully, Pilot Officer Hone was wounded and Adjutant Lafonte got the only consolation, a 109 'probable'. Tony Eyre was promoted to command and the Prime Minister was represented at the C.O.'s funeral at Whyteleafe by his personal bodyguard, Commander Thomson. Adjutant Bouquillard was then lost in a following mission as 615 joined in escorts with Nos. 1, 17, 56 and 249 Squadrons, all of which included ex-County of Surrey pilots.

It was 15th April before another combat ensued when Flight Lieutenant Dunning-White destroyed a Bf.109 over Dungeness, though he also had to abandon his machine over Dymchurch. Pilot Officer Blaize did not return from this mission and Fighter Command, in their wisdom, decided to send the squadron to Valley, in Anglesey, for a semi-rest, flying convoy escorts over the Irish Sea. Tony Eyre had come to the end of his operational tour and was relieved by Squadron Leader G. S. ff Powell-Sheddon, DFC, ex-242 Squadron Battle of Britain pilot. Two new pilots were lost, possibly due to technical troubles over the sea, and the only action was when Sergeants Hamilton and Roberts damaged an intruding Luftwaffe Ju.88, Hamilton being slightly wounded by return-fire. Another combat near Holyhead resulted in a second Ju.88 being damaged, a DFC for Flight Lieutenant Dunning-White being announced.

The C.O. left for Malta (later getting a DSO) and Squadron Leader D. E. Gillam, DFC, AFC, who had flown with 616 (South Yorkshire) and 312 (Czech) Squadrons, came to command. On 16th August popular Canadian Pilot Officer Albert Boulanger crashed and died in North Wales. On 26th August Flying Officer (as he then was) Mouchette and Sergeant Hamilton, chased a Ju.88 reconnaissance aircraft, putting one engine out of action and seeing it make a forced-landing near Old Kinsale Head, South of Cork, in neutral territory, where they had to cease firing. A Botha of Coastal Command crashed just offshore and, in a desperate endeavour to save the crew, twelve would-be rescuers died, including Leading Aircraftman Ford and Bannister of 615, the three men in the Botha also drowning in the treacherous waters.

A few days later Sergeant Maridor, another Frenchman destined to make headlines, joined the squadron and then came a welcome move to Manston, Kent, for a period of aggressive fighting with considerable success against enemy ships and a rewarding interlude when a rowing-boat containing six French volunteers for the allied cause was protected from Nazi interference. The squadron now acted as 'anti-flak' going ahead of our day bombers to try and silence enemy batteries and Pilot Officers Hamilton and the Australian Roberts, 'good pals, grand lads and great pilots', were lost attacking minesweepers and ground targets.

189. The Honorary Air Commodore with Sqdn Ldr D. E. Gillam, 1941.

Honorary Air Commodore the Rt. Hon W. S. Churchill brought Mrs Churchill to have tea with the squadron and to meet newcomers including Czech Sergeant Chaloupka who, soon after this, had to bale into the sea, being picked up by the Ramsgate rescue boat which was covered by 615's Hurricanes. On 2nd October, after attacking E-boats off Dieppe, the squadron went to the cinema in Canterbury to see a newsreel film of the Prime Minister's visit to their dispersal. Early next morning they hit seven flakships and an 8,000 ton merchantman before breakfast but, alas, Sergeant Chaloupka did not return. Three squadron Hurricanes were sent to Russia and as two Norwegians, recently escaped from their enemy-held country, joined on completing fighter training, a quick roll call showed Argentine, Australian, Canadian, French, English, Scots, Irish, Malayan, Norwegian, South African and Welsh pilots.

On 9th October, after sweeping the Belgian and French coastlines, destroying a 1,500 ton vessel, an enemy flak battery was silenced to allow Squadron Leader Gillam to fly into the Nouveau Basin, Ostend, to destroy two Heinkel 59s on the water before setting fire to their hangar. Five days later another He.59 was destroyed as the squadron accompanied the Airacobras of 601 (County of London) and Hurribombers of 607 Squadrons. Next morning four Bf.109s were shot down over Blankenberge and a fifth damaged, following which, according to squadron records, 'a most hearty breakfast was enjoyed!'

The Secretary of State for Air, Sir Archibald Sinclair, flew into Manston to express thanks to 615 and the squadron marked his visit by wiping out petrol storage tanks at Flushing and hitting four trawlers. The C.O. was wounded and Flying Officer Eric Aldous lost. Two more Heinkel 59s were destroyed at Ostend and a third damaged though flak got Flying Officer Strickland and Sergeant Potts and wounded Flying Officer Ford. Flight Lieutenant Hugo went in separately and blew up a gasometer. On 29th October General de Gaulle came to meet the squadron and, in particular, the Free French members, telling these pilots that they would soon form their own squadron (No. 340). On 9th November a lone Ju.88 dive-bombed Ramsgate and was then shot down by Sergeant Louis as it tried to get back to its base. On 22nd November came a Bar to his DFC for Flight Lieutenant 'Dutch' Hugo and next day he figured in a dramatic incident. Squadron Leader Gillam, although wounded in the legs and arms during an attack on a distillery, pressed on and Hugo dealt with the gun battery which had hit the C.O. Off Dunkirk, though, Gillam had to leave his crippled machine as Hugo 'fetched' the Air-Sea Rescue launch from the Goodwins. Then, as his aircraft was also disabled, he left two other pilots circling the C.O.'s dinghy, four Bf.109s being driven off in a fierce struggle to protect Gillam. Happily he was brought safely into Ramsgate harbour.

Next day a Tomahawk pilot of 26 Squadron was also protected as he waited in his dinghy to be rescued and the Air Officer Commanding, now Air Vice-Marshal T. Leigh-Mallory, sent congratulations and promoted Dutch Hugo to command No. 41 Squadron, a Spitfire unit. Flight Lieutenant Mohr, who had escaped from Norway, coming in as flight-commander. Telling 615 members that they had 'put Manston on the map' the Station Commander, Wing Commander Tom Gleave (now 'Chief Pig' of the famous Guinea Pig Club), read a letter from the Air Officer Commanding in which he said the squadron had made history by clearing the Channel of enemy shipping. Good news came in the form of a Red Cross advice that Sergeant Chaloupka was a prisoner of war and from Fighter Command that the Distinguished Service Order had been awarded to Squadron Leader Gillam.

Another well-deserved rest period took the squadron to Angle, with only an occasional reconnaissance Junkers to chase. Pilot Officer A. M. Fisher, a South African, lost his life during a convoy escort, a blow offset just a little by news of Distinguished Flying Medal awards to Sergeants Louis, Astley, and Finn. Then came a move to Portreath in Cornwall to fly out as far as Brest on escorts and offensives. Christmas Day brought a cable of greetings from Mr Churchill who was then visiting Washington, and Squadron Leader Gillam also left for the U.S.A., to lecture to American aircrews. Then came a move to Fairwood Common near Swansea, a DFC to Flight Lieutenant McCormack and the departures of two of the Norwegians to form and command Nos. 331 and 332 (Norge) Squadrons, which later topped the No. 11(F) Group scoreboard; a tribute, perhaps, to training with 615 Squadron!

Late in February 1942 warning came to personnel of a move overseas, pointedly brought home with vaccinations and inoculations. On 16th March a message from the Prime Minister:

I am sorry that I cannot see you all personally before you leave for overseas, to wish you well and to tell you how proud I am to be your Honorary Air Commodore. You have a very fine record and I am sure that you will maintain your high standard of devotion to duty, courage and skill. I hope you will continue to keep me informed of your accomplishments. All best wishes. Winston Churchill.

With a total strength of 401 officers and airmen, the squadron entrained at Swansea on 17th March, 1942, for Liverpool, there boarding a transport, disembarking at Bombay on 16th May. Then via Karachi or Calcutta (aircraft taking a different route) they finally reached Jessore, Bengal, on 17th June to begin reconnaissance of their sector (responsibility area). A further message from Mr

Churchill, via the Viceroy of India, read 'Please convey my good wishes to 615 Squadron. I am confident that they will win new distinctions Burma and India.'

Flight Lieutenant Holland left to command the neighbouring 607 Squadron (the unit with which 615 left for France in 1939) then, together, the squadrons flew offensive sweeps over Japanese held territory, hitting bridges, trains, river and road transports, and troops wherever they could be found. Al Horvath, the squadron's 'Yank', was lost and there was genuine regret for he was well-liked. On 6th December a move took 615 to Feni, Bengal, for raids as far into Burma as Akyab and Mungdaw, escorting Blenheims, Mohawks, and even the slow-moving Lysander. Christmas Day 1942 was a strange experience with temperatures akin to those in the Holy Land and cables were exchanged with Mr Churchill before the traditional waiting-upon-airmen ceremony. The pilots took off to beat-up Japanese machine-gun posts before they themselves did a little relaxing, with thoughts of Kenley and other home centres.

It was a tough blow when Squadron Leader B. L. Duckenfield, DFC, a 501 (County of Gloucester) Battle of Britain pilot, failed to return from a Magwe airfield sortie, Squadron Leader W. D. Williams, another Battle of Britain DFC, taking command. Pilot Officer Finn, DFM, was lost during successful sinkings of two river steamers early in January 1943 and Belgian pilot Flying Officer Ortmans was also lost. The satellite field was nicknamed Manston and sorties redoubled as the allies drove out the last Japanese from the Mayu peninsula. Unusual missions were to destroy a Wellington and a Hurricane, forced down and then camouflaged with trees by the Japanese, possibly for later use when serviceable. By March, though, the ex-enemy airfield at Maugdaw, re-named 'Ritz', was in use and for the first time the squadron was in combat with the Japanese Air Force, damaging or probably destroying two Army-01 aircraft known as 'Oscars'.

Beaufighters on photo-reconnaissance were escorted and river craft of all sorts and sizes were destroyed where known to be in enemy use. Information was received that Ortmans was safe and that he may have been shot-down by a captured Hurricane operated by a Japanese pilot. Leaflets were dropped, written in Bengali, to try and counteract the enemy's propaganda that Britain was merely exploiting the Indian people for her own ends. To commemorate the 25th Anniversary of formation of the Royal Air Force on 1st April, 1918, a small parade was held, before eleven squadron aircraft were scrambled on radar warning of an approaching Japanese formation. There were, in fact, thirty enemy bombers with fighter escort and in the resultant combats three Army-97 Mitsubishi 'Sally 2' bombers fell to 615's guns, with nine others damaged or probably destroyed, plus one enemy fighter damaged. Unfortunately

Flying Officer Ortmans, just back from his jungle adventures, was killed; he was later buried at Feni.

April was a month of 'Rhubarb' operations against ground targets of opportunity and then, as a pleasant change from sight of the Chindwin, a rest at Alipore, Calcutta from 7th May. Life in a modern block of flats suited everybody and All-India Radio was quick to have pilots of 615 and 607 to give talks on the theme 'Hurricanes over Burma' which were well received. The awards of a DFC to Flight Lieutenant Louis, DFM, a Bar to McCormack's DFC, and a DFC to Warrant Officer Chandler, a New Zealand pilot, helped morale, though this was never low, whatever the setbacks. Then, passing their trusty Hurricanes to No. 5 Squadron, both 615 and 607 pilots were flown to Karachi to pick up and fly back Spitfire Vc machines, a flight of $7\frac{1}{4}$ hours giving them useful practice with the new types. On 4th October Flight Lieutenant Louis was airborne on the first Spitfire scramble only to be beaten to the Japanese raider by No. 136 Squadron's aircraft which drove off the enemy, somewhat damaged.

Moving to Chittangong the squadron escorted Vultee Vengeance dive-bombers and on 8th November came the first kill with Spitfires when an Army-100 Nakajima 'Helen 2' was overhauled and shot down at 25,000 feet over Chiringa. On 10th November Flight Sergeant A. R. Hyde got another at 29,000 feet over Chittangong. Later that month eighteen of the 615/607 Spitfires climbed as high as 32,000 feet in training for Japanese recce machines on photographic missions. Enemy aircraft did not normally stay to fight it out but Pilot Officer H. L. A. Leonard, a straggler with engine trouble, had to bale out when jumped by the enemy. He trekked back to base through enemy lines to fly and fight again. On 28th November another Japanese fighter was damaged and next day an Army–99 Kawasaki 'Lily 2' probably destroyed, with four new types (later known to be the Navy–0 'Zero' or 'Zeke 52').

Earl Mountbatten called to thank the squadrons at Dohazari in East Bengal and the customary greeting for Christmas 1943 arrived from the Prime Minister with his thanks for goodwill messages during his illness. Boxing Day aptly saw a scrap when twenty-plus 'Sally' 'Oscar' and mixed Japanese fighters approached. Flying Officer Andrews and Flight Sergeant Chatfield claimed four enemy destroyed and one damaged but Sergeant Wright crashed in flames, thought possibly due to enemy action. On 16th January Flight Lieutenant Louis and Flying Officer Weggery out-manœuvred a Japanese 'Dinah' seventy miles east of base. With the move of the C.O. to Haifa, Egypt, for Staff College course, the Australian Squadron Leader D. W. McCormack was promoted to command. By February the squadron was flying from a paddy field strip at Nazir near the Burma border and had to destroy a Spitfire VIII as it lay in enemy country. In March a move to Silchar West (nicknamed 'Char') where there was smooth grass and, of course, tea gardens and the squadron enjoyed pleasant breaks in Mr McIvor's lovely home when off-duty.

April 25th/26th saw 'bags of joy' to quote squadron files when formations of Oscar aircraft were intercepted, with six probably destroyed or damaged. Wellingtons were escorted to hit Japanese airfields and by May, moving to Dergaon in Assam, the Spitfires equipped now with 90-gallon long-range tanks, flew cover to Douglas DC–3 Dakotas with supplies for the 14th Army. After moving first to Palel and then Sapam strip, one Oscar was confirmed destroyed with five damaged and enemy camps were 'sprayed' and Japanese trucks hit on the Tiddim Road with three more Oscar victories for the loss of Warrant Officer J. E. Payne, RAAF, who surprisingly turned up three days later after evading capture in enemy territory, a most commendable performance.

The Spitfire VIII was now received to replace the Vc and attacks on Japanese convoys increased the squadron score, though for the loss of Flying Officer Kelly. In came Flight Sergeant A. A. Payne, RAAF, twin-brother of the gallant warrant officer. On 10th August, 1944, there was stark tragedy when the squadron was ordered to fly its sixteen Spitfires from Palel to Calcutta: after about thirty miles the formation entered cumulo-nimbus cloud and the Spitfires were 'tossed about like so many leaves' to quote a survivor. Some pilots found themselves only 80 feet or so from the ground and the eight who managed to land safely did so with their hands cut to ribbons through gripping the controls. Of the eight Spitfires lost, four pilots, Squadron Leader McCormack, DFC and Bar, Flying Officer W. S. Bond, Pilot Officer M. Pain and Warrant Officer Chappell, all of the Royal Australian Air Force, lost their lives. Three baled out and one crash-landed.

With the squadron now at Baigachi, a new strip 28 miles NE. of Calcutta, Squadron Leader K. F. Gannon held the reins briefly before handing over to Squadron Leader T. H. Meyer. There was a flight, in company with 607 Squadron, for the Battle of Britain Day commemoration, the airmen parading below in Calcutta. After the cathedral service it was unanimously decided to set up a fund for a practical memorial to Squadron Leader McCormack and a cheque for 2,010 rupees was handed to the Chaplains' Department to pay for a stained glass window in McCormack's parish church at Seddon, Victoria. The usual cables were exchanged with the Prime Minister at Christmas and after co-operating with the Liberator bombers of No. 99 Squadron, RAF, members of 615 joined the cast of 'Handful of Stars' which ran for eight weeks on the American Broadcasting network, bringing hearty congratulations from the producer on the squadron's talent.

By February of 1945, flying from Nidania with the Spitfires now carrying bombs, attacks ahead of our troops were interspersed with anti-submarine patrols. Lieutenant-Commander D. B. Law, a famous Naval pilot, came from HMS *Emperor* to fly with 615 and with Flying Officer M. S. Fulford, RAAF, and other newcomers, the squadron joined No. 224 Group under Air Commodore the Earl of Bandon, a great pilot and most popular visitor to the squadrons. In April, from Prome Road, after flying from Ramree Island, the squadron helped roll back the Japanese and moved to Charra, Chakulia and Cuttack, celebrating VE Day and end of war in that far-away European theatre with the arrival of former C.O., Squadron Leader Duckenfield, released from captivity in Burma. On 10th June it was announced that 615's Spitfires would be handed to 135 Squadron and that, at Akyab, the 135 Squadron Thunderbolt fighter-bombers (nicknamed by the Americans 'The Jug' or 'The 7-ton milkbottle') would be taken over.

After some tactical reconnaissance flights and escorts to No. 84 Squadron's Mosquitos, the planned invasions of Malaya, Japan, and Jap-held territory were abandoned after the dropping of the two atomic bombs and VJ Day on 15th August, 1945. The squadron was now at Vizagapatam; and on 25th September it was disbanded with a parade after a letter from Air Chief Marshal Sir Keith Park, the Air Officer Commanding-in-Chief, Far East Air Force (the pilot who had escorted Churchill to Manston), had been read by the C.O., Squadron Leader P. J. Anson, DFC. It read:

> You have the enviable distinction of bearing the illustrious title 'Churchill's Own' a title those who bear the squadron's name in future will honour with pride. Air Ministry request that the numberplate of the squadron be returned to them so that 615 may be re-formed as part of the Auxiliary Air Force in England.
>
> During your tour in this theatre, 615 have played an important part and managed air superiority, which after the advent of Spitfires was unchallenged. While equipped with Hurricanes your squadron's achievements were most creditable in view of the inferiority of this aircraft to the Jap fighters. After re-equipping with Spitfires you did invaluable work from Chittangong and later performed magnificently at Palel, which at one time came under enemy fire.
>
> The squadron took part in operations continuously from December, 1942, except for periods of rest or re-equipment and the high standard of efficiency and keenness that it showed throughout was a fine example to all.

Thus for a brief period No. 615 did not exist and then, in June 1946, the newly constituted Auxiliary Air Force began to form and as

Kenley was considered unsuitable for the newer types of fighter, Biggin Hill, in Kent, became the squadron airfield (shared with 600 [City of London] Squadron) at weekends. The Spitfires XIVe and F.21 were the first post-war machines with Squadron Leader R. G. Kellett, DSO, DFC (who had led No. 303 [Polish] Squadron in the Battle of Britain), as C.O. His adjutant was Flight Lieutenant F. B. Sowrey, RAF, son of the Zeppelin Ace, and to encourage recruiting, the C.O. and adjutant decided to provide their own facilities for giving ground personnel air experience which single-seat fighters could not provide. From Aer Lingus a Walrus amphibian was purchased for £150, Kellett and Sowrey flying it from Dublin. In 1947 it took personnel to summer camp and from camp at Horsham St Faith to East Coast beaches. Putting down on the sea during one joyride it caused pandemonium; coastguards fired rockets, the Lowestoft lifeboat arrived and £5 donated to RNLI funds on the spot helped clear up an embarrassing situation. The Walrus is today exhibited in the Fleet Air Arm Museum at Yeovilton, Somerset.

190. Spitfire F.22s at Biggin Hill, 1950.

In 1948 the Spitfire F.22 was received and the following year Squadron Leader P. K. Devitt assumed command, he being relieved in turn by Squadron Leader Neville Duke, DSO, OBE, DFC, AFC, famous test pilot and record-breaker in the Hawker Hunter. In September 1950 came the conversion to the Gloster Meteor F.4. A summer camp at the wartime base, Manston, was followed by camps at Sylt, Oldenburg, Wunstorf and Celle, Germany, and Tangmere and Takali (Malta), then, in 1951, by the return of Squadron Leader F. B. Sowrey – now with the Air Force Cross for his fine work – to be commanding officer. From September 1951 the Meteor F.8 was used and some of the squadron formations were highly praised and much-publicised in aviation journals. In January 1954 Squadron Leader R. A. Eeles took command and the Honorary Air Commodore and the Queen Mother were only two of many V.I.P. visitors to Biggin Hill to meet the pilots and their groundcrews.

Much could be written, were space available, on the fine contribution of 615 members to military and civil aviation. Suffice it to say that the first C.O. became Air Commodore Sir Arthur V. Harvey, CBE, MP; another, Group Captain D. Gillam, rejoined 616 (South Yorkshire) post-war as an ordinary pilot; two other ex-C.O.s, Squadron Leaders Kayll and P. J. Anson, commanded 607 and 603 Squadrons respectively after the war. Air Chief Marshal Sir Christopher Foxley-Norris became Chief of Personnel and Logistics, Ministry of Defence, in January 1971; and Air Vice-Marshal F. B. Sowrey is Senior Air Staff Officer, Training Command, RAF, as this is written. On the civil side Squadron Leader Neville Duke contributed such fine books as *Test Pilot*, *The Sound Barrier* and other classics to our libraries and became Sir George Dowty's personal pilot in 1960. Ian Smith (of Pulborough, Sussex, not Rhodesia) flies airliners out of Gatwick as a change from aerobatting Meteors; and Hugh Merewether has the OBE for his fine flying for the Hawker Siddeley Group at Dunsfold. The third member of the Smith-Merewether-Judge Meteor formation, Flight Lieutenant 'Pee-Wee' Judge, did a fine job for Beagle Aircraft before his untimely death – a tremendous loss to British Aviation.

191. Sqdn Ldr Neville Duke, DSO, OBE, DFC, AFC.

What posterity owes to Flight Lieutenant J. H. Holloway, MBE, for his magnificent work for the Battle of Britain Fighter Pilots Association is incalculable, for he has made available for future generations the priceless collection of their autographs, and books such as *The Narrow Margin* on which the Battle of Britain film was based have relied on Flight Lieutenant Holloway's unique records, a labour of love from a pre-war member of the squadron.

When the Royal Auxiliary Air Force was disbanded in 1957, No. 615's C.O., Squadron Leader R. A. Eeles, joined the C.O.s of 600, 601 and 604 in a gallant battle to save the day. Members of Parliament were lobbied, Fleet Street was invoked, but to no avail, and with sincere regrets the men of 'Churchill's Own' the County of Surrey Squadron saw their Meteors flown away, the majority to be scrapped. In the Science Museum, though, and at RAF Binbrook, Lincolnshire, are displayed a Hurricane Mk.I L1592 and Spitfire F.22 PK664, flown by the squadron; reminders of a glorious past.

192. Sir Winston Churchill, OM, CH, MP, and Sqdn Ldr F. B. Sowrey, AFC.

REPRESENTATIVE SQUADRON AIRCRAFT

Avro Tudor		K6099 K6100 K6102
Hawker Audax		K5586
Hector		K8127 K8134
Gloster Gauntlet	II	K7854 RR–A K7948 M K7938 T K5357
Gloster Gladiator	I	K7976 KW–A K K7957 K8004 K8044
	II	N2302 N2312 N5581 N5900
Hawker Hurricane	I	L1689 P2768 P3111 KW–M R4194
	II	Z2703 KW–M AP530 (sent to USSR) HV828
Vickers-Supermarine		
Spitfire	Vc	JL108 MA395 MA650
	VIII	JF615 JG676 MD386
Republic Thunderbolt		
(P–47D–25)	II	KJ141 KL856 KW–D

Vickers-Supermarine
  Spitfire   XIV   NH792 SM829 RAV–U
                     F.21   LA215   RAV–A   LA306   LA313
                                  RAV–B
                     F.22   PK409 V6–L PK569 V6–S PK664
                                  V6–B
Gloster Meteor   F.4   VT182 V6–A VT270 V6–B VT285
                     F.8   WK810   E   WK984   B   WL162   J
                                WF685 WF714 (C.O.)

North American
  Harvard   IIb (AT–16)   FX208
Supermarine Walrus   G–AIZG   (formerly   L2301,   N18,
                                  EI–ACC)

From the time the Gloster Gauntlet was received the code RR was used and this was also on the Gladiators until outbreak of war when it changed to KW which was then used until disbanding in 1945. From 1946 the Reserve Command code of RAV was used but on transfer back to Fighter Command in 1948 the letter/figure V6 was carried on the Spitfires and Meteors. In 1951 codes were withdrawn and the squadron's coloured insignia of white rectangle with horizontal blue zigzag was carried until final disbandment.

    Badge: On a star of six points, an oak sprig fructed.

    Motto (translated): 'By our united force.'

502

(Ulster)

Squadron

In May of 1925, No. 502 Squadron began to form at Aldergrove as the first Special Reserve unit of Lord Trenchard's visionary plan to base squadrons near centres of population, with local part-time volunteers augmenting a nucleus of regular personnel. Why the number-plate allocated was not 500 or 501 has puzzled many but nothing can alter the fact that Ulster *was* the first. The airmen were billeted in Crumlin and on 9th June came two Vickers Vimy bombers (a type already seen in Ireland when Alcock and Brown touched down in Galway after making the pioneer direct Atlantic flight in 1919). Four days after Flight Lieutenant E. F. Turner, AFC, arrived to start recruiting, came Squadron Leader R. D. Oxland, the first commanding officer. An office was established in Old Town Hall Street and a grant made to form a squadron band.

On 1st December, Flying Officer Robert McLaughlin, DFC, a World War I pilot, became the first Special Reserve officer. March 1926 saw the first church parade at Killead Church and five Vimy aircraft did a round-Ulster publicity flight. Two months later the Air Ministry authorised the squadron to bear as its device the Red Hand of Ulster. Colonel J. D. Dunville, CBE, DL, worked marvels to enrol additional part-timers; this intrepid balloonist and huntsman seeing the total of airmen volunteers reach fifty. Wing Commander A. C. Wright, AFC, became C.O., and the records reveal that Flying Officer Tussaud caught his hand in the port airscrew during flight and was invalided from the Service. It is believed that he was recalled in 1939 and, promoted, did fine work commanding an Officer Training School at Uxbridge.

Visits were paid to factories to interest employers in the release of men for part-time RAF duties and the Battle of the Somme

193. Vickers Vimy, the first squadron machine.

anniversary (honouring the 36th Ulster Division) was 502's first public parade. Unfortunately Flying Officer Wing had to crash-land his Vimy which had to be written-off after a demonstration flight, but four passengers escaped injury. In September, though, Flying Officer Evans was hurt when he had to make a forced landing in his Avro 504N and died later in Masserne Hospital, Antrim; the first fatal casualty.

A new City Headquarters in Donegal Square South, complete with workshops, gymnasium and social facilities, worked marvels and new enrolments included three Special Reserve officers. The Bank of Northern Ireland gave a lead by offering staff leave on half-pay if they gained commissions and altogether there were 2,500 applications from the public for vacancies in the squadron. By 30th June, 1928, a complement of thirteen officers and ninety-seven airmen brought the reservist strength up to full establishment for the first time. A few days later came four Handley Page Hyderabad bombers to supplement the Avros and on 13th July Flight Lieutenant R. S. Sugden, AFC, won the first Ulster Air Race in a Lynx-Avro.

So keen were these part-timers that in March 1929 317 flying hours were logged, the highest for the Air Defence of Great Britain area. This brought a letter of commendation from Air Vice-Marshal H. C. T. Dowding, then Director of RAF Training. The funeral of Wing Commander Dunville, 'Father' of the squadron, at Holywood on 15th June, 1929, was a sad moment but the visit of No. 19 Squadron, RAF, for co-operation with their Siskin fighters, helped dispel the sadness of a great friend's passing.

Bombing targets were set up on Lough Neagh, the rafts skilfully navigated via the Lagan Canal by Flight Lieutenant (afterwards Air Commodore) B. D. Nicholas. In August a record 'cross-country' saw the squadron flying to Manston in Kent, a 900-mile round-trip. Squadron Leader C. L. King, MC, DFC, RAF, came in to command and the flying badge was awarded to Pilot Officer G. R. Montgomery (who rose to high rank during the war). For the Northern Ireland Golf Championships at Newcastle the squadron could only muster one entry – Pilot Officer G. F. Humphries – but he won the championship and the scratch cup!

Wing Commander F. P. Don came from No. 33(B) Squadron to take command and he left to assume command of the Cambridge University Air Squadron, in which many from Ulster gained their wings, including Air Vice-Marshal F. D. Hughes, CBE, DSO, DFC, AFC, now (1971) Commandant, Royal Air Force College. Into 502, to command, arrived Wing Commander R. T. Leather, AFC. In December 1931 the Hyderabads were flown over to No. 503 (Lincoln) Squadron, and 502 got the Vickers Virginia. Wing Commander L. T. N. Gould, MC, the next C.O., led the squadron as escort to HRH The Prince of Wales at the opening of Stormont in 1932 and, in 1933, flew formation for the new Belfast Dock ribbon-breaking ceremony.

In 1934 Flight Lieutenant G. P. Marvin left to join No. 58 (B) Squadron as a stepping-stone to high rank and, under Wing Commander J. C. Russell, DSO, 502 changed over to single-engined bombers with the Westland Wallace and Wapiti aircraft. Around this time the squadron adjutant was Flight Lieutenant Tom Gleave with Flying Officer T. F. U. Lang assistant adjutant. During 1940 Squadron Leader Gleave (who retired as a Group Captain with the CBE) was badly burned in combat and is today 'Chief Pig' of the magnificent Guinea Pig Club. Also playing a key part in the Battle of Britain was Wing Commander T. F. U. Lang, then a Controller at Headquarters No. 11 (Fighter) Group, who died in Australia after retiring from the Royal Air Force.

194. Squadron officers at summer camp, Hawkinge, 1938.

On 1st July, 1937, No. 502 (Ulster) Squadron was transferred into the Auxiliary Air Force, with only a small nucleus of regular personnel, the majority of air and ground complement being Ulstermen. Squadron Leader G. V. Tyrrell, MC, RAF, handed over command to Squadron Leader L. R. Briggs, a Special Reserve officer, and Hawker Hart and Hind aircraft paved the way for the Avro Anson as the squadron role was converted from a bomber designation to 'G.R.' (general reconnaissance) to form part of No. 18 Group of RAF Coastal Command.

When war came at last on 3rd September, 1939, No. 502 Squadron was at its war station carrying out anti-U-boat patrols and convoy escorts. The day after war broke out Terence Corry and John Harrison flew down to Roborough, Plymouth, to collect bomb-racks to carry the anti-submarine bombs on the Ansons. In November A Flight was detached to Hooton Park in Cheshire and here, on 19th January, 1940, was recorded the first war loss when Anson N5050 crashed on the Rhyl foreshore with the pilot seriously hurt and the other three aircrew killed. At this time the brothers Flight Lieutenants Terence and Brian Corry, directors of a Belfast timber firm, commanded the two flights, their AAF numbers 90033/34. Pilot Officer D. B. Hodgkinson began to make his mark and for a brief period the Blackburn Botha was used by the squadron. Attachments of Bomber Command Whitleys came to bolster Coastal forces and Pilot Officer Len Cheshire flew in with a 102 Squadron Whitley to fly with 502. Few would have guessed that this young pilot would end the war with VC, DSO and two Bars, DFC, or that after witnessing the second atomic bomb on Nagasaki, he would leave the Service to work for the under-privileged.

On 26th October, 1940 the liner *Empress of Britain* was sighted, ablaze from stem to stern, and her lifeboats were escorted until surface-craft rescued the survivors. Next day Flight Lieutenant Billings, flying one of the squadron's recently-arrived Armstrong Whitworth Whitleys, attacked a U-boat with a salvo of 250 lb bombs near where the liner had been torpedoed, but did not see evidence of the enemy's destruction. At this time the squadron was chosen to operate the first A.S.V. (Air-to-surface vessel: airborne search and homing radar, used for anti-U-boat and anti-shipping operations). Wing Commander Barkley of Holywood was the first pilot to make a successful radar landing by homing on to an A.S.V. beacon on returning from an operational flight, coming back sixty miles to Limavady with visibility less than 1,000 yards.

Flight Lieutenant Hunter McGiffin and his crew left for Beaulieu in the New Forest before going on to RAF St Athan, Glamorgan, for training with the top-secret radar gear and it was, in the event, Flight Lieutenant Terence Corry who was first in the squadron to pick up a U-boat with his A.S.V. On 30th November Flying Officer

L. R. de M. Thompson and his crew failed to return from patrol. In January 1941 Flight Lieutenant Billings, who had made the squadron's first war attack, did not come back from a sortie off the Scottish coast, the aircraft were operating out of Lossiemouth at this period. The next day Whitley T4168 had to make an emergency landing in Eire, two of the crew being interned with three reported missing.

195. Hawker Hart (T) with P/O W. H. McGiffin (left) and P/O J. Bell.

196. A Flight with Ansons at Hooton Park, Cheshire, April 1940.

By February 1941 one flight was established at Limavady, the other at Aldergrove, and winds were so strong that three Nissen huts became airborne one night. Wing Commander Tom Cooper managed to get long-range tanks approved to extend squadron patrols and a

U-boat was bombed, the Whitley was damaged by some accurate return-fire from the enemy guns and made a forced landing later without injury to the crew. In March, Squadron Leader Terence Corry left for No. 30 Wing, Iceland, and he later commanded a Beaufighter wing with great distinction. At Limavady, Sergeant A. W. Wood received the British Empire Medal – the first squadron decoration – for his gallantry on the occasion when the Whitley of which he was second pilot crashed into the sea near Castlerock. He swam ashore and ran barefoot along the railway line in search of help, getting an Army unit to the rescue of his comrades. He was later commissioned and rose to the rank of wing commander.

In April Whitley Z6553 crashed in Eire but Squadron Leader Brian Corry and his crew managed to bale out to safety and make their way back to base; Squadron Leader Corry borrowing a civilian suit from a Royal Ulster Constabulary member and returning to the wreckage to check that the top secret equipment was wrecked. It had, in fact, survived the crash so he immediately smashed it up so as to deny it to any enemy. Squadron Leader Bob Mooney came in from the Queen's University Air Squadron and Pilot Officer McCutcheon who was showing considerable promise later ranked as one of Coastal Command's Ace skippers.

On 17th July Wing Commander D. R. Shore, AFC, departed to take command of No. 612 (Aberdeen) Squadron and, en route to his new base, met a Focke-Wulf FW.200 four-engined Luftwaffe reconnaissance plane. Shore attacked and the FW.200 retreated into cloud, obviously seriously damaged. The Whitley was also crippled by return fire and, putting down on the sea to an excellent landing, the crew were later picked up by a ship. In August, Squadron Leader J. B. Russell reported as a flight-commander. On 3rd October 'G' of 502 was hit by a destroyer's fire and although badly wounded Sergeant Calder, the wireless operator, insisted on maintaining his anti-submarine watch until the aircraft landed. The following week Pilot Officer D. B. Collie, flying 'U' for Uncle, suffered an engine-failure on take-off and as he could not safely jettison his load, pulled the aircraft up a steep hillside, crash-landing without harm to the crew, though the Whitley burned out.

Next day the port engine of 'D' failed and Pilot Officer Southan calmly put the Whitley down on the sea, their dinghy being sighted by the *Port Wyndham* which brought the crew back. In November Flying Officer Collie experienced another engine-failure and again managed a successful landing – in a field at Prestland, SE. of Portrush, again without injuries. On the 30th, Flying Officer R. W. G. Holdsworth took off at 0609 hours, returning 1619 hours in aircraft Z9190 'B'. While flying in the area 46.55°N–0716°W, a U-boat was sighted on the surface and attacked. It was subsequently confirmed that this submarine was the U.206 (C.O. Opitz) and that it was sunk.

The Ministry of Defence confirmed (in 1969) that there is no record of an award to this officer in connection with this sinking.

The squadron was now operating from Chivenor in Devonshire and on 1st December came another outstanding patrol as Pilot Officer W. W. Cave took off at 0651 in Z9124 'T', landing back at 1638, reporting that at 1148 hours he had attacked a U-boat in position 4700°N–1135°W. The U.563 (C. O. Hartmann) was on the surface and replied with deadly cannon fire from the conning tower. On 18th December the Distinguished Flying Cross was awarded to Pilot Officer Cave on Admiralty's assessment of the evidence of this courageous low-level attack.

In January 1942 the squadron moved to Bircham Newton, Norfolk, with a detachment at St Eval, Cornwall, for Bay of Biscay sorties. On 4th February, 'M' did not return but through the Red Cross in Geneva news later came that Squadron Leader N. S. F. Davie and crew were prisoners of war. On the 12th, the day when *Scharnhorst* and *Gneisenau* the German battleships negotiated the English Channel and North Sea in terrible weather, Flight Lieutenant M. O. Weizmann signalled a 'Mayday' – that he was landing on the sea – but, tragically, the crew were not found. This brilliant pilot had devised homing systems and it was particularly sad that he did not live to see his father as Israel's premier.

Flying Officer Edward Cotton distinguished himself by shadowing the German convoy for over six hours during its passage up the North Sea, despite strong Luftwaffe and anti-aircraft opposition. Flight Sergeant V. D. Pope pressed home an attack in appalling conditions and Flying Officer Carmichael damaged an He.115 floatplane and was mightily relieved when an FW.190 fighter did not fire – presumably confusing the Whitley with a Dornier. Three aircraft had moved up to Langham for these operations and for their outstanding service on this eventful day (and for earlier attempts against U-boats) Flying Officer Cotton received the DFC and Flight Sergeant Pope (who was later commissioned) the Distinguished Flying Medal.

On 1st March, Squadron Leader J. B. Russell was promoted to command No. 172 Squadron (being awarded the DSO for his fine work with 502 and with his new squadron). Flying Officer Cave, DFC, sank an enemy trawler thought to be working with a U-boat and Squadron Leader T. R. Russell, replacement for his unrelated namesake, successfully depth-charged a surfaced U-boat just outside Spanish territorial waters. Pilot Officer Lonsdale sighted and attacked an Italian submarine and after 'E' had been hit by flak from a German ship, Sergeant Coates made an excellent belly-landing in the pitch-dark, with his second pilot wounded and the aircraft hydraulics shot away.

Pilot Officer Lonsdale, forced to ditch some sixty miles from

Land's End, was not seen again and, alas, another squadron machine, searching for this crew, also failed to return. The other crews redoubled their efforts throughout the summer of 1942 and Pilot Officer A. R. A. Hunt swept low over a submerging U-boat on 17th July, ignoring return-fire as he dropped six Torpex charges, seeing the stricken submarine's stern appear, then slide back into the sea. He had to leave at the limit of his fuel but a Lancaster of No. 61 Squadron sighted the same U-boat in a pool of oil and delivered another pinpoint attack, the enemy crew abandoned ship. Pilot Officer Hunt got a well-earned DFC and a few nights later had to crash-land on a beach in St Ives bay, after engine-trouble. The crew got away with minor injuries.

197. Whitley on patrol.

For the Dieppe Raid of August, four aircraft flew from Thorney Island, Sussex, to try and prevent U-boat interference. Also in August Flight Lieutenant L. A. Mackay had to ditch 'S' but fortunately 'A' and 'N' were nearby and he had his dinghy patrolled by an aircraft from No. 311 (Czech) Squadron. After eighteen hours the crew were picked up by a Sunderland of No. 10 (RAAF) Squadron. Next night Flight Lieutenant Cotton attacked a U-boat and although an oil patch some 200 yards wide spread over the water neither wreckage nor bodies were spotted. Leaflets were dropped on trawlers of the 'Tunnymen' warning them of RAF attacks if they did not show lights or neutral flags. In September 'E' was shot down by a Ju.88 over the Bay of Biscay and 'M' was in combat with an FW.200, driving off the four-engined machine with hits on its tail.

Pilot Officer McClintock located and bombed an enemy submarine and Flight Sergeant Ballard, returning to base with technical trouble, came out of cloud right over a surfaced U-boat which he promptly hit, leaving it with bows out of the water, appearing twice at a steep angle before disappearing. The George Medal was promulgated for Sergeant James Reynolds of Belfast for his bravery at St Eval some time earlier when he was on duty in the Flight Office at the time of an aircraft crash. Dashing out he saw a machine in flames and, being a first-class runner, arrived at the scene, 400 yards away, before anyone else. With no thought for himself he made his way into the flames and plunged through a door of the wrecked fuselage of the Hudson to try and rescue the crew. Ammunition was exploding in all directions and just as he reached the turret a most violent explosion – probably oxygen – blew him out of the aircraft. He was found, blinded, among the burning debris and narrowly missed being run over by the approaching fire tender. Two days later his sight returned and his gallantry remains an example to all who witnessed his courageous, though unavailing, attempt at saving life.

October was a fantastic month for the squadron with several successful attacks not only on submarines but on motor vessels and a complete enemy convoy, ships being left in flames. Flying Officer A. W. Wood, BEM, out 'Nickelling' (dropping leaflets on trawlers), was intercepted by three Ju.88s and although his aircraft was hit, managed to make his getaway, leaving one of the Junkers seriously damaged, if not destroyed. Signals of congratulation were received from the Air Officer Commanding No. 19 Group, also from the AOC-in-C. Coastal Command, Air Chief Marshal Sir Philip B. Joubert de la Ferté.

November opened with press-home attacks on Bordeaux shipping by Squadron Leader Cotton, Flying Officer Wood and Pilot Officer Hodgson. In January came DFCs for Flying Officers Hodgson and Grant, the first named earning his award for some magnificent shadowing and reporting which enabled the Royal Navy to sink 7,000-ton *Rhakotis* after a cruiser was 'homed' to the vessel by a Sunderland of No. 10 (RAAF) Squadron, old friends of 502 personnel. This single stroke deprived the Nazis not only of useful quantities of fats, vegetable oils, quinine bark, tea, rice and wolfram but also of 4,000 tons of rubber, sufficient for four armoured divisions for a year!

On 9th January, 1943, came one of the most important changes in squadron history when the Handley Page Halifax Mk.II arrived, a much appreciated honour when so many Coastal squadrons were still re-equipping with twin-engined machines. The personnel moved to Holmsley South, Hampshire, under Wing Commander J. C. Halley, the occasion notable for yet another DFC, this time to Flying Officer Cooper. There was keen competition to be the first to fly a 'Hallybag' on operations but, regrettably, a move to St Eval, Cornwall, brought early disasters as Pilot Officer L. J. McCullock and crew were reported missing and the very experienced Flying Officer A. Hodgson, DFC, was killed with his crew on take-off. April, however, saw Flying Officer Davey scoring hits on a surfaced U-boat, only to return to base after almost twelve hours' flying to be refused landing permission owing to weather. Diverted to Chivenor where weather was said to be better, the Controller there also refused, owing to low cloud. Davey thereupon climbed his Halifax to 5,000 feet and all baled out safely, the navigator and flight-engineer carrying their logs to the ground on Davey's orders, a fine performance by all.

Wing Commander J. C. Halley then set off, with five other aircraft, to participate in Belfast's 'Wings for Victory' Week, helping the city to a record achievement. Air Ministry advised that the all-up-weight must be restricted to 60,000 lbs, whereupon 512 Squadron decided to dispense with some armour-plating rather than reduce their load of bombs or depth-charges. In May several pinpoint attacks were logged and a Good Samaritan act by Flying Officer Cooper's crew who, on sighting a lifeboat with twelve occupants, dropped all the aircrew's emergency rations in a Mae West, including their personal orange juice when they saw there were children in the lifeboat. Flying Officer Clarkson used the newest 600 lb anti-submarine bomb against a U-boat, seeing a black oil patch when seventeen miles away from his attacking position. The C.O. flew tests with 'Boffins' at Boscombe Down's Aircraft and Armament Experimental Unit, keeping his Halifax airborne for 14½ hours, with fuel left for another 90 minutes, a useful pointer should longer sorties be necessary.

Squadron Leader T. R. Russell left on promotion and the British Empire Medal was awarded to Sergeant T. R. P. Roberts, with a Mention in Despatches for Flight Sergeant H. Adams. The Air Efficiency Award was promulgated for all who had joined the squadron as volunteer part-timers prior to 3rd September, 1939. Meteorological Flights were now entrusted to 502 Squadron in addition to its anti-shipping duties and when 'V' was attacked by a formation of four heavily-armed Ju.88s, Flying Officer Grant, DFC, skilfully outwitted the enemy fighters and one Ju.88 was shot into the sea, the other three immediately making off. On 30th July a pack of three U-boats was caught by a Sunderland and two of 502's Halifaxes, one enemy crew taking to their boats as their U-boat settled down slowly on an even keel to disappear from sight. On 2nd August Flying Officer Biggar attacked a German destroyer and the Inspector-General (Air Chief Marshal Sir Philip Joubert) came to congratulate the squadron and to fly with 502 on an operational mission. Unluckily this was uneventful, although Sir Philip spoke of the squadron's fine record of kills during his subsequent B.B.C. broadcast talk. The Ju.88s were now flying in bands of six, a tribute to the RAF's retaliatory power over the Bay of Biscay.

A Distinguished Service Order was announced for the C.O., Wing Commander Halley, on his departure to Headquarters, Coastal Command, for staff duties, and the DSO also came to Squadron Leader Davey, with DFC awards to Flying Officer Wood, BEM, and

Flight Lieutenant Van Rossum. In addition to the original Irishmen there were now Canadians, Dutchmen, Australians, New Zealanders, and, of course, English, Scots, and Welsh members, proud to be serving in the Ulster Squadron. On 8th December another move, this time to St David's, near Haverfordwest in South Wales, and on Christmas Eve eight machines took off to hit a vital enemy convoy. An Air Council Letter of Commendation followed, with the DFC for Flight Lieutenant A. W. Martin and a number of Mentions in Despatches for groundcrews in the New Year's Day Honours and Awards.

The first month of 1944 involved five tons of depth-charges being dropped on U-boats, with two claimed as disabled, despite atrocious weather. On 16th March the squadron was entrusted with the coverage from the air of an important Commando Raid, for which the War Office signalled congratulations. On 25th April, Canadian pilot Flight Lieutenant Holderness, AFC, in the light of his own flares, hit a U-boat which broke its back, our crew returning in high spirits notwithstanding extensive damage to their aircraft from return-fire. The following night Flying Officer Galbraith sighted two surface vessels and dropped 2,000 lbs of bombs, seeing one ablaze and the other beginning to burn as he left the area. The month concluded with a spate of 'gongs' when Flying Officer Galbraith was awarded both the DFC and the George Medal, the latter for his brilliant airmanship when, after being attacked by seven Ju.88s and with one crew member killed and another wounded, he nevertheless outflew the enemy formation and landed at base for a perfect touch-down.

Flight Sergeant Forbes, Galbraith's flight engineer, also scored a double, the DFM and George Medal, and 1st Lieutenant C. D. Kramer, United States Air Force, flying with 502, received the American Soldier Medal for Bravery. On 24th May, Squadron Leader C. A. Maton, one of the two flight-commanders, was promoted to command the squadron, a real landmark in Coastal Command history, for Wing Commander Maton was an air-gunner, the first, it was thought, to be so honoured. It was an extremely popular decision, for this South African (who just happened to be in England in 1939 when war came) was told then that he was far too old to fly. When at last authority relented he was commissioned and flew with No. 500 (County of Kent) Squadron, after which he did two tours in Fighter Command, relinquishing the rank of wing commander when posted to 502 Squadron for flying in September 1943.

For the eventful night of 5th/6th June, 1944 – D-Day – the squadron operated from Brawdy, South Wales, claiming two U-boat hits as the enemy was prevented from entering the Channel. Two DFC awards and nine Mentions in Despatches came to the squadron in the half-yearly Honours. On 20th June, Wing Commander

Maton's aircraft led a low-level raid on U-boats in St Peter Port, Guernsey, followed by 'Rangers' (offensive sorties far into Occupied Europe) to try and stop reinforcements from reaching the allied beaches in Normandy. A German destroyer, high and dry on the Isle de Batz, after damage in earlier attacks, was finally destroyed during a moonlight operation and co-operation with the Royal Navy brought the destruction of an enemy *Sperrbrechen*.

Losses, alas, were high at this peak time and on 11th September the squadron was instructed to move to Stornoway in the Hebrides, for a semi-rest, after three busy years in No. 19 Group's front line. A real blow was the loss of the C.O.'s machine (piloted by Flight Lieutenant C. D. Aidney, DFC, a Fijian) after a visit to Norway on 3rd October for an anti-shipping strike. A few days later a DSO was promulgated for Wing Commander Maton and a DFC for Squadron Leader D. M. Hannah, an Australian who rose to high rank in the RAAF on return to his native land after the war.

Wing Commander K. B. Corbould from 517 Squadron arrived to take command, and on 15th October Flight Lieutenant J. R. Howard was attacking a large vessel off the Norwegian coast when flak ignited a flare in the bomb-bay. One of the remaining bombs could not be jettisoned so the pilot headed for neutral Sweden with the bomb-doors still opened and flaps locked in the down position. When he found that the engines were behaving perfectly, the pilot turned away for a landing in Scotland, touching down safely at Milltown after managing to unlock the undercarriage, the Halifax saved for another day and the crew remaining free for further operations.

Daylight attacks were now being increased against enemy ships moving into Germany with much-needed supplies. The Swedish press revealed that the M/V *Kiel* bound for Hamburg with a cargo of sulphur and with a complement of German troops going home from Norway for leave, had been sunk, survivors being landed at Gothenburg, a confirmed success for 502 Squadron. Then, another blow, as the recently-appointed C.O., Wing Commander Corbould, fell victim to enemy gunfire. The popular Canadian, Squadron Leader Holderness, DFC, AFC, became C.O. on promotion and Flight Lieutenant Pruden, promoted flight-commander, received the DFC.

A beached U-boat near Vega was destroyed and a rare batch of DFC awards – five in one announcement – came for aircrews. On 15th December the B.B.C. arrived in force and the squadron pipe band came to the officers' mess to make recordings of 'The Sash' with vocal by the officers and 'The Wearing of the Green', without vocal! A more suitable moment for relaxation could hardly have been chosen, for the Air Ministry signalled that Wing Commander Maton and four of his crew were now known to be prisoners of war.

Christmas saw practical Greetings, as always, from the Territorial and Air Force Association of Northern Ireland, and with the arrival of the Halifax Mk.III what better place for bombing refresher training than Aldergrove, where the squadron was warmly welcomed back. It gave opportunity for the aircrews to entertain their hard-working ground personnel in traditional RAF manner, the Air Officer Commanding and many V.I.P. guests joining the celebrations.

By March 1945 with the end of the war in Europe in sight, the squadron's tonnage of bombs dropped on ships increased and Bars to DFCs were announced for Flight Lieutenant Rush and Flying Officer Lucy, with four DFCs to officers and a warrant officer. During April, 717 hours were flown and 86 tons of bombs left on German ships. Six more decorations, four DFCs, two DFMs, were signalled, the delight somewhat marred by news that Squadron Leader D. H. Pruden, DFC, and crew were missing, the last squadron casualties of the war. 'Strawberries', as messages of congratulation were known, came from the Air Council in thanks for 502's wonderful effort for, with 58 Squadron, RAF, it had dropped bombs on 186 occasions and the Admiralty estimated that the two Stornoway squadrons shared something over a million tons of enemy shipping sunk or damaged.

On 25th May came news of disbandment and the Honorary Air Commodore, Lord Londonderry, paid an official visit for a squadron photograph and party. A dramatic moment was the unexpected arrival of Wing Commander Maton with two of his crew, just flown from P.O.W. camp to England from where they had hitched a lift to Stornoway. Those aircrew members with service still to complete, transferred, in the main, to No. 206 Squadron at Leuchars, Scotland. Forty-one of 502's original ground personnel were still with the squadron.

The final note was sounded by the Air Council:

We have learned with great satisfaction that No. 502 (Ulster) Squadron, in addition to setting a high standard in the night anti-submarine and shipping role, established a fine accident-free record. In the past nine months 5,785 hours have been flown without a flying accident of any description.

So the squadron's wonderful war effort ended and the men returned to their homes or remained in the Service according to their terms of engagement. Then, in June of 1946, the Auxiliary Air Force was re-formed and there was no lack of volunteers at Aldergrove to help get 502 back into the air. The de Havilland Mosquito Canadian-built Mk.B.25 was issued initially with C.O. Squadron Leader W. Hunter McGiffin (who, like others, had risen

to higher rank during the war but was happy to rejoin in whatever
capacity was best for the squadron). In December 1947, the now-
Royal Auxiliary Air Force gave up the light-bomber role and 502
began to convert, still with the Mosquito, to night-fighters, flying the
NF.30s.

Summer Camp, 1947, had been held at Aldergrove but in 1948
it was at Horsham St Faith in Norfolk; where Corporal Carlisle
learned that his wife had produced twins. Unhappily, returning
from Horsham St Faith, Pilot (II) J. Campbell (employed by Combe
Barbour) with Corporal Walker, RAF, as passenger, crashed on
slopes south of Snowdon in a thunderstorm.

198. Summer camp, Tangmere, 1949. Hunter McGiffin (far left), Sqdn Ldr
Sheen third from right.

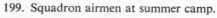

199. Squadron airmen at summer camp.

The squadron relied on an intake from Queen's University Air Squadron to supplement the nucleus of regulars and hard-core of wartime 502 members. Outstanding post-war personalities included Flight Lieutenant W. J. Gear, in charge of repairs and major inspections, Flight Lieutenant G. Gray the RAF adjutant and Flight Lieutenant A. Mail (Lisburn schoolmaster) the Auxiliary adjutant, with Flight Lieutenant P. G. Hill-Turner, RAF, the training officer and Flight Lieutenants R. E. Mooney (branch manager for a linen firm) and D. A. Ainsley, DFC (sales representative), the squadron flight-commanders. Corporal S. Turner was pipe major and many will recall the splendid flying at Sydenham and Aldergrove air displays of the late 1940s by such pilots as Hunter McGiffin, Flight Lieutenants C. G. Clark, DFC (aerobatics), G. MacDermott, DFC, and Flying Officers Cole-Baker, DFC, DFM, and R. Miskimmon, DFC.

Camps were held at Tangmere in 1949 and at Linton-on-Ouse in 1950 and, in accordance with AAF/RAuxAF policy, Squadron Leader McGiffin handed over command, this time to a regular officer, Squadron Leader D. F. B. Sheen, an Australian who had won the DFC and Bar in the Battle of Britain. In 1951 came the three-month call-up and the squadron was based at Aldergrove, then Acklington and Thornaby in the North of England. The Spitfire F.22 had replaced the Mosquito in 1948 and in 1951 the squadron again re-equipped, this time to fly the jet de Havilland Vampire.

200. Spitfire F.22 PK605.

Squadron Leader N. G. Townsend, DFC, a former RAF Volunteer Reserve pilot of Nos. 99 and 40 (Bomber) Squadrons, replacing Squadron Leader Pete Matthews, assumed command after serving post-war with 501 (County of Gloucester) and 612 (County of Aberdeen) Squadrons. Camps for 1952, 1953 and 1954 were at Biggin Hill, Kent, then at Sylt and Bruggen (two German airfields) and in 1954 came a glorious moment when, on Monday 24th May, at

RAF Aldergrove, His Excellency the Governor of Northern Ireland, Lord Wakehurst, KCMG, presented The Standard created by his late Majesty King George VI. The squadron's five battle honours, in scroll surrounding the badge, and with decorative border containing shamrock, rose, thistle and leek, were Atlantic 1939–44, Biscay 1941–44, Channel and North Sea 1942–45, Dieppe 1942, Baltic 1944–45. The Standard Bearer was Flying Officer I. A. Leinster with Standard Escorts Flight Sergeants A. Gibson and W. A. Burns. The Venerable J. R. McDonald, Archdeacon of Connor, conducted the consecration, supported by the Reverend A. J. Campbell and Reverend G. A. Miller.

Thanks to the 'Brookeborough Scheme' instituted in 1952, suitable men from Northern Ireland were offered two-year commissions in the Royal Air Force on condition that they joined 502 Squadron afterwards. Four candidates at least strengthened the squadron as a result and, as with all other RAuxAF squadrons, there was dismay at the news of the disbanding of the twenty flying units in 1957. Summer Camps at Gibraltar in 1955 and Driffield, Yorks, in 1956, had proved the squadron a most competent jet fighter team, commanded from 1956 by Squadron Leader J. H. Pearce, RAF, who had flown with 607 (County of Durham) and 611 (West Lancashire) Squadrons.

201. Squadron aircrews and groundcrews with Vampire FB.5s.

Viscount Brookeborough, Honorary Air Commodore, at a stand-down parade said: 'What you have done was well done. I do not feel it is lost. Your achievement will continue as an example in the years to come.' S. J. M'Aughtry, a member of 502 in the post-war period, spoke for many when he said:

Within a short time of joining 502 I had almost forgotten

my wartime squadron number – at camps 502 seemed, magically, to take over as the parent unit – to have accused 502 airmen of carrying squadron pride too far, or of assuming a superiority to which their unit's history did not entitle them, would have brought forth nothing but a blank stare. Not only was it indisputable that theirs was the best squadron on the airfield but that the fact should even have to be mentioned was beyond their comprehension. How did they get that way I shall never know. Why fitters and riggers worked twelve hours on a Sunday when regulations only called for eight – what drove the armourers to work eighteen hours daily at the Isle of Sylt Camp to keep Vampire cannons from stuttering – why 502's break-off after an exercise was so finely timed that it looked almost like mass suicide – reducing groundcrews of other squadrons to respectful silence.

The successors of the first Special Reserve airmen of 1925 worthily bore out the squadron motto 'I fear nothing' and saw their Vampires flown away with genuine regret. Let us hope that the Ulster Folk Museum's transport section will one day display as many of 502's types as possible to honour all who flew and maintained their machines.

Thanks to the tireless efforts of Tommy Cameron, reunions of all ranks, from the most junior A.C.2 to Group Captain Terence Corry, are held in Belfast. The Standard is now laid up in St Anne's Cathedral and former members from all parts of the world come there to see it. A few still fly, and Flight Lieutenant Norman Eccles, a Campbell College master, instructed the RAF Section of the Combined Cadet Force on Chipmunk trainers in the 1960s. The Ulster Squadron may not have acquired the glamour of the top-button-undone fighter boys but ask survivors of Churchill's 'Few' and you will be told that their hats are raised to 502 and other squadrons who flew obsolete aircraft over unfriendly waters, often unrewarded and under-publicised.

Post-war researches into enemy archives have yielded interesting additions to the facts recorded in the official squadron records and ought now to be added. From Marshal of the RAF Sir John Slessor (AOC-in-C Coastal Command 1943) we learn that U-boat U.462 sank after a direct hit from a 600 lb anti-submarine bomb using the Mark VIV bombsight; the only U-boat so destroyed in 1943. This was Flight Lieutenant Van Rossum's patrol of 30th July, 1943, which helped win him his DFC in 502 Squadron. From German Naval files it was discovered that U.206, sunk in the Bay of Biscay, 30th November, 1941, was not only a 502 victory but Coastal Command's first A.S.V. kill. Also that U.981, sunk in Bay of Biscay 12th August, 1944, was a 502 Squadron attack and finally that U.1060 sunk off Norway 4th November, 1944 was a shared success between 502 and No. 58 Squadrons. The records indicate that a total of four U-boats and three shared with other squadrons, seven in all, should be entered in the annals of 502 (Ulster) Squadron. Likewise the destruction of the Nazi Troop Carrier *Isar* of 9,026 tons carrying 1,500 soldiers. Despite destroyer escort J. R. Hutchinson of Knock, Belfast, saw two bombs explode in the hatches and patriots revealed later that many dead and wounded were put ashore from the badly damaged vessel. Of equal importance, the men saved by the squadron from lifeboats and dinghies – often unrecorded but a vital part of the unit's valiant contribution to the allied cause.

REPRESENTATIVE SQUADRON AIRCRAFT

Vickery Vimy		F9146 J7247
Handley Page Hyderabad		J7739 J7742 J8803
Vickers Virginia		J7434 J7560 J7706 K2323 K2658
Westland Wallace		K4338 K5073 K6014 K6020
Hawker Hart (T)		K6499
Hawker Hind		K6761 K6762 K6771 K6785
Avro Anson	I	N5049 N5050 N5063 N5064 N5104 N5109
Armstrong Whitworth Whitley	V	T4219 T4168 T5050 Z6553
	VII	Z9190 B (1st A.S.V. kill) Z9124 T
Handley Page Halifax		DT692 JP328 (V9–H)
Halifax	III	RG364 (V9–D)
Mosquito	B.25	KB565
	T.3	RR306 VP349
	NF.30	NT242 NT282 MV524
Spitfire	F.22	PK556 (RAC–T) PK605 (RAC–D) PK566 (V9–T)
DH. Vampire	FB.5	WA294 (V9–C) WA309 (V9–L) WG831 (V9–K)
	FB.9	WR128 A
Gloster Meteor	T.7	WF824 N

Before 3rd September, 1939, it is thought the code was KQ, changed on outbreak of war to YG, which was used until re-forming in Reserve Command when RAC was allotted. On transfer into Fighter Command it became V9 but by 1953 the squadron's own insignia of blue rectangle with red lightning flash was carried, first on the nose but, when the code was discontinued, also on the tail-booms of Vampires.

Badge: A red hand erased – taken from the arms of Ulster but erased instead of couped.

Motto (translated): 'I fear nothing'.

616
(South Yorkshire)
Squadron

IT WAS AT Doncaster's airport on 1st November, 1938, that Squadron Leader the Earl of Lincoln began to form a new bomber squadron of the Auxiliary Air Force. He had served with 609 (West Riding) Squadron, Yeadon, and as his first officers had Pilot Officers G. E. Moberley also from 609, and E. F. St Aubyn from 503(B) Squadron, Waddington. A hard-core of regular officers and airmen arrived under Flight Lieutenant D. S. Radford, adjutant/flying instructor, with Flight Lieutenant H. M. Pim, MC. On 10th November came six Hawker Hinds, two Avro Tutors and two Avro 504N's from No. 50(B) Squadron, Waddington. Five days later 616 was transferred into Fighter Command. Flying Officer the Hon C. J. F. Win joined for administrative duties and on 5th December, as flying training commenced, a big recruiting drive was launched.

On 30th January, 1939, Gloster Gauntlets were received and Flight Lieutenant R. G. Kellett, an experienced pilot of 600 (City of London) Squadron joined the South Yorkshire unit. History was made on 26th March when Mr K. Holden flew solo and a month later the C.O. was awarded the RAF flying badge. Following a successful Empire Air Day on 20th May some Fairey Battles were flown in to speed the training of pilots and by 10th June it was possible to put one flight into the air. On 17th/18th June Messrs H. S. L. Dundas and H. Casson went solo and the Marquess of Titchfield, MP, accepted appointment as Honorary Air Commodore. Summer Camp was at Manston, Kent, during which all Auxiliaries were called up and, on 24th August, embodied into the Royal Air Force, returning to Doncaster to take up their war station. On 18th September Squadron Leader W. Beisiegel assumed command and a batch of trained pilots was posted in to make up the operational strength including Flight Lieutenant D. E. Gillam, AFC. As the squadron moved over to Leconfield in October, Pilot Officer O. Gradon was left in charge at Doncaster.

202. Gloster Gauntlet.

Spitfires Mk.I were taken over from No. 66 Squadron and by early January 1940 the South Yorkshire pilots were flying their first war patrols, escorting our merchant convoys along the North Sea. Co-operation with our bomber squadrons greatly helped both fighter pilots and bomber crews but it was during a convoy escort that the first loss was suffered when Flight Lieutenant Tony Wilson, leading a section of three, descended through cloud to locate shipping and was never seen again, a great blow to a young squadron. His place as a flight-commander went to Flight Lieutenant Gillam and when the 'Phoney War' at last turned into the Nazi blitzkrieg of 10th May, the squadron stood ready to repel attacks on Yorkshire, but these did not come immediately. On 26th May came orders to fly into Rochford, Essex to relieve No. 74 Squadron which had been much involved with the patrols over Calais and Dunkirk.

Within minutes of refuelling at Rochford, 616 Squadron had twelve Spitfires flying alongside Nos. 19 and 65 Squadrons between Dunkirk and Gravelines. Squadron Leader M. Robinson, from 602 (City of Glasgow) Squadron, was the new C.O., on the departure of Wing Commander Walter 'Bike' Beisiegel to RAF Coltishall to be Sector Controller. On 28th May, although jumped by about thirty Messerschmitt 109s, the new C.O. managed to survive by taking brilliant evasive action, crashing unhurt at Manston. Meanwhile, Pilot Officers Holden and Scott had scored the squadron's first successes with a Bf.109 destroyed and another claimed as probable. When Flying Officer Moberley landed he also claimed two enemy destroyed. Sergeant Ridley was wounded and two Spitfires were damaged.

For several days the squadron shared the patrols over our soldiers on the beaches. It was not until 1st June, though, that further combats ensued, when Ken Holden shot down another Bf.109 with a second 'probable', whilst Flying Officer Bell, separated from the others in a mêlée, attacked a force of eight Messerschmitts in formation, shooting down one before he, too, was brought down, to be picked up from the sea by the Royal Navy. All this happened before breakfast and at 8.25 a.m. the squadron took off again, led by Gillam, 'enjoying a real party', to quote their own words, for this time they mixed it with the Luftwaffe's bombers over our evacuation ships. On landing they claimed one Junkers Ju.88 and one Heinkel He.111 destroyed, two 88's as 'probables', with seven bombers claimed as damaged, some of which were unlikely, it was thought, to have made it back to their bases.

203. Spitfire I's landing at Rochford, 1940.

The Air Officer Commanding No. 11 (Fighter) Group, Air Vice-Marshal Keith Park, sent a signal of congratulation for the squadron's determined patrolling on 2nd and 3rd June during poor visibility. On the 4th came tragedy when Pilot Officer E. S. Scott, who had shown tremendous promise, crashed when trying to land. 5th June was an uneventful day with the Miracle of Dunkirk accomplished and next day the squadron returned to Leconfield. There was a fortnight's lull before action when Flying Officer Bell, patrolling between Hull and base, intercepted a lone He.115 which jettisoned its bombs and streaked for home with smoke pouring out as a result of Bell's attack.

Night-fighting in a Spitfire was uncommon but we had very few radar-equipped Blenheims at this time and so when Pilot Officer

D. S. Smith destroyed an He.111K soon after midnight on 26th June it was a most commendable performance. Three nights later Pilot Officer Marples was scrambled just before 1.00 a.m. and, between Pickering and Driffield at 10,000 feet, sighted an He.111 which he chased to Hornsea. He gave it two short bursts and later heard that the Luftwaffe crew had been picked up from the sea.

On 3rd July Pilot Officer Dundas (a great character, always referred to as 'Cocky') destroyed a Do.17 when in company with Flying Officer Moberley and Flight Sergeant Bernard. A second raider was claimed as damaged. Convoy protection was still a priority, interspersed with the task of giving a newly-formed fighter squadron – No. 249 – some dog-fighting practice. This was to show a dividend when, on 16th August, Flight Lieutenant J. B. Nicolson of 249 gained Fighter Command's only Victoria Cross over Gosport in combat with a Messerschmitt Bf.110.

With the airfield waterlogged whenever it rained, a start was made on concrete runways, which limited the landing area available but failed to keep the squadron grounded. Squadron Leader Robinson and Sergeant Ridley drove off Ju.88s attacking convoys and then came another grievous blow as Pilot Officer R. A. Smith was killed when he crashed three miles from the airfield. On 15th August the squadron was ordered to go to Flamborough Head with all speed and there, thanks to our early-warning radar, it was waiting as some fifty Ju.88s with Bf.110 escort flew towards our coast (in poor formation, according to squadron records). From 20,000 feet the squadron dived down and soon had eight Junkers claimed as in the sea with half-a-dozen seriously damaged and turning back to their Scandinavian bases. This was the claim that day although post-war checks indicate that the other squadrons involved also claimed some of these machines. No matter; the Luftwaffe's Luftflotte 5 is now known to have lost nine Ju.88s and eight Bf.110s that afternoon, in addition to eight He.111s (which 616 did not claim) and never again attempted to hit the North East of England in strength during daylight.

It was no surprise when a few days later came orders to move into Kenley, Surrey, to share the defence of London against the enemy's pre-invasion attacks. On 22nd August, over Dover, twelve Messerschmitt Bf.109s dived on Green Section of three Spitfires: Flying Officer Dundas, his aircraft in flames, parachuted down slightly wounded in leg and arms. Sergeant Philip Wareing, who claimed one of the Messerschmitts, was himself shot down near Calais on the 25th and taken prisoner. Almost at the same time his friend Sergeant Westmoreland was also shot down and killed near Canterbury as Flying Officers Bell and Moberley, with Sergeant Ridley, were claiming successes against a force of Messerschmitt Bf.109s.

Sergeant Wareing – the first of the squadron to become a prisoner

– was flown to Germany for interrogation, after which he spent almost three years in various Prisoner of War Camps. In December 1942, he made a magnificent escape bid, eventually reaching England from Sweden in January 1943 to receive a well-earned Distinguished Conduct Medal. He was commissioned and, after lecturing on his escape to help other aircrews, became an instructor. He was the only one of 'The Few' who was shot down and captured during the Battle of Britain who managed to escape. As this is written (in 1971) he lives in Cornwall.

204. Flt Lt Philip Wareing, DCM.

    Next day only seven Spitfires were immediately serviceable and, directed to a raid over Dungeness just before noon, they arrived too late for the bombers and ran into about fifty Bf.109s. As the remaining five Spitfires joined up, another thirty Messerschmitts arrived and in half a minute Flying Officer Moberley and Sergeant Ridley were killed. Pilot Officer Walker and three others were wounded and five Spitfires were written-off with another damaged. Flight Lieutenant Gillam was the only pilot to claim a victory. It was two days before another combat took place and again it was Gillam who chased a Bf.110 to within five miles of France before shooting it into the Channel. Next day (30th) Flying Officer Bell was killed near West Malling, Kent, and Sergeant J. Hopewell's Spitfire was also destroyed at Kenley though he was unhurt in the crash-landing after combat.

    In addition to Hopewell's destruction of a Bf.109, Flying Officer D. S. Smith destroyed a second over the Thames Estuary and Pilot Officer 'Buck' Casson, after attacking a third, found himself alone and climbed up over Kent to await the Luftwaffe bombers returning from London, getting in bursts of fire into two Heinkels. Flight Lieutenant Gillam claimed a Messerschmitt Bf.109 and another on 31st August. Buck Casson's Spitfire was damaged by return-fire from a Do.17 over Kenley but he landed unhurt and his machine was repairable.

Next day Gillam and Hopewell were in combat with Bf.109s and 110s, claiming two enemy probably destroyed though Gillam was forced to bale out near Gravesend, which cost the squadron a valuable Spitfire. The squadron was now sent to Coltishall near Norwich for a rest and Squadron Leader Billy Burton, ex-66 Squadron, took over as C.O. Flight Lieutenant Gillam was posted to 312 (Polish) Squadron and was replaced by Flight Lieutenant McFie from 611 (West Lancashire) Squadron. Another incoming young pilot was Pilot Officer J. E. Johnson from 19 Squadron and who could then have forecast that, without a single victory in 1940, he would end the war as the RAF's top-scoring pilot.

By 9th September the squadron was at Kirton-in-Lindsey, Lincolnshire, joined by Pilot Officer Maitland-Thompson (who later transferred to night-fighters, commanding 604 [County of Middlesex] before losing his life after VE Day in a car accident in Europe). Convoy patrols enabled new pilots to gain experience before flying with the newly-created No. 12 Group 'Balbo', a wing of up to five squadrons, a controversial idea suggested by Squadron Leader Douglas Bader and approved by his Air Officer Commanding, then Air Vice-Marshal Trafford Leigh-Mallory. Unfortunately, though, 616 did not see action until 27th September when Ken Holden and Sergeant Copeland had combats with Bf.109s. In this engagement Pilot Officer D. S. Smith crashed after battling with 109s and, severely wounded, died next day in Faversham Hospital, a sad loss of one of the most experienced pilots.

To enable 616 to re-build its depleted forces, one flight left for Ringway, Manchester, the other flight busily engaged in bringing to operational standard seven new NCO-pilots from training units, including Sergeants Le Cheminant and McCairns. The Battle of Britain virtually ended, a rare burst of activity on 5th November saw Flight Lieutenant Jones wounded during a combat with an He.111 off Spurn Head. As the enemy bomber fell into the Humber, Jones, losing blood from a gaping wound, managed to land without coming to further harm.

A batch of Polish pilots joined the squadron as troopships leaving Liverpool were protected, the duties shared with No. 71 (Eagle) Squadron. On 15th January, Pilot Officer J. E. Johnson returned from hospital after attention to a damaged shoulder which had kept him out of action and celebrated his return by damaging a Do.17, the first of his many combats. Pilot Officer Marples' 21st birthday party was followed by a visit from the irrepressible George

Formby and on 26th January, 1941, to help implement Churchill's directives, the squadron flew down to Tangmere, Sussex, taking over the Spitfire IIs from 65 Squadron. Part of Bader's Wing, comprising 145, 610 (County of Chester) and 616 Squadrons, the task was to escort our day bombing raids, alternating with 'Rhubarb' sorties.

205. 610 and 616 Squadrons, Tangmere Wing, June 1941. *Front row from left:* Flt Lt Crowley-Milling, Flt Lt Lee Knight, Sqdn Ldr K. Holden (610), Wg Cdr Bader, Gp Cpt Woodall, Sqdn Ldr Burton (616), Flt Lt Casson, F/O Marples, P/O Gray. *Second row:* P/Os Mallon, Lintott, Hugill, Stoop, Gaze, Murray, Hepple, Johnson (last two and third row unidentified).

Early in May the squadron moved to Westhampnett, a grass field satellite to Tangmere. On 5th May Flying Officers Buck Casson and Marples scored hits on a Ju.88 at dusk; Casson's machine was hit by return-fire and he baled out into Littlehampton. On the 17th Cocky Dundas destroyed one of a trio of Bf.109s attacking Worthing and on 6th June, amid much regret, albeit with good wishes, Ken Holden left on promotion to command 610 Squadron at nearby Tangmere. Flight Lieutenant E. P. P. Gibbs came from 56 Squadron as a new flight-commander and the squadron continued its bomber escorts with few combats – the Luftwaffe rarely accepted a challenge unless to try and finish off a straggling flak-hit bomber in hopes that the fighters could not get down in time to join in.

On 21st June Squadron Leader Burton shared a Messerschmitt 109 with a 145 Squadron pilot but Pilot Officer Brown was lost on this mission. Next day – as the Germans invaded the USSR – Pilot Officer Marples got a Bf.109 and Buck Casson and Sergeant Beedham shared another. 'Johnnie' Johnson then got his first confirmed victory, and with the squadron's fiftieth success came Distinguished Flying Cross awards to Squadron Leader Burton, Cocky Dundas and Ken Holden. Four days later Sergeant McCairns' machine was badly disabled but he coolly nursed it down without further damage. On 3rd July, over Lille, Sergeant Douglas Crabtree (ex-501 [County of

Gloucester] Squadron) was shot down but, after months of incredible adventures in Occupied Europe, he returned to England, complete with detailed drawings of an arms' factory on cigarette-papers, risking his life to carry this information. The factory was duly bombed, Crabtree was commissioned, became an instructor but, sad to relate, lost his life flying a civilian aircraft in 1950.

206. Douglas Crabtree (centre back) with
the patriot family who sheltered him.

Spitfire Vb's, with the 1,440 h.p. Merlin engine and with two 20-mm cannons and four 0.303 machine-guns, replaced the Mk.II's, giving 374 m.p.h. at 13,000 feet against the 357 m.p.h. of the earlier type. Pilot Officer 'Hip' Hepple and Sergeant Smith shot down Bf.109s and Canadian Sergeant Bowen shared an Hs.126 with a 610 pilot. On 5th July Flight Lieutenant McFie was forced down, and damaging his ankle in a hard landing, was soon captured by waiting enemy soldiers. Next day Sergeant McCairns had to crash-land on the beaches near Dunkirk. His sliding hood jammed but, luckily, the aircraft did not catch fire and he was released from the cockpit by German soldiers and eventually reached a prisoner of war camp. He escaped, was recaptured but escaped again and, after one of the war's most thrilling solo journeys, got to England via Spain and Gibraltar in April 1942. Awarded the Military Medal and commissioned he lectured for a time and then pleaded to be allowed to fly with the Special Duties Squadrons. For his splendid work piloting Lysanders into and out of Occupied Europe he was awarded the Distinguished Flying Cross and two Bars; he then managed to fly

Tempest fighters, with No. 3 Squadron, in the closing days of April 1945 being credited with two enemy aircraft destroyed. The French Government later gave him the Croix-de-Guerre for his secret sorties carrying 'Joes' (the special agents).

Flight Lieutenant Dundas took over McFie's flight and Squadron Leader E. P. P. Gibbs, promoted to take over a command, was forced down, with Sergeant Morton, on 9th July. Squadron Leader Gibbs evaded capture and returned to fly again, and wrote an amusing book *It's further via Gibraltar* after the war. On 11th July, Sergeant Smith, having oxygen trouble, dived out of formation and, to his delight, found a row of twenty Ju.87 dive-bombers parked on an airfield. He destroyed two and damaged others, using up his ammunition on a German E-boat as he crossed the Channel.

On 1st August a DFC was promulgated for McFie, languishing in a P.O.W. camp, and then came a double blow as Douglas Bader, the wing leader, and Buck Casson failed to return, both being reported as captured in due course. The squadron escorted the Blenheim which dropped a spare artificial leg for Bader and a ray of sunshine was news of Sergeant Crabtree's arrival at the British Embassy in Madrid. No. 616 Squadron was certainly leading the field in escape and evasion. At the same time 'Johnnie' Johnson was adding to his tally and, almost coinciding with his promotion and appointment as a flight-commander, came his DFC, with one to Hip Hepple and a third to the absent Buck Casson, now a prisoner, Air Vice-Marshal Leigh-Mallory came to present the squadron badge and to announce a Distinguished Flying Medal for New Zealand pilot Sergeant West.

Squadron Leader Billy Burton was replaced as C.O. by Squadron Leader Colin Gray, a New Zealander, credited already with sixteen kills and wearing the DFC and Bar under his wings. Cocky Dundas came to the end of his operational hours and left for No. 59 Operational Training Unit to instruct, his replacement being Flight Lieutenant R. W. Oxspring, a Battle of Britain pilot in 66 Squadron. Flight Lieutenant Marples returned from rest to learn of his own DFC and in early October the squadron patrolled a corridor over which ships due to exchange prisoners disabled and ill, were to cross. The Nazis went back on their word and men from both sides were, alas, returned to their camps.

Sergeant J. G. West, DFM, was commissioned, and on the day the squadron returned to Kirton-in-Lindsey, news came that Sergeant McKee, missing since 14th August, was in Gibraltar, yet another feather in the squadron cap. Flying down to West Malling, Kent, to participate in offensives, and sending pairs to operate from Coltishall, kept operational pilots busy as newcomers were trained for action. Some left to strengthen squadrons in Malta and the Middle East and Squadron Leader H. L. I. Brown (ex-609 [West Riding] Squadron) came to relieve Colin Gray who had scored his 17th victory leading the squadron and who ended the war as New Zealand's top scorer with 27½ confirmed destroyed and with the DSO and a second Bar to his DFC. After the war he was granted a permanent commission in the RAF.

207. 616 Squadron, Kirton-in-Lindsey, December 1941. *From left:* Wg Cdr Walker, Flt Lt Heppell, Sqdn Ldr Gray, F/O Bowen, Flt Lt Johnson (in cockpit), F/O Murray (standing far right), P/O West (on wing).

Free French pilots arrived at King's Cliffe near Wittering, Northants, then came another move, to Matlaske, Norfolk, from where escorts were flown to 'Whirlibombers', Westland Whirlwind fighters carrying bombs against targets in Holland. In April 1942 came the Spitfire VI for high-flying sorties, 616 being chosen to get this version. On 25th May came the first combat at height as Pilot Officer Brown damaged a Dornier over Leicester, but he was hit in the right eye by perspex shattered by the bomber's fire. He made a perfect landing at North Luffenham, Rutland, where the eye was removed. Brown's only comment 'When can I fly again?'

On 31st May eleven Spitfires took off to cover the return of bombers from Cologne after the first 'Thousand Plan' attack. A U-boat was sighted but could not be attacked as the order was to protect any lame-duck aircraft against pursuing Luftwaffe fighters. On 1st July came a Bar to his DFC for Johnnie Johnson and then, to the dismay of all squadron members, he left to take command of 610 (Chester) Squadron, his score being six confirmed and a damaged enemy aircraft whilst with 616 Squadron. Flight Lieutenant Gaze kept up the good work with one aircraft destroyed and one damaged over the Channel and a move was made to Great Sampford, Essex, to allow the Spitfires to gain maximum altitude and then become top cover for the 'Circus' operations of combined bombers and fighters hitting NW. Europe to help, particularly, our Russian allies by preventing the Luftwaffe from reinforcing units attacking the USSR.

On 18th August came a move to Hawkinge near Folkestone for the next day's Dieppe Raid, during which four patrols were flown and a total of 75 hours, flying time logged. A Do.217 was destroyed and six Focke-Wulf 190s fought and damaged. Flight Lieutenant Gaze was promoted to command 64 Squadron and with a move now to Ipswich, 616 Squadron escorted Boeing B–17 Flying Fortresses to St Omer and elsewhere, climbing on the 9th September to 39,000 feet to intercept a Ju.86P photo-reconnaissance machine which made off on sighting the Spitfires. Back to Tangmere on 23rd September in time for Pilot Officer Large to get an FW.190 and for Flight Sergeant Cooper (from Kenya) to find himself in his dinghy only four miles from Calais. As the rest of the squadron protected him against enemy fighters, a Walrus amphibian of our air-sea rescue squadrons landed on the sea and picked him up.

A DFC for Pilot Officer Large was followed by departure of Flight Lieutenant Fifield to take command of 131 Squadron and Squadron Leader Brown also got a DFC, mainly for leading some ground-strafing attacks the squadron's tally of locomotives destroyed rising with every mission flown. Christmas Day 1942 saw standing patrols against possible enemy intruders but the other officers and NCO-pilots entertained the groundcrews at the aptly named Richmond Arms where traditional Yorkshire fare was laid on. Pilot Officer Blanchard returned from patrol with propeller tips bent back where he had hit the sea, but he landed without difficulty. On 2nd January, 1943, a move to Ibsley in the New Forest with Squadron Leader G. S. K. Heywood in command, and a Bar to Squadron Leader E. A. O. Gaze's DFC for his work before leaving 616.

208. The squadron at Exeter in 1943.

Escorts to bombers attacking Cherbourg was followed by a close-escort to the Liberator taking Mr Churchill from Casablanca after the top-level conference, on its last leg into England. Exercises with the Army and cover for Hurribombers hitting German shipping kept crews busy and Squadron Leader P. W. Lefevre, DFC, arrived as C.O. only to become part of a triple blow as he and both flight-commanders were posted missing after a Brest operation escorting Ventura light-bombers. Happily once again it was not long before news filtered through that Squadron Leader Lefevre was alive and well and living in Gibraltar! Air Commodore the Marquis of Titchfield (later Duke of Portland) came to see his squadron and Squadron Leader P. B. 'Laddie' Lucas, DFC, famous international golfer, took over, only to be promoted to lead a wing and Flight Lieutenant L. W. Watts, the A Flight commander, was promoted to command.

Honoured by being chosen to escort King George VI into Northolt after his flight from North Africa, the squadron took Whirlibombers to St Peter Port, Guernsey, to attack shipping. Squadron Leader Watts received the DFC and Flying Officer M. Cooper, survivor of the Calais dinghy incident, was brought down near Triqueville airfield after engine failure but was back in England in five months, thanks to the gallant French patriots. A newcomer, Flying Officer 'Paddy' Flynn, DFC, was a 'Catafighter' Hurricane pilot who had destroyed an FW.200 four-engined reconaissance plane before baling out on a Murmansk Convoy and he came at a time of move to Exeter to re-equip with Spitfire VII's with ceiling to 43,000 feet, maximum speed 408 m.p.h. Missions were flown from Ford, Sussex, West Malling and Hawkinge, Kent, pre-Normandy invasion attacks against enemy airfields and gun sites, with only the occasional combat; Pilot Officer Clerc, Free French, was awarded the Croix-de-Guerre with Palm. In May 1944, from Fairwood Common near Swansea, the squadron was briefed to destroy trains, barges, road transports and everything associated with the German Army in France. Locomotives, staff cars, gun-posts, radar stations and other targets fell to the guns of 616's Spitfires and on D-Day, 6th June, over the Brest peninsula, the squadron destroyed aircraft on their French airfields plus to locos and four military trucks, but returned without Flight Lieutenant Graves, DFC, who later tele-phoned from Plymouth, having been picked up from the sea by the Navy.

By 15th June the first squadron machine was landing on the improvised airstrips in France to refuel and press on far into Occupied Europe in search of the Luftwaffe. At this time, though, came the top-secret news that 616 Squadron was to be the first allied unit to fly jet aircraft! At Culmhead, away from prying eyes, the first pilots began training on two Gloster Meteors (which were originally named Thunderbolt, until the Americans brought over their aircraft of that name). Aircraft EE213G and 214G (the 'G' suffix meaning that a guard must always watch a grounded machine) were in use and Wing Commander Andrew McDowall (who had gained the DFM and Bar as a Sergeant-Pilot of 602 Auxiliary Squadron) took over the jet flight, accompanied by Wing Commander H. J. Wilson, AFC (who, after the war, broke the world speed record in a Meteor). A Spitfire operational flight was also maintained at Manston, Kent, to deal with the V.1 flying bombs.

209. Sqdn Ldr Andrew McDowall, DFM and Bar.

On 27th July history was made as Flying Officer 'Dixie' Dean was ordered off to intercept a doodlebug, only to be talked-down by Control when balloon barrages threatened danger. However, this was only a short postponement for on 4th August Flying Officer Dean caught up with one of the pilotless bombs near Tonbridge, Kent, only to find that his guns would not fire. Determined to destroy it, Dean carefully edged his 400 m.p.h. Meteor under the wing of the next V.1 and, pulling up sharply, overturned the enemy missile which exploded four miles from Tenterden, the first enemy brought down by an allied jet fighter! A few minutes later Flying Officer Rodger put two bursts of cannon into another V.1 which blew up near Tenterden. By 10th August Dixie had scored a hat-trick of flying bombs.

During August the entire squadron changed over to Meteors and by the time the Germans had been driven from the main launching areas in the Pas de Calais, 616 Squadron had a score of thirteen confirmed V.1 successes. Now, though, they faced the possibility of combat with the Luftwaffe's Messerschmitt Me.262 jet fighters and, for experience to help both British and American pilots, four Meteors were attached to Debden, Essex, to 'engage' Mustangs and Thunderbolts escorting USAAF bombers, this enabled the Americans to work out tactics against possible interceptions by the Me.262. By the end of the year, 616 Squadron, re-equipped with the Meteor III, moved into RAF Colerne, near Chippenham, Wiltshire. One flight flew to Brussels Melsbroek on 4th February, 1945, to operate from airfield B.58, first flying over allied airfields and troop positions so that our forces could identify the British jets. On 27th March the squadron moved to B.77 at Gilze-Rijen, between Breda and Tilburg in Holland, and on 13th April to B.91 at Nijmegen. Flying Officer Cooper was first to attack German transports, the speed of his dive 'foxing' German flak gunners completely. By 20th April, the jets were operating far into Germany, based at Quackenbrucke, some 45 miles SW. of Bremen, where the 'No Frat' rule will be well-remembered by those who served there. A Ju.88 became the first piloted enemy aircraft to be destroyed but this was on the ground, at Nordholz, where buildings were also wiped out despite return-fire. A Meteor pilot found his name in the squadron Line book for including in his report the remark 'I could easily have put my wheels down and taxied along the flak bursts!'

210. Meteors at Lübeck.

A move to Fassburg was marked by the tragic deaths of Squadron Leader Watts, DFC, and Flight Sergeant Cartmel who were thought to have collided in thick cloud. On 1st May a record was set when, during 26 sorties, 13 German transports were claimed destroyed with 25 others damaged under the leadership of Wing Commander W. E. Schrader, DFC, and Squadron Leader E. A. O. Gaze, DFC (who had returned after flying with 486 [N.Z.] and 41 Squadrons, to finish the war with his old squadron). During one of the final battles of the war a section of four Meteors attempted to engage Focke-Wulf 190s in combat only to receive the unfriendly attentions of Spitfires and Tempests who, apparently, mistook the Meteors for Messerschmitt 262s. This caused the Meteors to lose the chance of writing a page of history but, on 2nd May, a small consolation when a Fieseler Storch was encountered by a solitary Meteor. After some brilliant evasive action by the Luftwaffe pilot he ran out of altitude, made a forced landing and ran from the machine which was then destroyed by the Meteor's fire. This is thought to be the one and only combat of a squadron Meteor and the war in Europe ended without a jet-versus-jet engagement. 3rd May saw 616 Squadron at Lüneburg, hitting another 46 transports as the enemy tried in vain to seek safety in Denmark and Norway. Between 3rd and 7th May a few more transports and grounded aircraft were added to the score, and a Bar to his DFC was promulgated for Wing Commander Schrader.

VE Day, 8th May, saw a short thanksgiving parade and then stand-down and next day Squadron Leader Gaze was flying the FW.190 and also a Siebel 204 transport, bringing back a thousand eggs to the delight of the airmen. Several pilots then flew the Luftwaffe's Me.262 jets and when Marshal Zhukov of the U.S.S.R. arrived in Frankfurt for a big allied air display, it was 616 Squadron's Meteors which provided the highlights. A Bar to the DFC was announced for Squadron Leader Gaze and Mentions in Despatches for Flying Officers Dean, Rodger and Wilson. Then, on 29th August, 1945, word came that the squadron was to disband so that it could re-form as soon as possible as part of a post-war Auxiliary Air Force.

In June 1946, at RAF Finningley, near Doncaster, an immediate emotional response was provoked and ex-airmen from offices and shops, the railways, the banks, the schools, the steelworks, rushed to volunteer. Company directors, commercial travellers, men from all walks, were suddenly re-united in a common desire, to see No. 616 (South Yorkshire) Auxiliary Squadron a strong and useful part of our country's post-war defence.

Several of the pre-war veterans joined, along with wartime members, and Squadron Leader Ken Holden, DFC, of Selby, was appointed C.O.; with pilots like Group Captain Denis Gillam, DSO and Bar, DFC and two Bars, AFC; Buck Casson, DFC; Jim McCairns, DFC and two Bars, MM, Croix-de-Guerre; and Maurice Clark, DFC (who had flown Halifax bombers from Burn, Yorkshire), all keen to come, with far lower ranks than they had held during the war. This applied also to ground personnel where ex-officers cheerfully opted for duties as NCOs just to be part of the squadron again. The first post-war machine was the Mosquito NF.30, with the Airspeed Oxford trainer to get the pilots operational.

In 1948 the first summer camp was held at RAF Tangmere, following a 1947 dinner at the Danum Hotel, Doncaster, when Nos. 401 and 438 Squadrons, Canadian Auxiliary Air Force, had steaks flown to London Airport to be picked up by a squadron Oxford, a splendid gesture. News then came that the role was to be changed to that of a day fighter squadron – a popular announcement. Sad it was, though, that on Sunday 13th June, 1948, Flying Officer J. A. Mc-Cairns and his passenger, Aircraftman Shaw, lost their lives when engine failure caused the Mosquito to make an emergency landing. It was a particular blow for Flight Lieutenant Maurice Clark, for Jim McCairns was one of his firm's District Managers and was in line for the General Manager's post – no man contributed more to the fine record of 616 Squadron than did this gallant escaper and 'Moon Squadron' pilot and his funeral was a memorable occasion. In December 1948 the Freedom of Entry into the County Borough of Doncaster 'on all ceremonial occasions with all customary privileges' was conferred on the squadron and the Scroll of Freedom with an inscribed silver salver handed to Squadron Leader Holden by the Mayor, Alderman P. Judd.

211. The boss and his boy: F/O Maurice Clark and Flt Lt Jim McCairns on McCairns' wedding day.

In this same month came the Meteor III and, later, the Mark F.4. In 1950 Squadron Leader L. H. Buck Casson assumed command and was awarded the Air Force Cross for his magnificent airmanship over many years. In accordance with RAuxAF custom, Buck in turn handed over, in 1954, to Squadron Leader W. G. Abel, RAF, who had flown Sunderland flying-boats before instructing on jets at the RAF College. Group Captain Bader, CBE, DSO, DFC, who had known the squadron so well in war, came to open Town Headquarters in Sheffield and then, in March 1957, came the unbelievable news that the Royal Auxiliary Air Force squadrons were to be disbanded.

At RAF Finningley, the post-war airfield, is Meteor F.8 painted as WH456 of 616 although it is, in reality, WL168 once with 604 Squadron. Also kept at Finningley the Scroll of Freedom and the squadron's silver plate with other items of squadron property and history. Complete records are not available, alas, but it is known that at least eleven DFCs, one DCM, one MM, one DFM, one AFC, two Croix-de-Guerre and several Mentions in Despatches were gained by members for service with 616. Some reached high rank and one must here mention Air Vice-Marshal J. E. Johnnie Johnson CB, CBE, DSO and two Bars, DFC and Bar, now retired and a Deputy Lieutenant for Leicestershire. The contribution made by the South Yorkshire Squadron was in the very highest tradition of the Royal Air Forces and remains a proud and important part of county history.

REPRESENTATIVE SQUADRON AIRCRAFT

Hawker Hind		K5403 K5481 (T) L7195
Gloster Gauntlet	II	K5313 K5338 K5364
Vickers-Supermarine		
Spitfire	I	L1055 N3269
	IIa	P7435 P7732
	Vb	P8477 P8694 VB W3560
	VI	BR922 BS149 YQ–B BS448
	VII	MB769 MD101 YQ–C MD107
Gloster Meteor	I	EE214 EE220 YQ–G EE229 YQ–W
	III	EE245 YQ–C EE243 EE276 YQ–T
de Havilland	NF30	NT508 RAW–E NT590 RK936
Mosquito		RAW–H
Gloster Meteor	F.3	EE348 RAW–D EE386 EE393
	F.4	EE594 VT183 N
	F.8	WA781 W WH307 M WH464
		WK883 J WL166 B
	T.7	WH120 F

Until outbreak of war the squadron's fighter aircraft bore the code letters QJ but from September 1939 these changed to YQ, carried until disbandment in 1945. On re-forming in 1946 the code was the Reserve Command's RAW allocation, reverting in 1948 to YQ. With the Meteor F.8 in 1951 a squadron insignia of a green rectangle with two yellow diamonds superimposed was worn either side of the fuselage. It is of passing note that whereas the genuine squadron Spitfire at Coltishall carries the code ZH–T of 266 (Rhodesia) Squadron, with which the aircraft also served, another Historic Aircraft Flight Spitfire VB serial AB910, though never with 616 Squadron, wears the code QJ–J. Some will tell you that this stands for test pilot Jeffrey Quill (who handed the machine over to the RAF) and others will say it is for No. 92 Squadron (a unit with Yorkshire links in post-war years). Many ex-members, though, when they see this Spitfire in the air will square their shoulders and claim it as a South Yorkshire aircraft – and who will blame them?

Badge: A Yorkshire rose.

Motto (translated): 'No rose without a thorn'.

613
(City of Manchester)
Squadron

THE 'BABY' OF the Auxiliary Air Force, as it was then known, was the squadron formed on 1st February, 1939, at Ringway, Manchester, as part of No. 22 (Army Co-operation) Group, Fighter Command, administered by the East Lancashire Territorial Army and Air Force Association. The full title was No. 613 (East Lancashire [City of Manchester]) Squadron, but was generally known as 613 (City of Manchester) Squadron. Edgar Rhodes was appointed to command and gazetted squadron leader, with Flight Lieutenant D. C. R. Macdonald and Pilot Officers Redington and Gow as the regular RAF adjutant and instructors. There were more than 1,200 applications for about one hundred airmen vacancies, enabling a careful selection to be made for ground personnel. Messrs J. G. S. Haig, I. T. Whipp, P. Wilson, G. F. H. Webb, P. H. Grummack, G. W. Jackson, L. Macintosh, G. Buckley, A. Kershaw, F. Pilling, H. Toft, J. M. Horsley, R. Stone and Dr B. P. Robinson were the first volunteers to be commissioned and by Empire Air Day on 20th May, 1939, there was enough enthusiasm for a display, following a launching ceremony on 11th May when Alderman E. J. Hart, the Lord Mayor, had broken a bottle of champagne against the undercarriage of the first machine. Hawker Hind trainer K5473 and some locally-built Avro Tutors had then arrived.

The Air Display was somewhat marred by the crash of a Lysander from Catterick, flown by Pilot Officer H. G. Malcolm who fractured his skull. It was thought he would never fly again, but nursed back to health by a member of the Voluntary Aid Detachment, Miss Helen Swan, Malcolm later rejoined his squadron and married Helen. On 4th December, 1942, Wing Commander Hugh Malcolm led ten Bisley light-bombers against a Luftwaffe airfield in Tunisia and was awarded a posthumous Victoria Cross.

On 6th August the squadron travelled to Hawkinge, Kent, for summer camp, taking two Hinds and four Tiger Moths, the Secretary of State for Air, the Rt. Hon Sir Kingsley Wood, MP, paying a visit to the camp. On 25th August 613 Squadron was embodied into the Royal Air Force and on the outbreak of war the nine Auxiliary officers and seventy Auxiliary airmen were backed by five regular officers, fifty-five regular airmen and eight civilians. On 2nd October, at full-strength of 18 officers and 169 airmen, the squadron moved to Odiham, Hampshire, to continue training on a mixture of Hawker Hector and Westland Lysander two-seat Army Co-operation machines. The Hector was an all-metal biplane, fabric covered, powered by one 805 h.p. Napier Dagger engine, maximum speed 187 m.p.h. at 6,500 feet, armament one Vickers gun forward, one Lewis gun aft, with two 112 lb bombs or supply containers below the wings. The Lysander was a high-wing strutted monoplane powered by a

212. Hawker Hind, the first squadron aircraft.

213. Hawker Hector.

Bristol Mercury XII of 890 h.p., maximum speed 219 m.p.h. at 10,000 feet, two fixed machine guns forward and one manually operated in the rear cockpit, all 0.303. Six light bombs or supplies could be carried below stub wings.

On 1st January, 1940, Squadron Leader A. F. Anderson assumed command and in April came more Lysanders from 225 Squadron, together with Pilot Officers P. P. C. Barthropp and P. Le Cheminant. Supply drops to the Irish Guards provided useful training until, on 14th May, following the invasion of the Low Countries, the squadron was thrown into operations and ordered to ferry aircraft to Amiens-Glisy, then to move into Hawkinge, the grass airfield near Folkestone. On 25th May six Hector aircraft of 613 attacked a battery of large enemy field guns four miles SW. of Calais, high dive-bombing and, despite accurate flak, the mission was successful though two Hectors were damaged. Next day six Hectors returned to the attack, five of them again bombing successfully, one returning with engine trouble. On the 27th the Lysander flight of six machines dropped supplies to the soldiers trapped in Calais, flying at only 200 feet, with the Hectors and some Skuas of the Fleet Air Arm as escorts.

Never did airmen go into battle flying such obsolete machines but the spirit was unequalled as machine-gun posts were knocked out by the Hectors, the enemy pouring a hail of return-fire into the slow-moving aircraft. One Hector (K8116) crash-landed near Dover and although Pilot Officer Jenkyns scrambled out unhurt, his air-gunner, 903229 LAC Brown, died later, and so Manchester lost her first Auxiliary airman, who gave his life trying to help soldier-comrades holding the Calais perimeter.

214. Westland Lysanders.

With the completion of the miraculous Dunkirk evacuation the squadron was withdrawn to Nether Thorpe on the edge of the Sherwood Forest, to help reorganise the British Army for the battles ahead. At last the need for airmen and soldiers to combine forces had been proved – at high cost. Wing Commander J. N. T. Stephenson was the new C.O. and photographic reconnaissance flights were interspersed with occasional coastal patrols involving training in mobility as the squadron moved from airfield to airfield covering Army convoy movements in Yorkshire. On 6th September, Pilot Officer G. L. Edmonds was landing Lysander P1692 at Firbeck when he hit a moving lorry taking part in the same exercise. The aircraft overturned and caught fire; Sergeant Lethan escaped but the pilot was only rescued after some heroic work by L.A.C. Farley and A.C. Coop. Tragically he died later in Worksop Hospital; 613's first officer casualty.

With the Luftwaffe now battering away as a prelude to the intended invasion of England, the need for an air-sea rescue organisation to pick up pilots from the sea became a priority and it was 613's Lysanders which, from Martlesham Heath, Suffolk, paved the way for what was soon nicknamed 'The Salvation Navy' as the squadron led high-speed launches to pilots in their dinghies or Mae West lifejackets, returning many of 'The Few' to fly and fight again in the Battle for Britain.

On 16th June, 1941, Wing Commander Viscount Acheson was appointed to command and soon afterwards came North American Harvard trainers before the squadron received its first Curtiss Tomahawk tactical reconnaissance and ground attack fighter, a revolutionary change with top speed of 345 m.p.h. at 15,000 feet and with six 0.303 guns, four in the wings and two in the fuselage; powered by an Allison 1,040 h.p. V engine. One of the last Lysander tasks, the gas-spraying of troops near Beverley, resulted in the loss of aircraft V9434 and the deaths of Pilot Officer R. I. Millan and air-gunner Lethan (who had narrowly escaped death on 6th September, 1940).

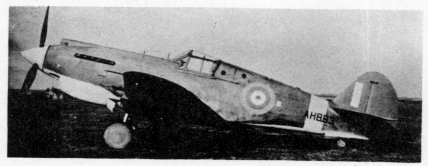

215. North American Tomahawk.

On 4th April, 1942, the squadron moved to Twin Woods near Bedford; then with the Tomahawk considered of more use in the Middle East another move was made, to Ouston near Sunderland, there to re-equip with the North American Mustang fighter-bomber, maximum speed 390 m.p.h. and with four 0.50 and four 0.303 guns; the early machines, though, powered by the Allison engine and only suitable for low-level work. Wing Commander Burt Andrews, a South African, took over, with three United States Air Force pilots attached to help bring the squadron to operational efficiency. On 11th December, 1942, a detachment moved into Odiham and from there flew 'Rhubarb' sorties into enemy-occupied Europe. Photo-recces were then flown up to thirty miles inside occupied territories, the Mustangs attacking airfields, transports and defence points on the way out; these operations were given the code-name 'Popular' and provided splendid training for the future.

On 14th and 23rd January, 1943, the squadron detachments, flying from southern airfields against the Dieppe-Fécamp areas, scored enormous successes, Army Co-operation Command confirming that twenty-five locomotives had been destroyed or seriously damaged, together with some grounded Luftwaffe machines, for no loss to 613. Valuable photographs were secured for the work now proceeding at top-secret establishments where a return to Europe was being planned. Air Commodore the Duke of Kent, with his equerry, Group Captain Lord Willoughby de Broke, MC, AFC, pre-war auxiliary and ex-C.O. 605 (County of Warwick), visited the squadron to congratulate members, one of the Duke's last engagements before he lost his life en route to Iceland in a Sunderland flying boat.

216. North American Mustang.

19th March, 1943, was a red-letter day with a return to Ringway, the twelve Mustangs contrasting in appearance and speed with the Armstrong Whitworth Whitleys being used at the airport for the training of our airborne forces and of agents soon to parachute into Europe. Manchester's 'Wings for Victory' got a real boost with a Briefing being staged in the windows of Kendal-Milne's store and a Mustang on exhibition in Piccadilly. The Lord Mayor entertained the squadron following Lord Trenchard's taking of the salute at an impressive parade which included local war workers. The original of the squadron's badge, signed by King George VI, was handed to the Lord Mayor for safe-keeping; and, with some thrilling low-level flying over the city, the squadron was en route to Wellingore, Lincolnshire, from where they were to fly close escort missions to Coastal Command's Beaufighters and No. 2 Group's Ventura bombers attacking Dutch coastal shipping and Luftwaffe airfields in Holland.

On 3rd May, 1943, No. 487 (NZ) Squadron's Venturas were briefed to wipe out Amsterdam power station in daylight, a formidable task with large forces of Focke-Wulf 190 and Messerschmitt 109 fighters based nearby. The Mustangs escorted the bombers to the Dutch coast and there, alas, a blunder occurred, for as the Mustangs retired, out of fuel, the take-over Spitfires also withdrew, having reached their rendezvous point early, consequently using up their petrol too soon. The Venturas pressed on alone and all were shot down. After the war, on the evidence of Dutch patriots and surviving aircrew, Wing Commander Len Trent, DFC, was awarded the VC for his leadership of that raid. He counts himself extremely fortunate, for he was just leaving the tunnel at Stalag Luft III in 1944 when the mass escape was discovered. Fifty of the officers ahead of him were executed by the Gestapo.

On the day of the Mustang escort to the Venturas the last pre-war Auxiliary officer left when Flight Lieutenant G. Buckley, the A Flight commander, was posted away, a group photograph being taken to mark his founder-membership. During May, several Focke Wulf 190s were shot down by 613 and when King George VI visited RAF Digby for an investiture, a squadron Mustang was flown over so that the C.O. could explain this powerful new weapon to His Majesty. On 29th May the squadron moved into Fighter Command from Army Co-operation Command (which had been formed in 1940) and moved to Portreath, Cornwall, to provide escorts for Coastal Command's Mosquitos hitting U-boats and also to cover air-sea rescue operations in the Bay of Biscay. In August a special mission was flown over the North Sea to protect Danish vessels bringing patriots to England following proclamation of martial law in Denmark.

The Distinguished Flying Cross was awarded to Flight Lieutenant W. T. Hawkins, a New Zealand pilot, for his successes against the enemy fighters, flying with 613 from Snailwell in Suffolk. Ground personnel were now moved to Sculthorpe, Norfolk, for intensive training, as aircrews moved to Lasham, Hampshire, where they learned that 613 Squadron was to get the 'Wooden Wonder' de Havilland Mosquito fighter-bomber. Any fears the pilots may have had of coping with this fast twin-engined machine were dispelled when the first of the squadron machines arrived, flown in by a diminutive Air Transport Auxiliary lady-pilot! Wing Commander K. H. Blair, DFC, arrived to command with Squadron Leaders R. N. Bateson, DFC, and C. W. Newman as flight-commanders. Veteran of pinpoint raids, Squadron Leader Parry, DSO, DFC and Bar, kept the training programme up to schedule and HRH Prince Bernhard of the Netherlands came to thank the squadron for their fine work in support of his country's liberation. Lasham's Station Commander, Group Captain (later Air Marshal Sir Leslie) Bower flew with 613 and by 19th December No. 2 (Bomber) Group, 2nd Tactical Air Force, was able to put the squadron on the operational roster.

217. Sqdn Ldr Bateson's Mosquito.

From that day, almost unceasingly until the end of January 1944, 613 Squadron aircraft attacked the 'Noball' targets. Cunningly concealed and camouflaged they called for expert navigation and bombing and on 31st January, 1944, the Chief of the Air Staff sent a signal to 613: 'Please congratulate squadron on very successful attacks. The results are outstanding and I hope they can be maintained.' The Air Officer Commanding-in-Chief, 2nd Tactical Air Force, Air Marshal Sir Arthur Coningham, and the Air Officer Commanding No. 2(B) Group, Air Vice-Marshal Basil Embry, added their thanks for the squadron's work.

On 6th February, 1944, Group Captain Bower and two other 613 Squadron machines were hit by the guns of a flak-train but Squadron Leader Charles Newman dived down and blew the train to smithereens. Group Captain Bower crash-landed near Newhaven as the others escorted him back. Happily he and his navigator got clear as the Mosquito burst into flames. Lasham now became the base of No. 138 Airfield, 138 Wing comprising Nos. 613, 305 (Polish), 320 (Dutch) and 107 Squadrons and Wing Commander Bateson took over the squadron reins as the first night-intruder sorties saw the destruction of many Luftwaffe aircraft on their aerodromes. Air Chief Marshal Sir Trafford Leigh-Mallory, Air Commander-in-

Chief of the Allied Expeditionary Air Force (of which 613 was now part), came to meet the squadron and it was no surprise to Wing Commander 'Bob' Bateson when, in April, he was instructed to take his crews to Swanton Morley in Norfolk, for a 'hush hush' task.

When the crews reported for briefing the presence of the Inspector-General, Royal Air Force, and the Air Officer Commanding stressed the mission's importance, and the uncovering of detailed models, with supporting photographs, made clear the necessity for the most accurate low-level bombing ever carried out. It was the Kunstzaal Kleizkamp Art Gallery, close to the Peace Palace, in The Hague, where the Gestapo were keeping the records of all Dutch families, from which they selected those to go to concentration camps or forced labour units, and where they could obtain details of patriots' relatives for torture and execution when reprisals were sought. It was absolutely vital that these records be destroyed with the minimum loss of Dutch life. Success would be measured, not in yards, but in feet and inches.

On 11th April, flying at only fifty feet, Wing Commander Bateson led six Mosquitos, the plan being for three pairs to come in at two-minute intervals dropping high-explosives and incendiary bombs. Bateson led the first pair in, skimming house tops, making straight for the target building. A German sentry on duty at the front door screamed with horror as he threw away his rifle and ran for his life. Flight Lieutenant P. C. Cobley, in the second plane, saw his leader's bombs going 'right in the front door'. A parade was in progress in the yard behind the building and some off-duty soldiers were playing football. No further goals were scored as Cobley's aircraft scattered troops in all directions with more bombs, right on target. Squadron Leader Newman led in the next pair. The house was now partly obscured by smoke but he and his colleague dropped incendiaries across it. Last in were Flight Lieutenant V. A. Hester and a Dutch pilot. Hester attacked with incendiaries and delayed-action high-explosives but the Dutchman's bombs hung up. Despite two more circuits and runs over the target he could not release them and had to return home without scoring a hit.

It was only at the end of the attack that spasmodic and inaccurate flak came up, for the Germans had been taken completely by surprise. Reconnaissance photographs showed that the target building had been reduced to rubble while neighbouring houses in the Schveningse Weg were untouched. Dutch officials faked thousands of cards and thus threw the records upon which the Nazis depended into inextricable confusion. Wing Commander Bateson received a well-merited Distinguished Service Order and Squadron Leader Newman, Flight Lieutenant Hester, and Flying Officer Standish (Bateson's navigator) all received the DFC. On 1st May the B.B.C. broadcast 'The House in the Hague', a first-hand account by Wing Commander Bateson and on the 4th they met His Majesty King George VI and went on to the Netherlands Embassy where Wing Commander Bateson and Flying Officer Standish received the Netherlands Flying Cross.

On 25th May Flight Lieutenant J. G. Oliver, reported missing in January, returned to the squadron, having made his way back through Occupied Europe, aided by patriots, adding another memorable page to the achievements of the City of Manchester Squadron. When at last D-Day dawned, 613 aircraft were bombing positions behind the beaches, flying forty-three day and night sorties on 6th June, preventing interference with allied landings wherever they could. On the promotion of Group Captain Bateson to command No. 140 Wing, Wing Commander Charles Newman became C.O. and the intrepid Air Vice-Marshal Embry showed his confidence in 613 by flying one of their aircraft under various noms-de-plume, often as 'Flying Officer Smith', for there was a price on his head following his own escape from the enemy in France in 1940.

Nazi S.S. barracks SE. of Limoges were razed in support of the Maquis, with twenty direct hits. One Mosquito was brought down but Flight Lieutenant House and Flying Officer Savill were assisted through Occupied France, over the Pyrenees into Spain and down to Gibraltar, from where they were soon back to fly again. In the Battle of the Falaise Gap the squadron played a decisive role and during the ill-fated Arnhem landings the squadron attacked enemy

218. Squadron at Cambrai-Epinoy, January 1945. *Front row left to right:* Major Brown, Flt Lt Ellis, Flt Lt Coward, Flt Lt Topliss, Flt Lt Hanbury, Flt Lt Morris, Sqdn Ldr Duncan, Wg Cdr Lucas, Sqdn Ldr Gardner, Flt Lt Knight, F/O Stevens, Flt Lt Walker, unknown, unknown, Capt Winterschladen. *Second row:* Flt Lt Wesson, F/O Morris (behind), F/O Edgar, Flt Sgt Parfitt, F/O Gates, unknown, Flt Lt Capon, Flt Lt Grey, unknown, unknown, P/O Muir, Flt Lt Shepherd, Flt Lt Wishart, P/O Vick, unknown, F/O Dean. *Third row:* immediately left of shield Flt Sgy Nemry, unknown, W/O Wilshire, right of shield F/O Dean, P/O Higginson, F/O Bieri, unknown, Flt Lt Holloway, F/O Dickens, Flt Lt Quevatre. *Back row:* NCOs and ground staff including Flt Sgt Hellings, Flt Sgt McPhail, and Flt Sgt Webb.

barracks in support of our paratroopers, several decorations being awarded. A move took the squadron to Hartford Bridge (now Blackbushe airfield) where the King and Queen arrived for an open air investiture. In December came the move to Epinoy and Wing Commander J. S. Hamilton was relieved as C.O. by Wing Commander P. B. 'Laddie' Lucas, DSO, DFC, a veteran of Malta.

Squadron patrols now probed deep into Germany and during the enemy offensive in the Ardennes at Christmas 1944, the squadron flew two sorties a night to relieve the onslaught against the American forces pinned down. As the Nazis were thrust back across the Rhine, squadron sorties reached Berlin and when Laddie Lucas handed over to Wing Commander W. C. Duncan, an unprecedented happening was an all-ranks presentation to Laddie who had endeared himself to the squadron from the start. After the war he became Member of Parliament for Brentford and Chiswick and has worked hard for civil aviation. On Wing Commander Duncan's departure, Wing Commander Charles Newman returned to his old command and on the anniversary of D-Day the squadron flew in salute over the Arromanches beaches where, a year earlier, their bombing had saved many allied lives. The squadron's last operational sortie had, in fact, taken place on 26th April and after some weeks it was decided to disband 613 Squadron and let No. 69 Squadron take over their Mosquitos and any personnel with time to serve.

219. Headquarters and Wing officers No. 2 (B) Group, Brussels, June 1945, including former 613 officers: Gp Cpt Leslie Bower, front row second left; fourth left Gp Cpt Bob Bateson; centre, AV-M Basil Embry; third row far right, Wg Cdr Charles Newman.

On 1st November, 1946, at the original base, Ringway, Manchester, No. 613 (City of Manchester) Auxiliary Squadron began to re-form under Squadron Leader J. S. Morton, DFC and Bar, a one-time RAF Volunteer Reserve pilot with No. 603 (City of Edinburgh) Squadron in the Battle of Britain, who gained his DFC flying Spitfires, the Bar was awarded for night-fighting with 219 Squadron. Wing Commander Edgar Rhodes (the first C.O.) was on hand to help recruiting, plus a nucleus of regular RAF officers and airmen to strengthen the Thursday evening and weekend auxiliaries. Ten Spitfire XIVs and two Harvard trainers arrived, and the squadron gradually settled down to the pre-war routines with summer camps at Horsham St Faith, Manston, Thorney Island, and Takali, Malta. In 1947, on the death of Lord Derby, who had been the Honorary Air Commodore for many years, Sir Roy Dobson, CBE, FRAeS, JP, became the squadron's Honorary Air Commodore. In 1949 Spitfire F.22's arrived, and in March 1951 the de Havilland Vampire FB.5's. Squadron Leader Morton was relieved by Squadron Leader J. B. Wales who, sad to relate, later lost his life while testing an Avro Shackleton.

220. Harvard, IIB, Ringway, 1950.

Because of Ringway's growing volume of civilian air traffic Sir Roy Dobson arranged for the jet training to take place at nearby Woodford Aerodrome, the Avro (now Hawker Siddeley) field, and Sylt, in Northern Germany, and Gibraltar were added to the squadron's summer camping sites. Then, in 1957, came the decision to disband the Royal Auxiliary Air Force squadrons and special permission was given for the squadron to march through Manchester with fixed bayonets on Saturday 2nd March. The Lord Mayor, Councillor H. Sharp, read a resolution expressing the Council's appreciation of the squadron's services, before, during, and after World War II. Sir Roy Dobson replied, and during the ceremony 613 Squadron's Vampires flew a salute. Silver tankards were handed to the 138 officers and men (including Sir Roy) and a silver salver to the widow of Squadron Leader J. B. Wales. The '613 Squadron Trophy' presented by the City was passed to Messrs A. V. Roe for yearly presentation to the best apprentice.

221. All ten Vampires airborne, 20th November, 1954.

In 1966 a commemorative plaque was unveiled in the central concourse of Ringway Airport, by the Lord Mayor, in the presence of Sir Roy Dobson, Wing Commanders Edgar Rhodes, Laddie Lucas and 'Paddy' Barthropp, and many former members of the squadron. The plaque is of quarter-inch laminated float glass 4 feet 6 inches high and 5 feet 3 inches in width. On an obscure sandblasted ground the squadron badge has been hand painted in its heraldic colours, the wording hand cut and filled with pigment. The centre of the badge is the fleur de lys. In World War I the arms of Manchester were changed to the fleur de lys as the crest of the Manchester regiment because the arms were too intricate for service use. In 1939 permission was given by the Lord Mayor and Corporation of Manchester and the Hon Colonel of the Manchester Regiment to use the fleur de lys in the squadron's badge to represent the City of Manchester. In 1939 a competition was held for the best suggestion for the motto. Pilot Officer G. F. H. 'Sandy' Webb won the competition by unanimous vote with *Semper Parati* – 'Always prepared'. Wing Commander G. F. H. Webb, DFC and Bar, was killed, alas, when leading a fighter squadron over Germany towards the end of the war. Designed by the College of Arms and signed by King George VI the badge was received by the squadron in June 1939. There have been two alterations since then. In 1947 the Auxiliary Air Force was honoured to receive the title Royal Auxiliary Air Force. In 1953 on the occasion of Queen Elizabeth II's accession the Queen's Crown surmounted the badge instead of the King's Crown. Since the disbandment of the squadron the badge now rests at an Air Defence Headquarters.

Awards gained by squadron personnel are extremely difficult to verify as some were promulgated after personnel had been posted to other units or for personnel joining whose decorations had been won before reaching 613 Squadron. It is thought, however, that 4 Distinguished Service Orders, 44 Distinguished Flying Crosses, 2 Air Force Crosses, and 1 George Medal were credited to the squadron. In addition, 2 Commanders, 4 Officers, and 4 Members of the Order of the British Empire owe their honours entirely or in part to their association with 613; a truly remarkable record for the 'baby' squadron. Many ex-members reached high rank in the Royal Air Force including Air Marshal Sir Peter de Lacey Le Cheminant, KCB, who moved from 613 to 614 Squadron and gained the DFC (and Bar in Korea); Air Vice-Marshal 'Bob' Bateson, CBE, DSO, DFC; Air Commodores F. O. Barrett, CBE, DFC, and Charles Burt-Andrews, CB, CBE. Some who left the Service carved useful niches in post-war 'Civvy Street' including Wing Commander P. P. C. Barthropp, DFC, AFC, who left 613 to join another AAF unit, No. 602 (City of Glasgow), to fly with distinction in the Battle of Britain. His generosity to the RAF Benevolent Fund in donating valuable prizes for the Battle of Britain Ball is typical of the concern of surviving members of 'The Few' for the welfare of dependants of those who have died in peace and war during RAF service.

REPRESENTATIVE SQUADRON AIRCRAFT

Hawker Hind		K5379 K5473 (T)
Hawker Hector		K8116 K8127 K8138 K9689
Westland Lysander	I	P1692 R2572
	II	L4779 L4791
	IIIa	V9434
North American Tomahawk		AH905 AH931 AK118
North American Mustang	I	AG365 AG443 AG564 AG495 SY–1

de Havilland		HJ666 HP927 (Hague) HX828 LR275
Mosquito	FB.VI	LR366 SY–L (Hague) LR355 (Wg Cdr Bateson) NS844 (Sqdn Ldr Newman) MM408 (Hague) NT134 PZ194 PZ222 RS600 LR376 (Hague)
Supermarine Spitfire	FR.XIV	NH637 D NH785 E NH918 F TX983 J
	F.22	PK406 A PK564 K PK543 F PK599 K
North American Harvard	IIb	KF387 I KF470
de Havilland Vampire	FB.5	VV602 B VV616 K VZ271 H WA301 A
Gloster Meteor	T.7	VW452 '3' WA637 '4' WF778 '5'

Squadron aircraft were coded SY during World War II but post-war carried at first the code RAT which was changed to Q3 from 1949 when rejoining Fighter Command. The Q3 code was, uniquely, retained on the Vampires when an official insignia of horizontal bars coloured green, yellow, green was carried on the tailbooms.

Apparently no authentic squadron machine now exists although a Hector-wreck in Eire *could* be a former 613 aircraft. Let us hope it is restored and also that, one day, a Tomahawk in squadron colours joins the RAF Museum to mark this type's link with the Auxiliaries.

Badge: In front of two wings conjoined at base a fleur de lys – based on the badge of the Manchester Regiment (see above).

Motto (translated): 'Always ready'.

Postscript

AFTER THE QUEEN and the Duke of Edinburgh had received more than eighty commanding and senior officers of the RAuxAF and Air Divisions of the RNVR at Buckingham Palace on 16th March, 1957, each officer was given, on leaving, a signed copy of a message from the Queen. The message handed to the RAuxAF officers read as follows:

I have welcomed this opportunity of taking leave of the commanding officers and senior Auxiliary officers of the squadrons of the Royal Auxiliary Air Force which are being disbanded and of sending them this message of appreciation and thanks to all their officers, airmen and airwomen.

The history of the Auxiliary Air Force has been a glorious one. The first Auxiliary squadrons were included in the air defence of Great Britain in 1925. By the outbreak of war in 1939 the Auxiliary fighter coastal, and balloon squadrons formed an integral and vital part of our forces. It was aircraft of these squadrons which shot down the first enemy bombers over this country; and Auxiliary squadrons were heavily engaged in the air over Dunkirk and throughout the Battle of Britain. Later they were to win battle honours over the Atlantic, in Malta, North Africa, Sicily and Italy, the Arakan and Burma, and in Normandy, Belgium, Holland and Germany.

After the war the fighter squadrons were reconstituted as the Royal Auxiliary Air Force and the traditional spirit of voluntary service found new outlets with the formation of A.O.P. and field squadrons, fighter control and radar reporting units, some of which are to remain in being and provide further opportunities for voluntary service.

The association of the force with my family has always been close. I was proud to become Honorary Air Commodore of Nos. 603, 2603 and 3603 (City of Edinburgh) Squadrons in 1951 and to succeed my father as Honorary Air Commodore-in-Chief of the Royal Auxiliary Air Force in 1952. [King George VI succeeded King Edward VIII as Honorary Air Commodore-in-Chief.] Members of my family have always treasured their association with Auxiliary squadrons as honorary air commodores.

I wish as Air Commodore-in-Chief to thank officers, airmen and airwomen of the Royal Auxiliary Air Force for all that they have given to the service of the country by their enthusiasm, their spirit and their devotion in peace and war. It is a sad day when it is necessary to tell so many that it is no longer possible to use their services on the duties they have assumed so willingly. I wish them to know that they can look back with pride and satisfaction to service well done.

This book does not cover the post-war No. 622 Squadron formed at Blackbushe in 1950 for transport duties; nor does it include the AOP units mentioned by the Queen, Nos. 661, 662, 663, 664, 666 Squadrons with their Austers and Tiger Moths. They, too, have disbanded, and any reader who wishes to play a part in the Royal Auxiliary Air Force today should communicate with Wing Commander L. E. Robins, RAuxAF, No. 1 (County of Hertford) Maritime Headquarters Unit at Northwood, Middlesex. There are also No. 2 (City of Edinburgh) Maritime Headquarters Unit, Edinburgh, and No. 3 (County of Devon) Maritime Headquarters, Mountbatten, Plymouth, for those within reach. These Units co-operate with the RAF in the defence of our country, continuing the volunteer tradition of the pre-war AAF.

Former members of AAF/RAuxAF squadrons will like to know that The Esher Trophy (a bronze figure of Perseus by Sir Alfred Gilbert, presented by the late Viscount Esher) is at RAF, Henlow, in store for the RAF Museum, due to be opened at Hendon in November 1972. The Cooper Trophy (a bronze figure of an athletic young man holding aloft the RAF flying badge, designed by Gilbert Bayes) was presented by Wing Commander Geoffrey Cooper in commemoration of the sacrifice and devotion of the Auxiliary Air Force in the Battle of Britain, and of his friend Flying Officer Peter Henry Basson, killed over Holland on 24th July, 1942. On the side are the words 'They shall mount up with wings as eagles'. Winners of the two trophies were:

ESHER

Year	Squadron	Year	Squadron
1926	601	1929	602
1927	605	1930	605
1928	601	1931	605

Esher Trophy Winners continued

1932	604	1949	604
1933	605	1950	603
1934	605	1951	616
1935	605	1952	610
1936	604	1953	615
1937	604	1954	609
1938	603	1955	500
1948	604		

COOPER

1948   601 Squadron, Sqdn Ldr H. S. L. Dundas
1949   502 Squadron, Flt Lt W. Bowden
1950   600 Squadron, Fg Off J. N. Haslewood
1951   615 Squadron, no name quoted
1952/3   no contest
1954   500 Squadron, no name quoted
1955   602 Squadron, no name quoted
1956   610 Squadron, no name quoted

Thanks are due to Group Captain The Hon Peter Vanneck, OBE, AFC, ADC, DL, RAuxAF (who succeeded Air Commodore Michael Birkin, CBE, DSO, DFC, AFC, as Inspector of the RAuxAF in 1962 after flying in 601 Squadron), also to Mr. L. A. Manwaring, PA to DGM, Ray Lee, Assistant Keeper, RAF Museum, and Wing Commander David Bennett ARAeS (who inspected the Cooper Trophy, with Southampton University Air Squadron, the present holders; since it became an inter–UAS trophy). It is a pity that individual names are not recorded after 1950 but readers who were associated with the 1951–56 events will be able to add the details.

It is good to know that there will be an AAF/RAuxAF tribute in the Royal Air Force Museum and where better than at Hendon, pre-war 'home' of Nos. 600, 601 and 604 Squadrons. Some links are also maintained at a few TAVR Centres and at RAF stations Church Fenton and Finningley. There was never, it seems, an approved distinctive badge for the AAF or RAuxAF but there was an RAuxAF tie – designed by Michael Birkin – still available from Lewins in Jermyn Street, London, to those entitled to it. Let us hope it will be worn for many years to come!

July 1972   L.H.